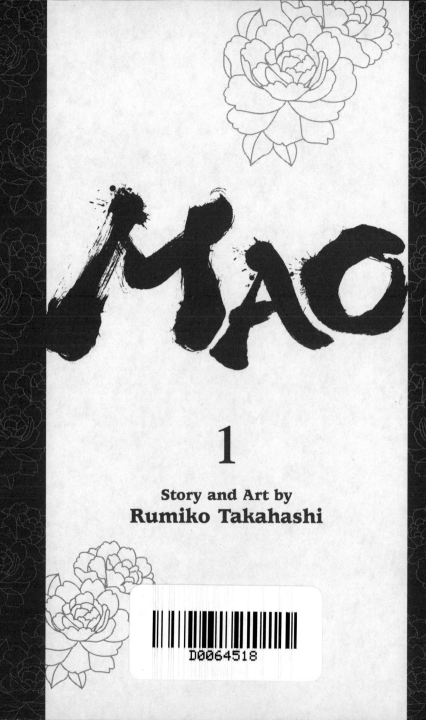

MAO

1

Story and Art by
Rumiko Takahashi

CONTENTS

Chapter 1: Nanoka •••••••••••••••••••••••••• 5

Chapter 2: Mao •••••••••••••••••••••••••••••• 43

Chapter 3: The Other Side of the Gate •••••••• 73

Chapter 4: The Faceless Viscount ••••••••••••• 97

Chapter 5: Spider Lady •••••••••••••••••••• 115

Chapter 6: The Accursed •••••••••••••••••• 133

Chapter 7: The Sinkhole •••••••••••••••••• 153

Chapter 8: Power Over Life And Death •••••• 171

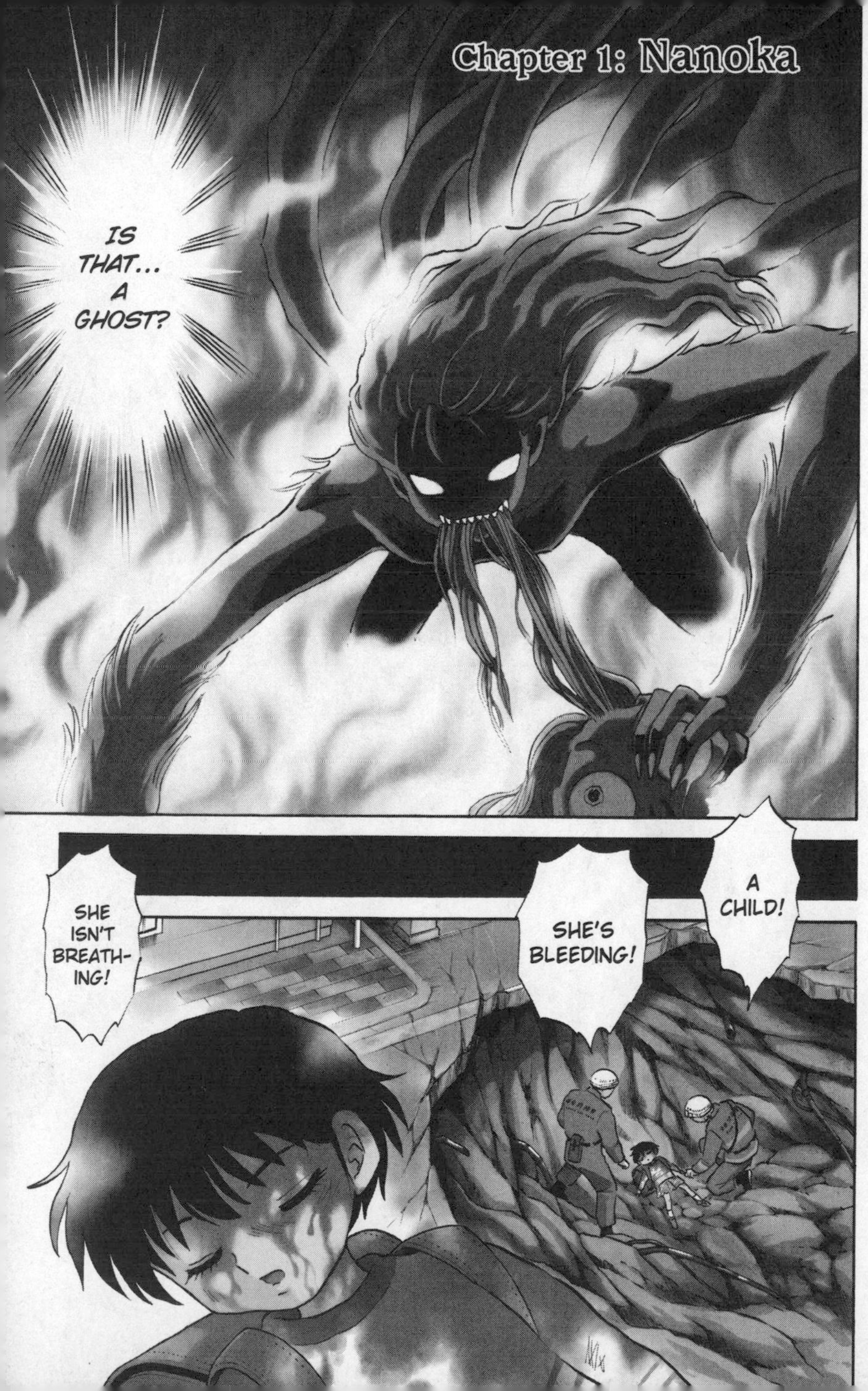
Chapter 1: Nanoka
IS THAT... A GHOST?
A CHILD!
SHE'S BLEEDING!
SHE ISN'T BREATH-ING!

Chapter 1: Nanoka

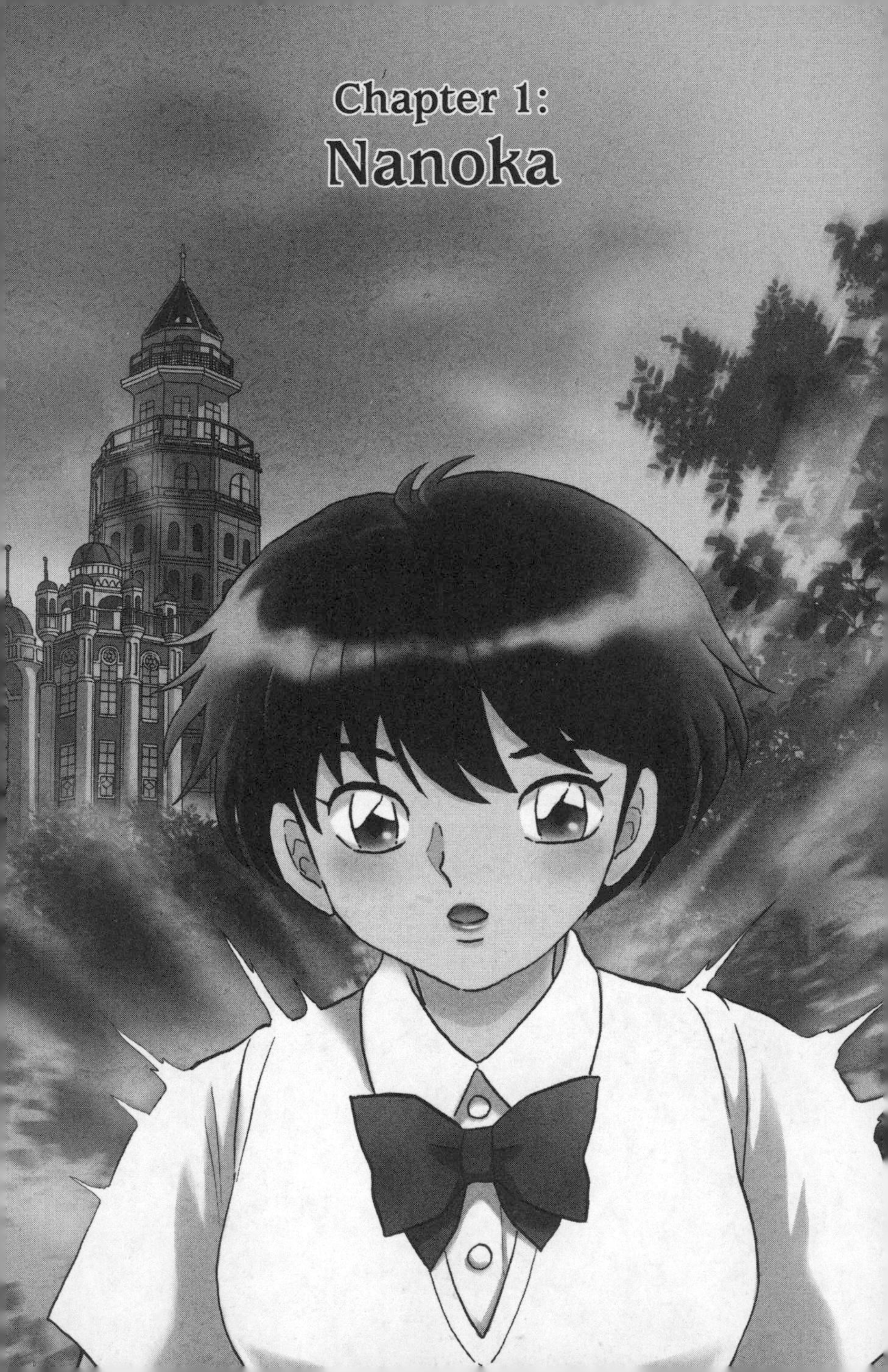

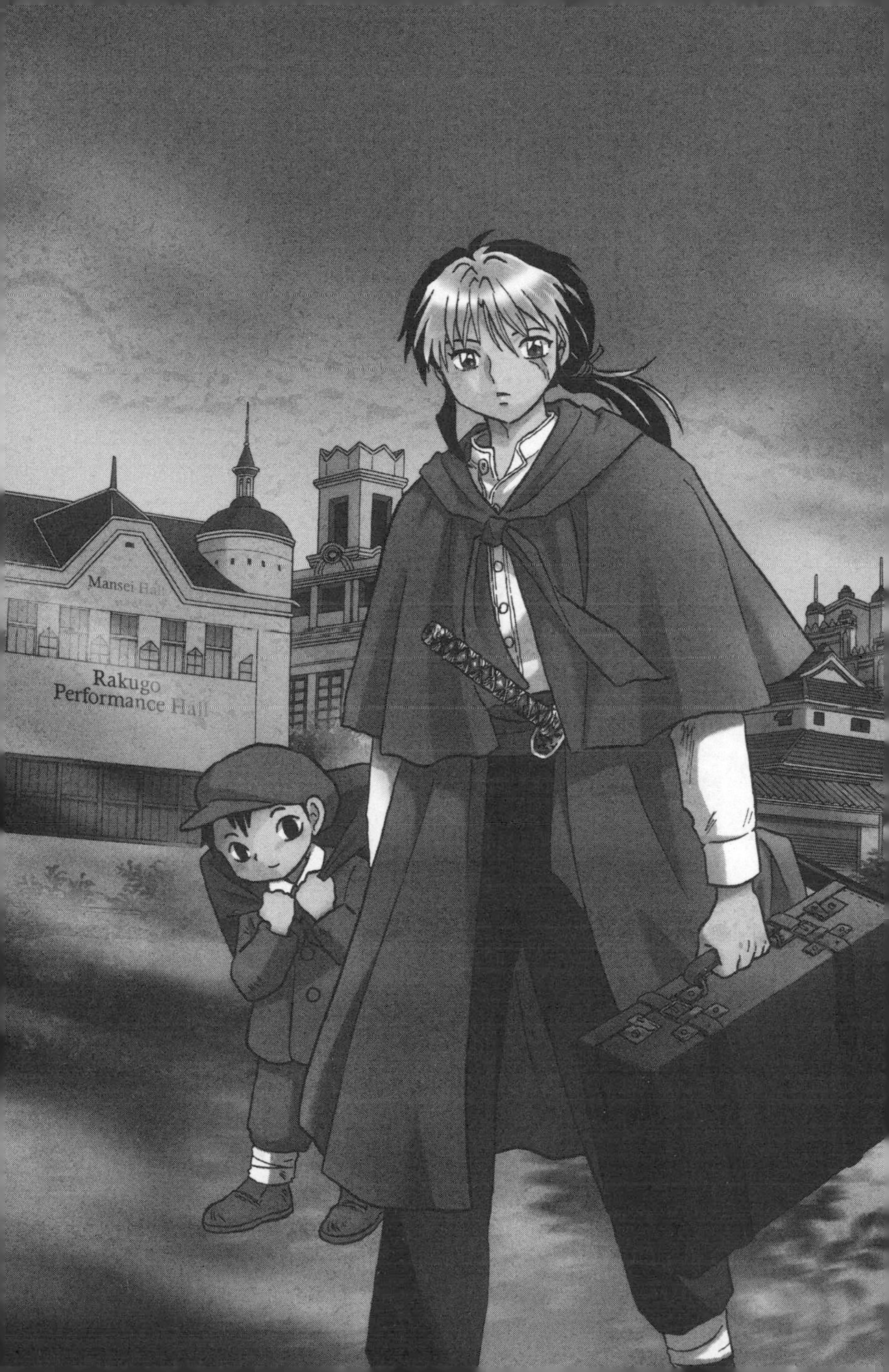
Mansei Hall
Rakugo
Performance Hall

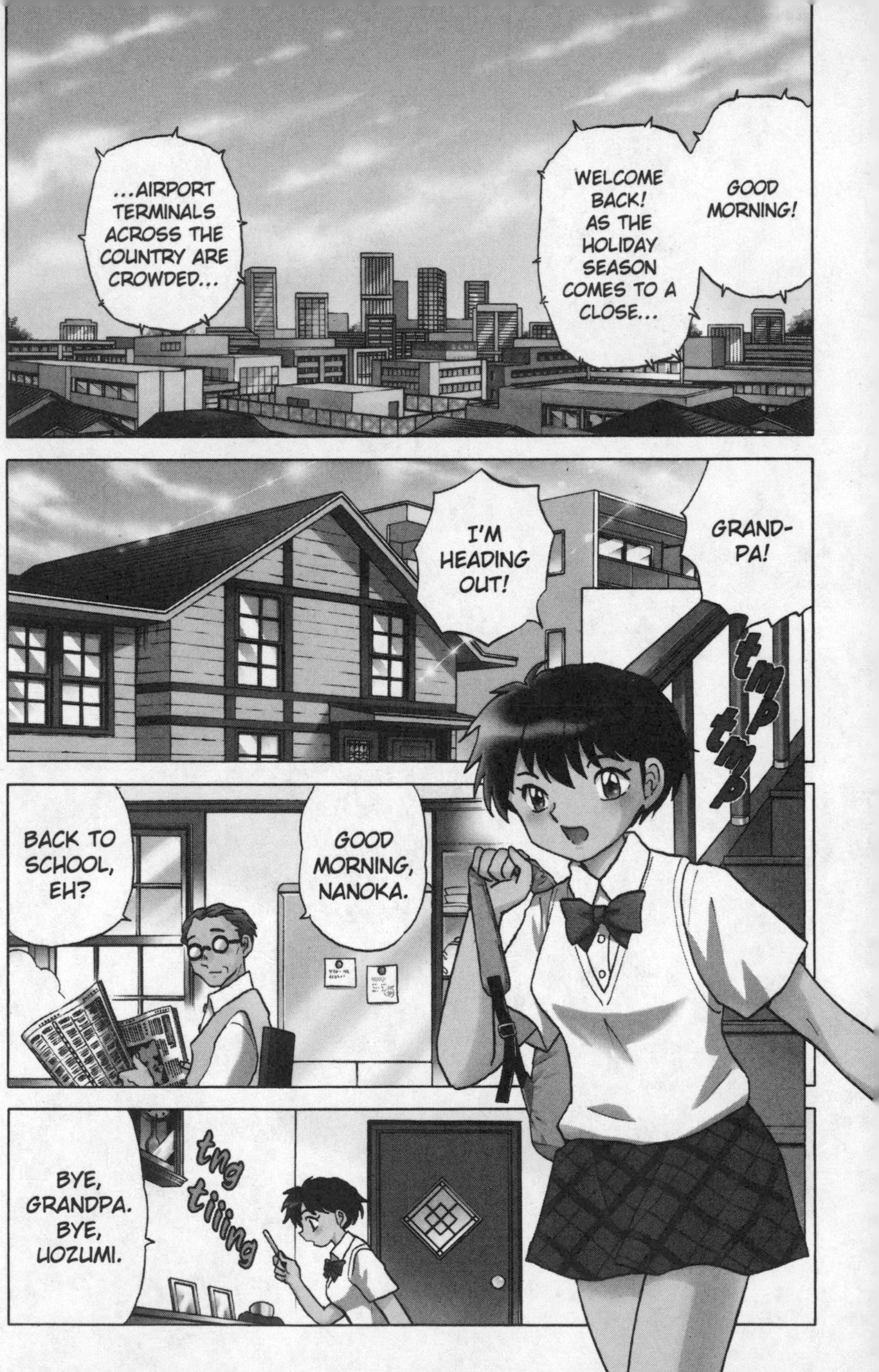
GOOD MORNING!
WELCOME BACK! AS THE HOLIDAY SEASON COMES TO A CLOSE...
...AIRPORT TERMINALS ACROSS THE COUNTRY ARE CROWDED...
GRAND-PA!
I'M HEADING OUT!
tmp tmp
GOOD MORNING, NANOKA.
BACK TO SCHOOL, EH?
tng tiiing
BYE, GRANDPA. BYE, UOZUMI.

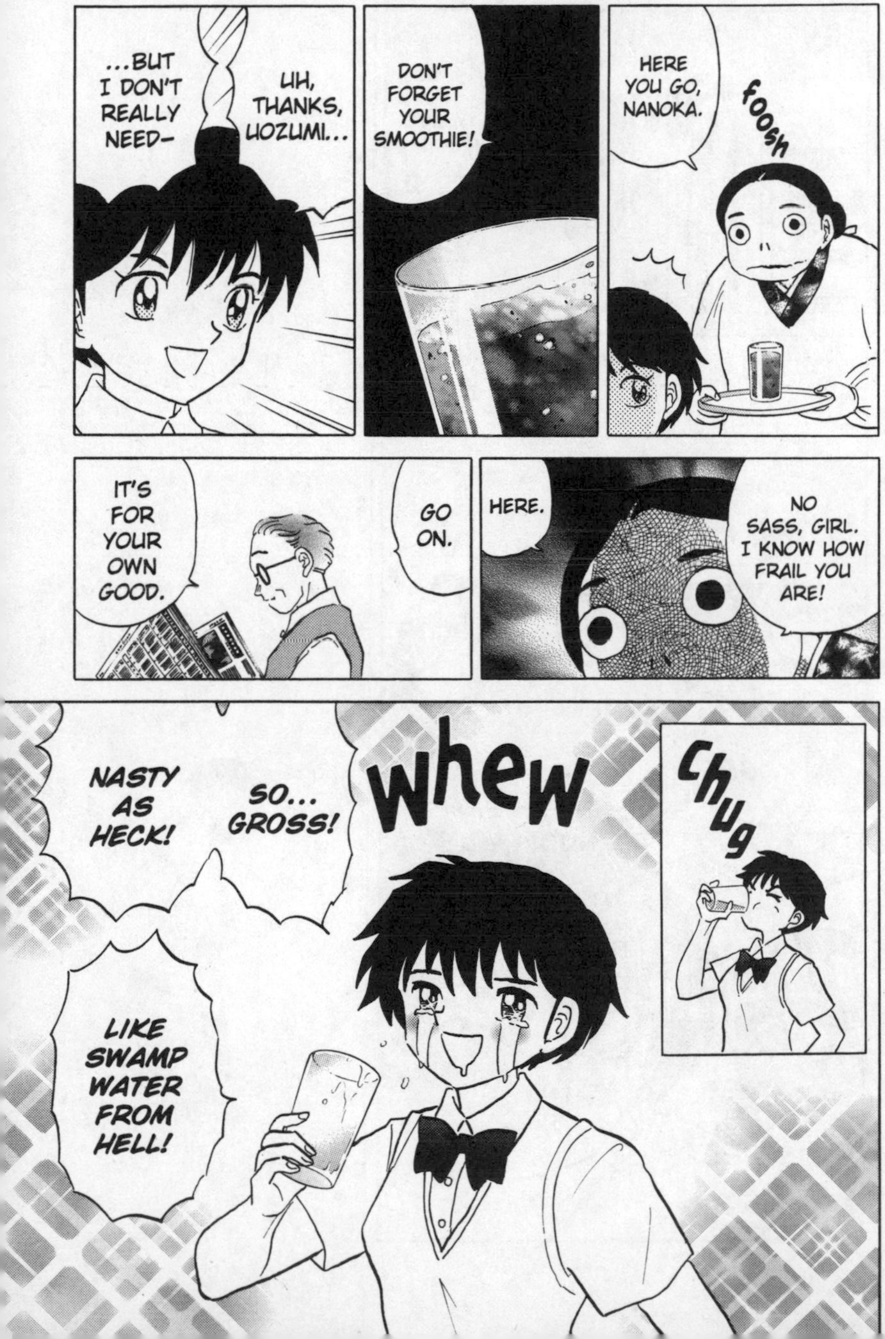
HERE YOU GO, NANOKA.
foosh
DON'T FORGET YOUR SMOOTHIE!
UH, THANKS, UOZUMI...
...BUT I DON'T REALLY NEED–
NO SASS, GIRL. I KNOW HOW FRAIL YOU ARE!
HERE.
GO ON.
IT'S FOR YOUR OWN GOOD.
chug
whew
SO... GROSS!
NASTY AS HECK!
LIKE SWAMP WATER FROM HELL!

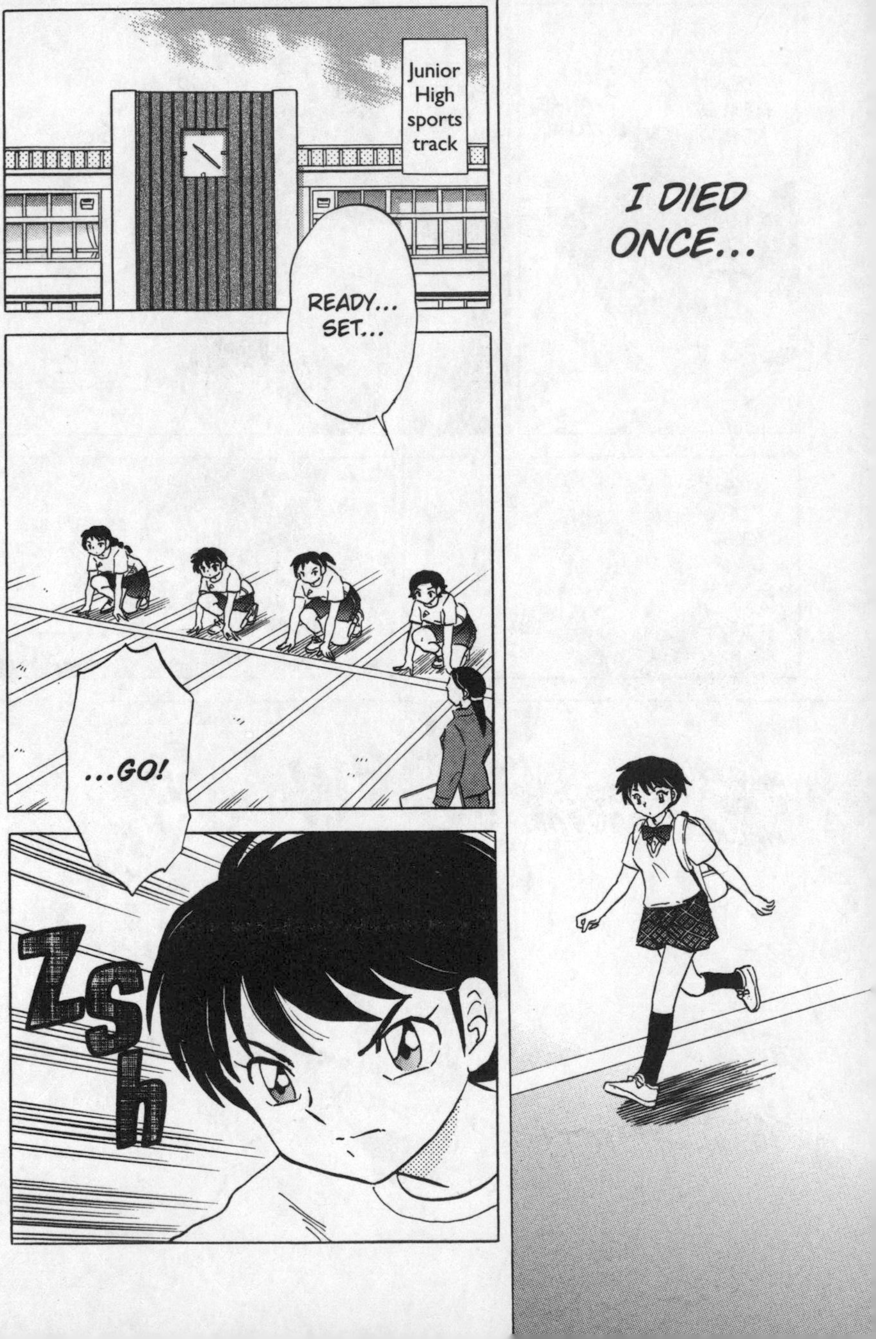
I DIED ONCE...
Junior High sports track
READY... SET...
...GO!
Zsh

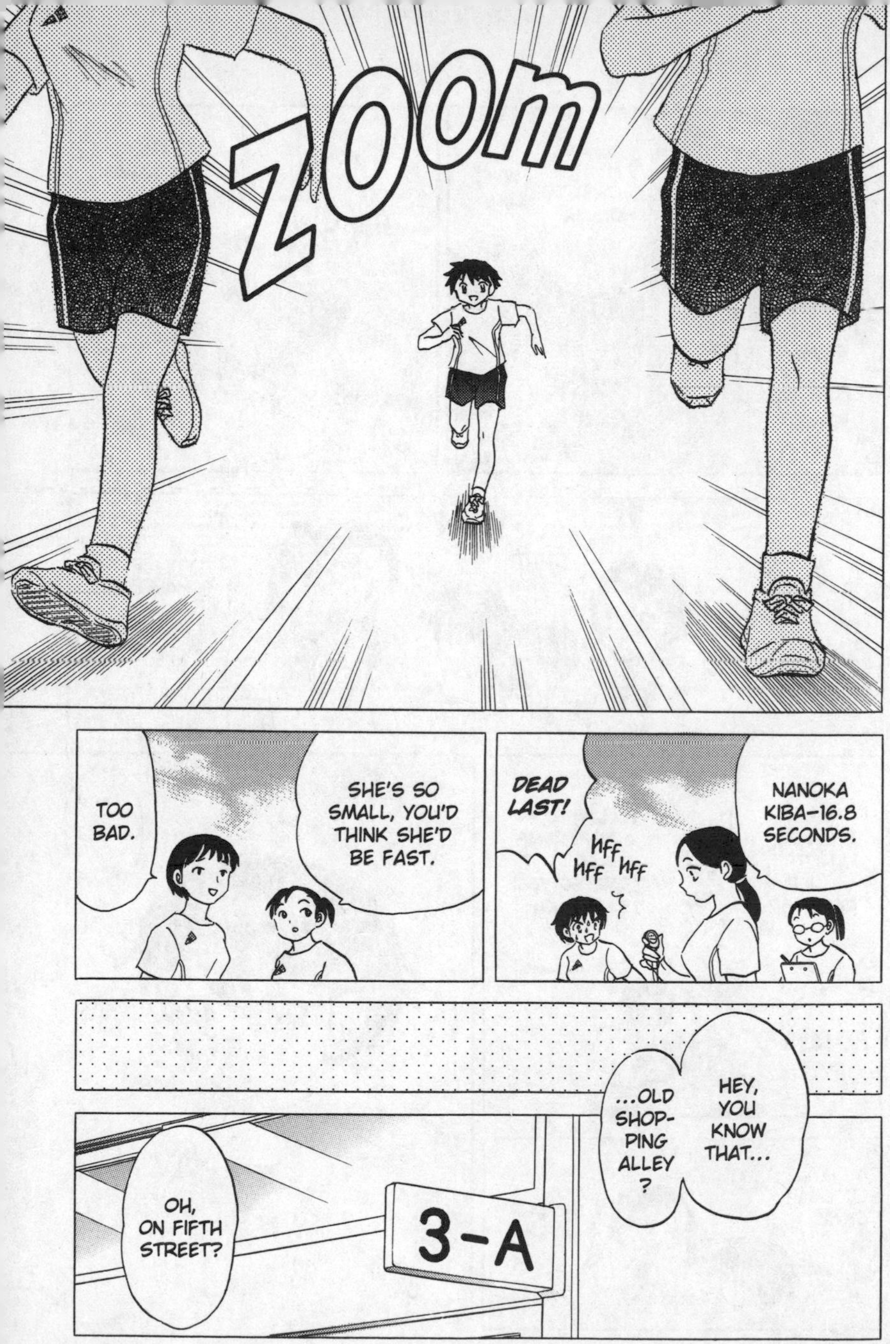
ZOOM
NANOKA KIBA–16.8 SECONDS.
DEAD LAST!
HFF HFF HFF
SHE'S SO SMALL, YOU'D THINK SHE'D BE FAST.
TOO BAD.
HEY, YOU KNOW THAT...
...OLD SHOP-PING ALLEY?
3-A
OH, ON FIFTH STREET?

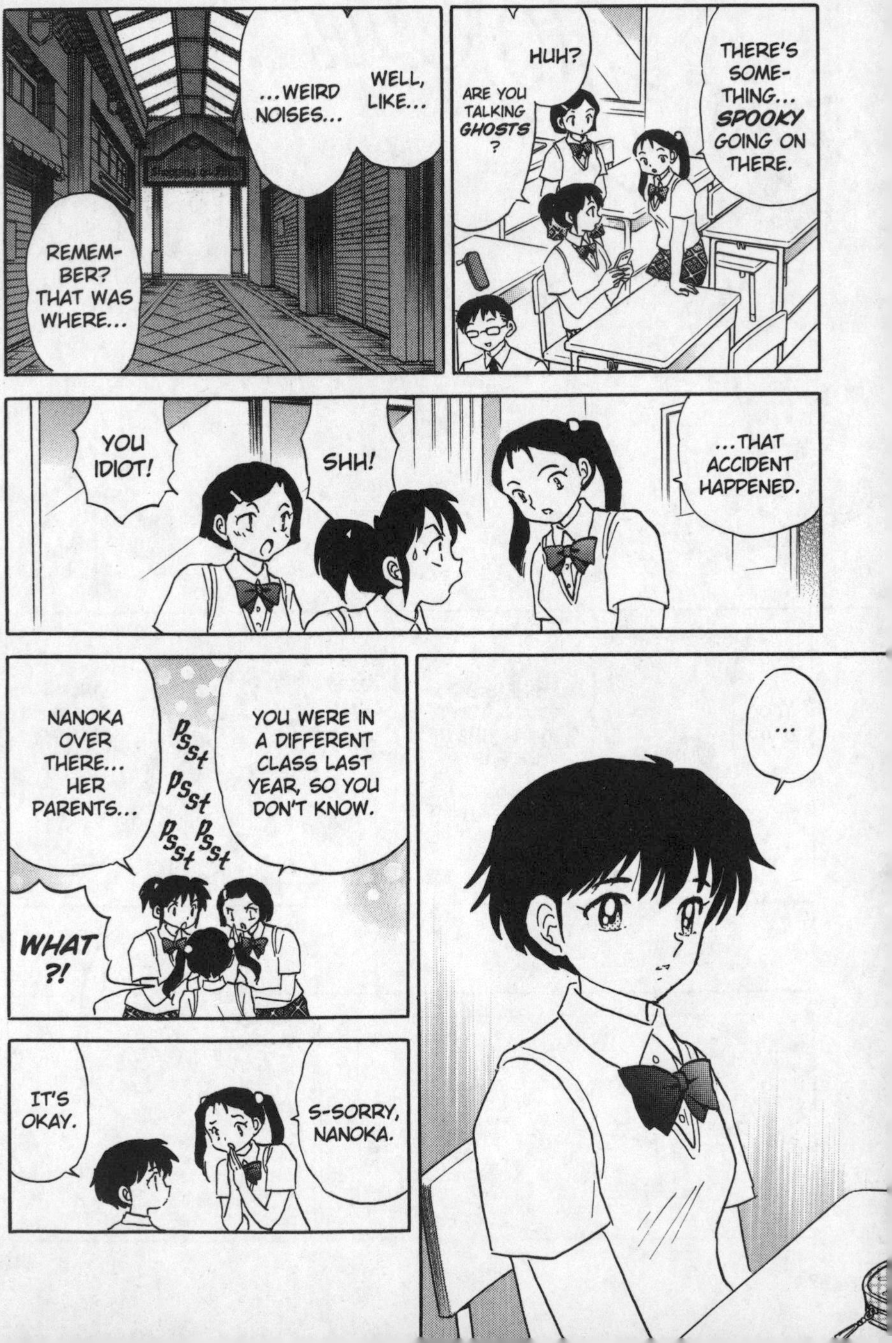
THERE'S SOME-THING... SPOOKY GOING ON THERE.
HUH?
ARE YOU TALKING GHOSTS?
WELL, LIKE...
...WEIRD NOISES...
REMEMBER? THAT WAS WHERE...
...THAT ACCIDENT HAPPENED.
SHH!
YOU IDIOT!
...
YOU WERE IN A DIFFERENT CLASS LAST YEAR, SO YOU DON'T KNOW.
PSST PSST PSST PSST
NANOKA OVER THERE... HER PARENTS...
WHAT?!
S-SORRY, NANOKA.
IT'S OKAY.

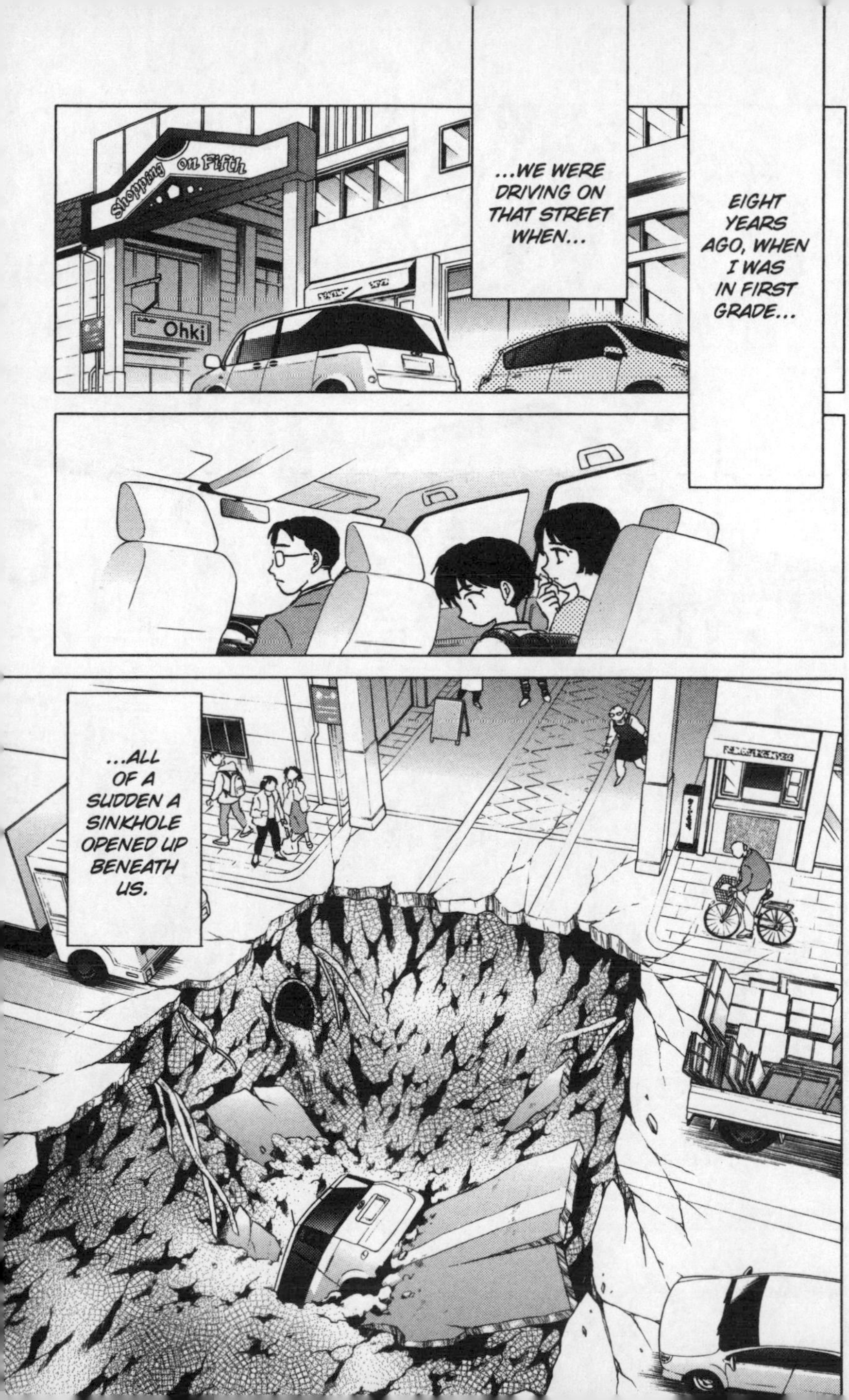

EIGHT YEARS AGO, WHEN I WAS IN FIRST GRADE...
...WE WERE DRIVING ON THAT STREET WHEN...
Shopping on Fifth
Ohki
...ALL OF A SUDDEN A SINKHOLE OPENED UP BENEATH US.

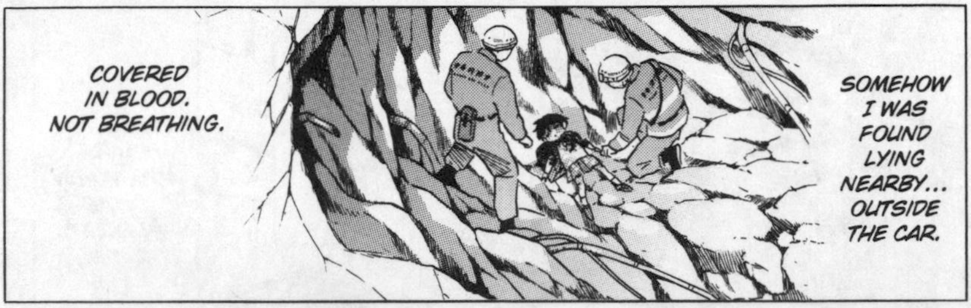
SOMEHOW I WAS FOUND LYING NEARBY... OUTSIDE THE CAR.
COVERED IN BLOOD. NOT BREATHING.

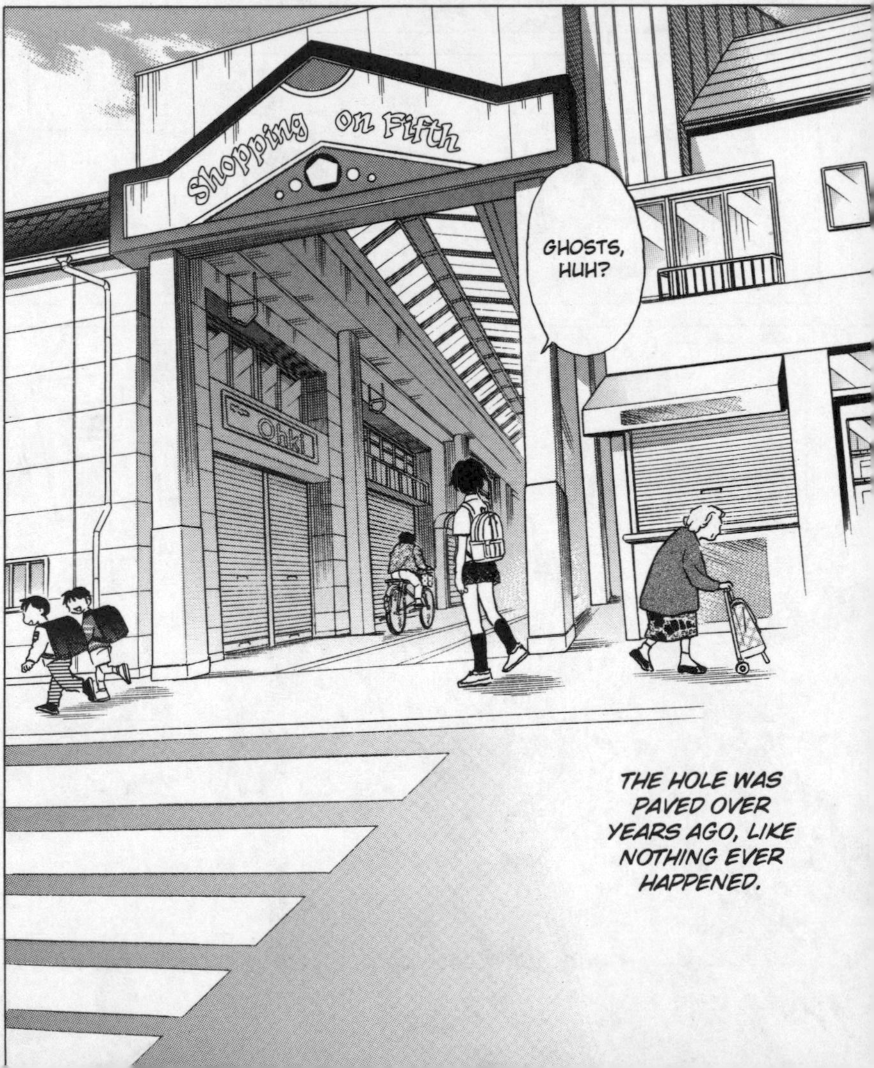
Shopping on Fifth
GHOSTS, HUH?
Ohki
THE HOLE WAS PAVED OVER YEARS AGO, LIKE NOTHING EVER HAPPENED.

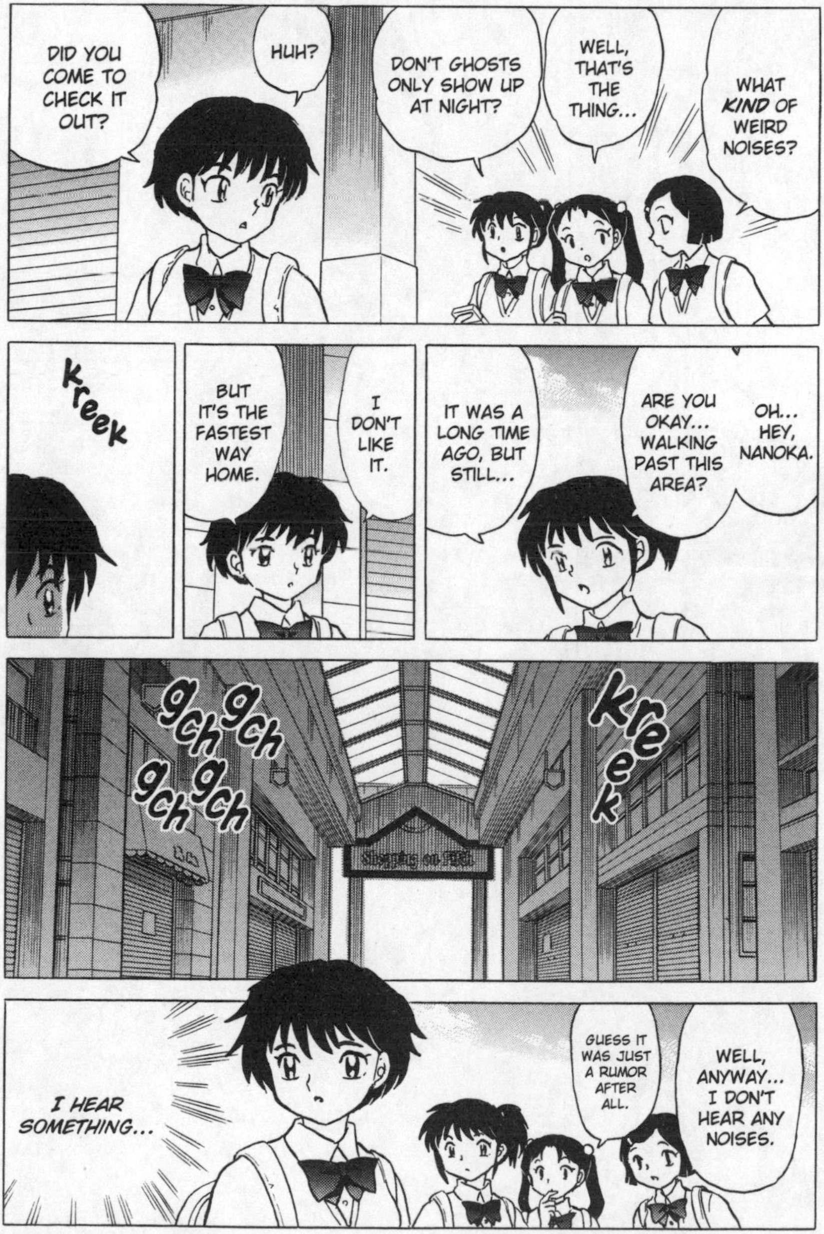

WHAT *KIND* OF WEIRD NOISES?
WELL, THAT'S THE THING...
DON'T GHOSTS ONLY SHOW UP AT NIGHT?
HUH?
DID YOU COME TO CHECK IT OUT?
OH... HEY, NANOKA.
ARE YOU OKAY... WALKING PAST THIS AREA?
IT WAS A LONG TIME AGO, BUT STILL...
I DON'T LIKE IT.
BUT IT'S THE FASTEST WAY HOME.
kreek
kreek
gch gch gch gch
WELL, ANYWAY... I DON'T HEAR ANY NOISES.
GUESS IT WAS JUST A RUMOR AFTER ALL.
I HEAR SOMETHING...

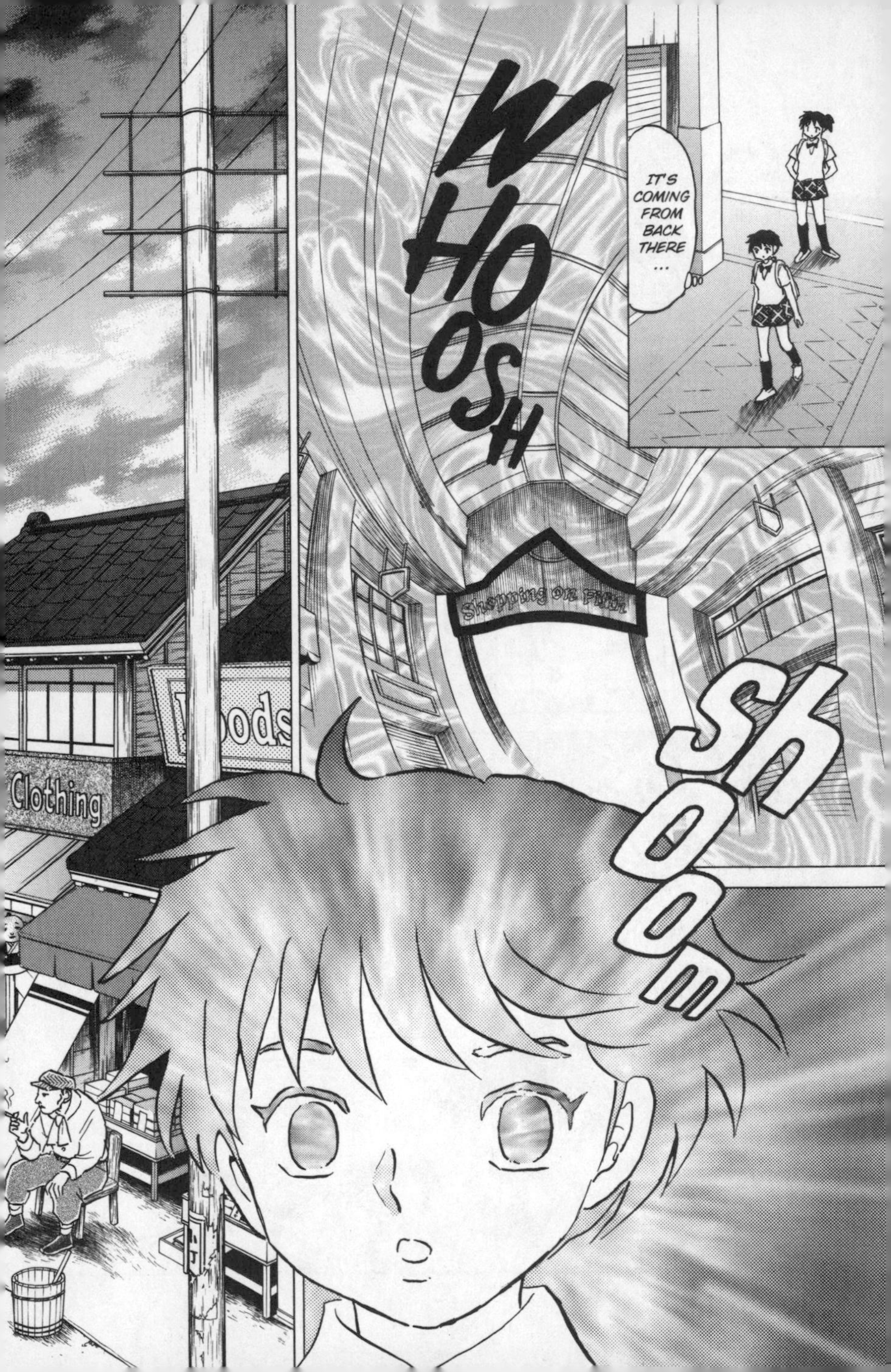
IT'S COMING FROM BACK THERE ...
WHOOSH
Shopping on Fifth
SHOOOM
Clothing

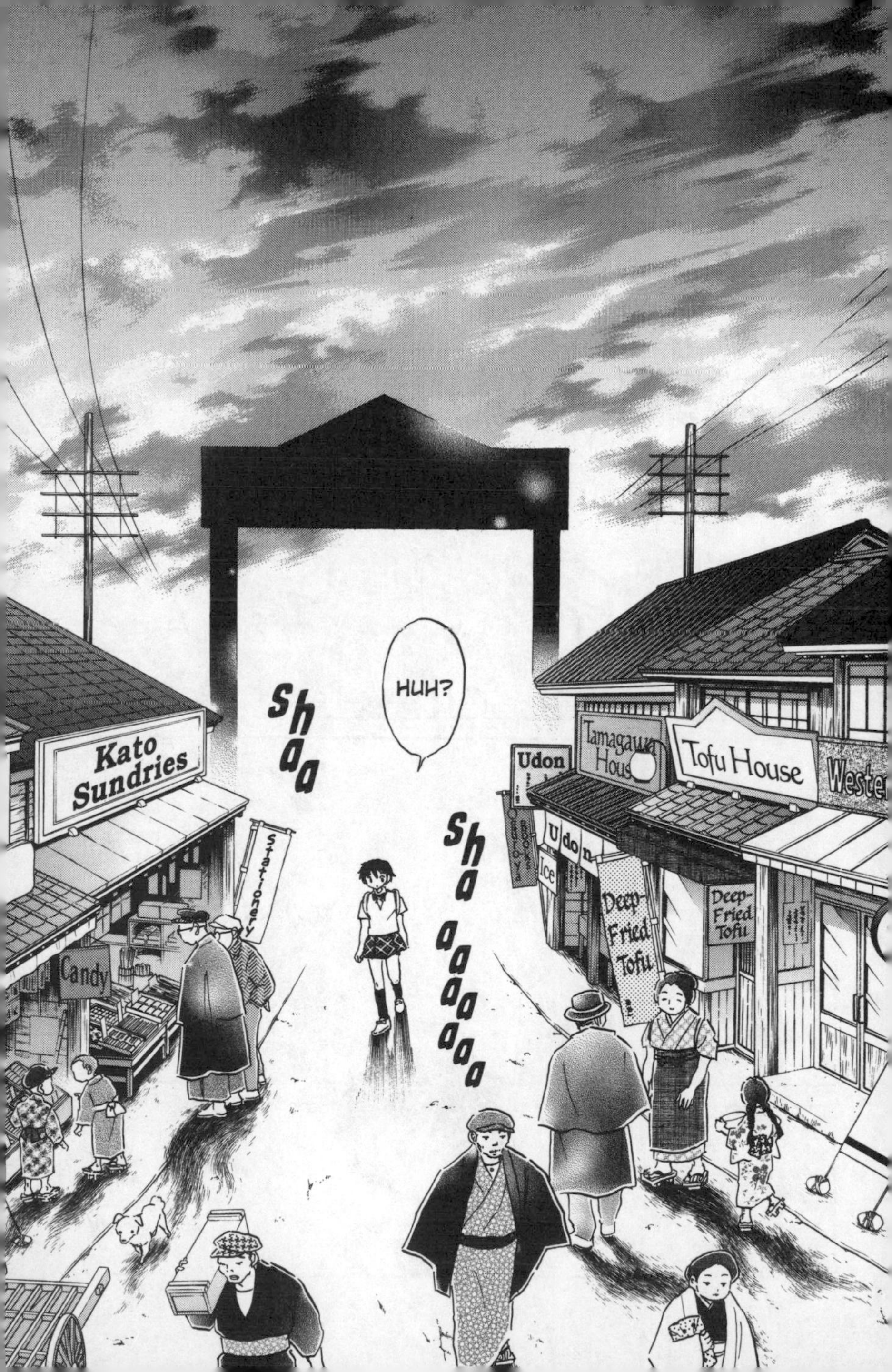
Tofu House
Tamagawa House
Udon
Udon
Ice
Deep-Fried Tofu
Deep-Fried Tofu
HUH?
Shaaaaaaaa
Shaa
Kato Sundries
Stationery
Candy

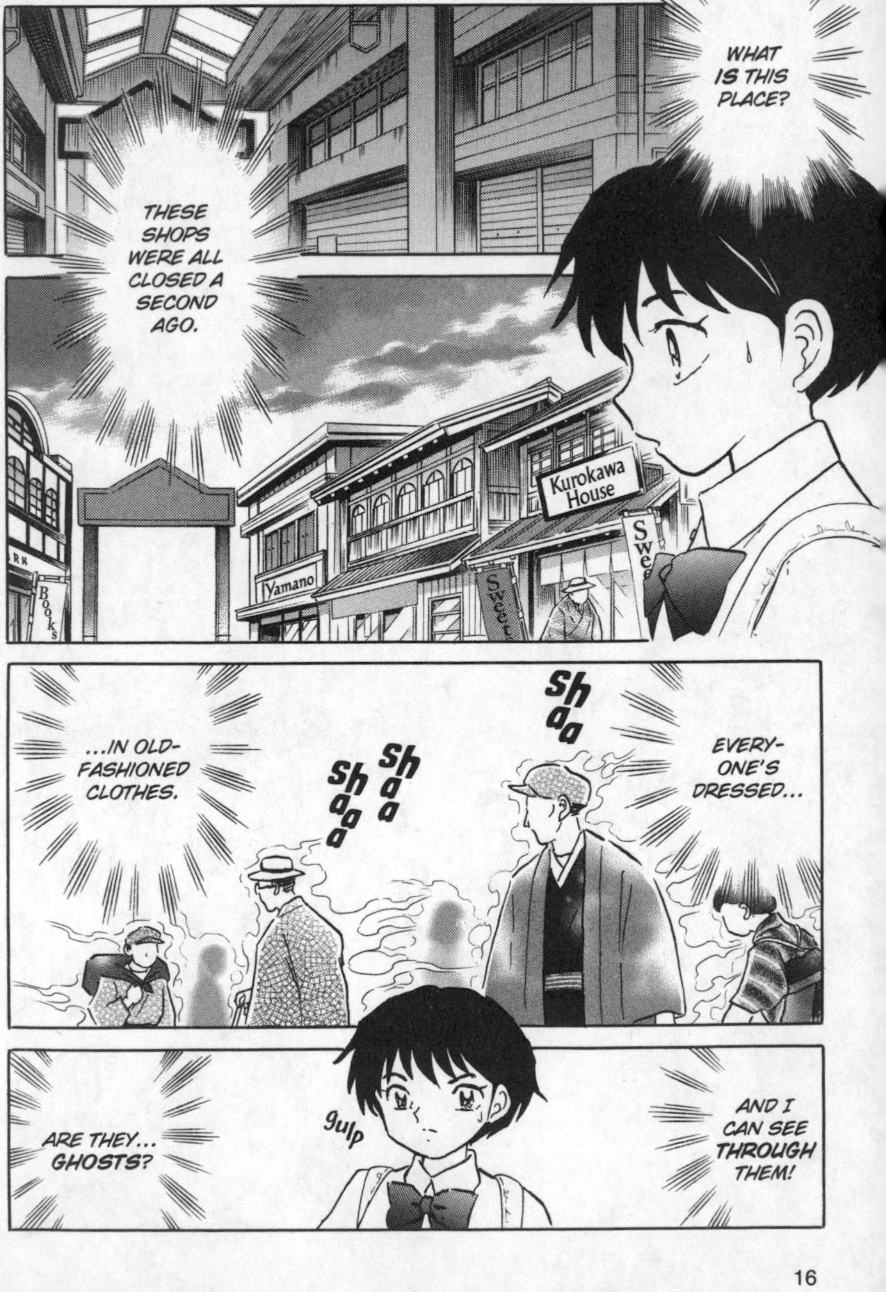
WHAT IS THIS PLACE?
THESE SHOPS WERE ALL CLOSED A SECOND AGO.
Kurokawa House
Yamano
Books
Shaa
Shaa
Shaa
EVERY-ONE'S DRESSED...
...IN OLD-FASHIONED CLOTHES.
AND I CAN SEE THROUGH THEM!
gulp
ARE THEY... GHOSTS?

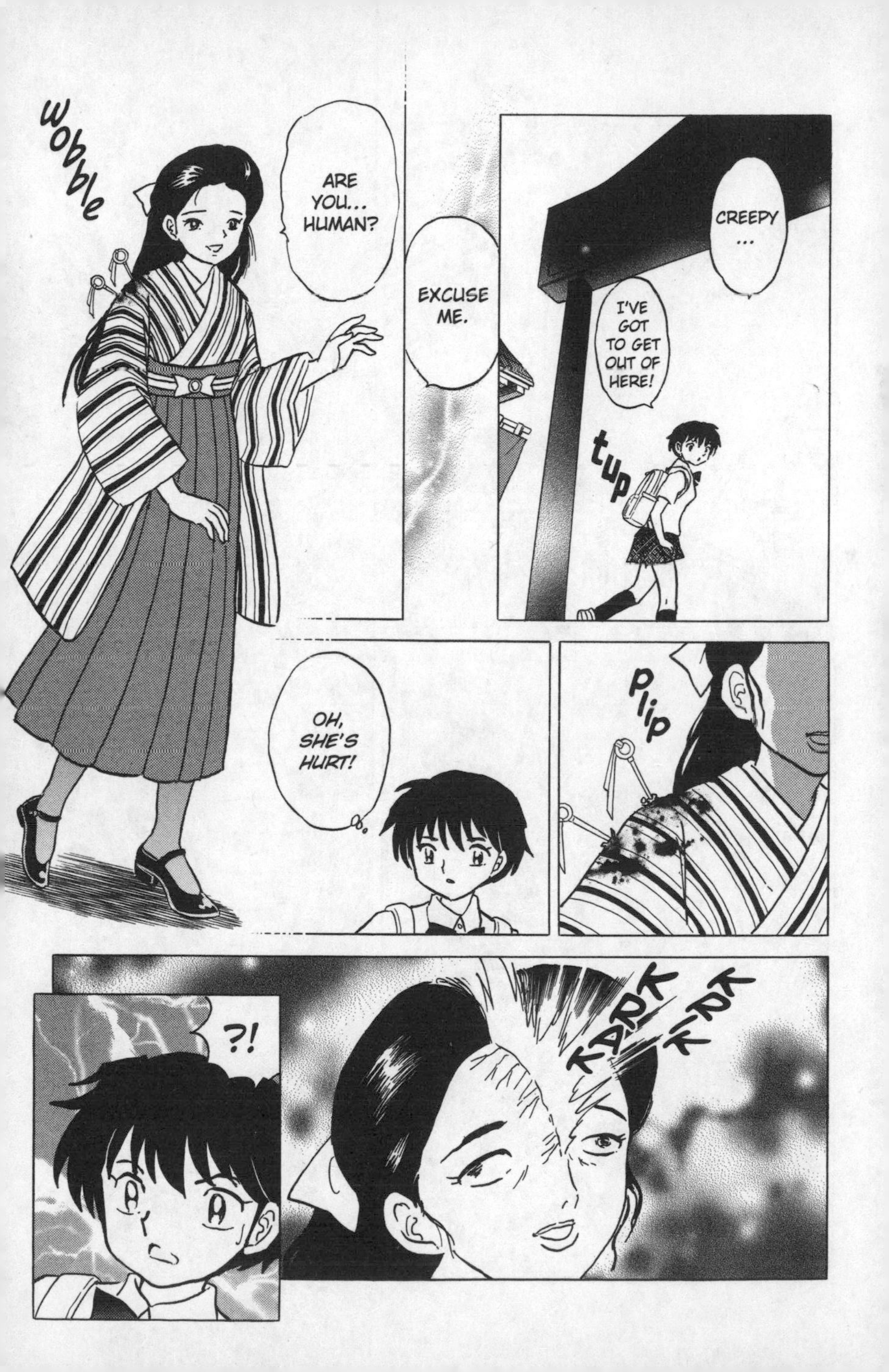

CREEPY ...
I'VE GOT TO GET OUT OF HERE!
tup
EXCUSE ME.
ARE YOU... HUMAN?
wobble
plip
OH, SHE'S HURT!
KRAK
KRIK
?!

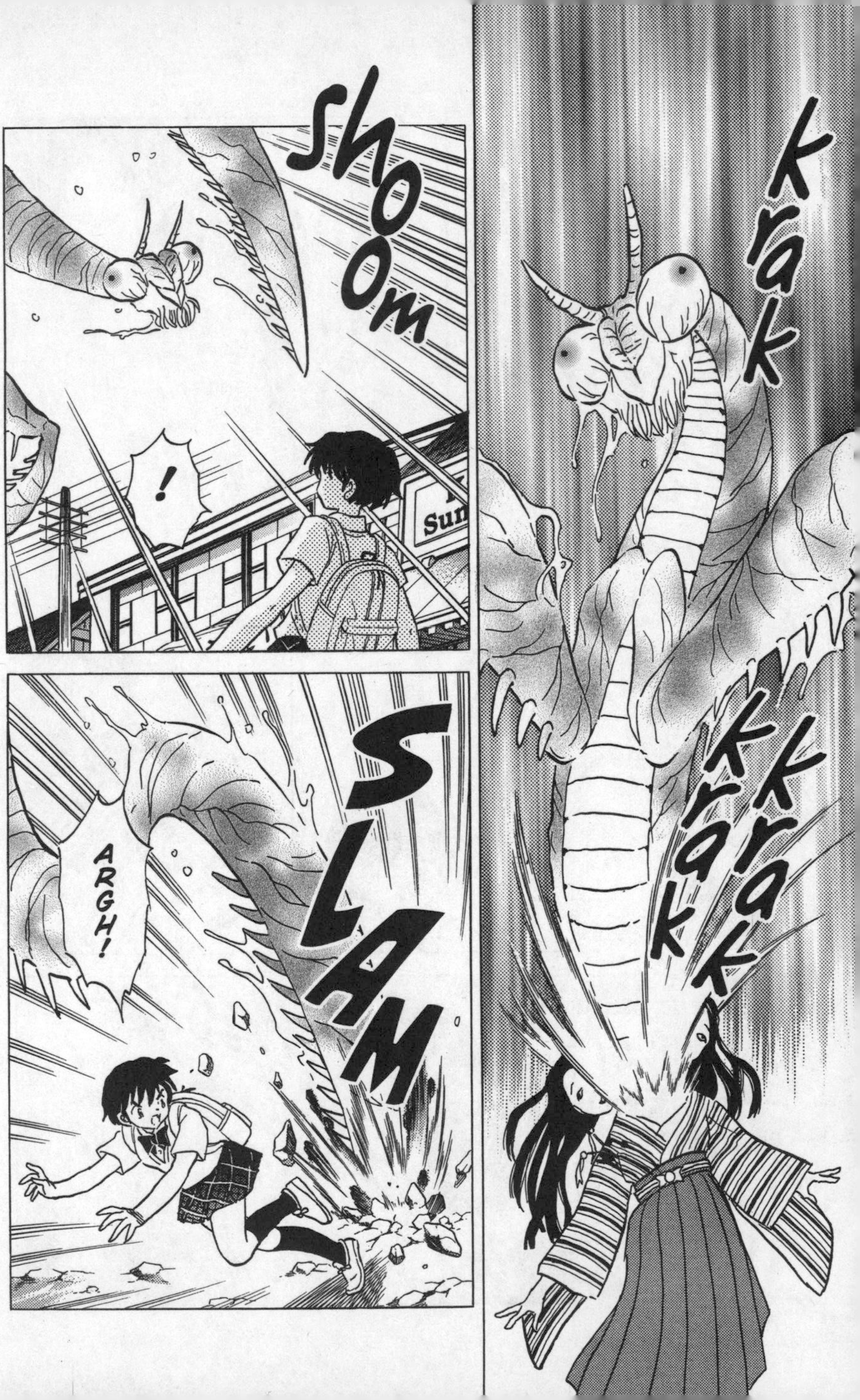
krak
krak
krak
SHOOM
!
Sun
SLAM
ARGH!

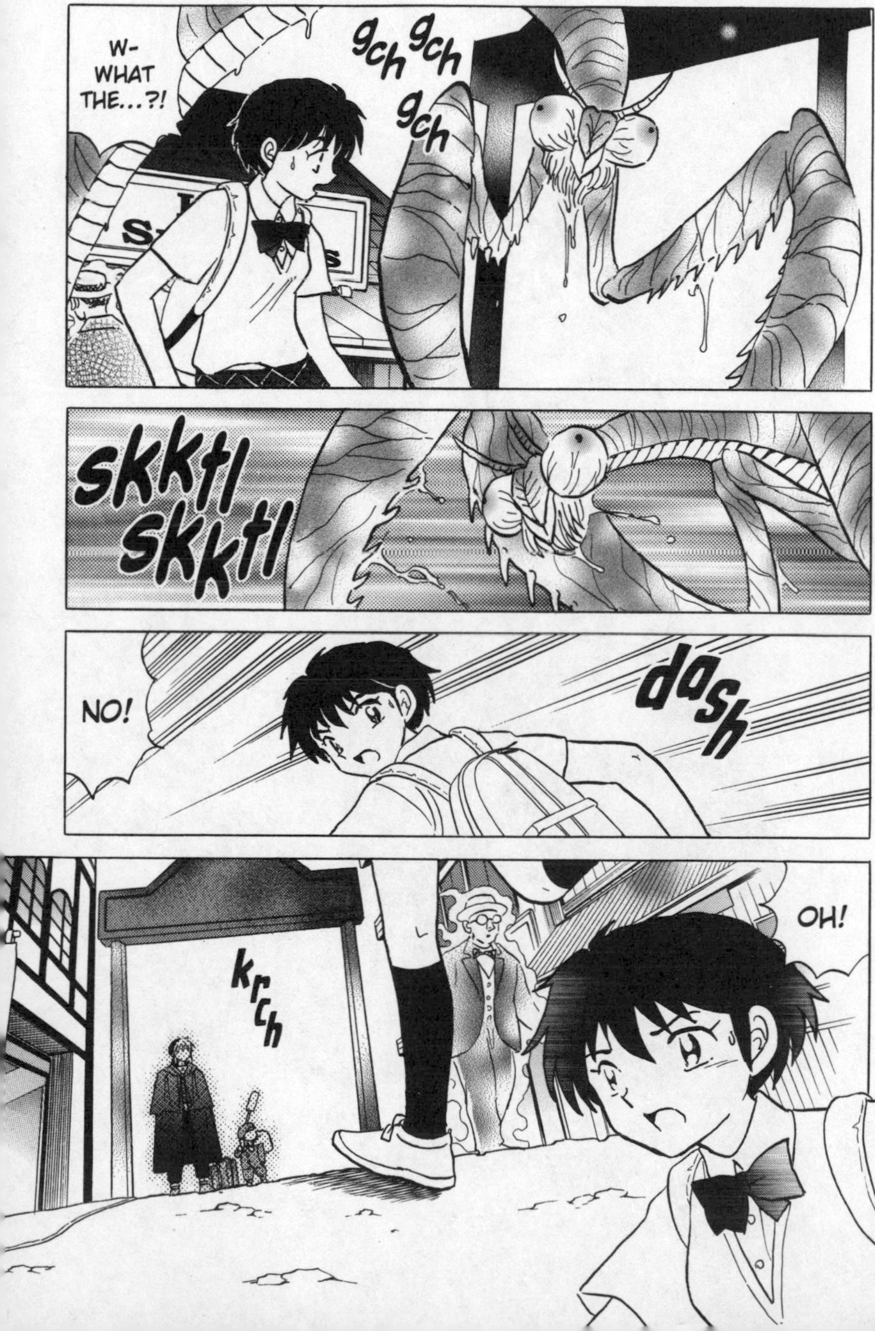
gch gch gch
W- WHAT THE...?!
skktl skktl
dash
NO!
OH!
krch

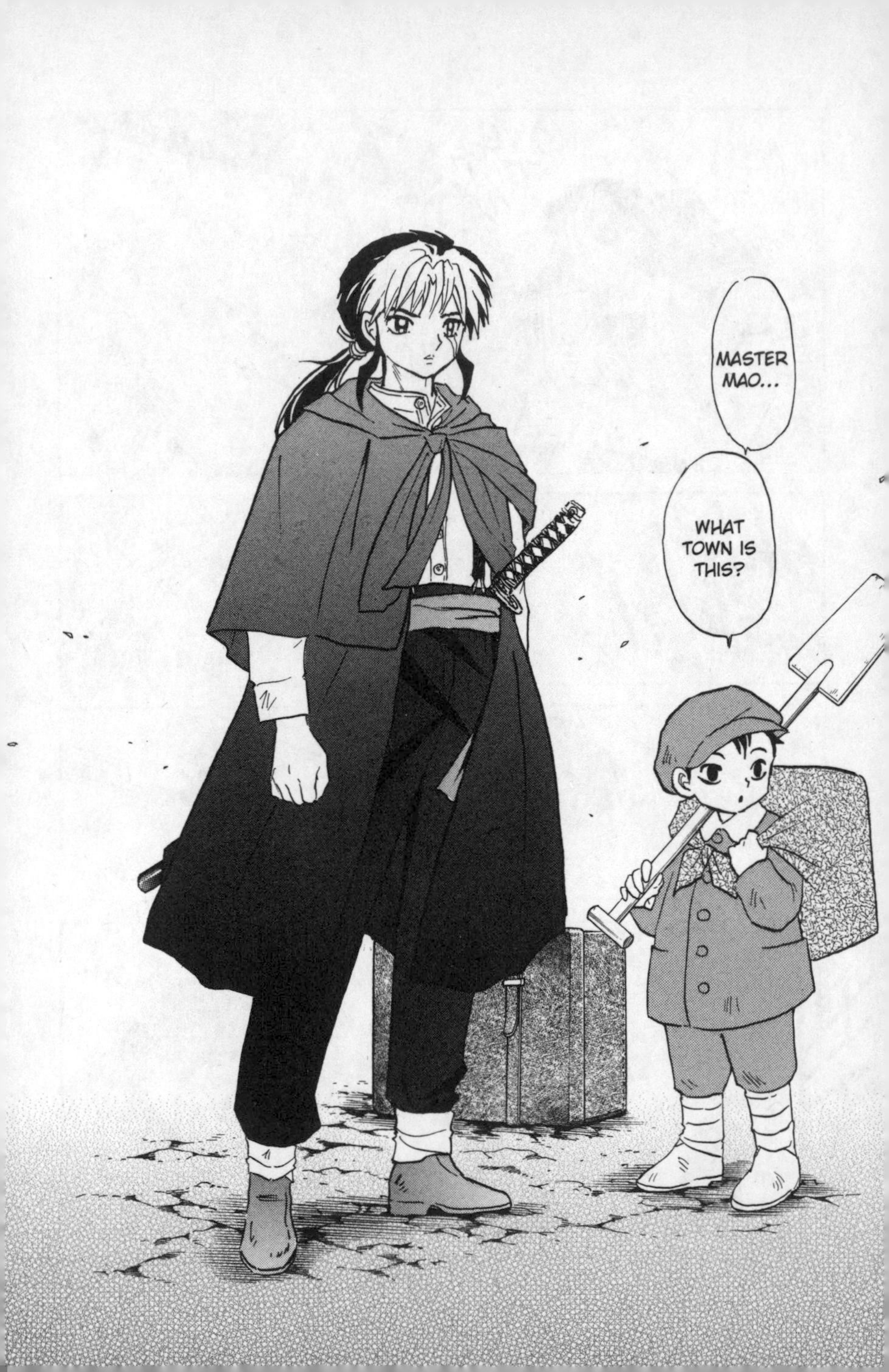
MASTER MAO...
WHAT TOWN IS THIS?

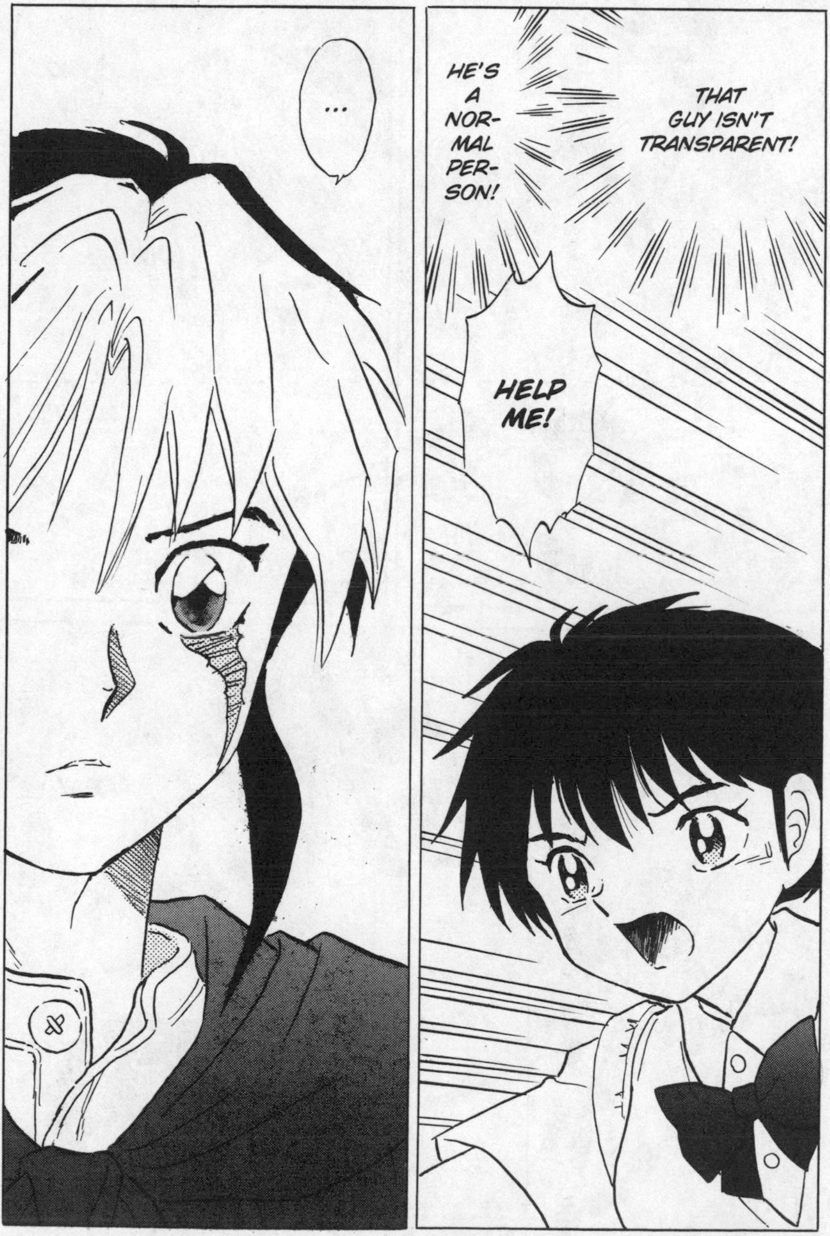
THAT GUY ISN'T TRANSPARENT!
HE'S A NOR-MAL PER-SON!
HELP ME!
...

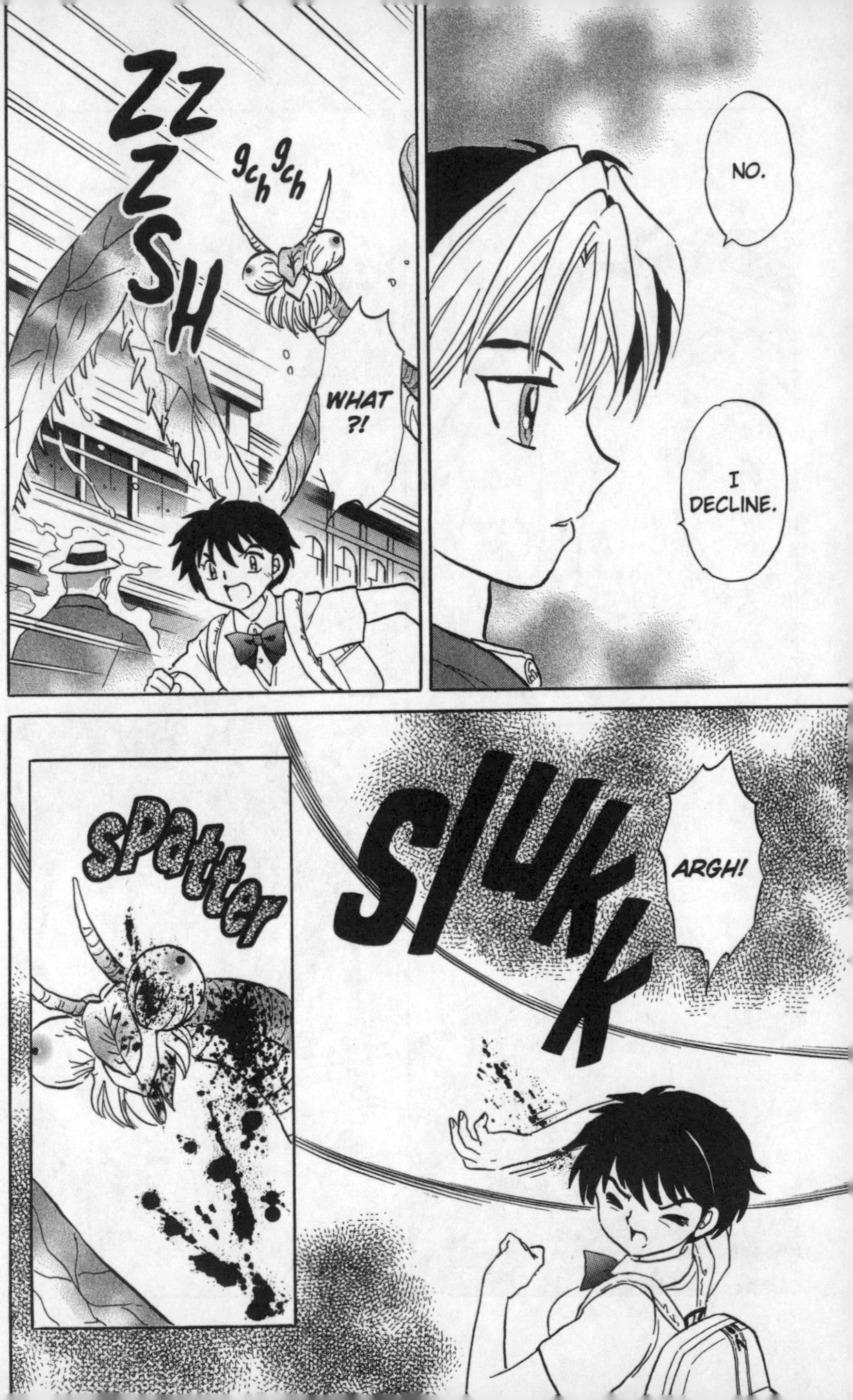
NO.
I DECLINE.
ZZZSH
gch gch
WHAT?!
SLUKK
ARGH!
sPatter

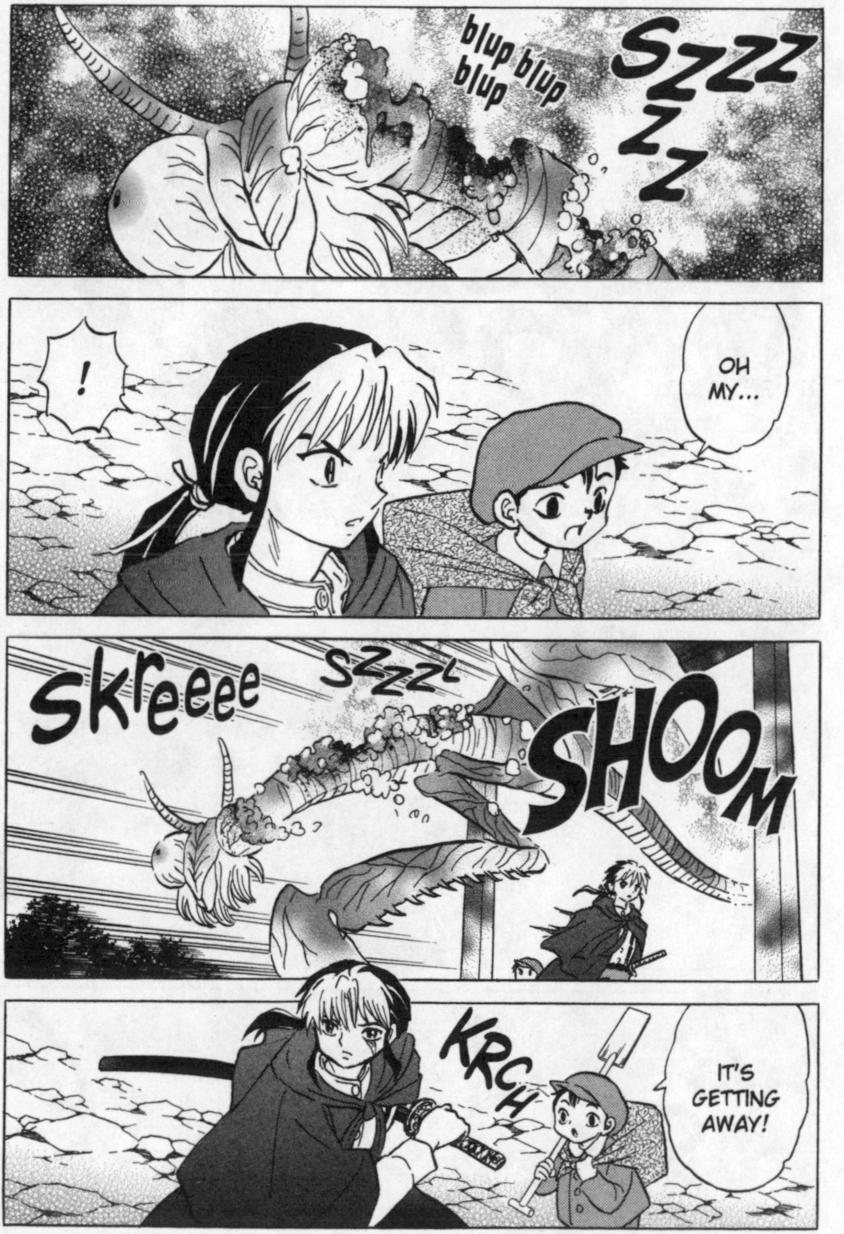
SZZZZ Z Z
blup blup
blup
OH MY...
!
SHOOM
SZZZL
SKREEEE
IT'S GETTING AWAY!
KRCH

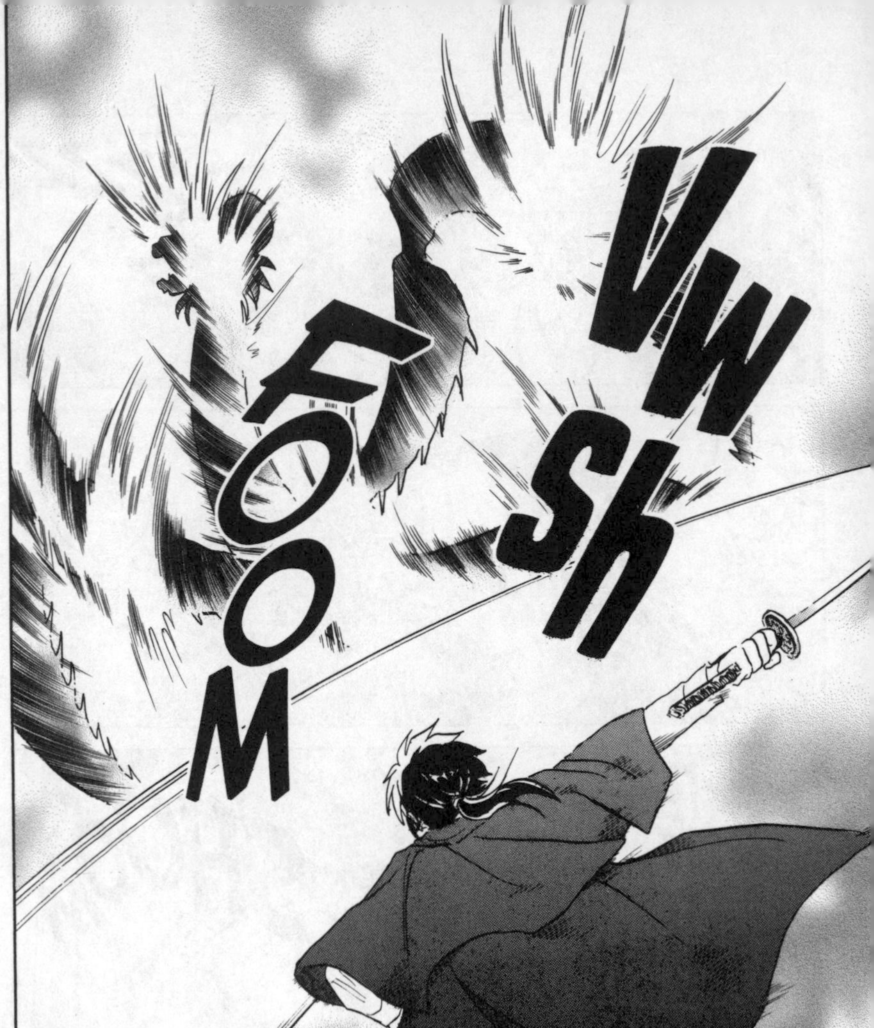
VWSH
FOOM
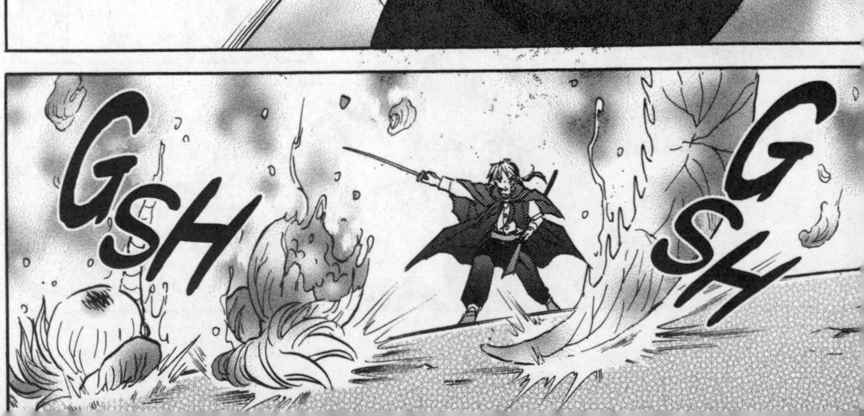
GSH
GSH

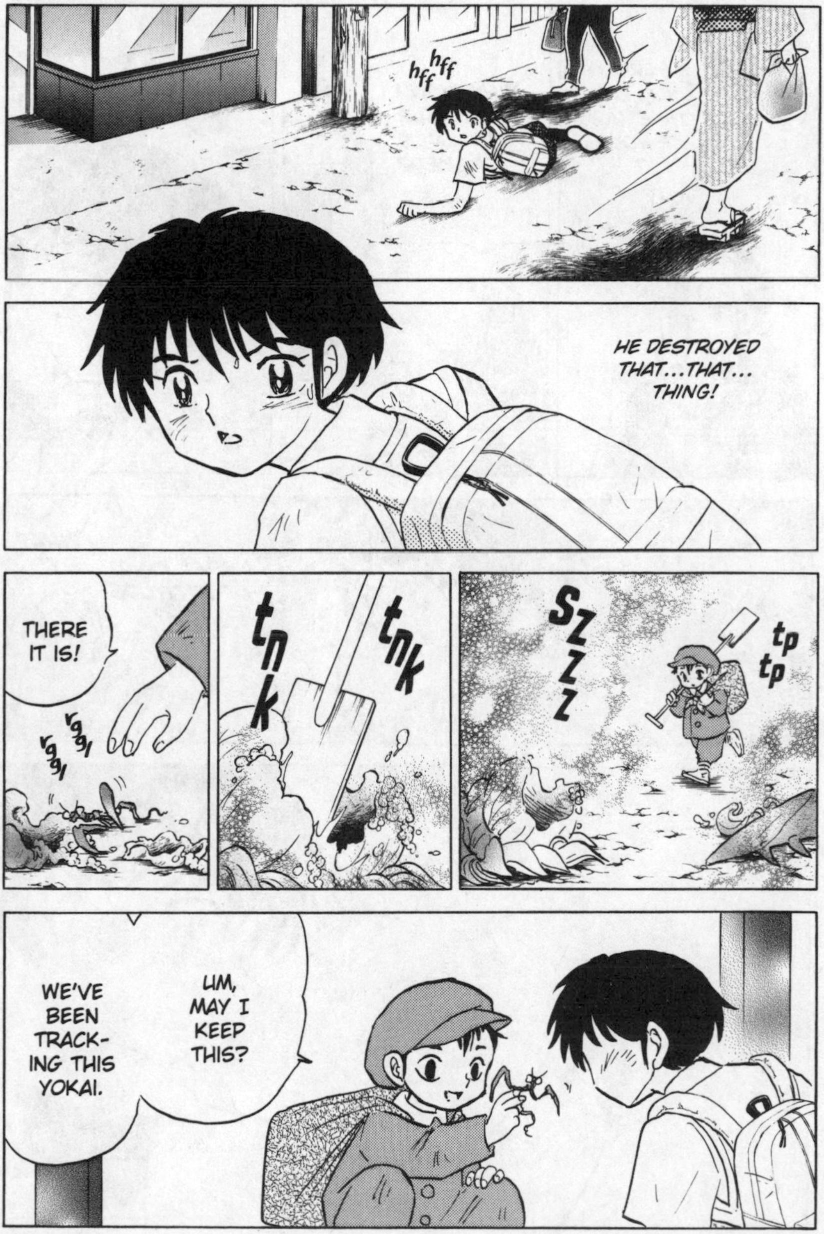
hff hff
HE DESTROYED THAT...THAT... THING!
SZZZ
tp tp
tnk tnk
THERE IT IS!
rggl rggl
UM, MAY I KEEP THIS?
WE'VE BEEN TRACK-ING THIS YOKAI.

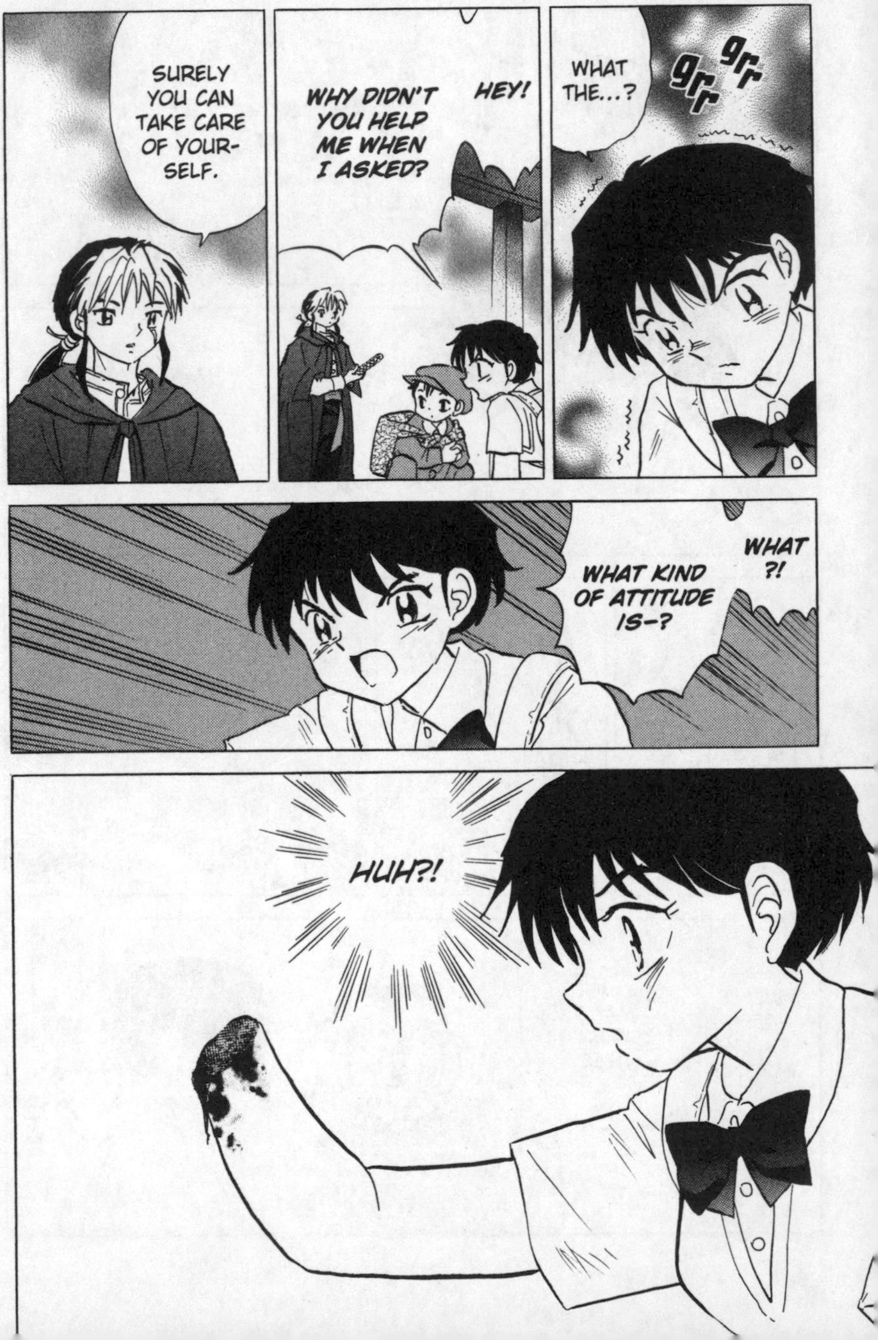
WHAT THE...?
grr grr
HEY!
WHY DIDN'T YOU HELP ME WHEN I ASKED?
SURELY YOU CAN TAKE CARE OF YOUR-SELF.
WHAT ?!
WHAT KIND OF ATTITUDE IS–?
HUH?!

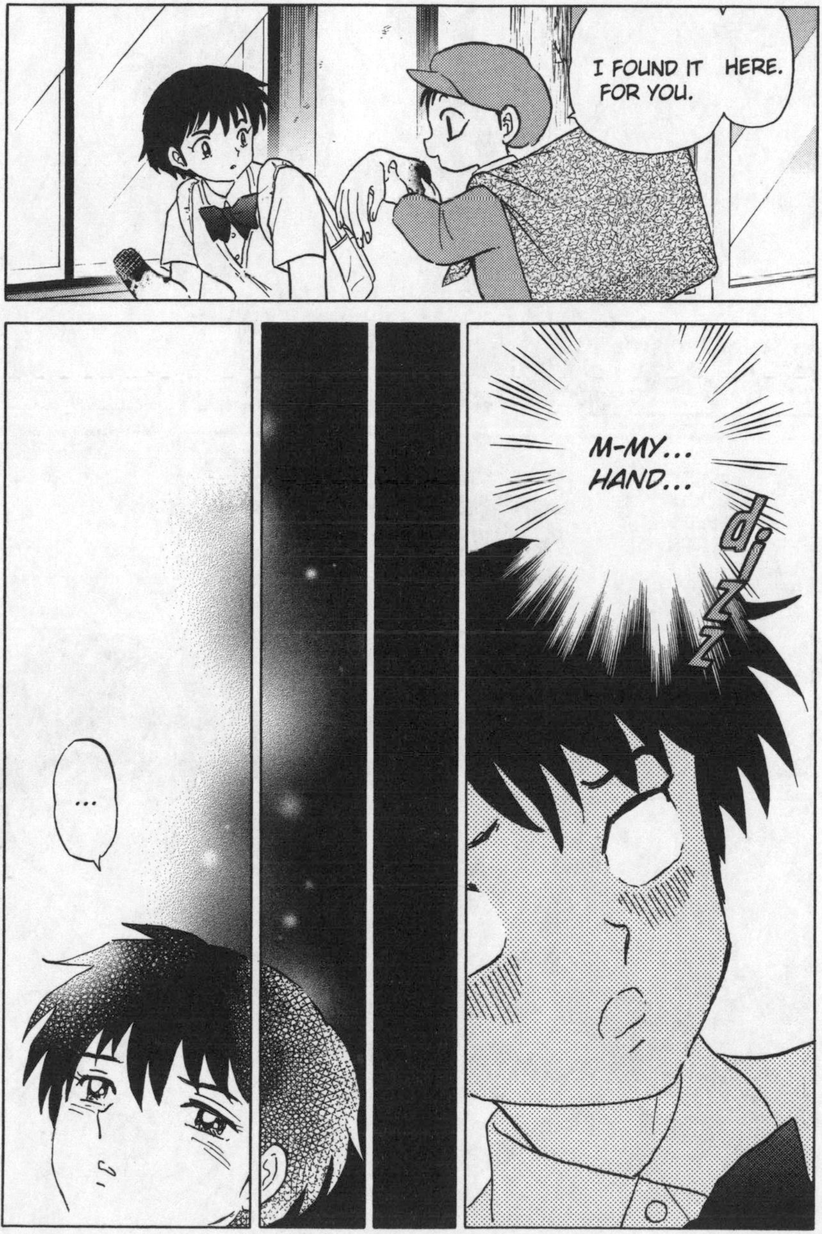
I FOUND IT FOR YOU. HERE.
M-MY... HAND...
dizzz
...

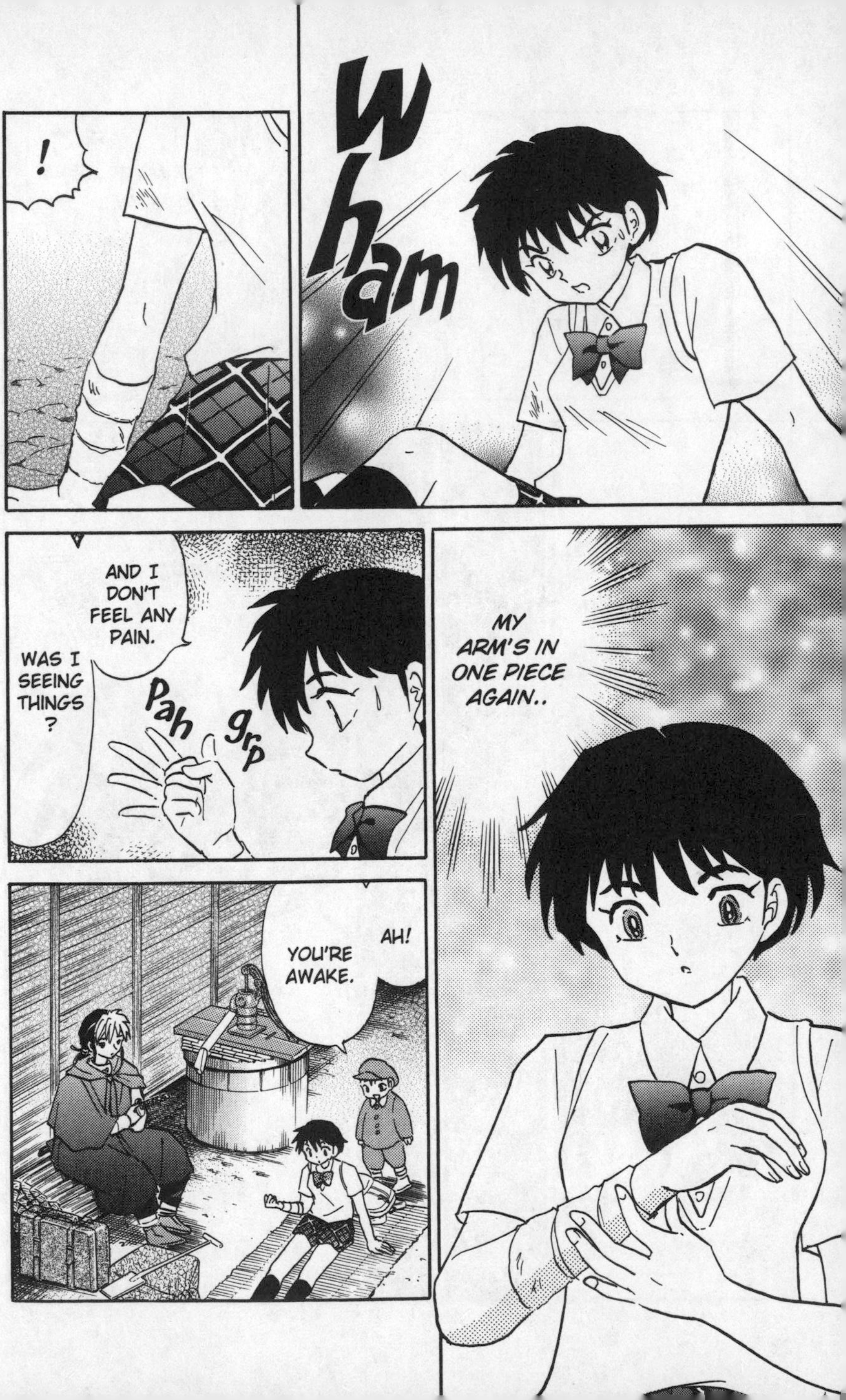

wham
!
MY ARM'S IN ONE PIECE AGAIN..
AND I DON'T FEEL ANY PAIN.
WAS I SEEING THINGS?
grp
Pah
AH!
YOU'RE AWAKE.

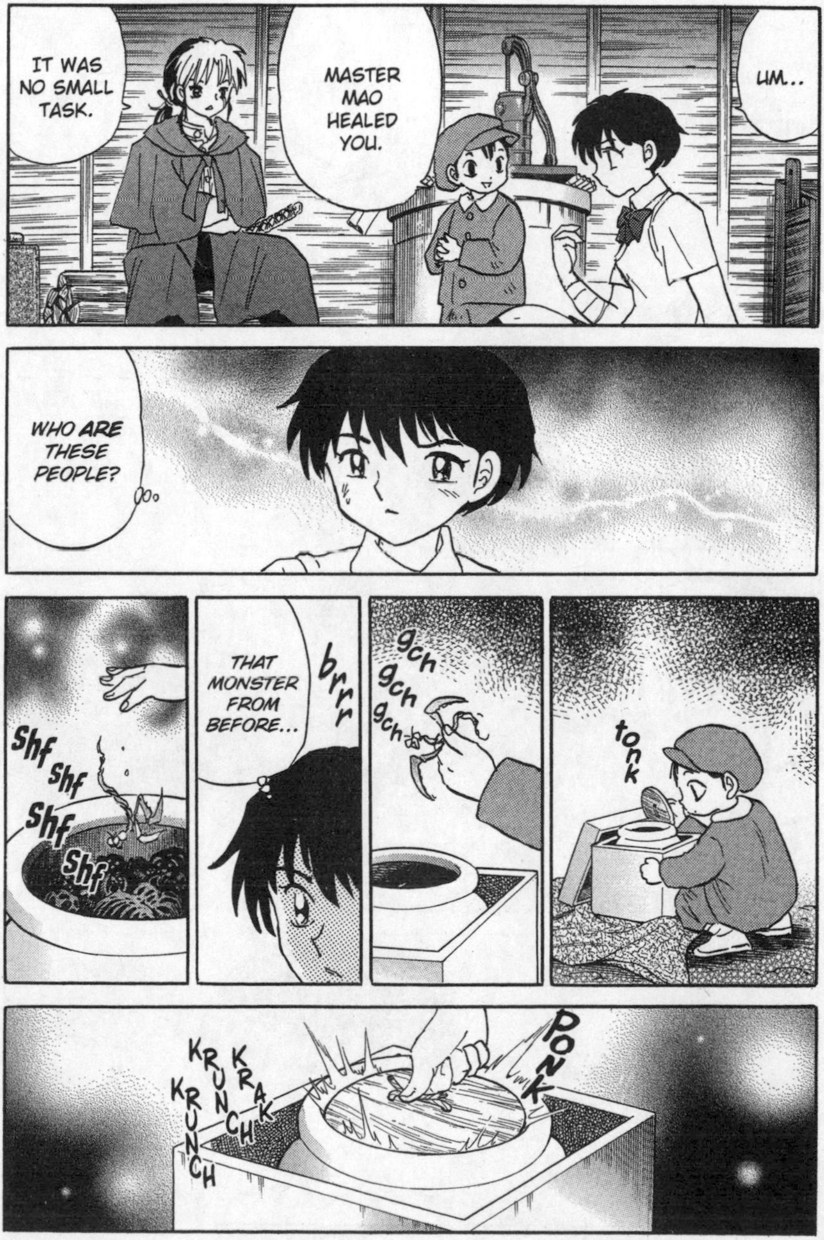
UM...
MASTER MAO HEALED YOU.
IT WAS NO SMALL TASK.
WHO ARE THESE PEOPLE?
tonk
gch gch gch
brrr
THAT MONSTER FROM BEFORE...
shf shf shf shf
PONK
KRAK
KRUNCH
KRUNCH

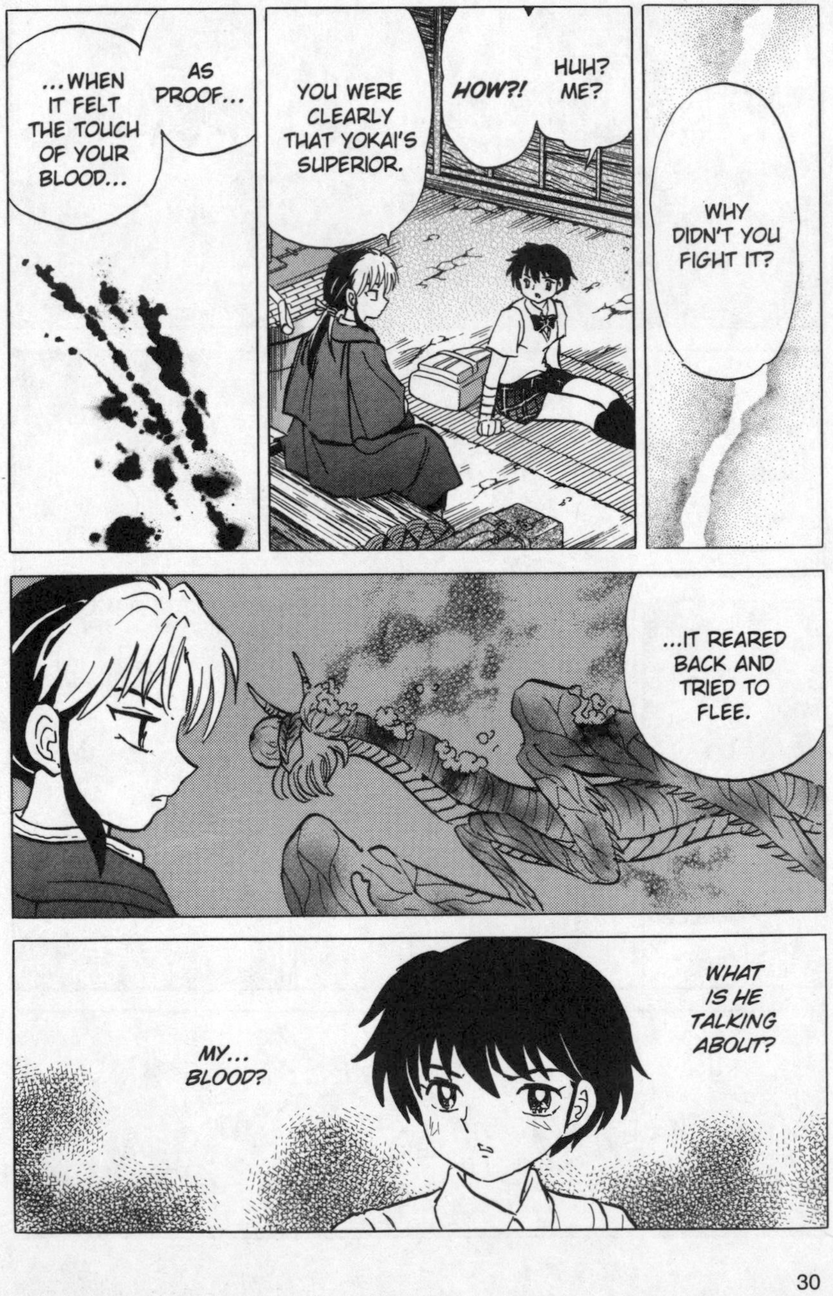
WHY DIDN'T YOU FIGHT IT?
HUH? ME?
HOW?!
YOU WERE CLEARLY THAT YOKAI'S SUPERIOR.
AS PROOF...
...WHEN IT FELT THE TOUCH OF YOUR BLOOD...
...IT REARED BACK AND TRIED TO FLEE.
WHAT IS HE TALKING ABOUT?
MY... BLOOD?

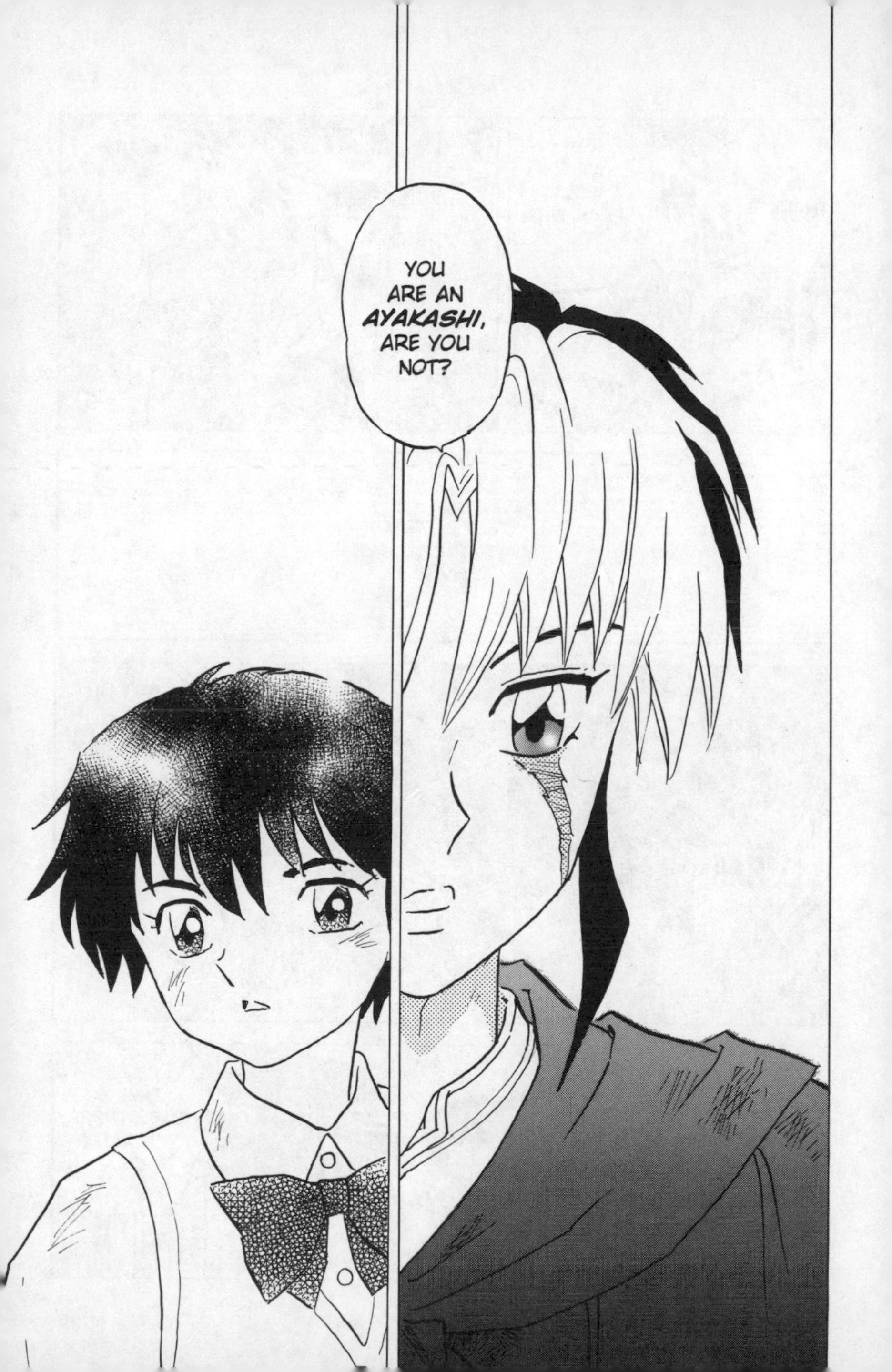
YOU ARE AN AYAKASHI, ARE YOU NOT?

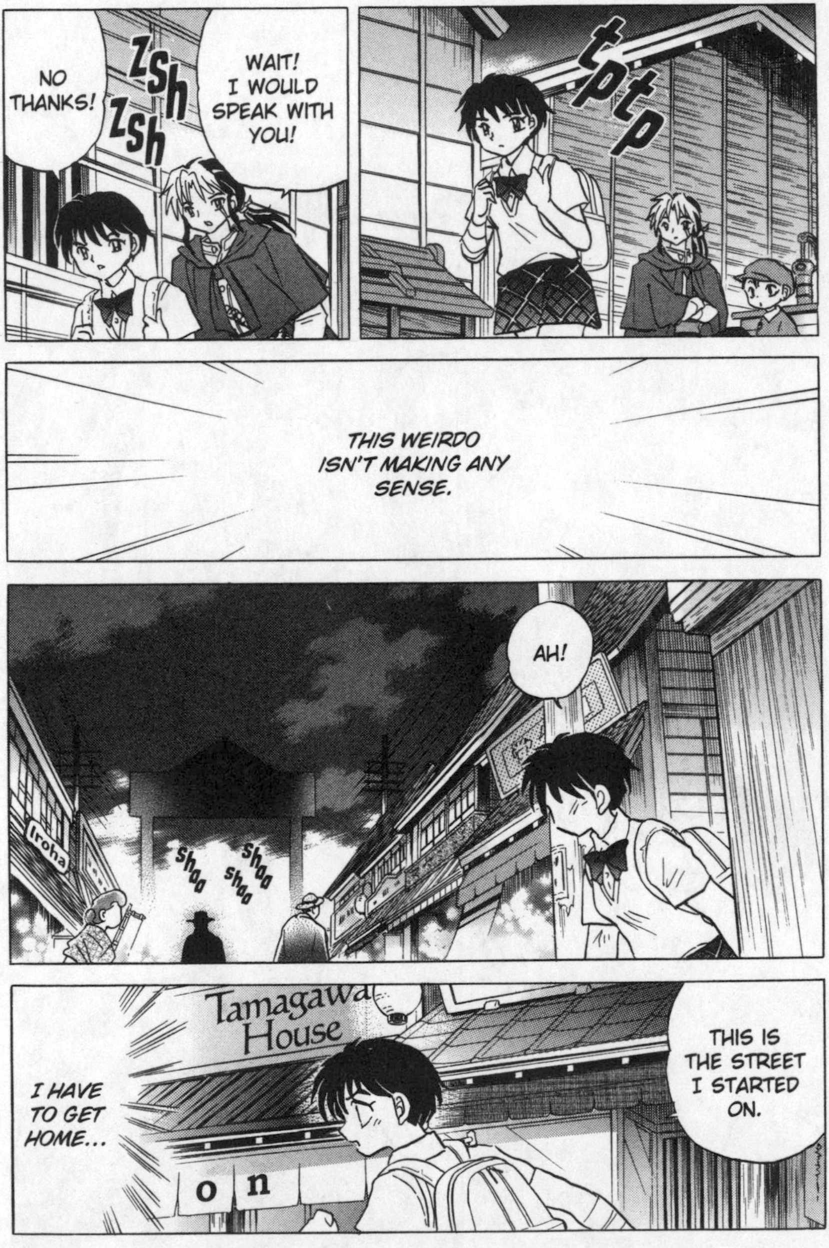
tptp
WAIT! I WOULD SPEAK WITH YOU!
zsh zsh
NO THANKS!
THIS WEIRDO ISN'T MAKING ANY SENSE.
AH!
shaa shaa shaa
Iroha
THIS IS THE STREET I STARTED ON.
Tamagawa House
I HAVE TO GET HOME...
o n

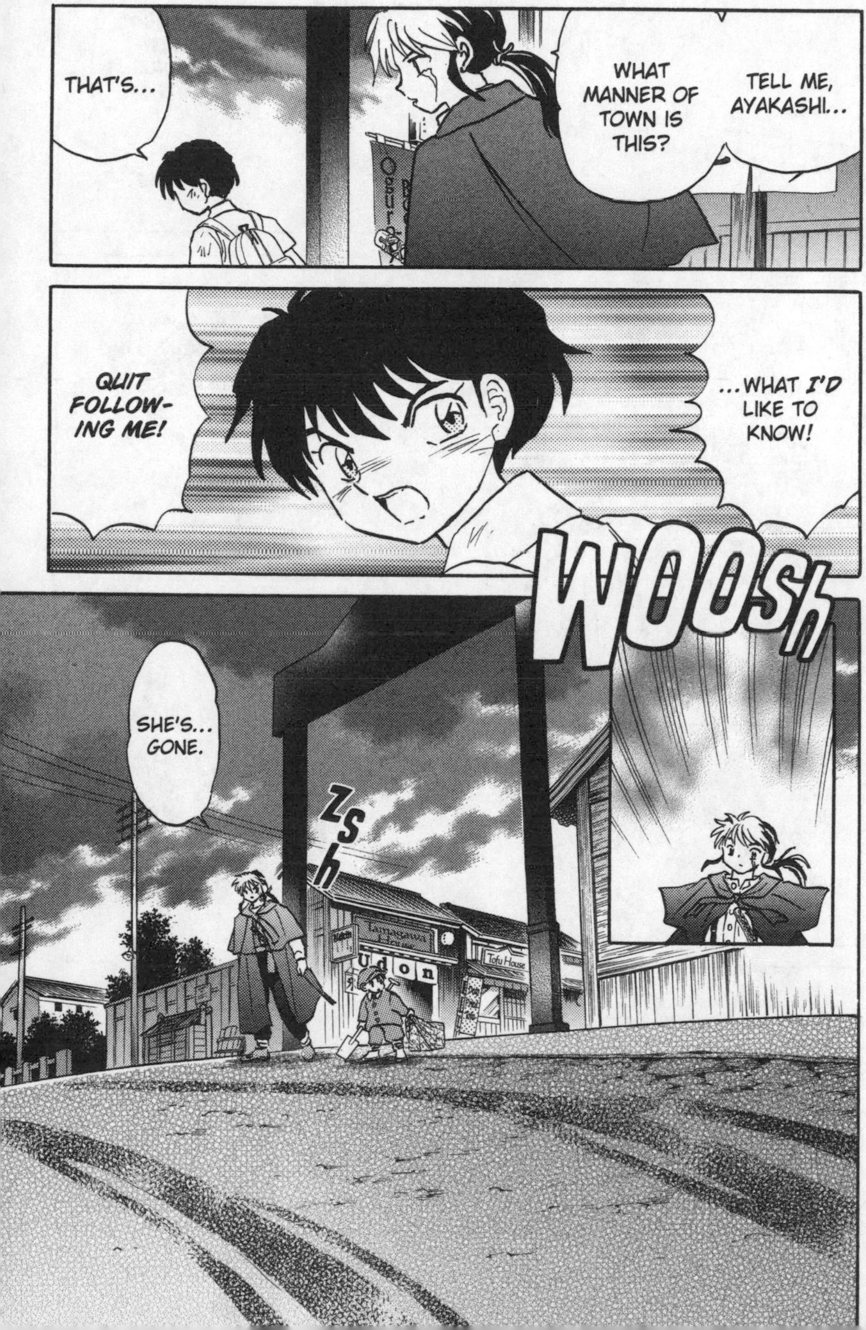
TELL ME, AYAKASHI...
WHAT MANNER OF TOWN IS THIS?
THAT'S...
...WHAT *I'D* LIKE TO KNOW!
QUIT FOLLOWING-ING ME!
WOOSH
SHE'S... GONE.
ZSH
Udon
Tofu House

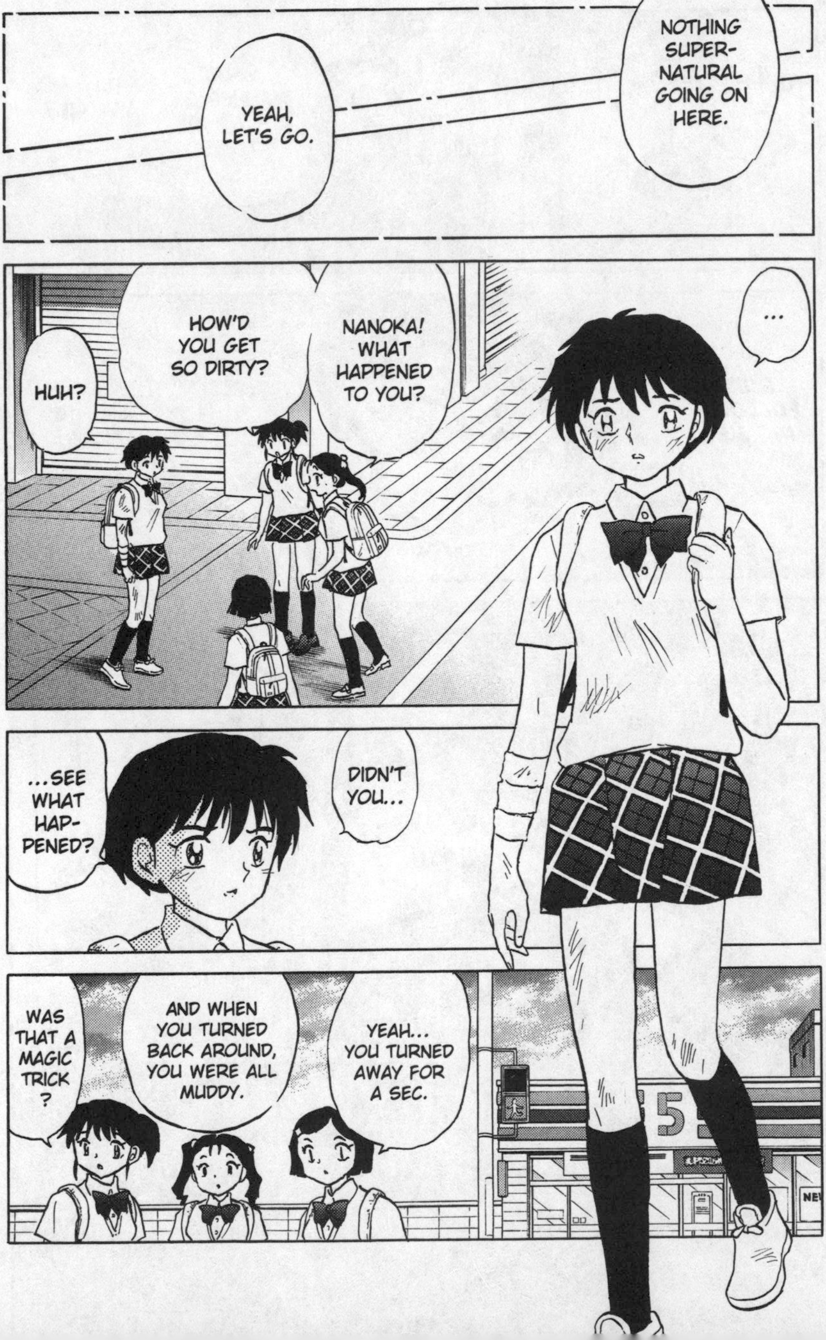
NOTHING SUPER-NATURAL GOING ON HERE.
YEAH, LET'S GO.
...
NANOKA! WHAT HAPPENED TO YOU?
HOW'D YOU GET SO DIRTY?
HUH?
DIDN'T YOU...
...SEE WHAT HAP-PENED?
YEAH... YOU TURNED AWAY FOR A SEC.
AND WHEN YOU TURNED BACK AROUND, YOU WERE ALL MUDDY.
WAS THAT A MAGIC TRICK?

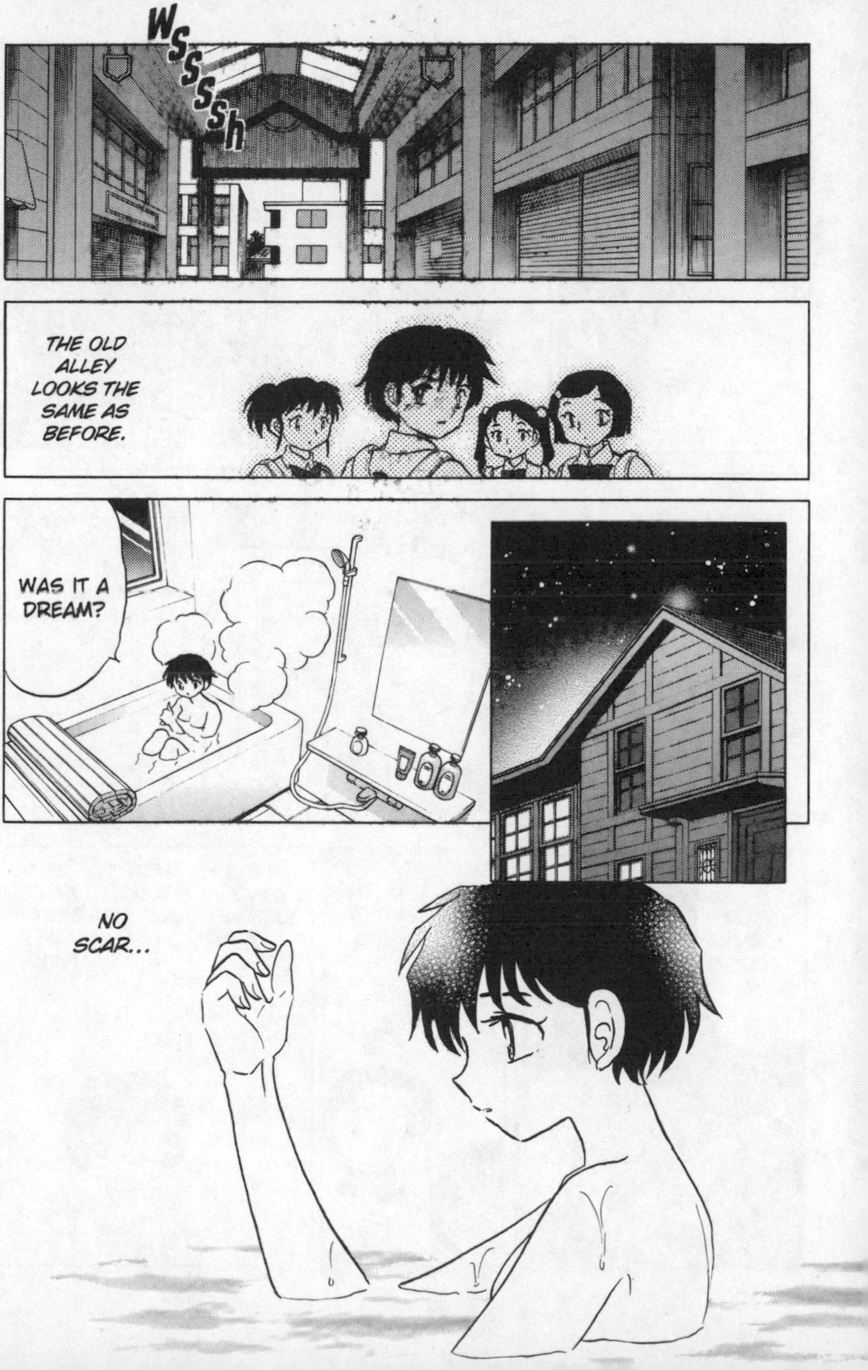
WSSSSh
THE OLD ALLEY LOOKS THE SAME AS BEFORE.
WAS IT A DREAM?
NO SCAR...

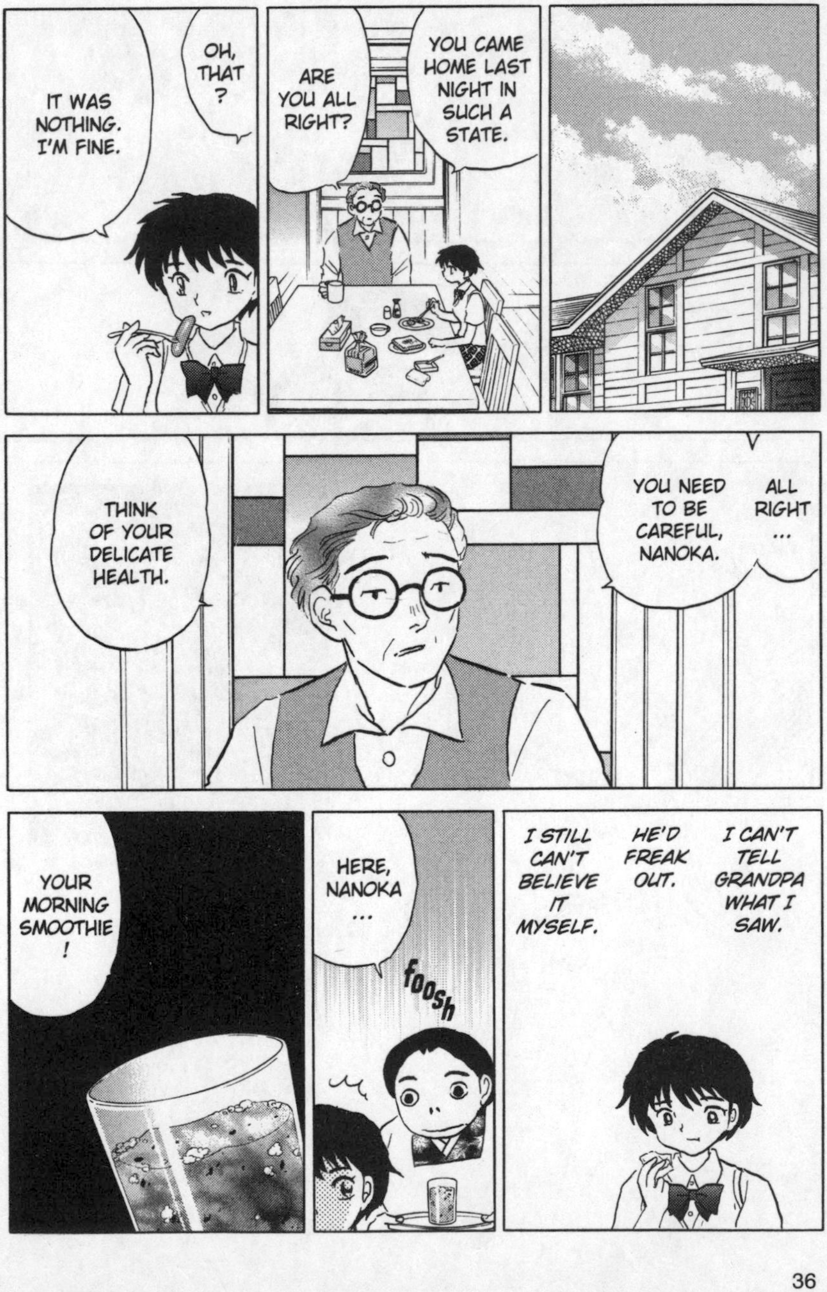
YOU CAME HOME LAST NIGHT IN SUCH A STATE.
ARE YOU ALL RIGHT?
OH, THAT?
IT WAS NOTHING. I'M FINE.
ALL RIGHT ...
YOU NEED TO BE CAREFUL, NANOKA.
THINK OF YOUR DELICATE HEALTH.
I CAN'T TELL GRANDPA WHAT I SAW.
HE'D FREAK OUT.
I STILL CAN'T BELIEVE IT MYSELF.
HERE, NANOKA ...
foosh
YOUR MORNING SMOOTHIE!

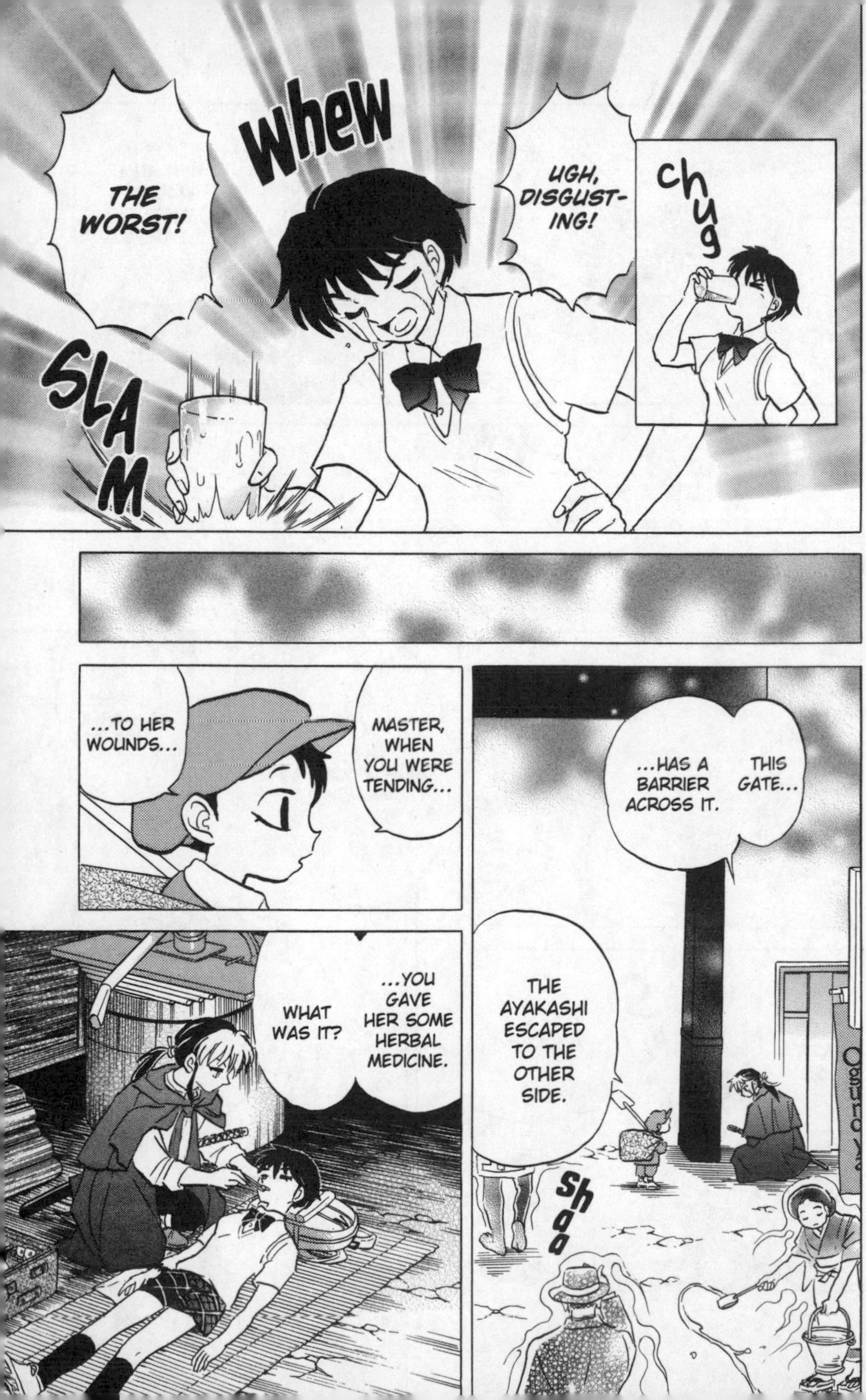
chug
UGH, DISGUST-ING!
whew
THE WORST!
SLAM
THIS GATE...
...HAS A BARRIER ACROSS IT.
THE AYAKASHI ESCAPED TO THE OTHER SIDE.
shaa
MASTER, WHEN YOU WERE TENDING...
...TO HER WOUNDS...
...YOU GAVE HER SOME HERBAL MEDICINE.
WHAT WAS IT?

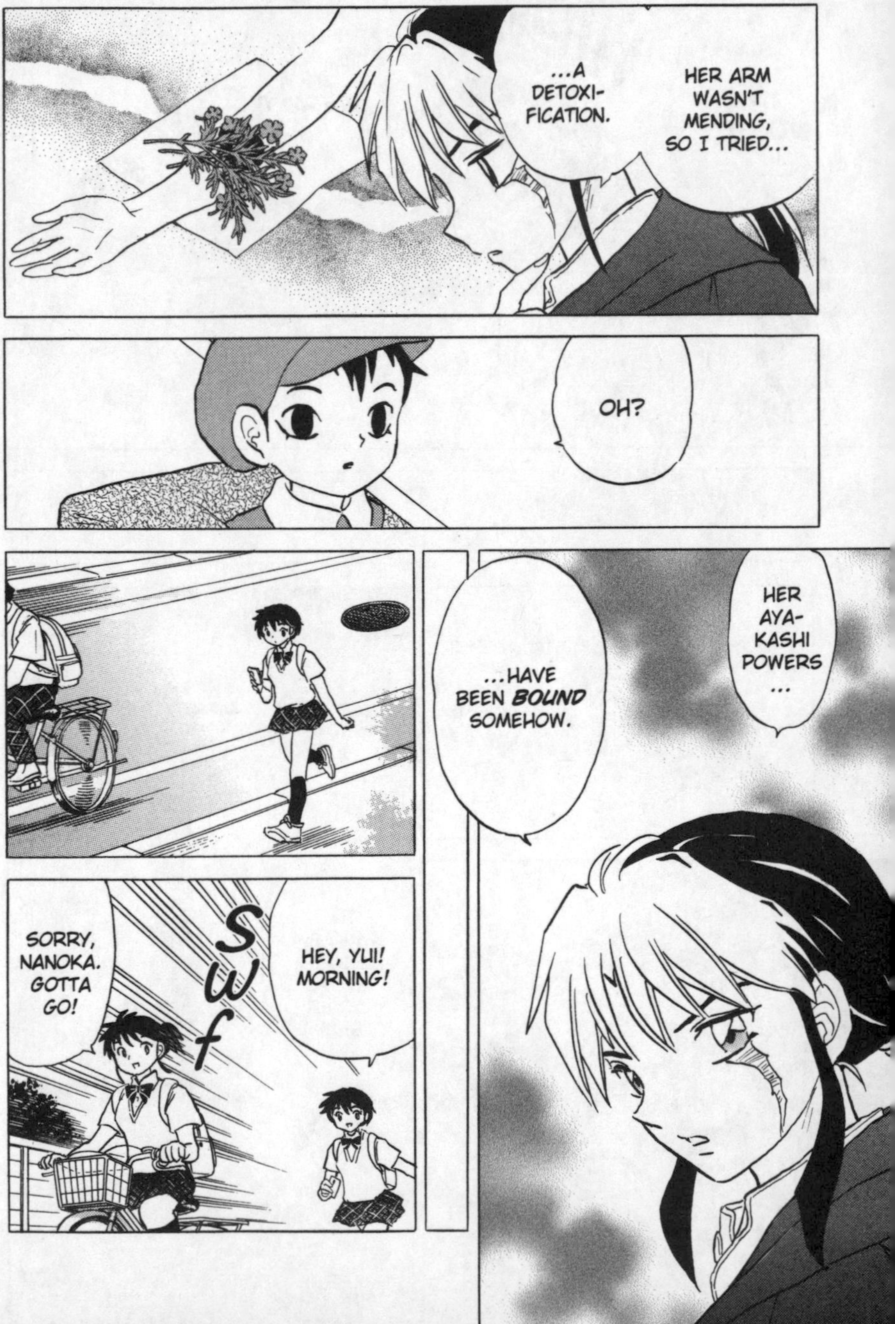

HER ARM WASN'T MENDING, SO I TRIED...
...A DETOXI-FICATION.
OH?
HER AYA-KASHI POWERS ...
...HAVE BEEN *BOUND* SOMEHOW.
HEY, YUI! MORNING!
SWF
SORRY, NANOKA. GOTTA GO!

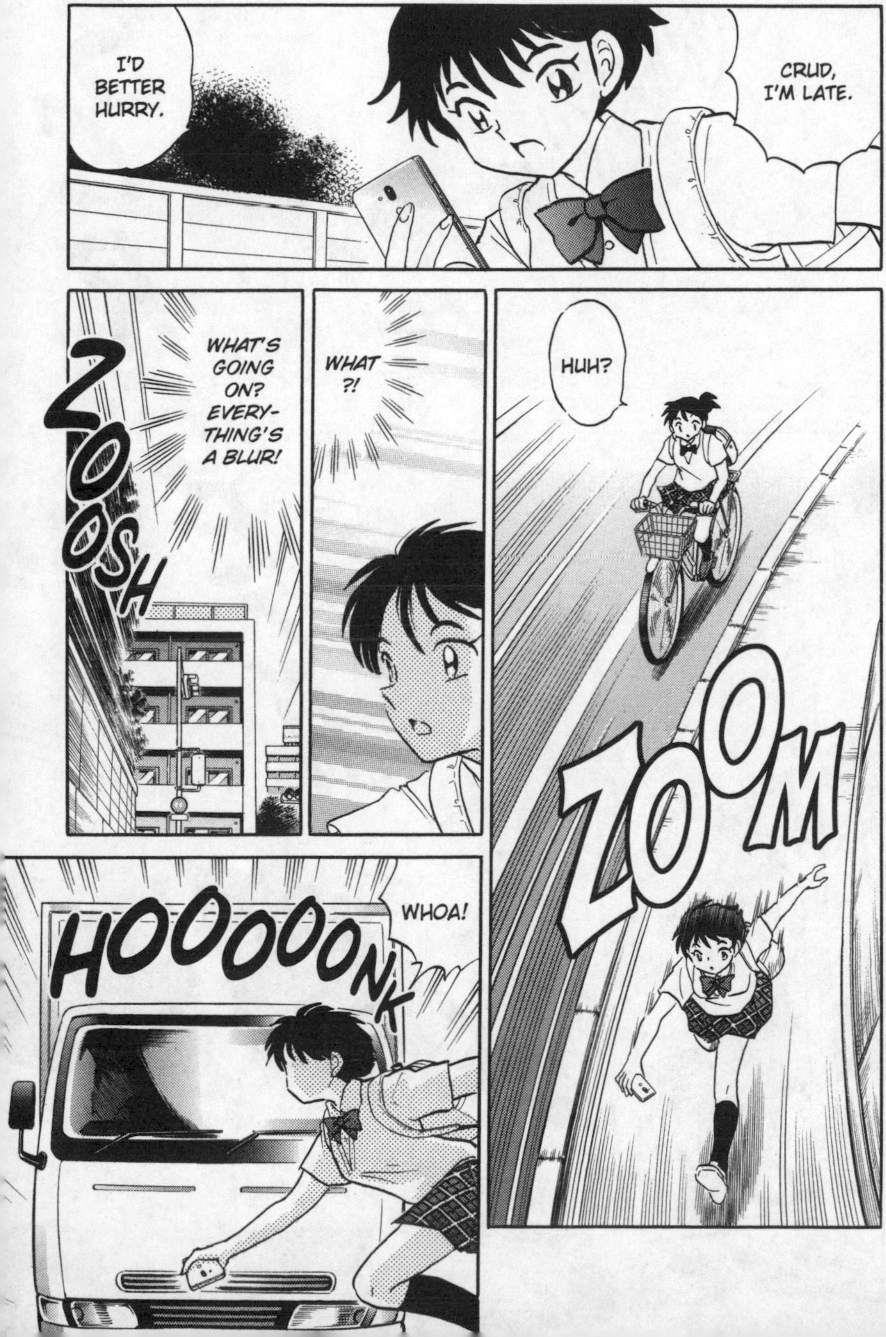
CRUD, I'M LATE.
I'D BETTER HURRY.
HUH?
ZOOM
WHAT ?!
ZOOSH
WHAT'S GOING ON? EVERY-THING'S A BLUR!
WHOA!
HOOOOONK

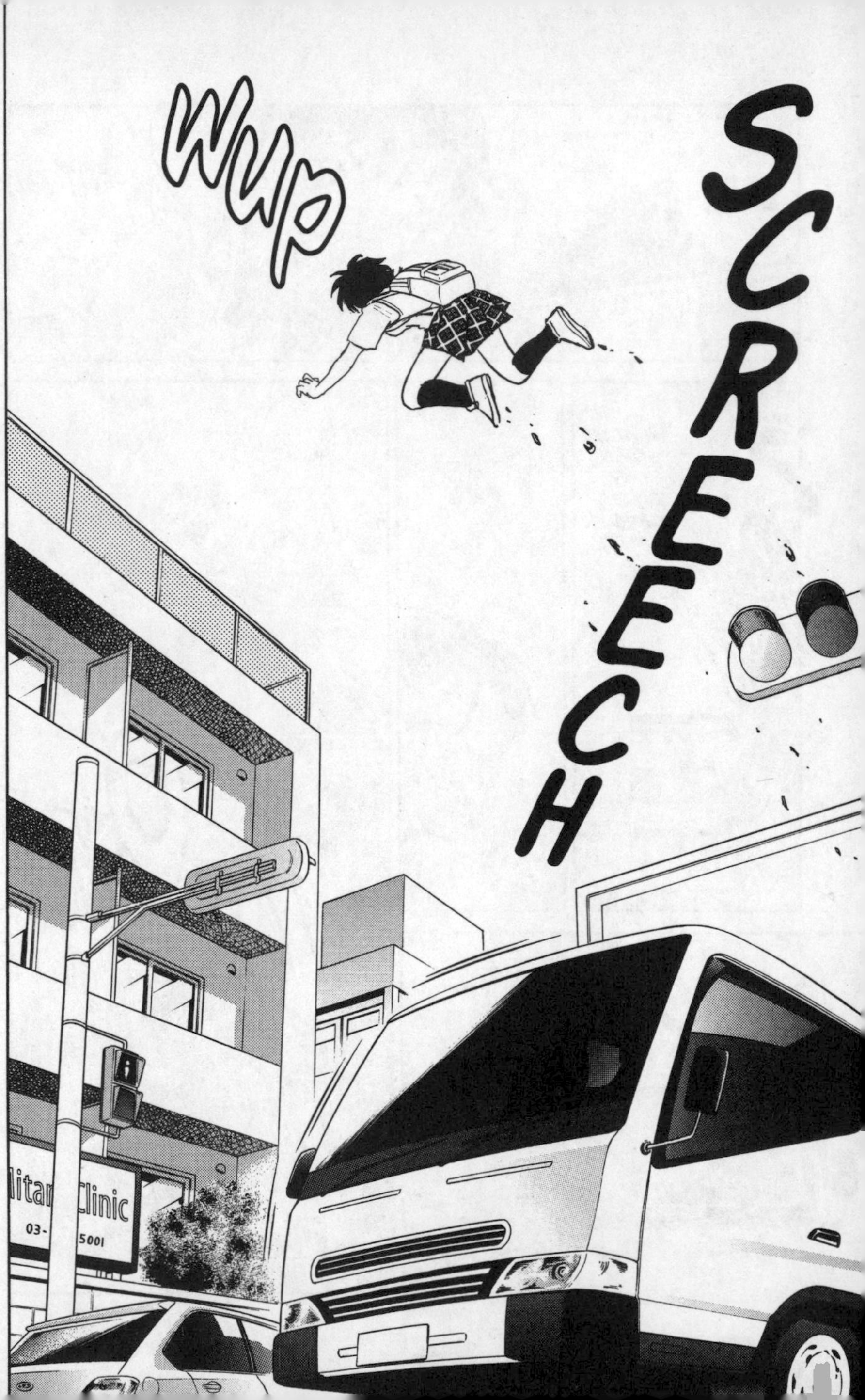
SCREEECH
Wup
Clinic
03-
5001

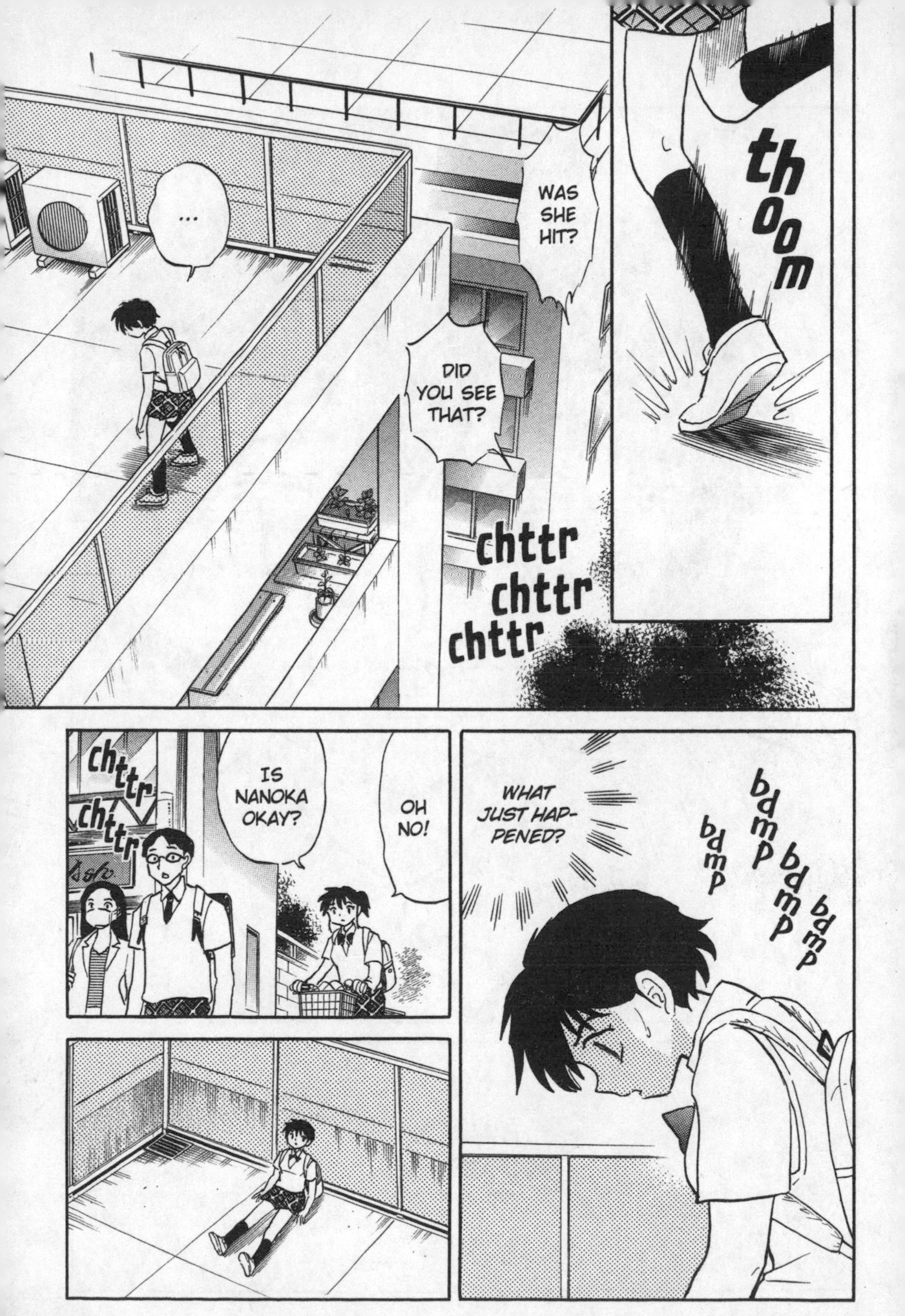
thoom
WAS SHE HIT?
...
DID YOU SEE THAT?
chttr chttr chttr
bdmp bdmp bdmp bdmp
WHAT JUST HAP-PENED?
OH NO!
IS NANOKA OKAY?
chttr chttr

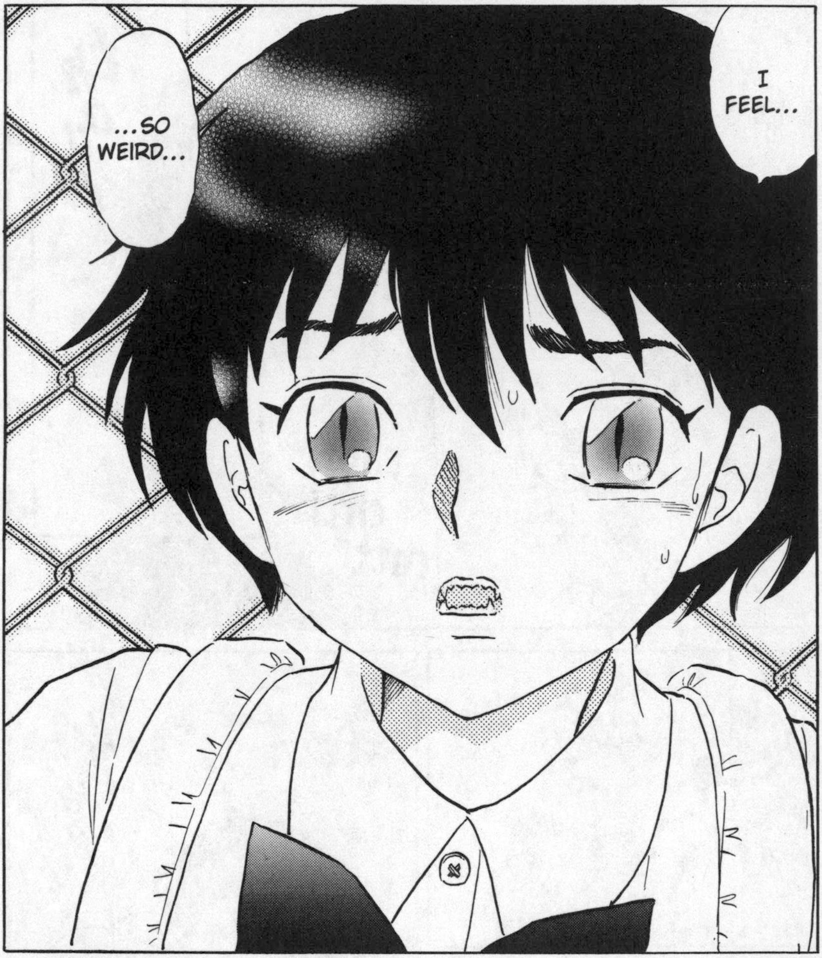
I FEEL...
...SO WEIRD...
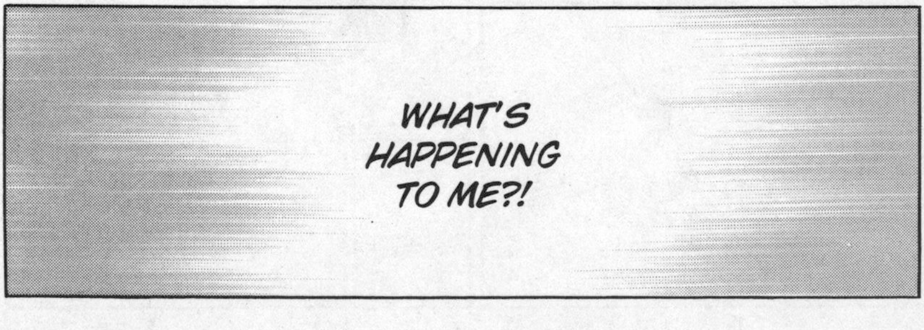
WHAT'S HAPPENING TO ME?!

Chapter 2:
Mao

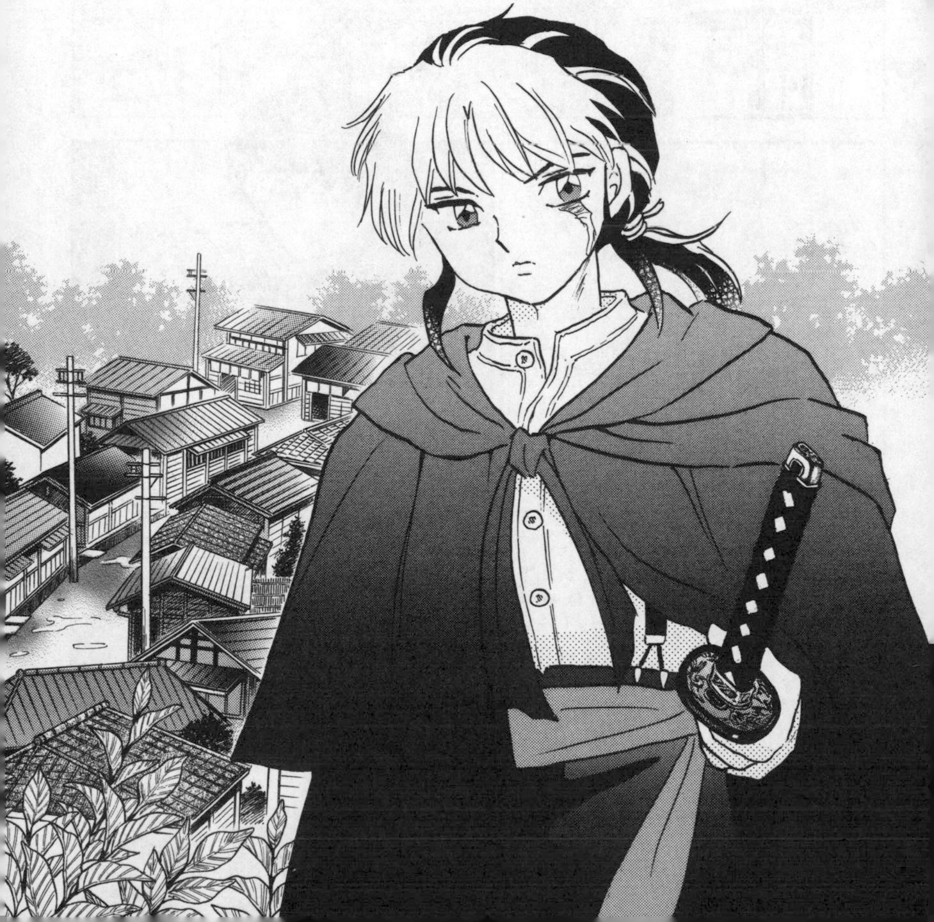

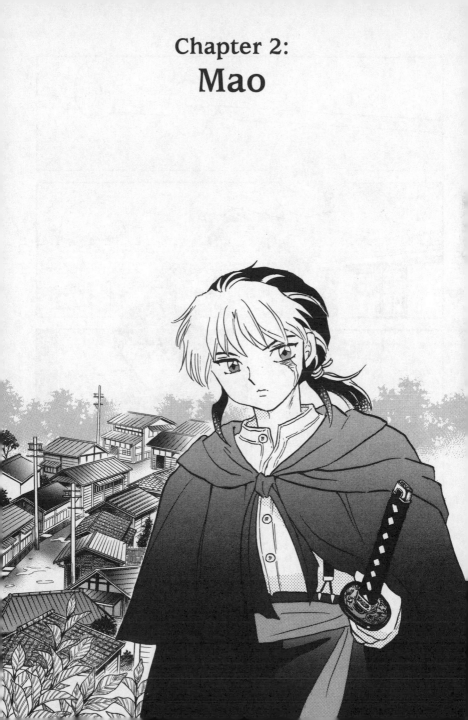

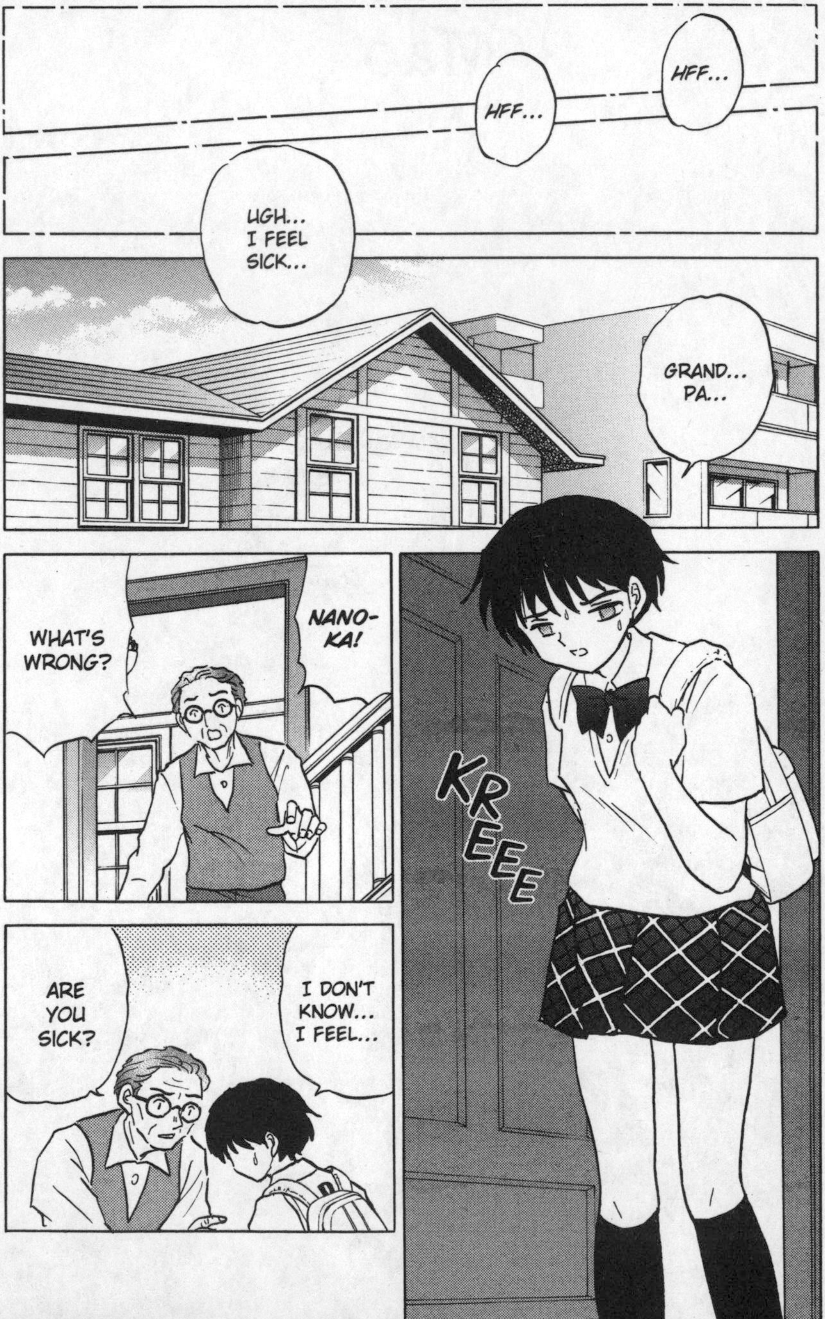
HFF...
HFF...
UGH... I FEEL SICK...
GRAND... PA...
KREEEE
NANO-KA!
WHAT'S WRONG?
I DON'T KNOW... I FEEL...
ARE YOU SICK?

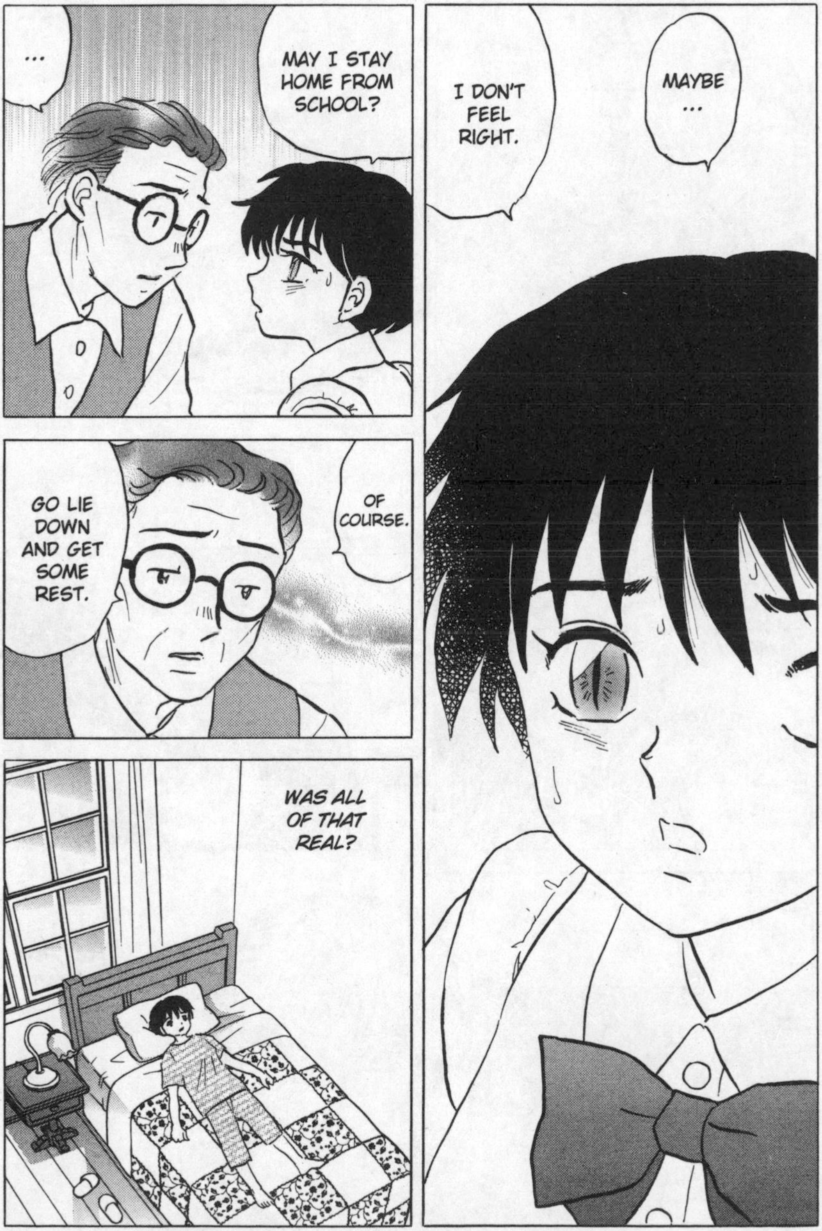
MAYBE ...
I DON'T FEEL RIGHT.
MAY I STAY HOME FROM SCHOOL?
...
OF COURSE.
GO LIE DOWN AND GET SOME REST.
WAS ALL OF THAT REAL?

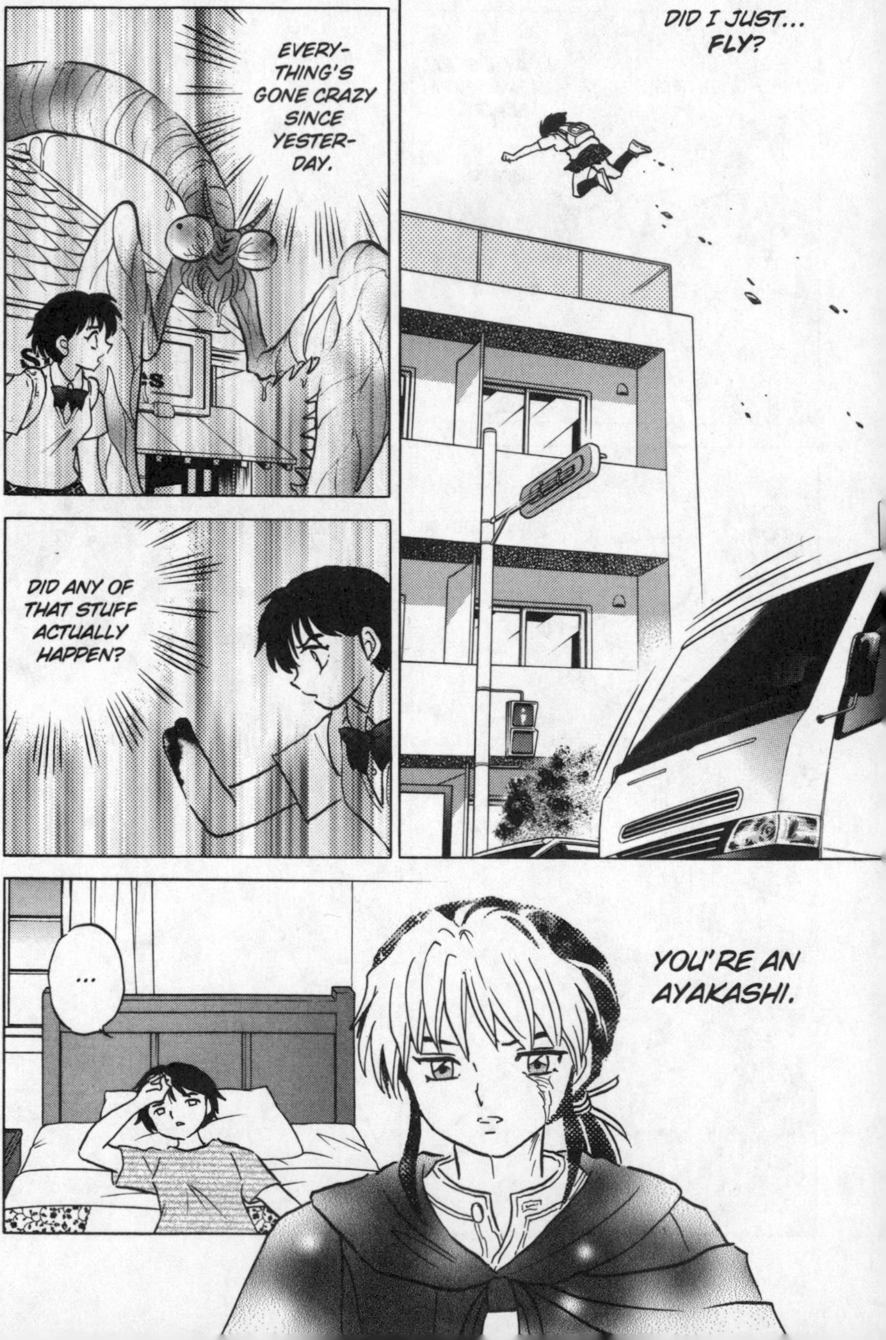
DID I JUST... FLY?
EVERY-THING'S GONE CRAZY SINCE YESTER-DAY.
DID ANY OF THAT STUFF ACTUALLY HAPPEN?
YOU'RE AN AYAKASHI.
...

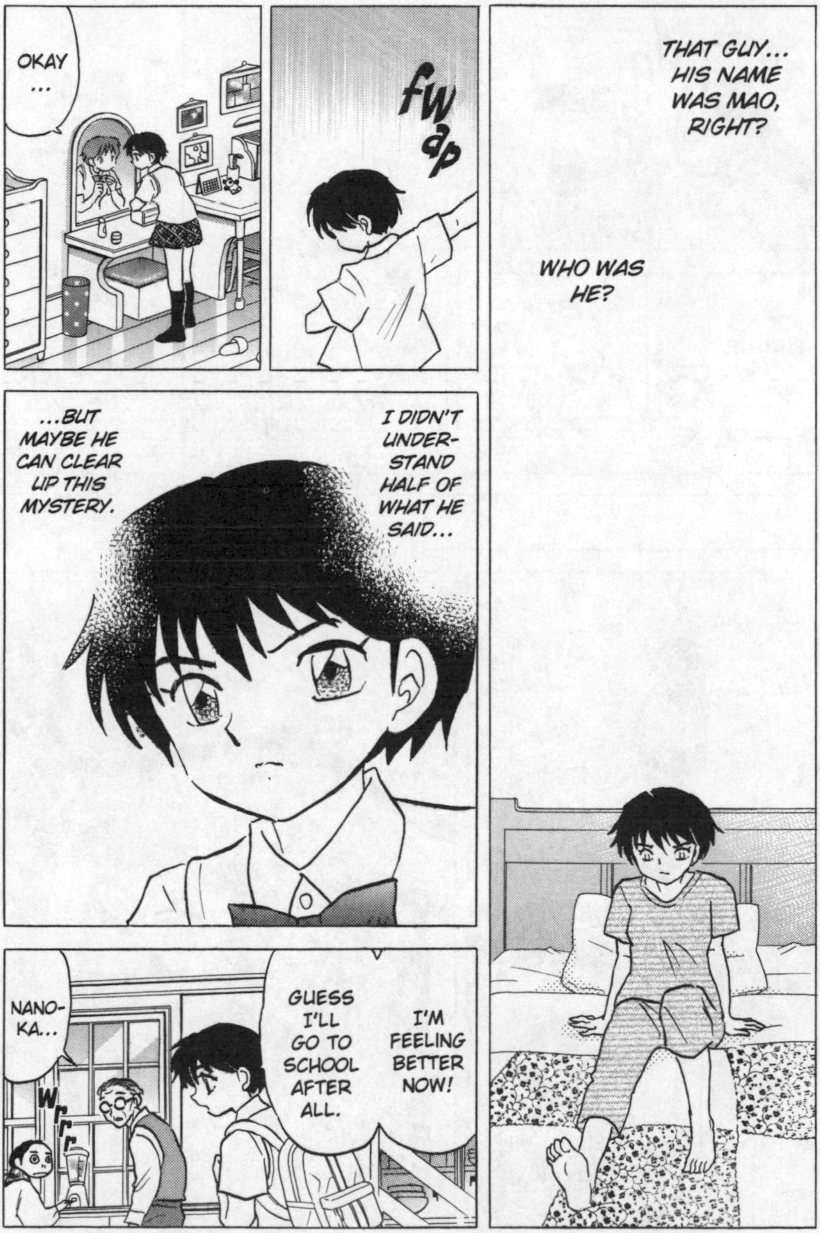
THAT GUY... HIS NAME WAS MAO, RIGHT?
WHO WAS HE?
fwap
OKAY ...
I DIDN'T UNDER-STAND HALF OF WHAT HE SAID...
...BUT MAYBE HE CAN CLEAR UP THIS MYSTERY.
I'M FEELING BETTER NOW!
GUESS I'LL GO TO SCHOOL AFTER ALL.
NANO-KA...
Wrrr

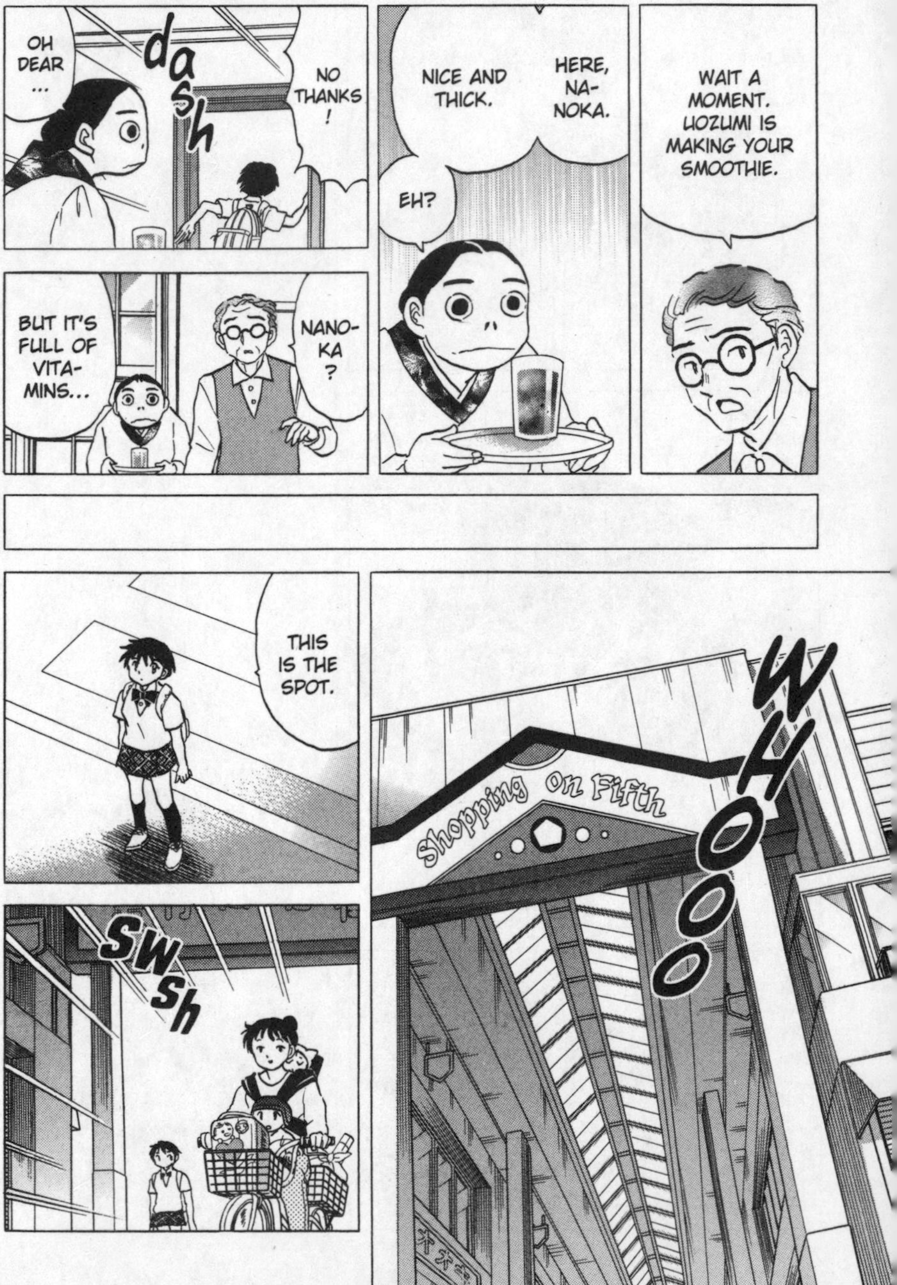
WAIT A MOMENT. UOZUMI IS MAKING YOUR SMOOTHIE.
HERE, NA-NOKA.
NICE AND THICK.
EH?
NO THANKS!
dash
OH DEAR ...
NANO-KA?
BUT IT'S FULL OF VITA-MINS...
WHOOOOO
Shopping on Fifth
THIS IS THE SPOT.
SWSh

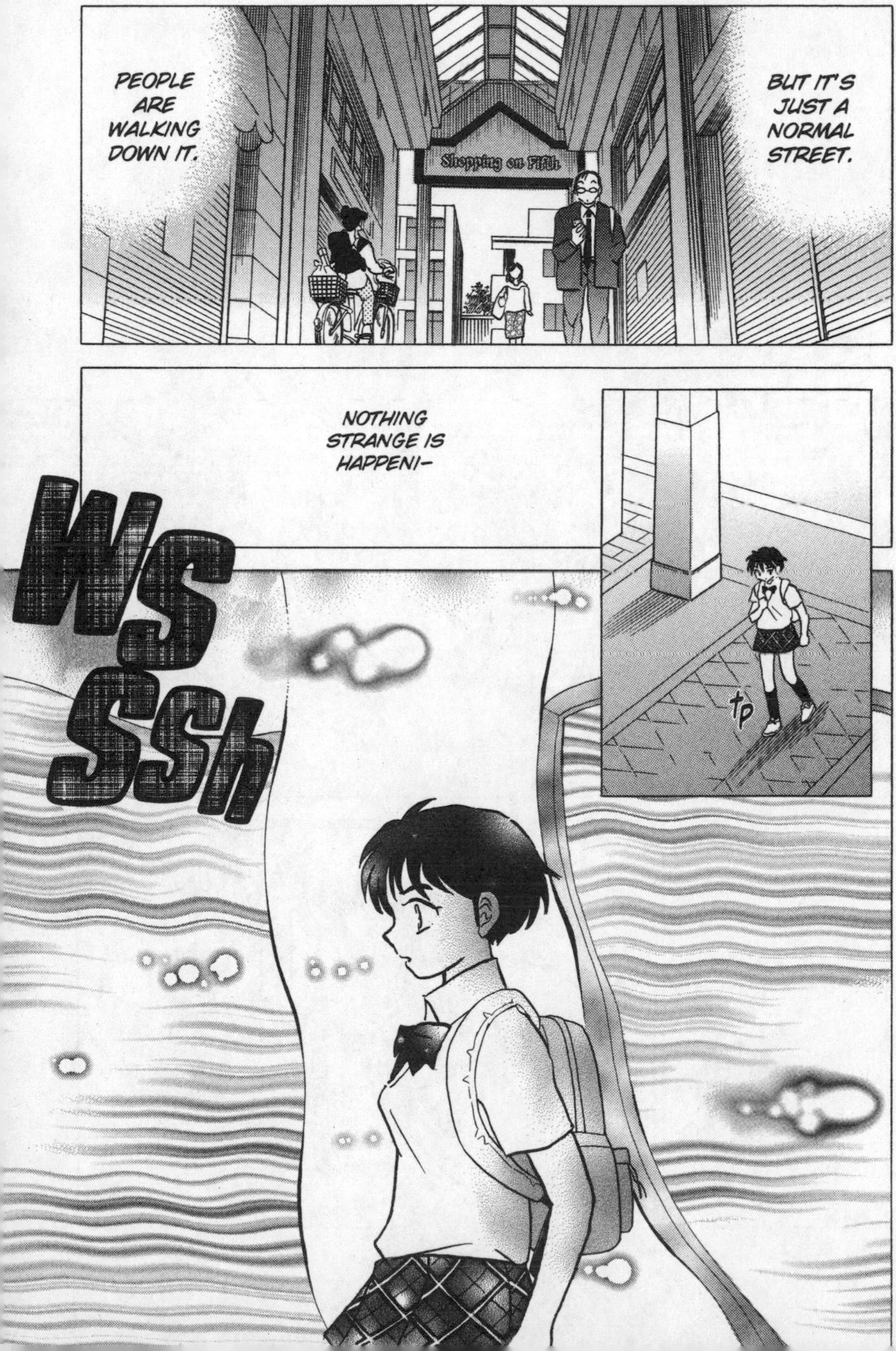
BUT IT'S JUST A NORMAL STREET.
PEOPLE ARE WALKING DOWN IT.
Shopping on Fifth
tp
NOTHING STRANGE IS HAPPENI-
WS SSh

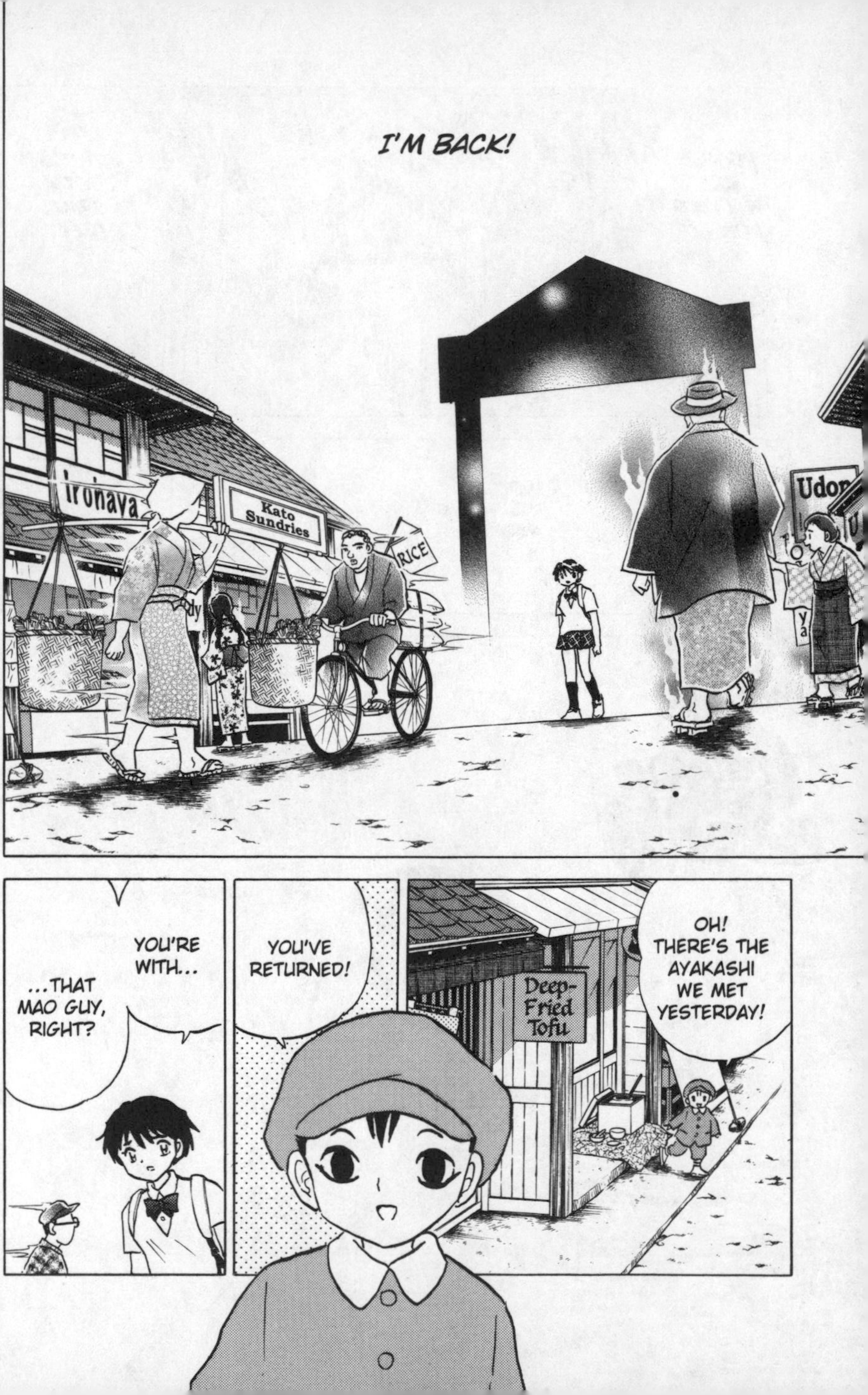
I'M BACK!
Irohaya
Kato Sundries
RICE
Udon
OH! THERE'S THE AYAKASHI WE MET YESTERDAY!
Deep-Fried Tofu
YOU'VE RETURNED!
YOU'RE WITH...
...THAT MAO GUY, RIGHT?

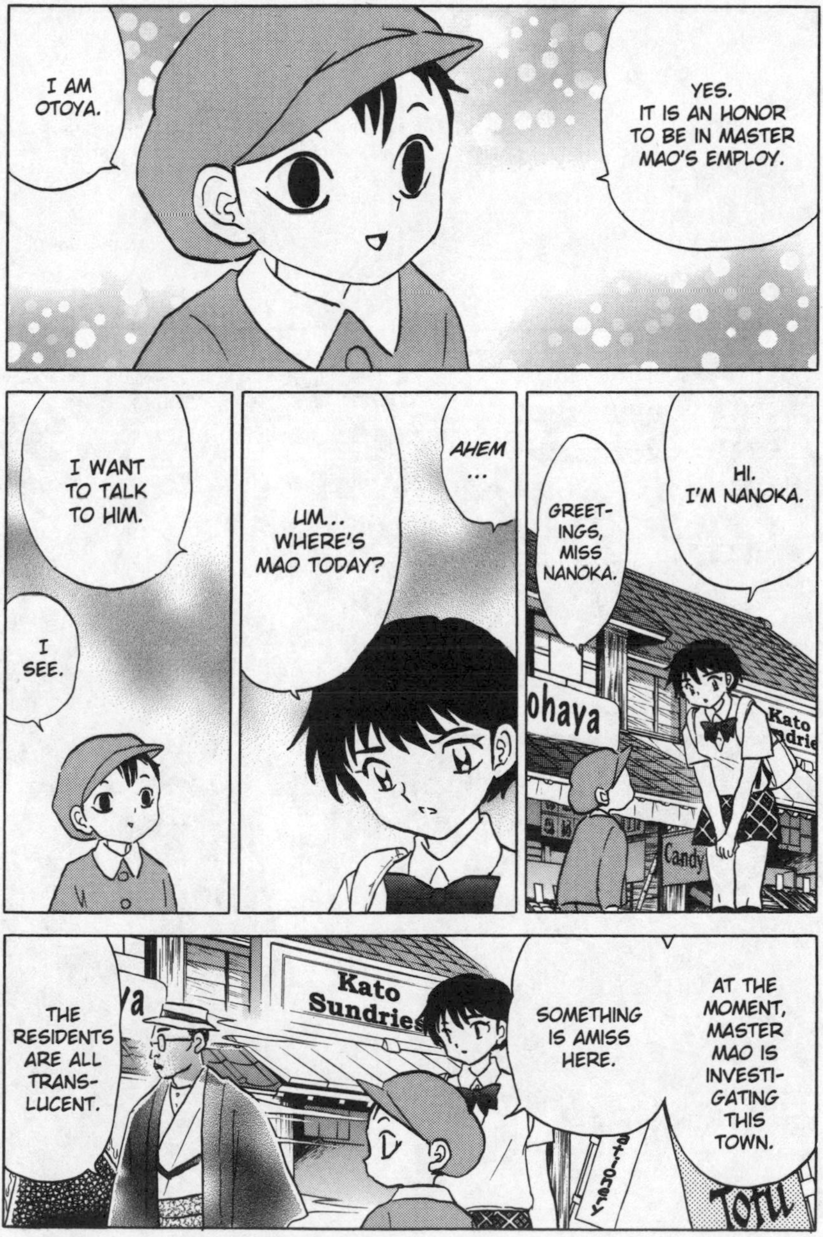
YES. IT IS AN HONOR TO BE IN MASTER MAO'S EMPLOY.
I AM OTOYA.
HI. I'M NANOKA.
GREETINGS, MISS NANOKA.
Candy
AHEM ...
UM... WHERE'S MAO TODAY?
I WANT TO TALK TO HIM.
I SEE.
AT THE MOMENT, MASTER MAO IS INVESTIGATING THIS TOWN.
Toru
SOMETHING IS AMISS HERE.
Kato Sundries
THE RESIDENTS ARE ALL TRANSLUCENT.

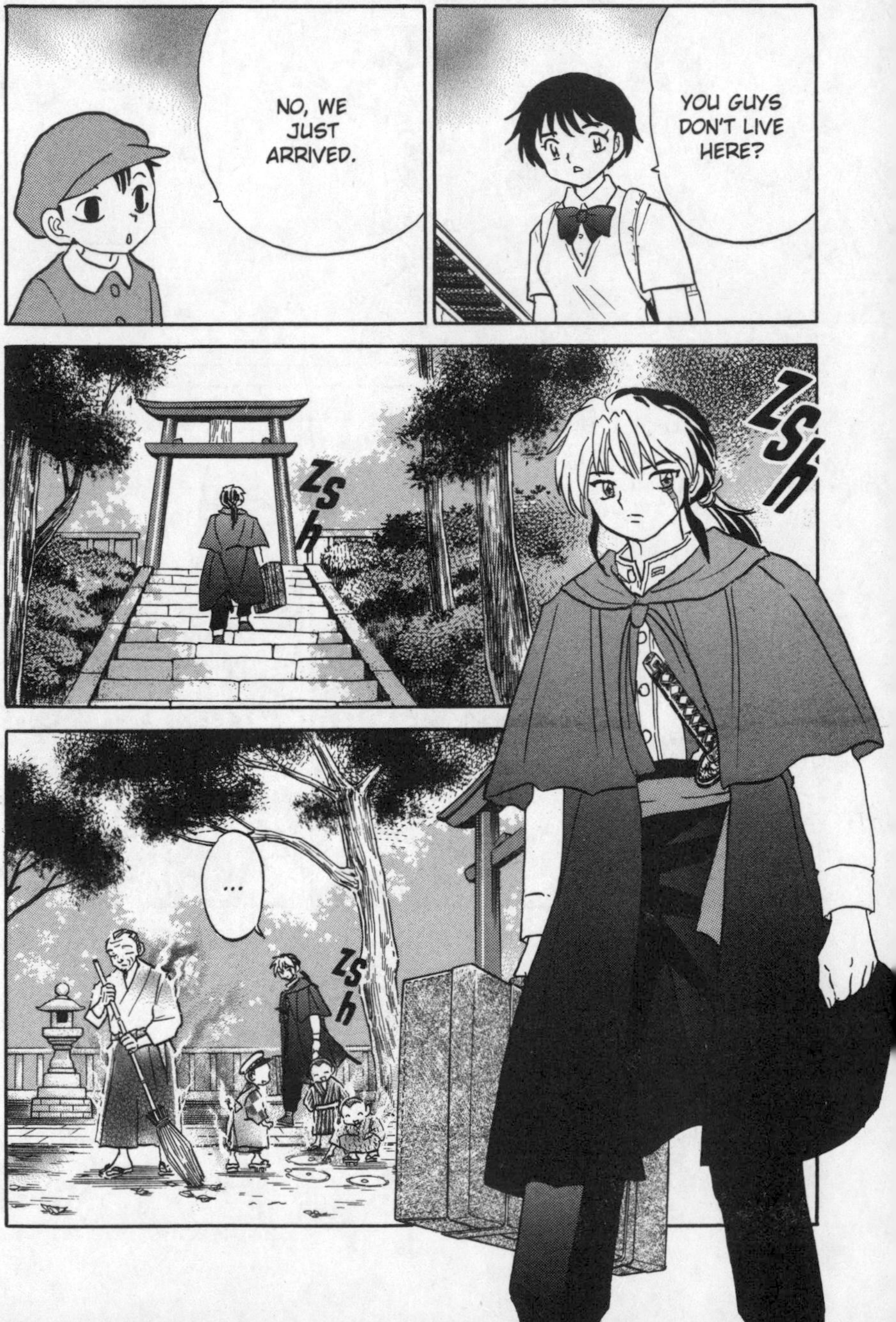
YOU GUYS DON'T LIVE HERE?
NO, WE JUST ARRIVED.
ZSH
ZSH
...
ZSH

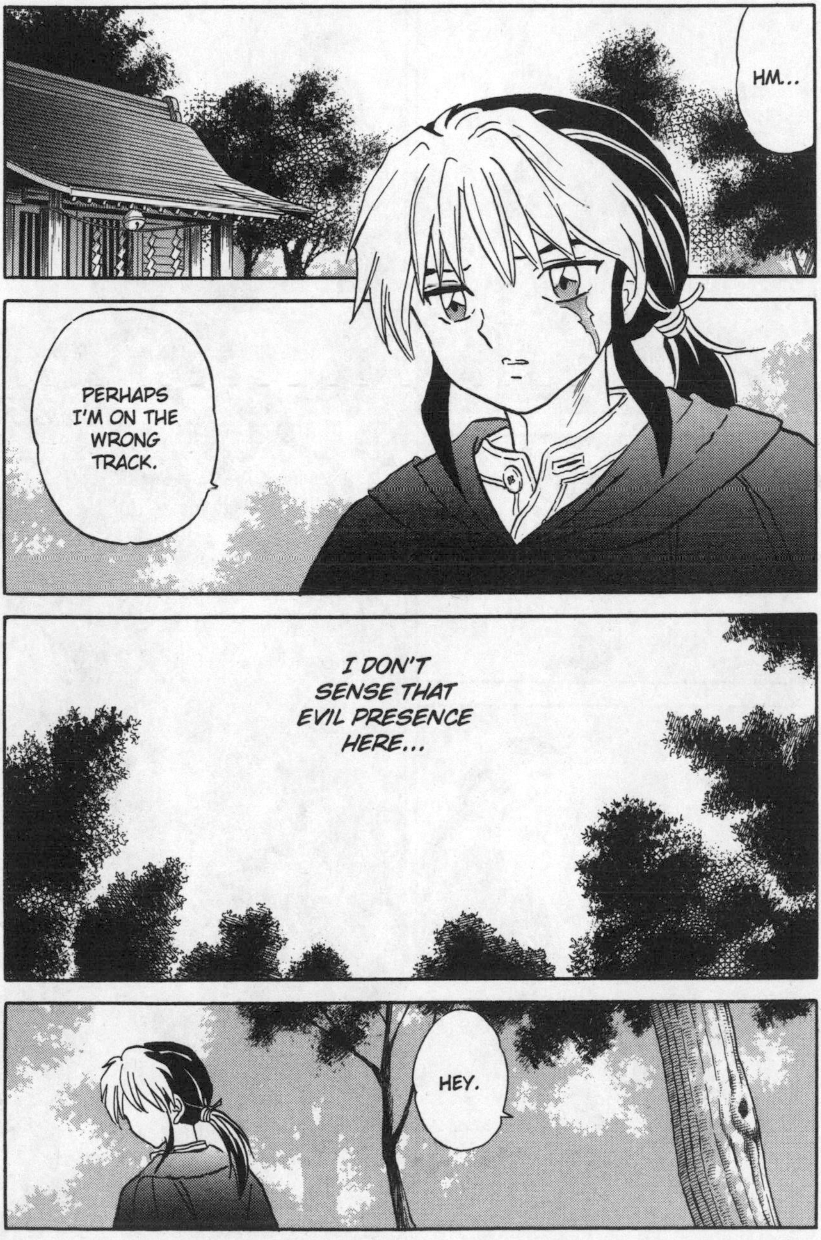
HM...
PERHAPS I'M ON THE WRONG TRACK.
I DON'T SENSE THAT EVIL PRESENCE HERE...
HEY.

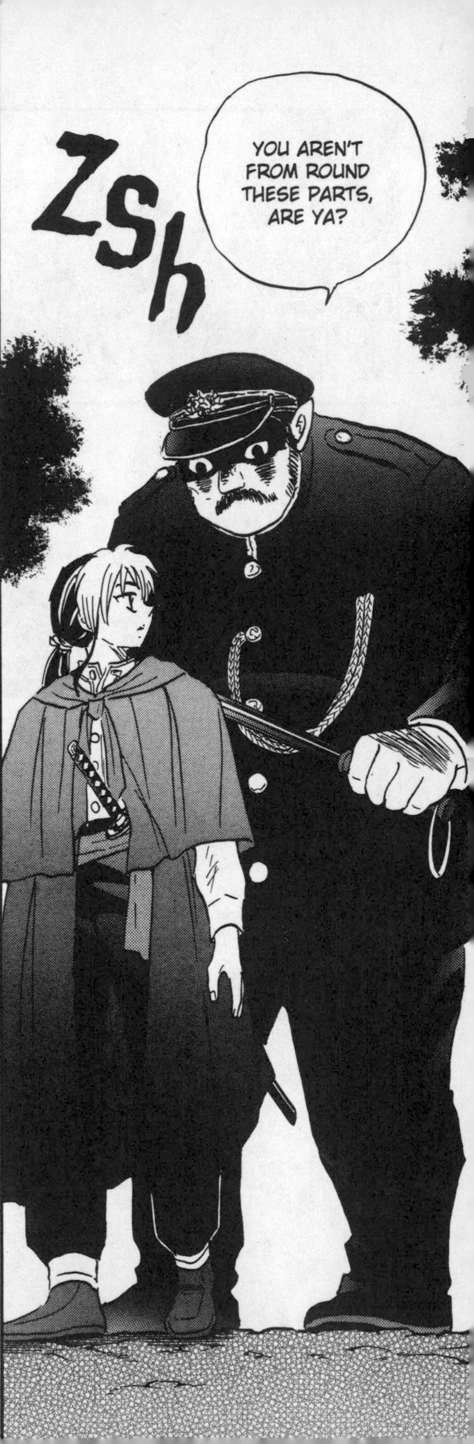
YOU AREN'T FROM ROUND THESE PARTS, ARE YA?
ZSh

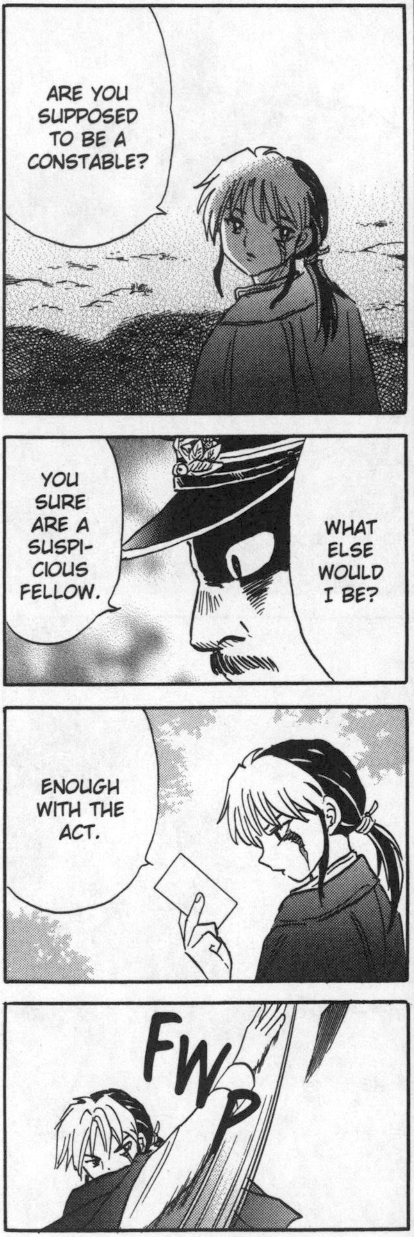
ARE YOU SUPPOSED TO BE A CONSTABLE?
WHAT ELSE WOULD I BE?
YOU SURE ARE A SUSPICIOUS FELLOW.
ENOUGH WITH THE ACT.
FWP

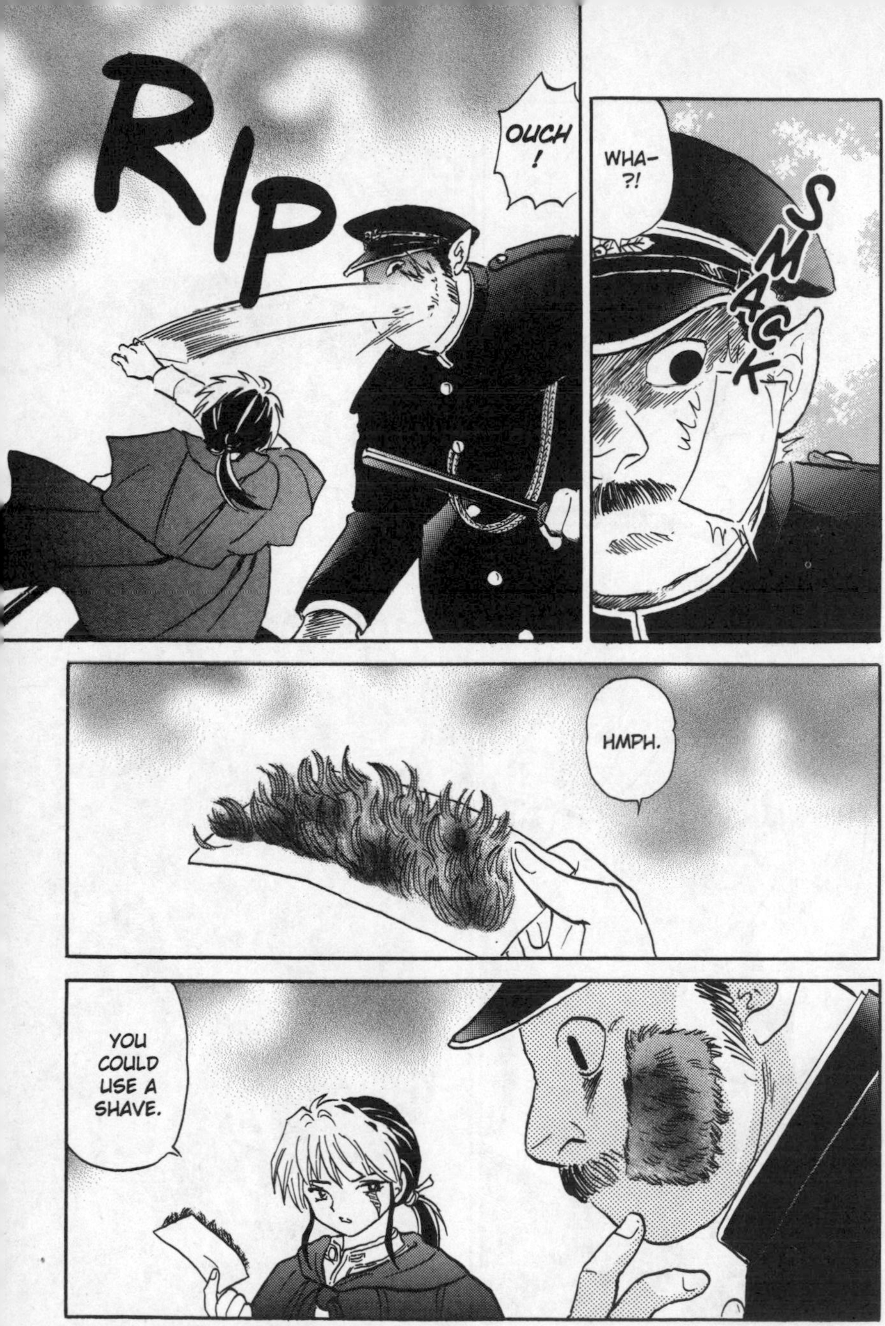
WHA-?!
SMACK
RIP
OUCH!
HMPH.
YOU COULD USE A SHAVE.

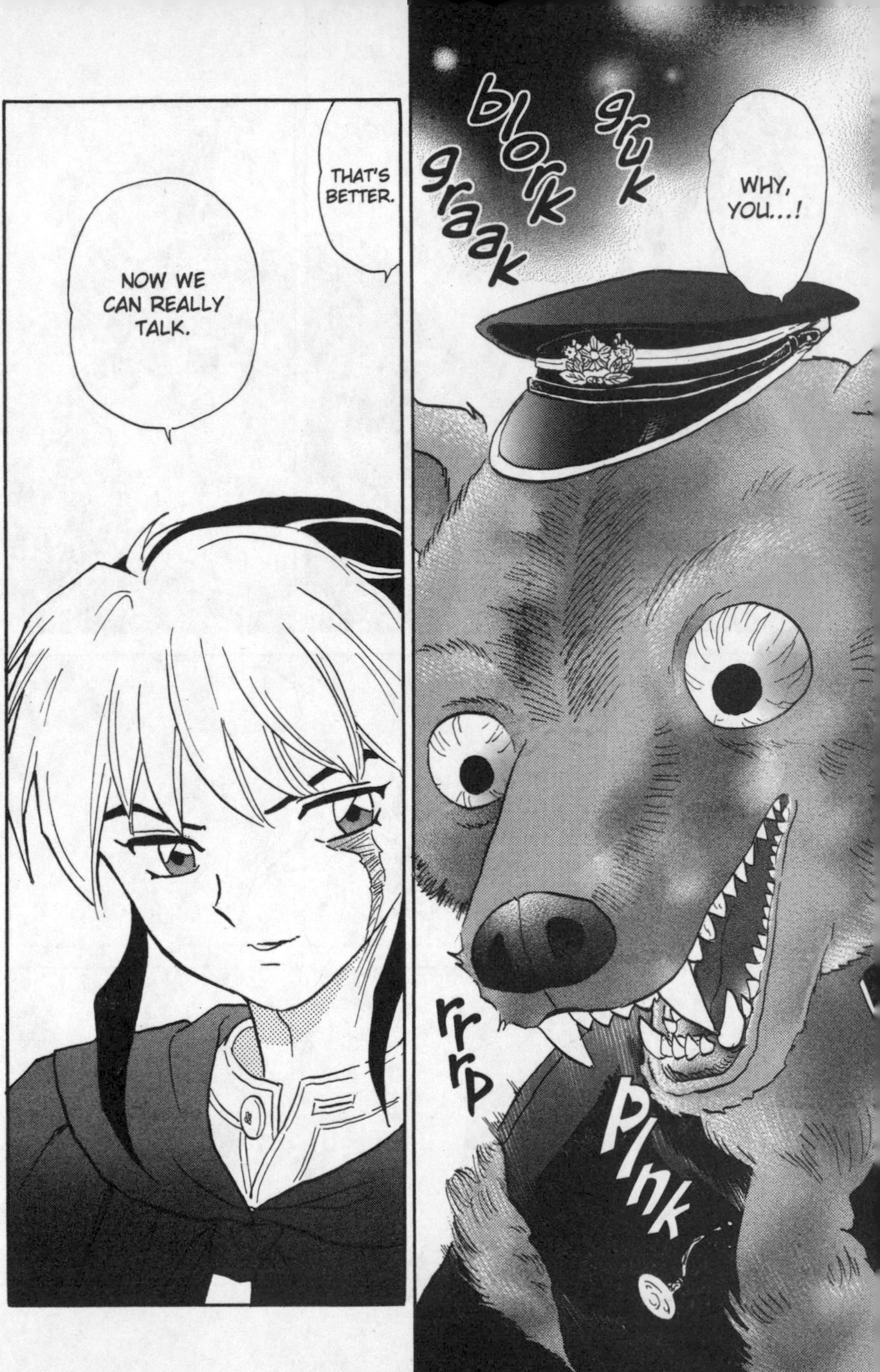
WHY, YOU...!
gruk
blork
graaak
rrrp
plink
THAT'S BETTER.
NOW WE CAN REALLY TALK.

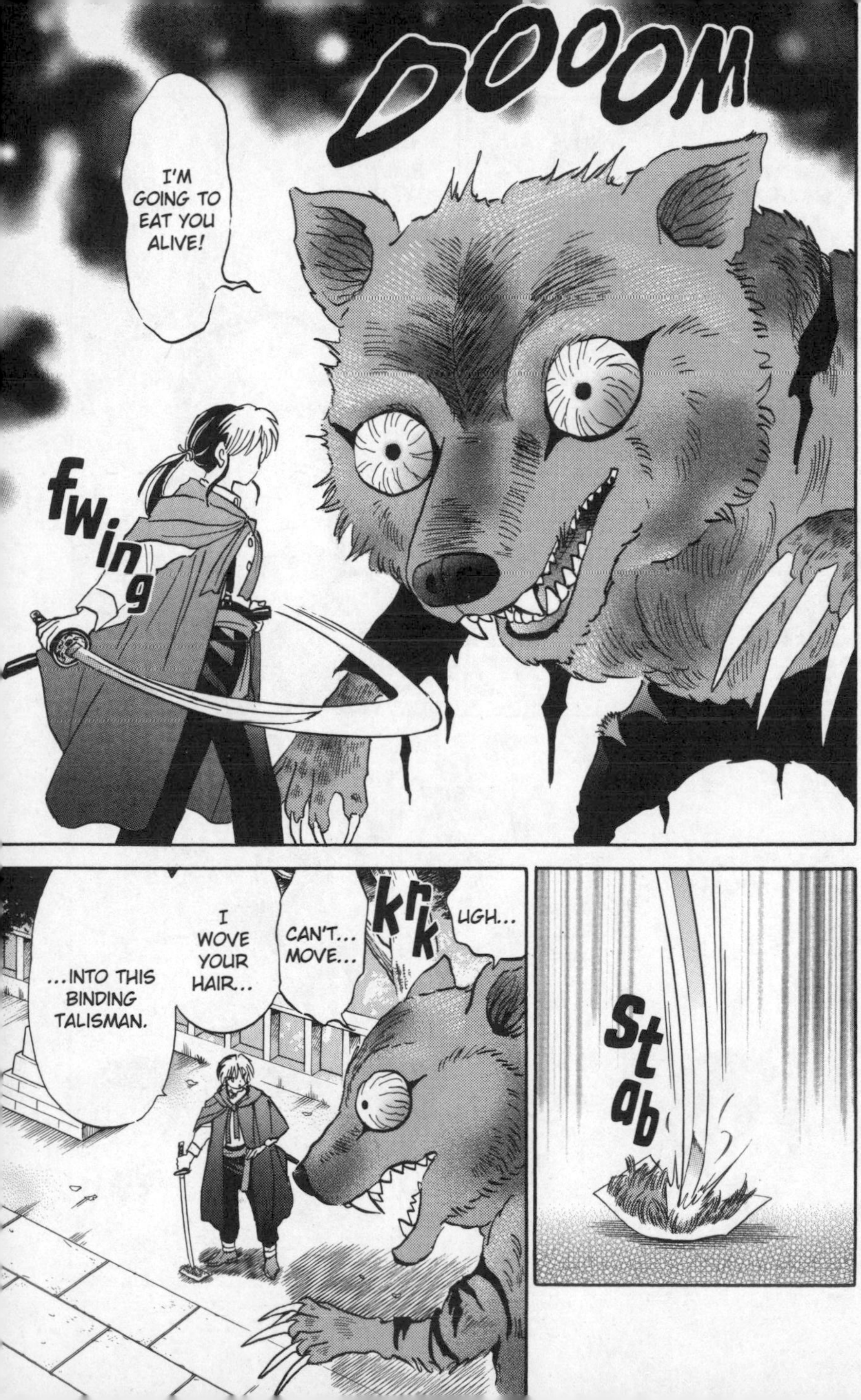
DOOOM
I'M GOING TO EAT YOU ALIVE!
fwing
Stab
UGH...
krk
CAN'T... MOVE...
I WOVE YOUR HAIR...
...INTO THIS BINDING TALISMAN.

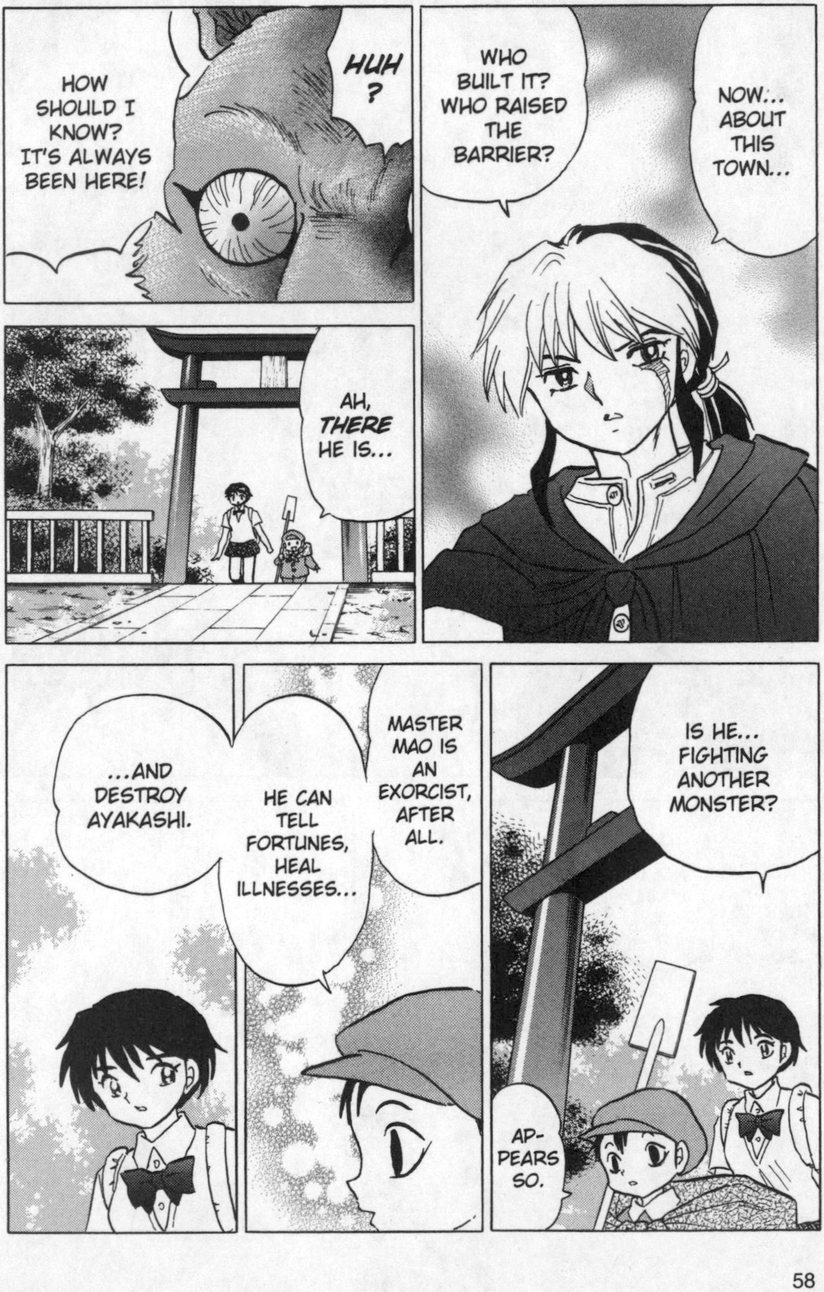
NOW... ABOUT THIS TOWN...
WHO BUILT IT? WHO RAISED THE BARRIER?
HUH?
HOW SHOULD I KNOW? IT'S ALWAYS BEEN HERE!
AH, *THERE* HE IS...
IS HE... FIGHTING ANOTHER MONSTER?
AP-PEARS SO.
MASTER MAO IS AN EXORCIST, AFTER ALL.
HE CAN TELL FORTUNES, HEAL ILLNESSES...
...AND DESTROY AYAKASHI.

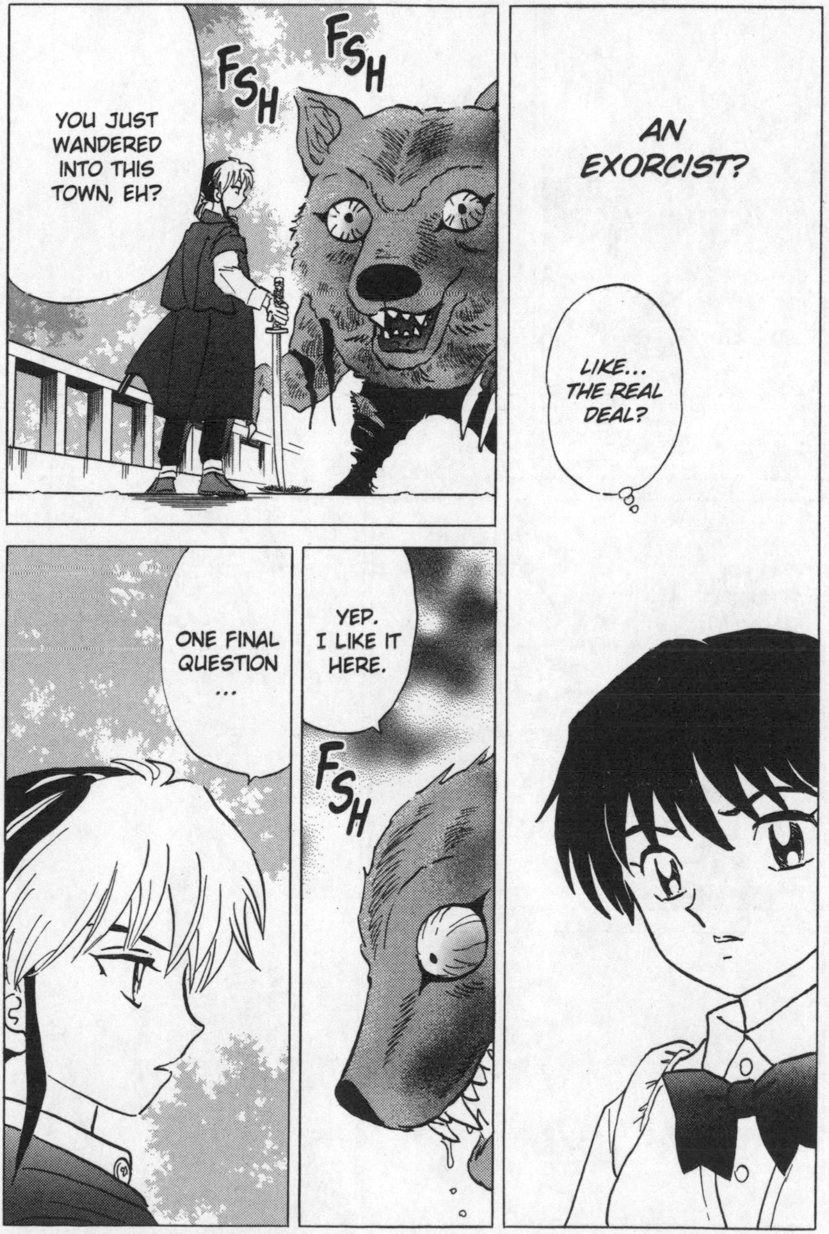
AN EXORCIST?
LIKE... THE REAL DEAL?
FSH
FSH
YOU JUST WANDERED INTO THIS TOWN, EH?
YEP. I LIKE IT HERE.
FSH
ONE FINAL QUESTION ...

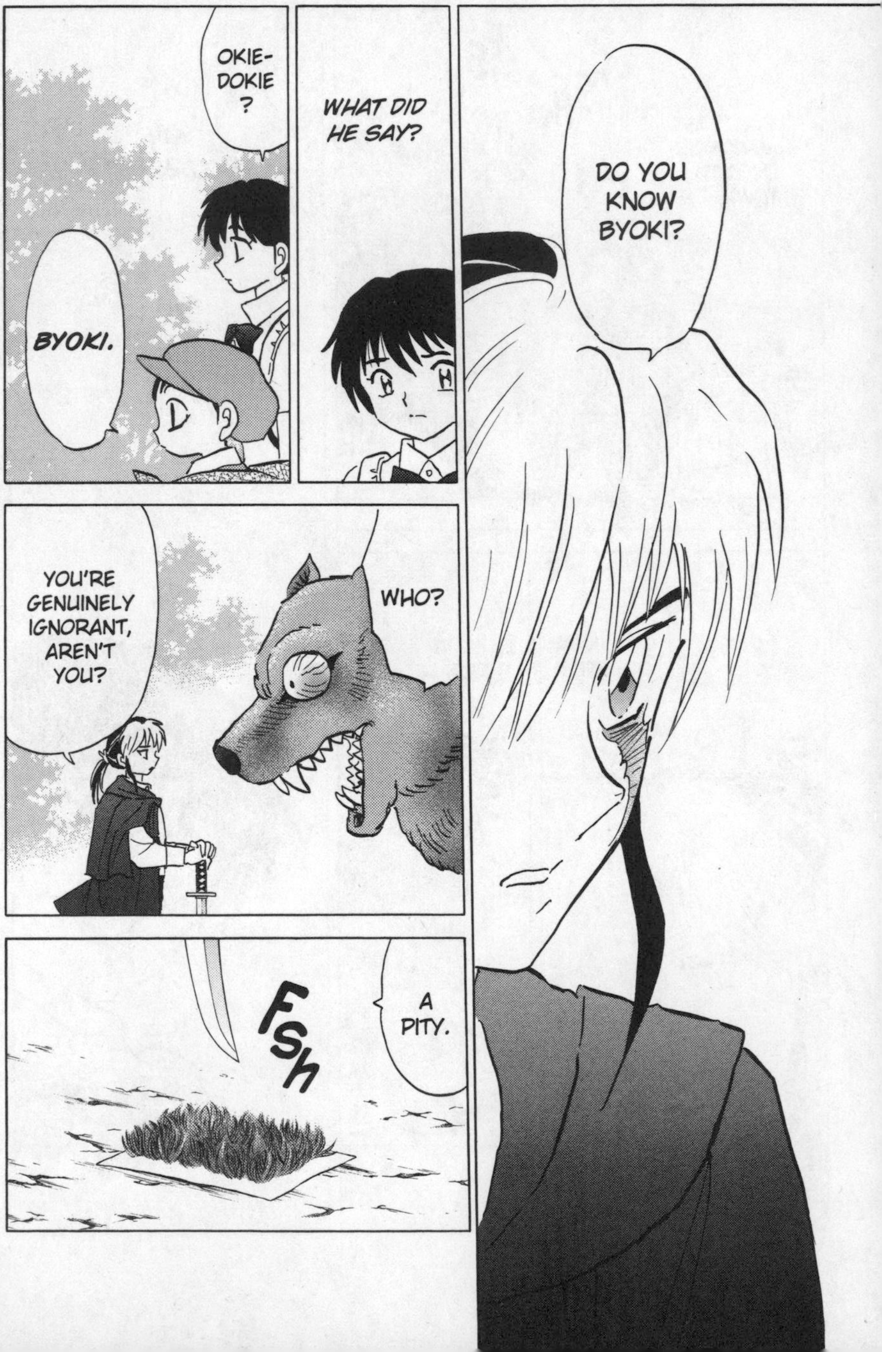
DO YOU KNOW BYOKI?
WHAT DID HE SAY?
OKIE-DOKIE ?
BYOKI.
WHO?
YOU'RE GENUINELY IGNORANT, AREN'T YOU?
A PITY.
Fsh

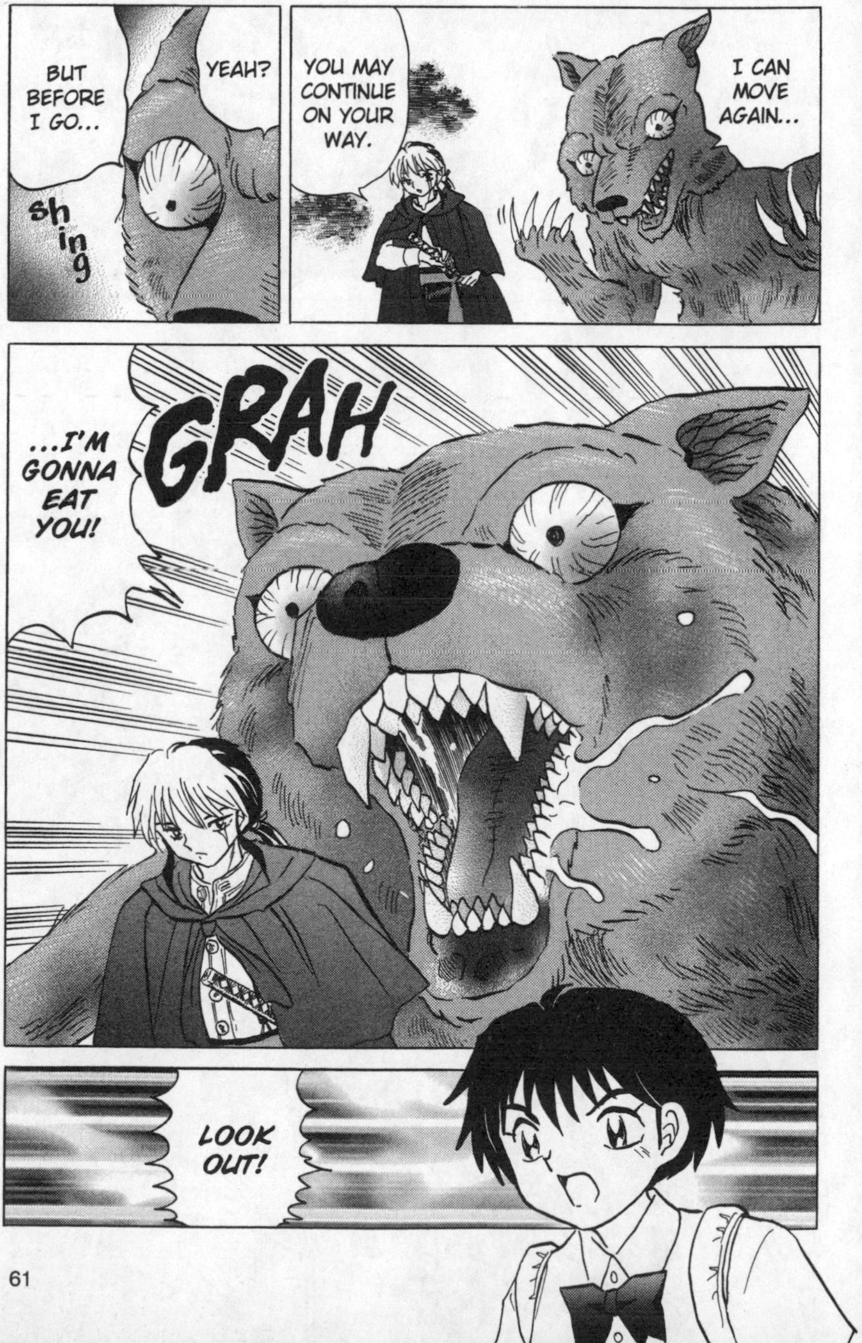
I CAN MOVE AGAIN...
YOU MAY CONTINUE ON YOUR WAY.
YEAH?
BUT BEFORE I GO...
shing
GRAH
...I'M GONNA EAT YOU!
LOOK OUT!

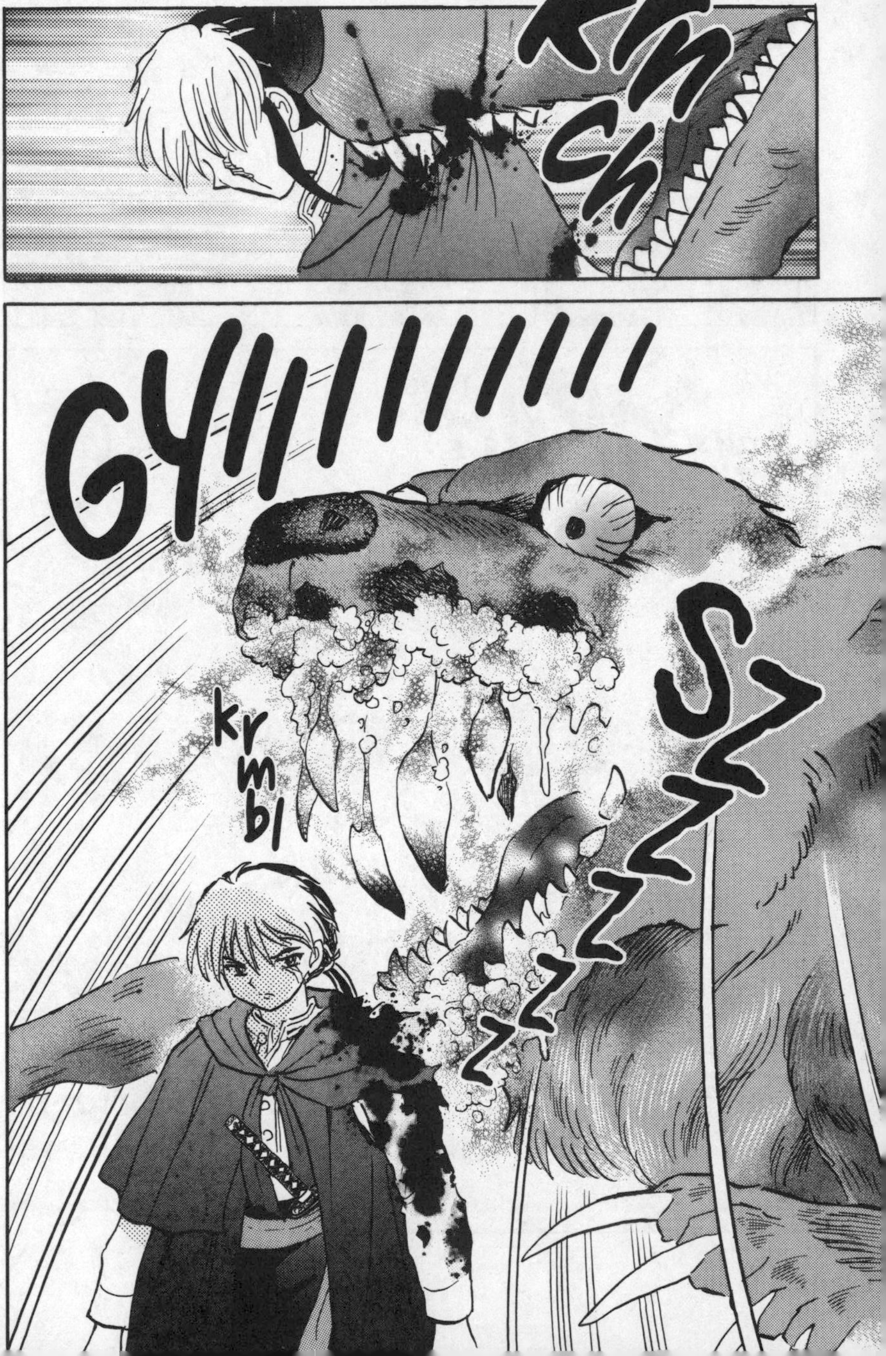
KRNCH
GYIIIIIIIII
SZZZZZZ
krrmbl

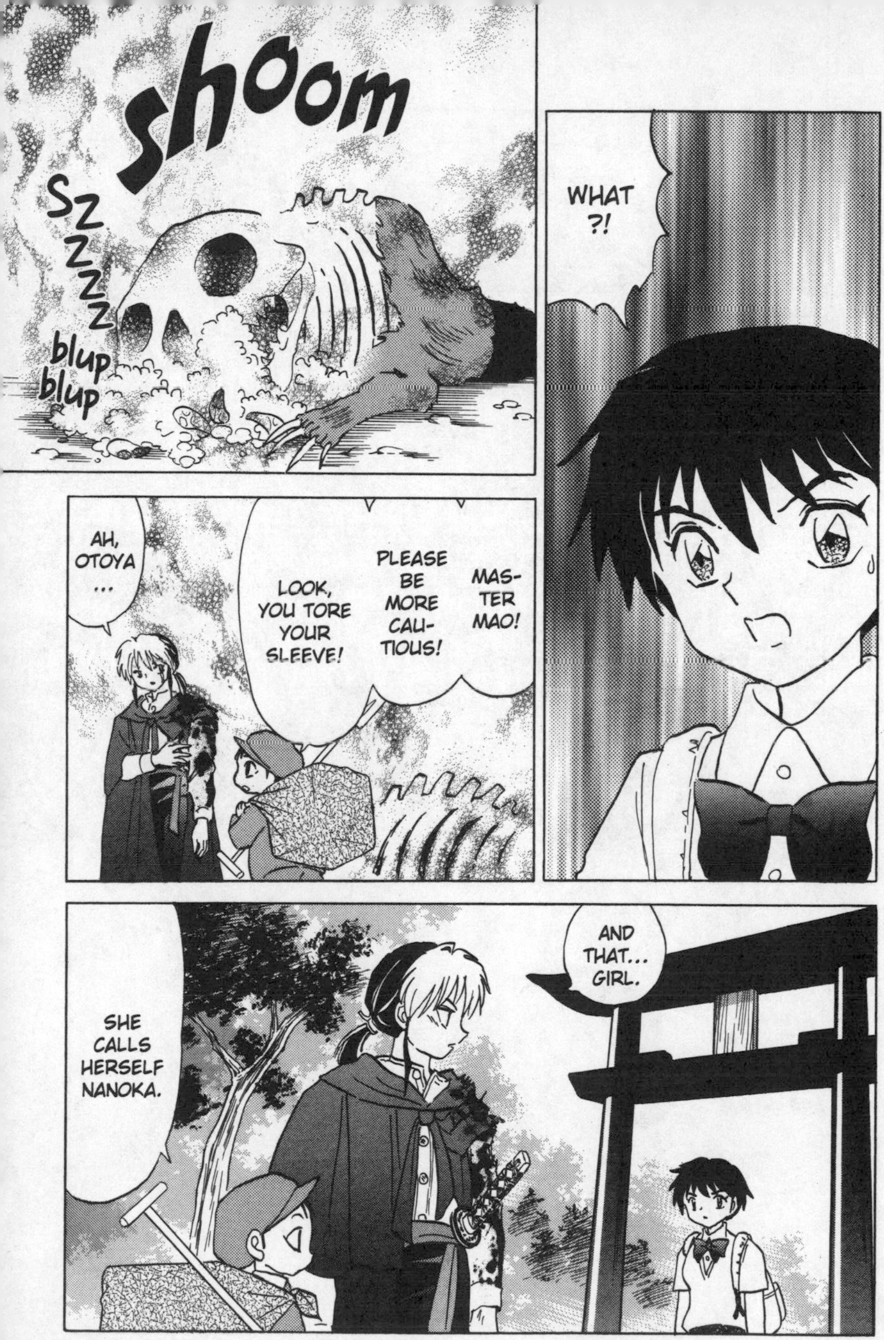
WHAT ?!
shoom
SZZZZZ
blup blup
MAS-TER MAO!
PLEASE BE MORE CAU-TIOUS!
LOOK, YOU TORE YOUR SLEEVE!
AH, OTOYA ...
AND THAT... GIRL.
SHE CALLS HERSELF NANOKA.

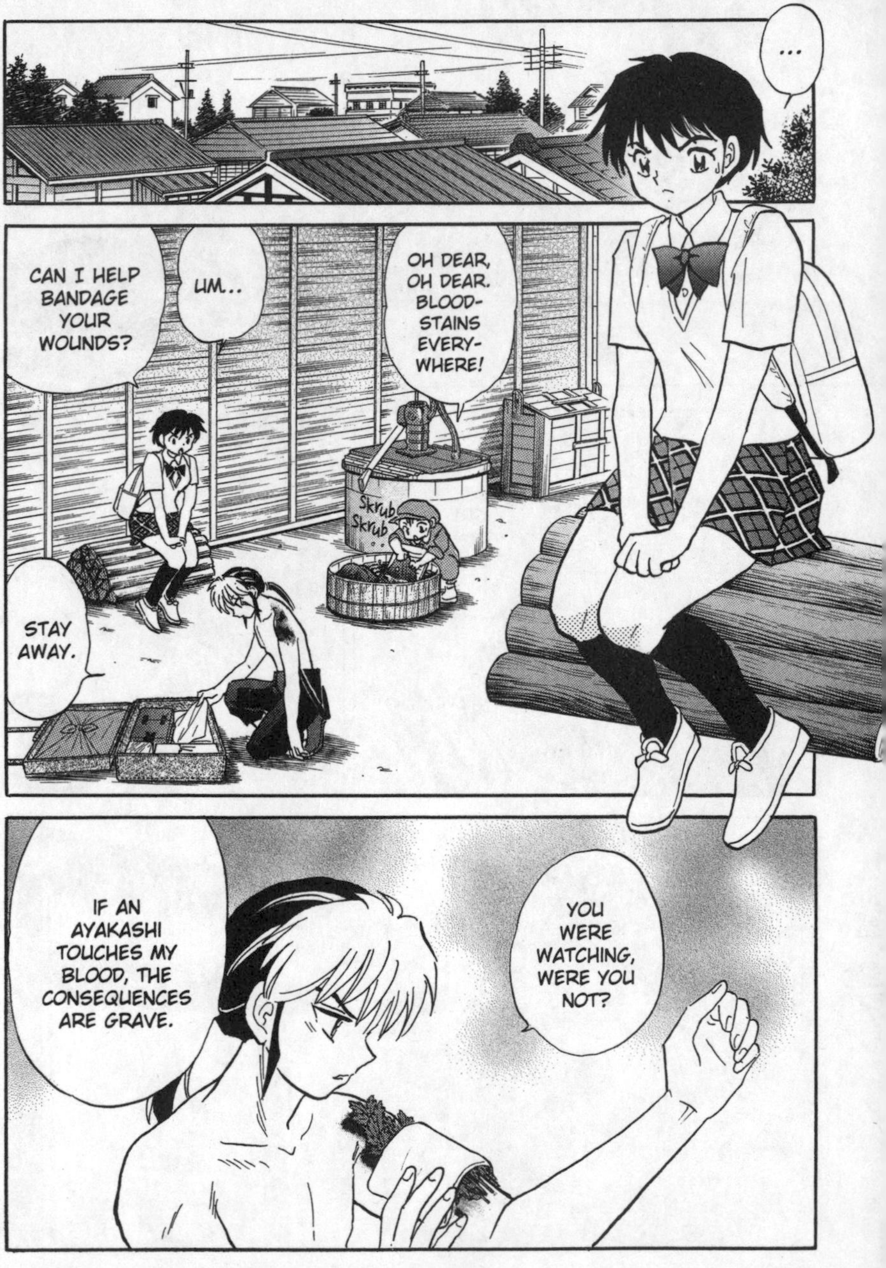
...
OH DEAR, OH DEAR. BLOOD-STAINS EVERY-WHERE!
UM...
CAN I HELP BANDAGE YOUR WOUNDS?
Skrub Skrub
STAY AWAY.
YOU WERE WATCHING, WERE YOU NOT?
IF AN AYAKASHI TOUCHES MY BLOOD, THE CONSEQUENCES ARE GRAVE.

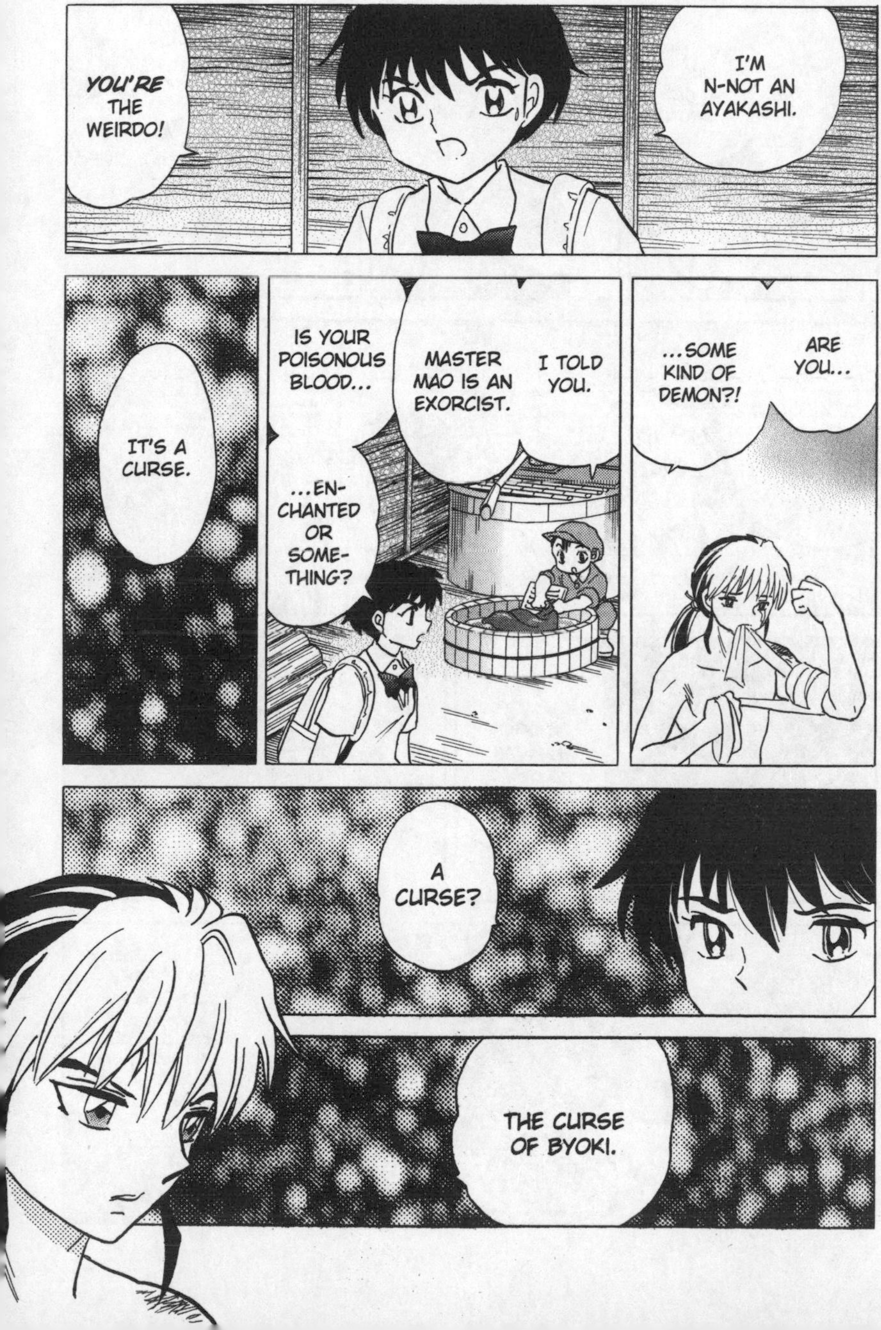
I'M N-NOT AN AYAKASHI.
YOU'RE THE WEIRDO!
ARE YOU...
...SOME KIND OF DEMON?!
I TOLD YOU.
MASTER MAO IS AN EXORCIST.
IS YOUR POISONOUS BLOOD...
...EN-CHANTED OR SOME-THING?
IT'S A CURSE.
A CURSE?
THE CURSE OF BYOKI.

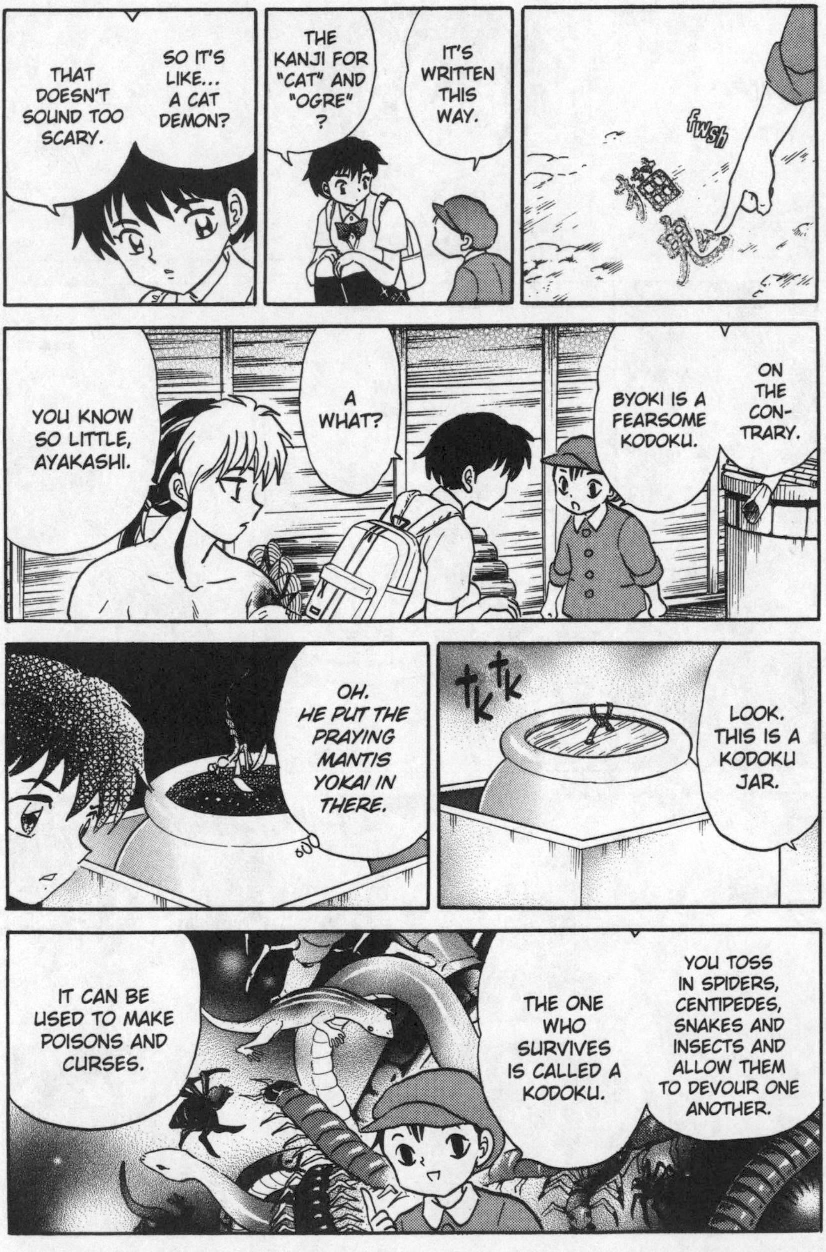
fwsh
猫鬼
IT'S WRITTEN THIS WAY.
THE KANJI FOR "CAT" AND "OGRE"?
SO IT'S LIKE... A CAT DEMON?
THAT DOESN'T SOUND TOO SCARY.
ON THE CON-TRARY.
BYOKI IS A FEARSOME KODOKU.
A WHAT?
YOU KNOW SO LITTLE, AYAKASHI.
tk tk
LOOK. THIS IS A KODOKU JAR.
OH. HE PUT THE PRAYING MANTIS YOKAI IN THERE.
YOU TOSS IN SPIDERS, CENTIPEDES, SNAKES AND INSECTS AND ALLOW THEM TO DEVOUR ONE ANOTHER.
THE ONE WHO SURVIVES IS CALLED A KODOKU.
IT CAN BE USED TO MAKE POISONS AND CURSES.

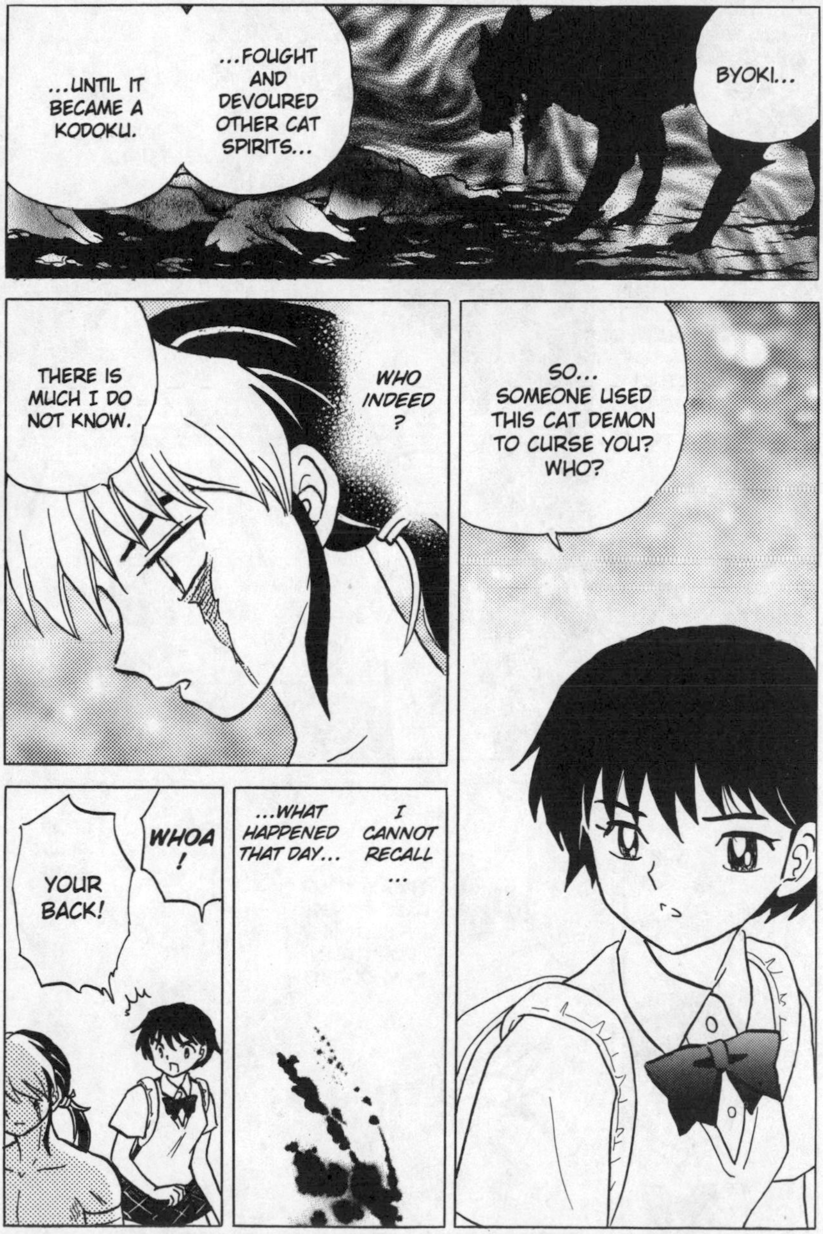
BYOKI...
...FOUGHT AND DEVOURED OTHER CAT SPIRITS...
...UNTIL IT BECAME A KODOKU.
SO... SOMEONE USED THIS CAT DEMON TO CURSE YOU? WHO?
WHO INDEED?
THERE IS MUCH I DO NOT KNOW.
I CANNOT RECALL...
...WHAT HAPPENED THAT DAY...
WHOA!
YOUR BACK!

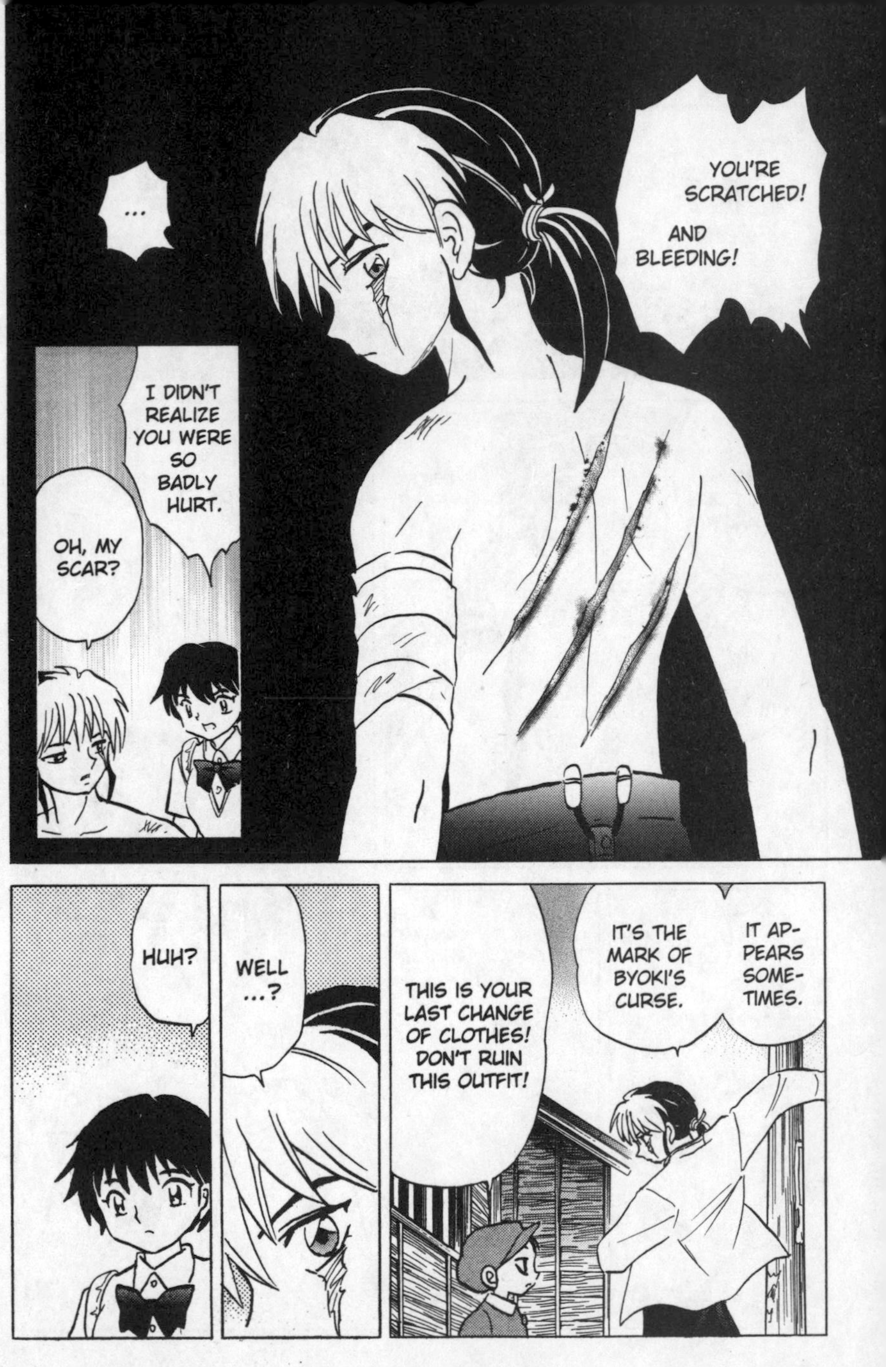
YOU'RE SCRATCHED!
AND BLEEDING!
...
I DIDN'T REALIZE YOU WERE SO BADLY HURT.
OH, MY SCAR?
IT AP- PEARS SOME- TIMES.
IT'S THE MARK OF BYOKI'S CURSE.
THIS IS YOUR LAST CHANGE OF CLOTHES! DON'T RUIN THIS OUTFIT!
WELL ...?
HUH?

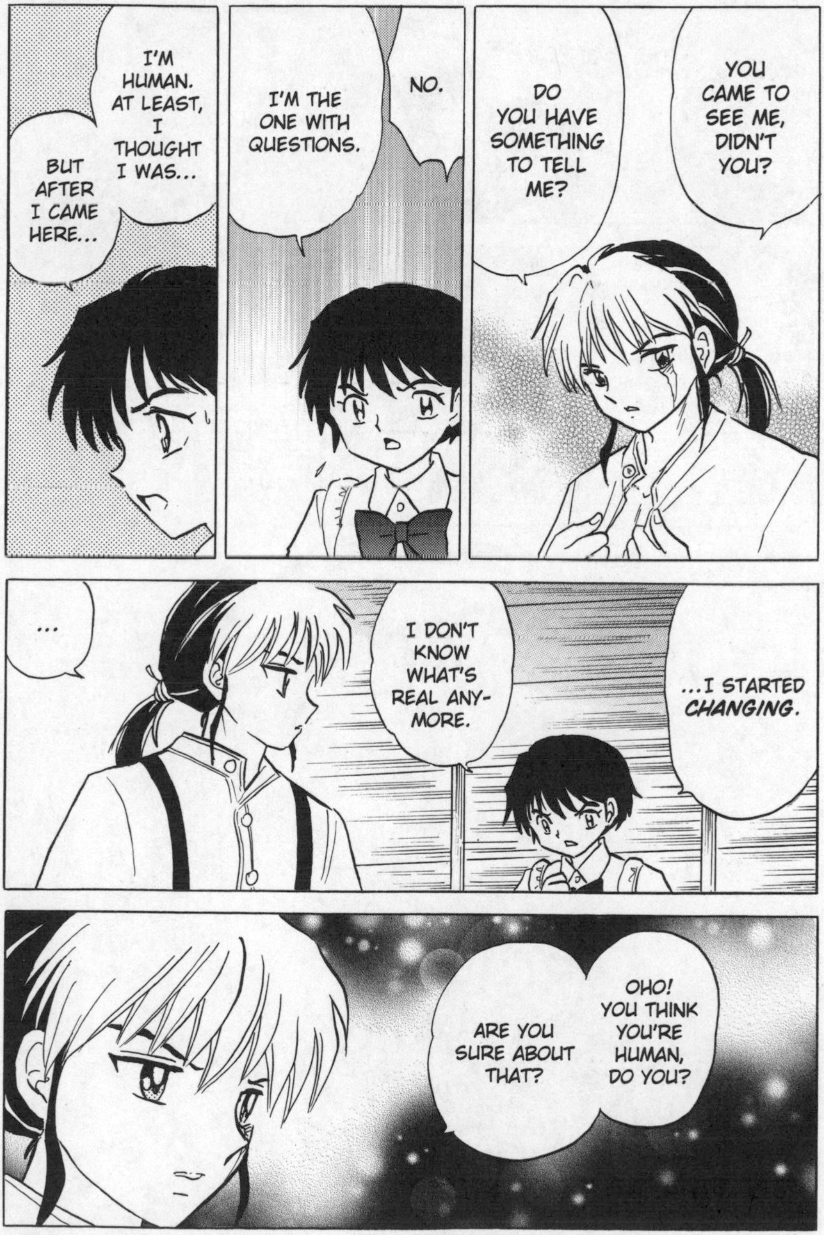
YOU CAME TO SEE ME, DIDN'T YOU?
DO YOU HAVE SOMETHING TO TELL ME?
NO.
I'M THE ONE WITH QUESTIONS.
I'M HUMAN. AT LEAST, I THOUGHT I WAS...
BUT AFTER I CAME HERE...
...I STARTED *CHANGING*.
I DON'T KNOW WHAT'S REAL ANY-MORE.
...
OHO! YOU THINK YOU'RE HUMAN, DO YOU?
ARE YOU SURE ABOUT THAT?

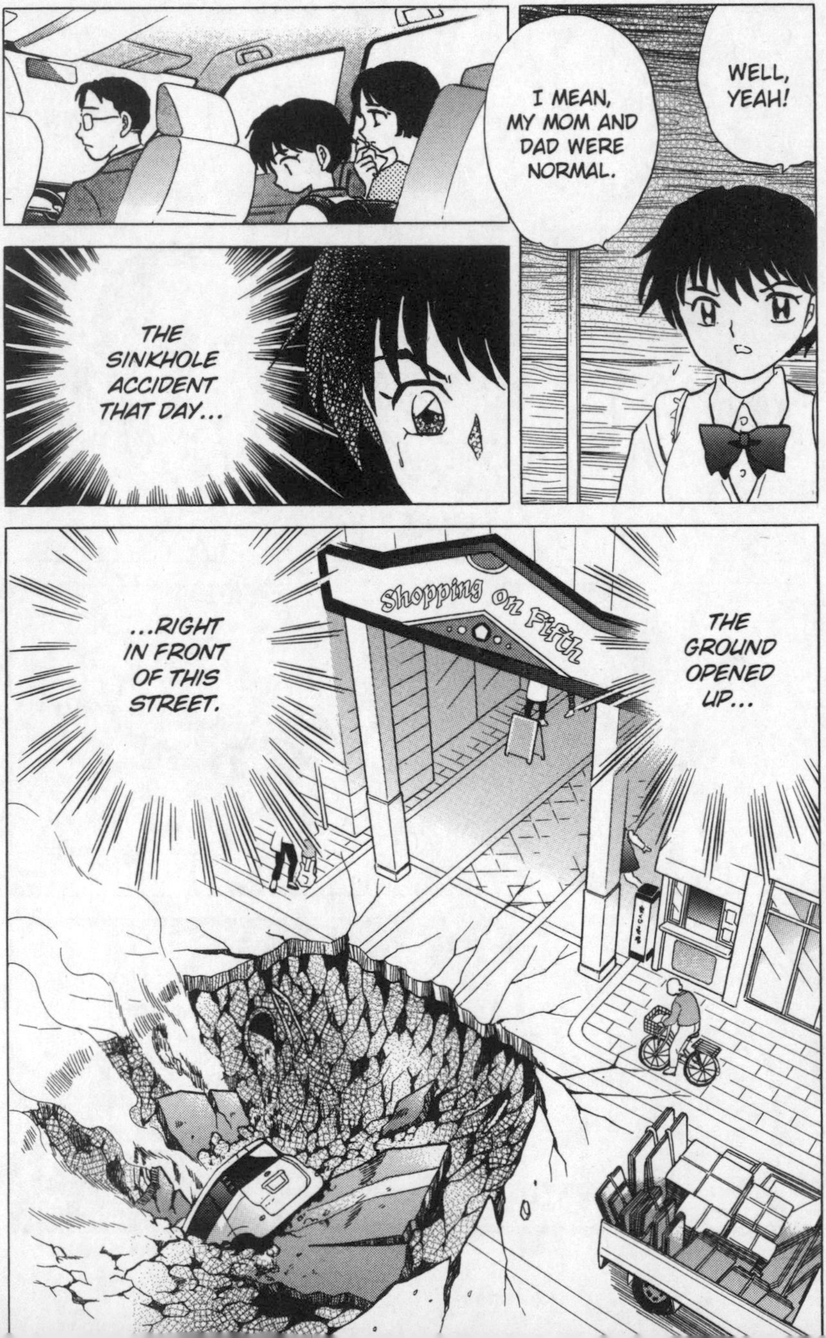
WELL, YEAH!
I MEAN, MY MOM AND DAD WERE NORMAL.
THE SINKHOLE ACCIDENT THAT DAY...
THE GROUND OPENED UP...
...RIGHT IN FRONT OF THIS STREET.
Shopping on Fifth

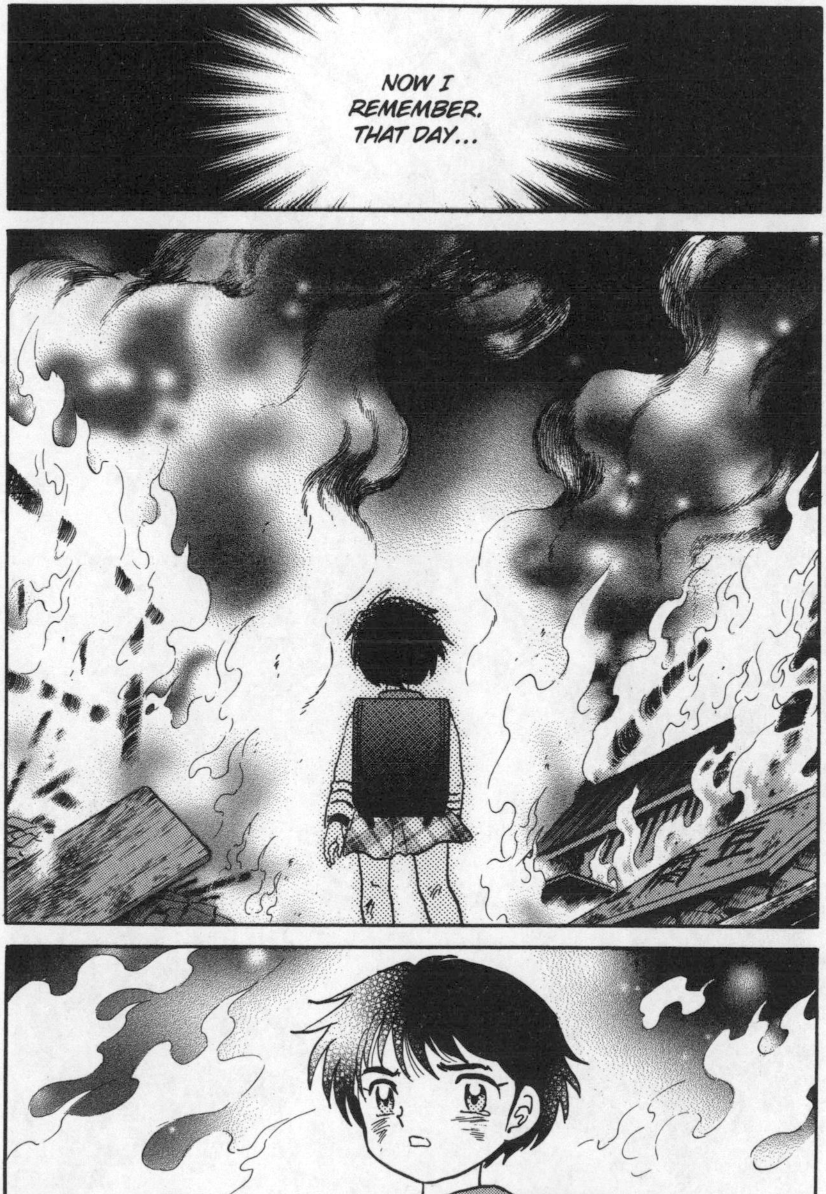
NOW I
REMEMBER.
THAT DAY...

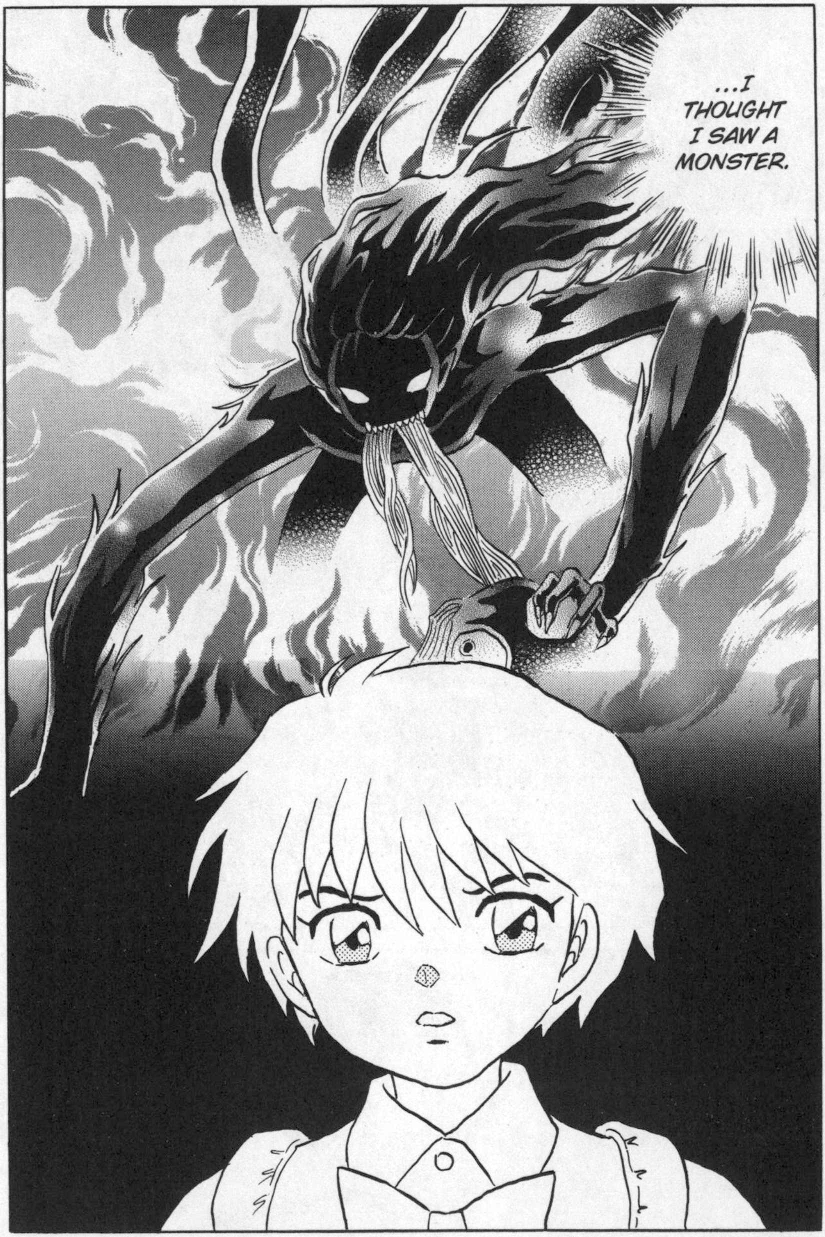
...I THOUGHT I SAW A MONSTER.

Chapter 3:
The Other Side of the Gate

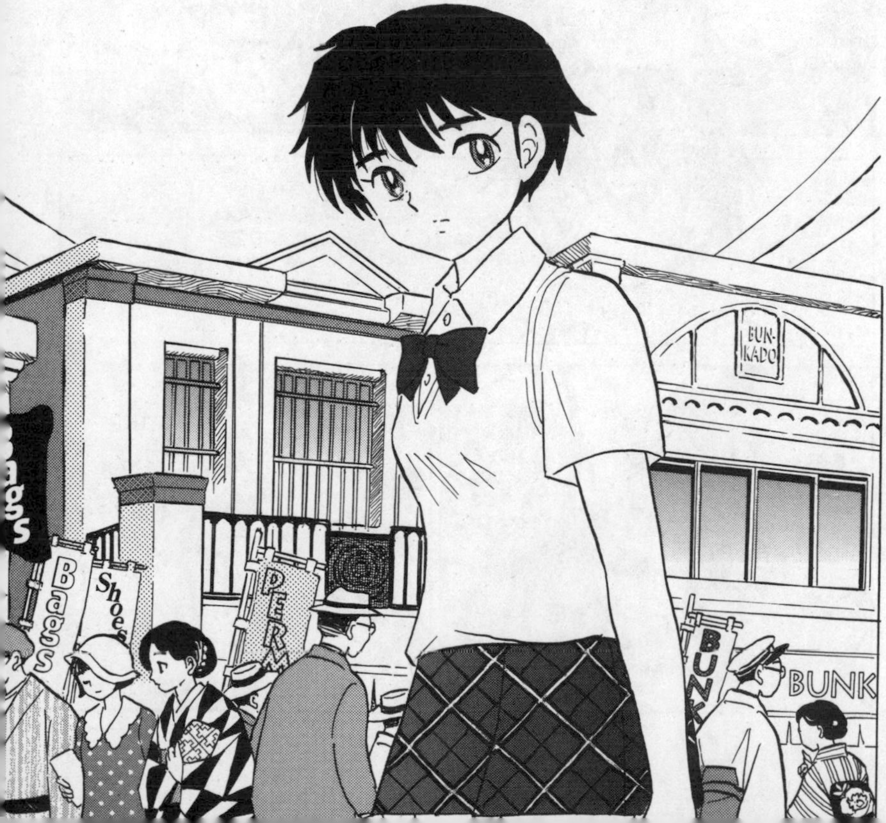
BUN-
KADO
Shoes
BUNK

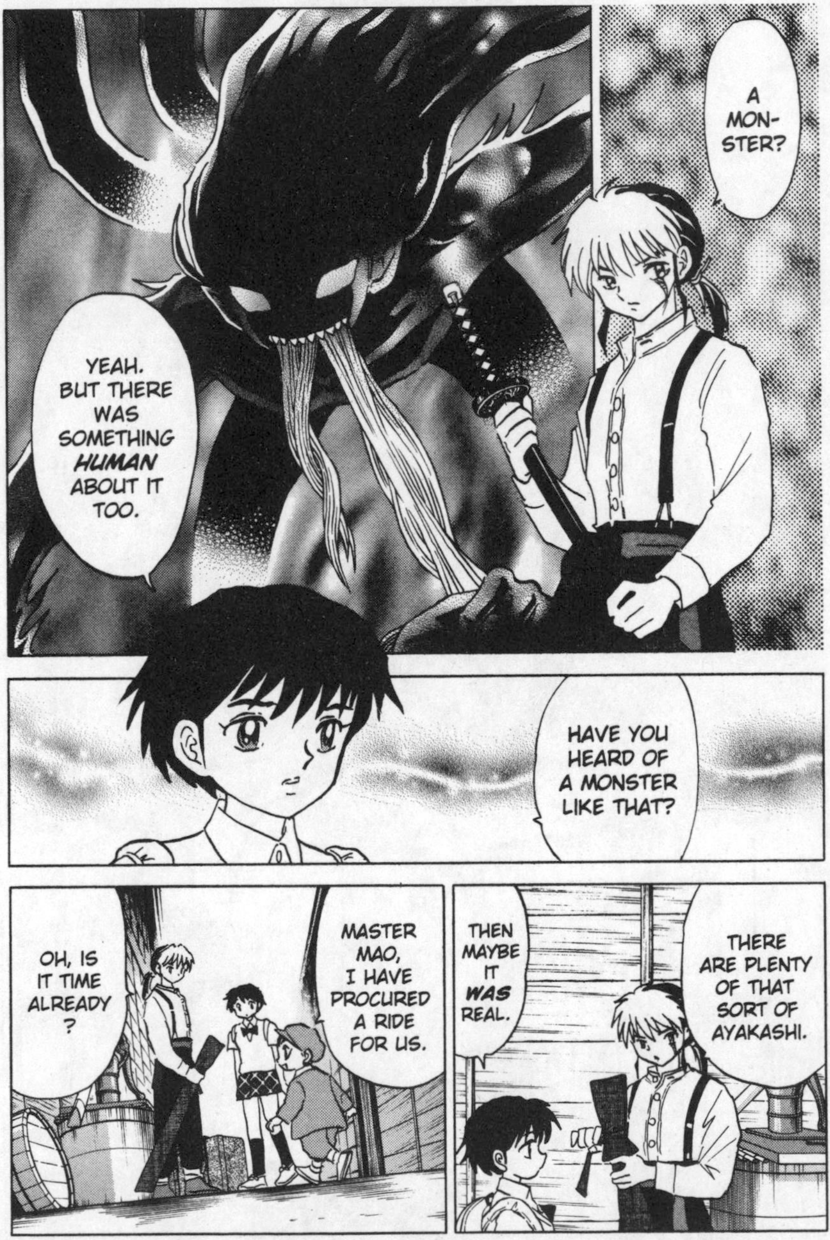
A MON-STER?
YEAH. BUT THERE WAS SOMETHING *HUMAN* ABOUT IT TOO.
HAVE YOU HEARD OF A MONSTER LIKE THAT?
THERE ARE PLENTY OF THAT SORT OF AYAKASHI.
THEN MAYBE IT *WAS* REAL.
MASTER MAO, I HAVE PROCURED A RIDE FOR US.
OH, IS IT TIME ALREADY?

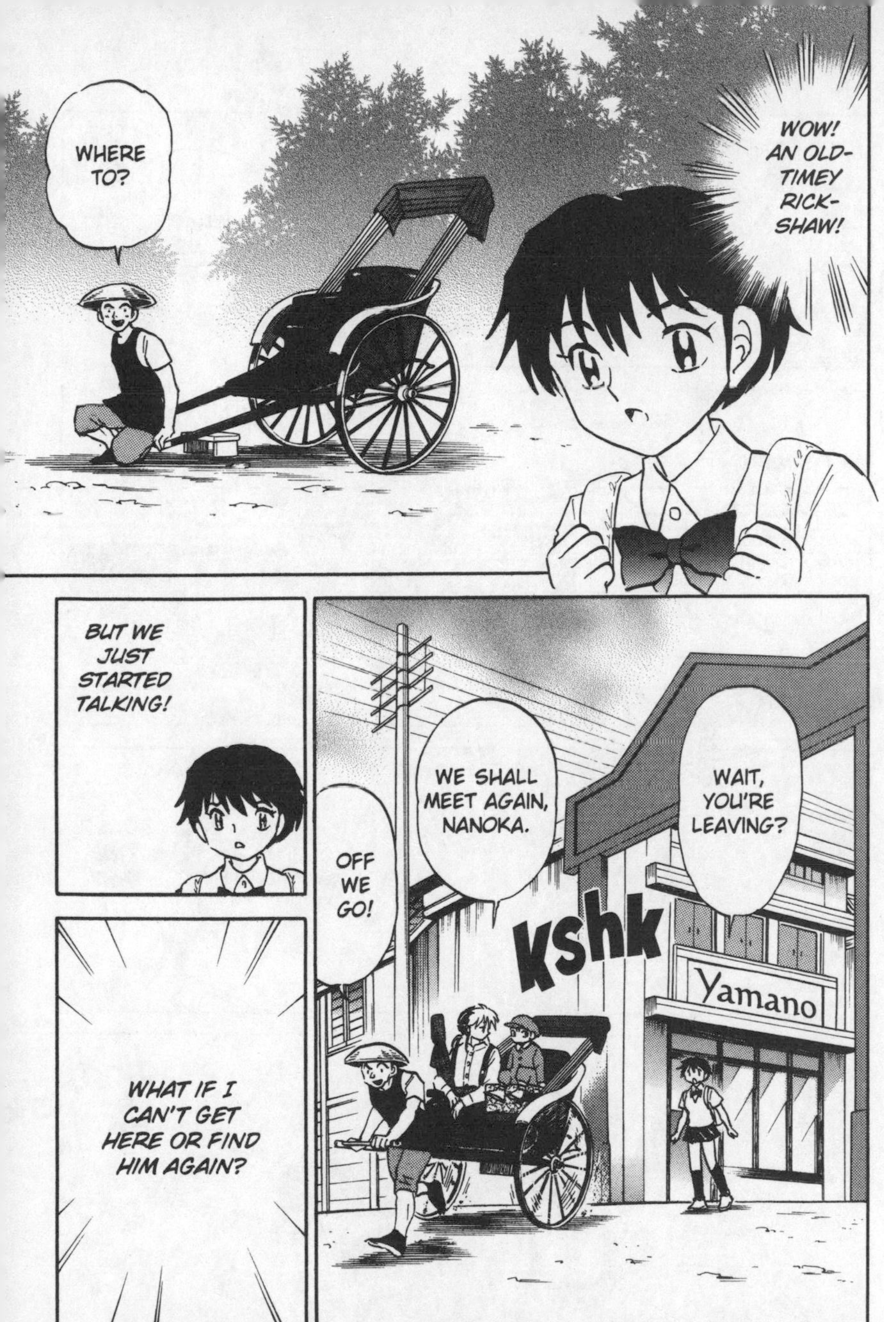
WOW! AN OLD-TIMEY RICK-SHAW!
WHERE TO?
WAIT, YOU'RE LEAVING?
WE SHALL MEET AGAIN, NANOKA.
OFF WE GO!
KSHK
Yamano
BUT WE JUST STARTED TALKING!
WHAT IF I CAN'T GET HERE OR FIND HIM AGAIN?

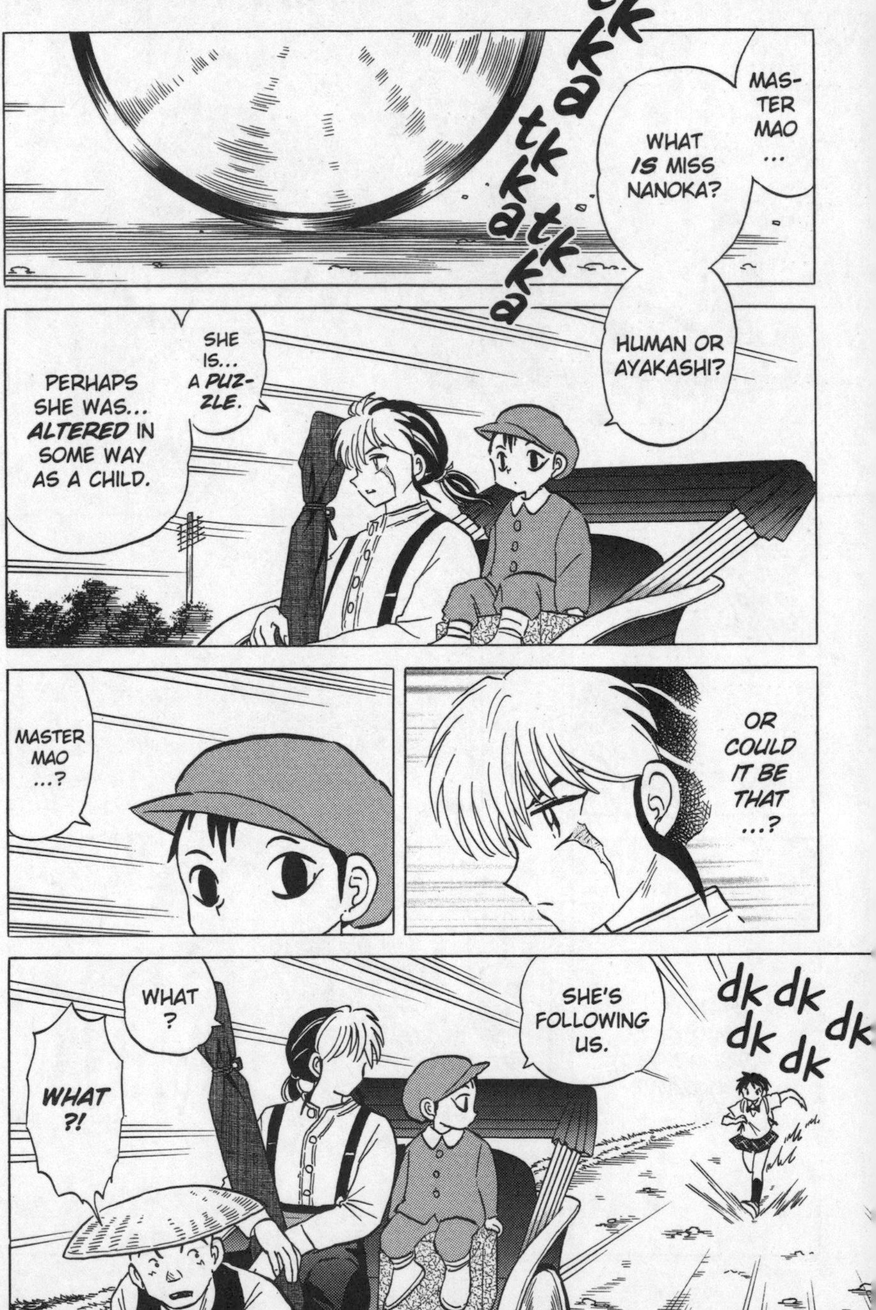
tk ka tk ka tk ka tk ka
MAS-TER MAO ...
WHAT IS MISS NANOKA?
HUMAN OR AYAKASHI?
SHE IS... A PUZ-ZLE.
PERHAPS SHE WAS... ALTERED IN SOME WAY AS A CHILD.
OR COULD IT BE THAT ...?
MASTER MAO ...?
dk dk dk dk dk
SHE'S FOLLOWING US.
WHAT ?
WHAT ?!

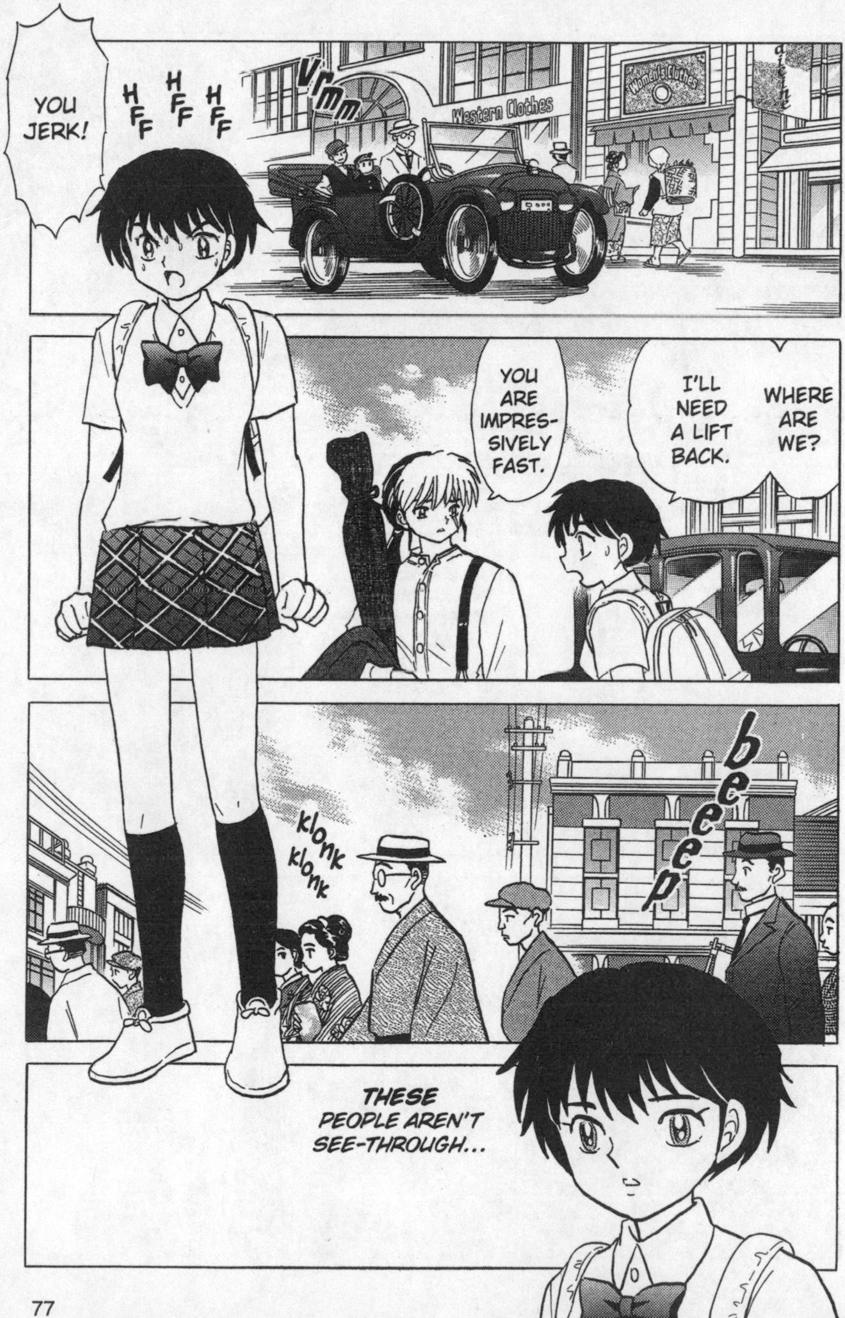
Women's Clothes
Western Clothes
vrmm
HFF HFF HFF
YOU JERK!
WHERE ARE WE?
I'LL NEED A LIFT BACK.
YOU ARE IMPRES-SIVELY FAST.
beeep
klonk klonk
THESE PEOPLE AREN'T SEE-THROUGH...

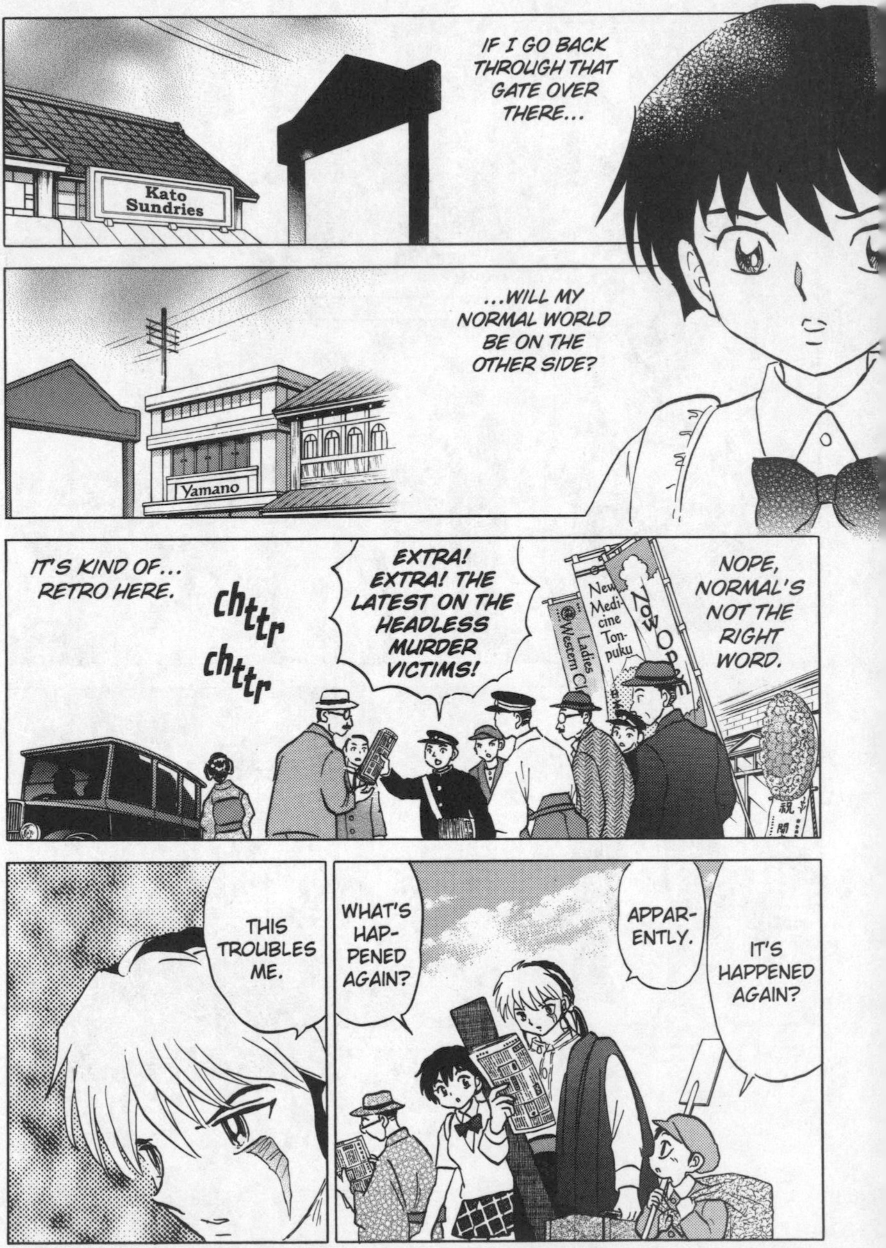
IF I GO BACK THROUGH THAT GATE OVER THERE...
Kato Sundries
...WILL MY NORMAL WORLD BE ON THE OTHER SIDE?
Yamano
NOPE, NORMAL'S NOT THE RIGHT WORD.
New Medi-cine Ton-puku
EXTRA! EXTRA! THE LATEST ON THE HEADLESS MURDER VICTIMS!
chttr chttr
IT'S KIND OF... RETRO HERE.
IT'S HAPPENED AGAIN?
APPAR-ENTLY.
WHAT'S HAP-PENED AGAIN?
THIS TROUBLES ME.

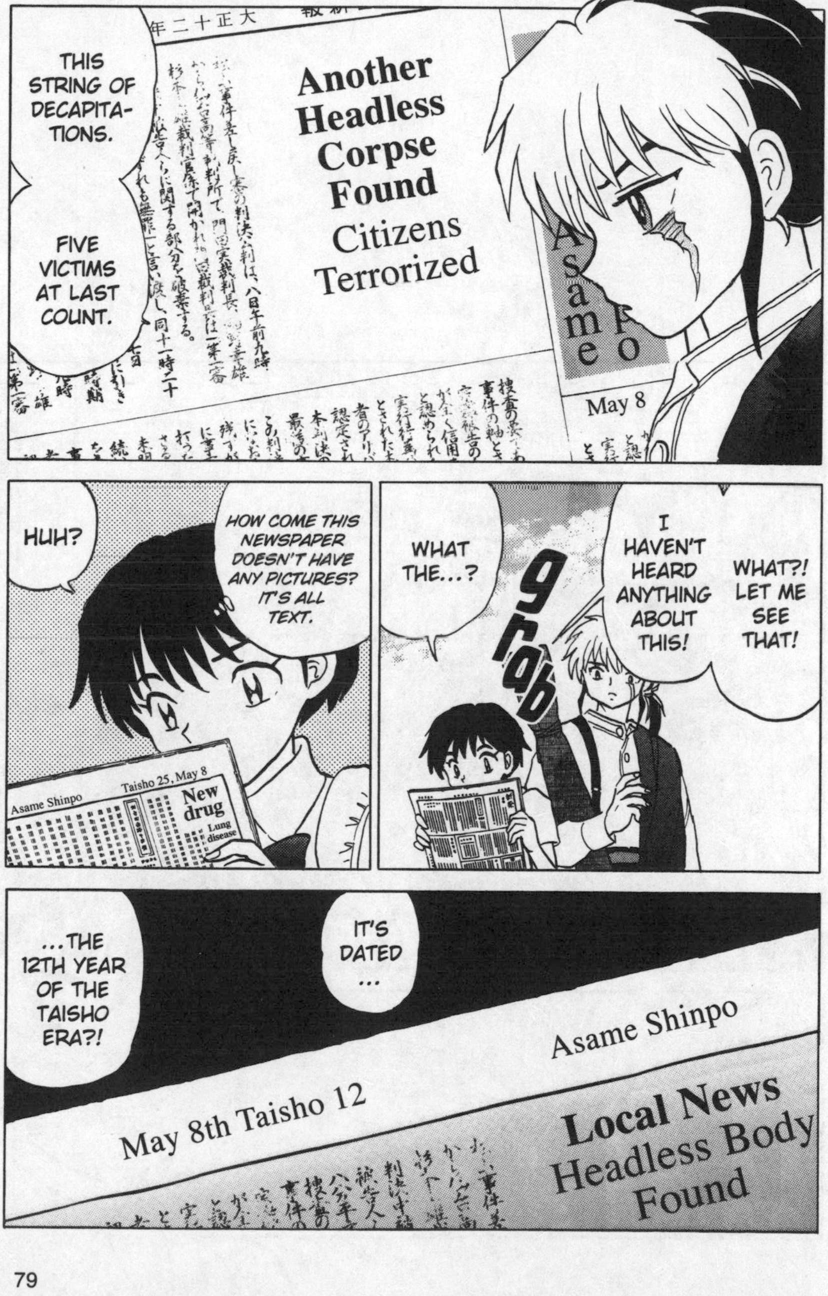
Another Headless Corpse Found
Citizens Terrorized
Asame Po
May 8
THIS STRING OF DECAPITATIONS.
FIVE VICTIMS AT LAST COUNT.
WHAT?! LET ME SEE THAT!
I HAVEN'T HEARD ANYTHING ABOUT THIS!
grab
WHAT THE...?
HOW COME THIS NEWSPAPER DOESN'T HAVE ANY PICTURES? IT'S ALL TEXT.
HUH?
Asame Shinpo
Taisho 25, May 8
New drug
Lung disease
IT'S DATED ...
...THE 12TH YEAR OF THE TAISHO ERA?!
Asame Shinpo
May 8th Taisho 12
Local News
Headless Body Found

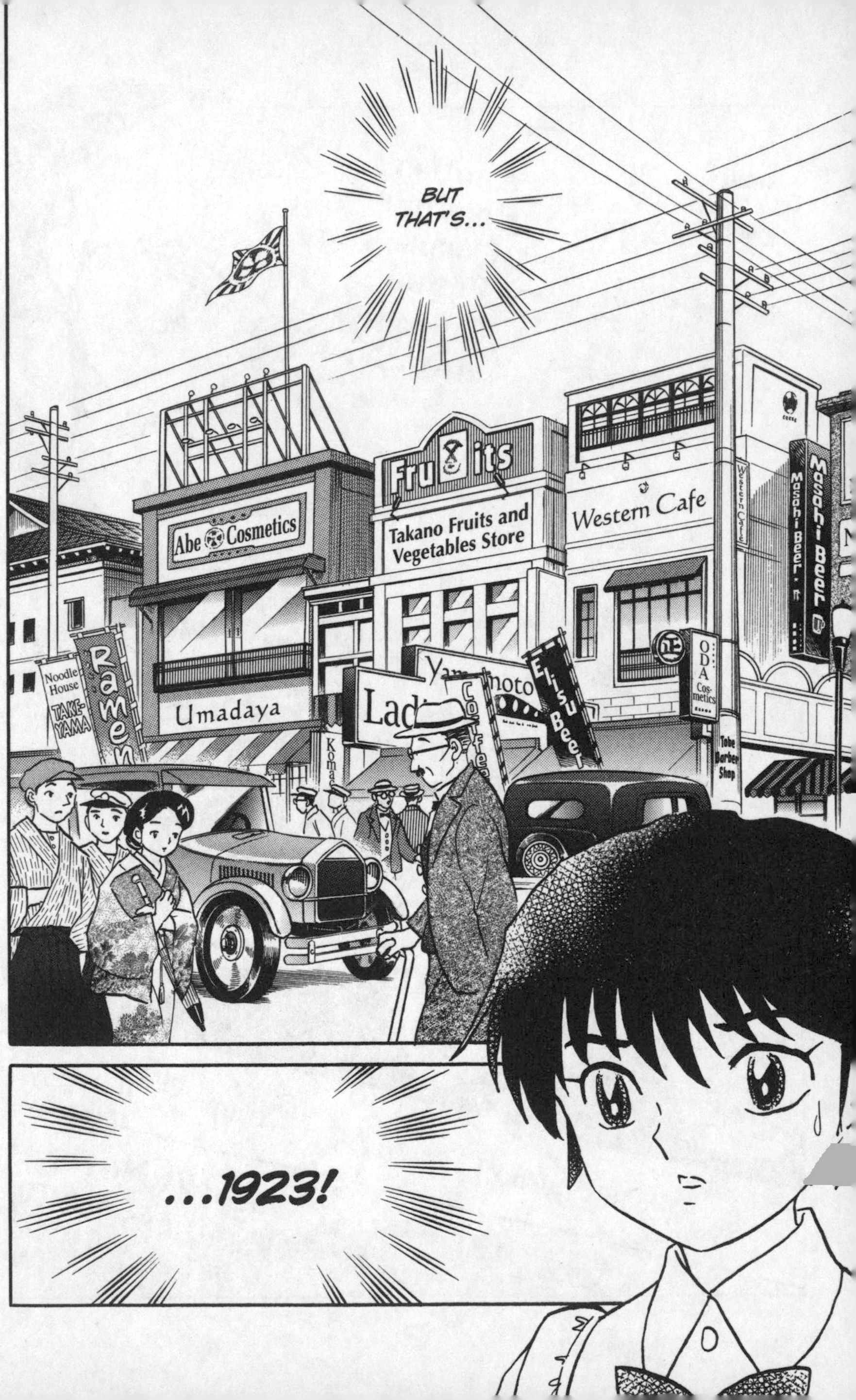
BUT THAT'S...
Abe Cosmetics
Fruits
Takano Fruits and Vegetables Store
Western Cafe
Masahi Beer
Noodle House TAKE-YAMA
Ramen
Umadaya
ODA Cosmetics
Tobe Barber Shop
...1923!

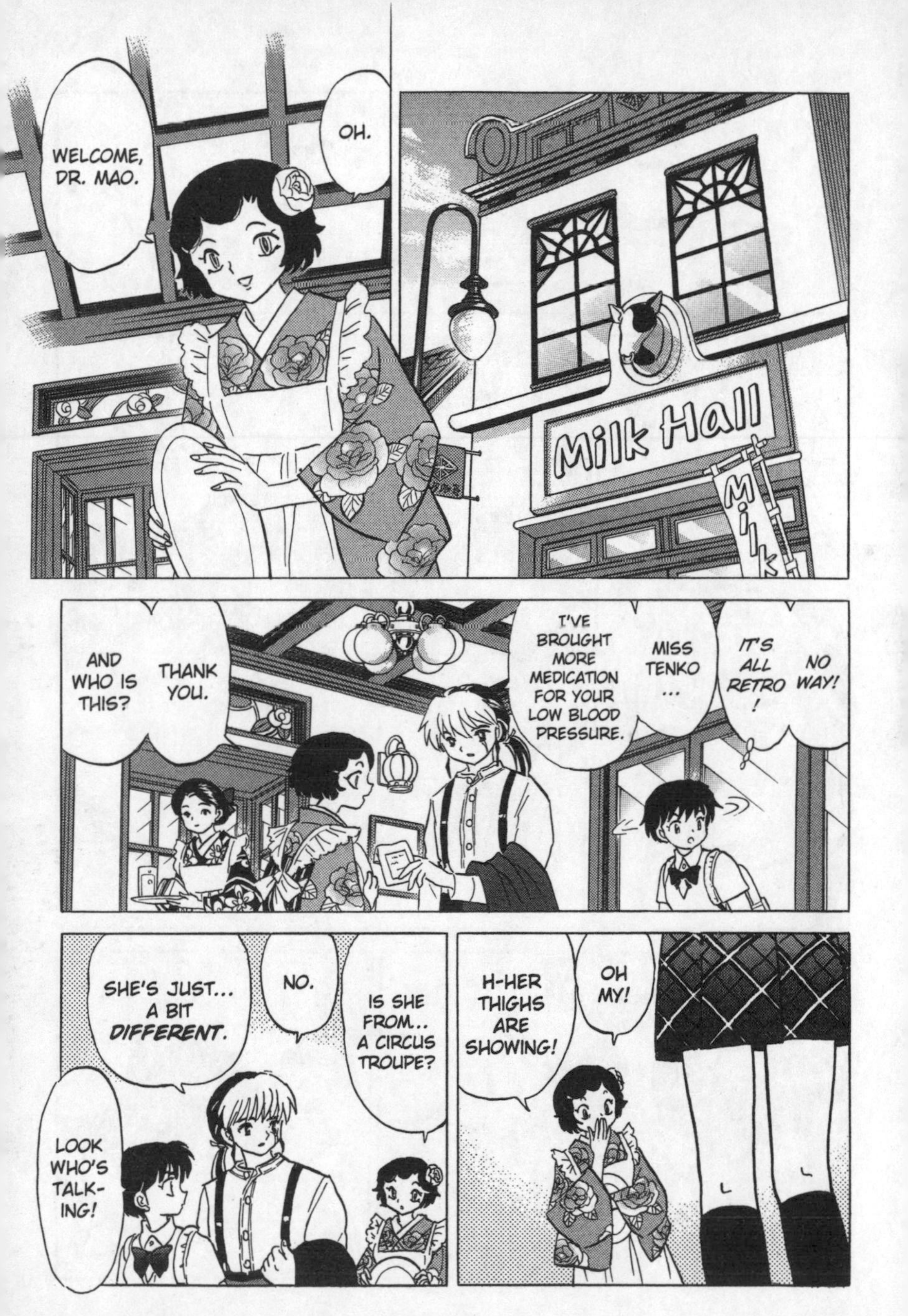
Milk Hall
Milk
OH.
WELCOME, DR. MAO.
NO WAY!
IT'S ALL RETRO!
MISS TENKO...
I'VE BROUGHT MORE MEDICATION FOR YOUR LOW BLOOD PRESSURE.
THANK YOU.
AND WHO IS THIS?
OH MY!
H-HER THIGHS ARE SHOWING!
IS SHE FROM... A CIRCUS TROUPE?
NO.
SHE'S JUST... A BIT *DIFFERENT*.
LOOK WHO'S TALK-ING!

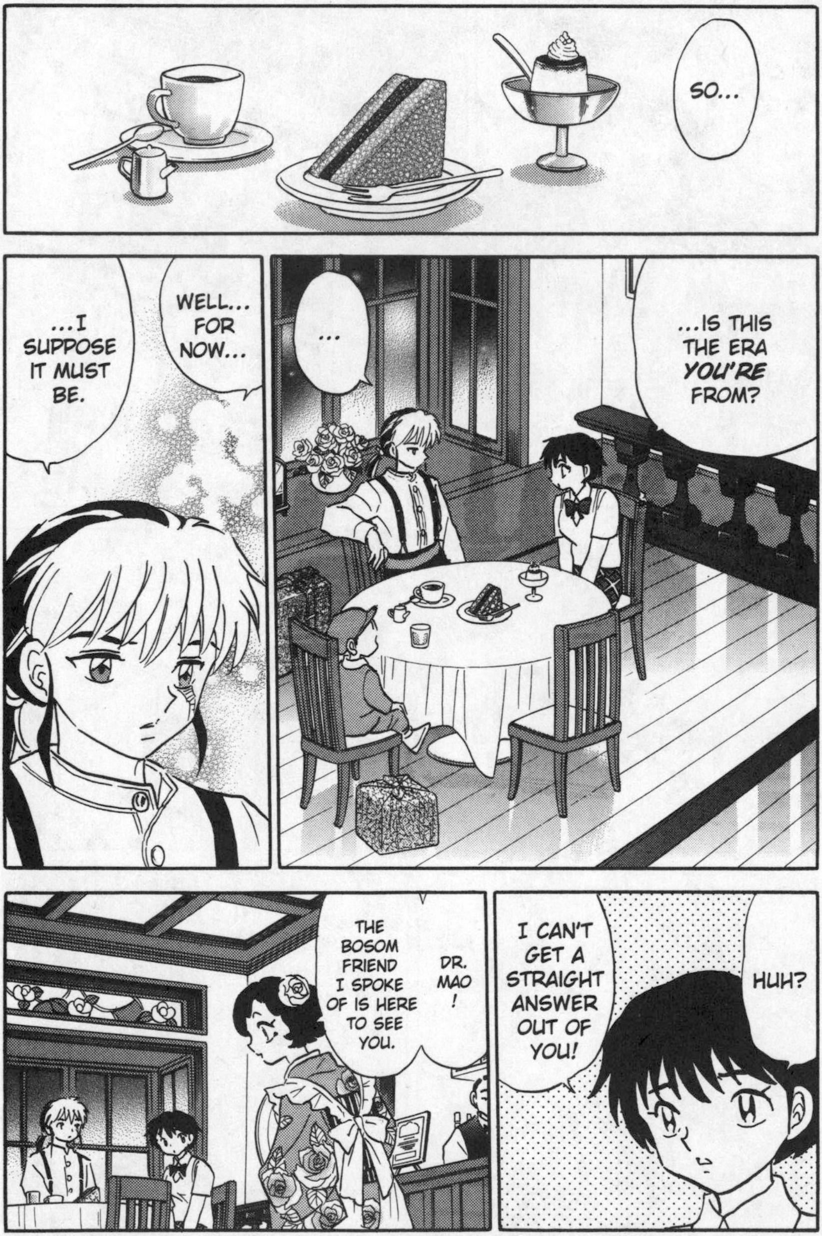
SO...
...IS THIS THE ERA *YOU'RE* FROM?
...
WELL... FOR NOW...
...I SUPPOSE IT MUST BE.
HUH?
I CAN'T GET A STRAIGHT ANSWER OUT OF YOU!
DR. MAO!
THE BOSOM FRIEND I SPOKE OF IS HERE TO SEE YOU.

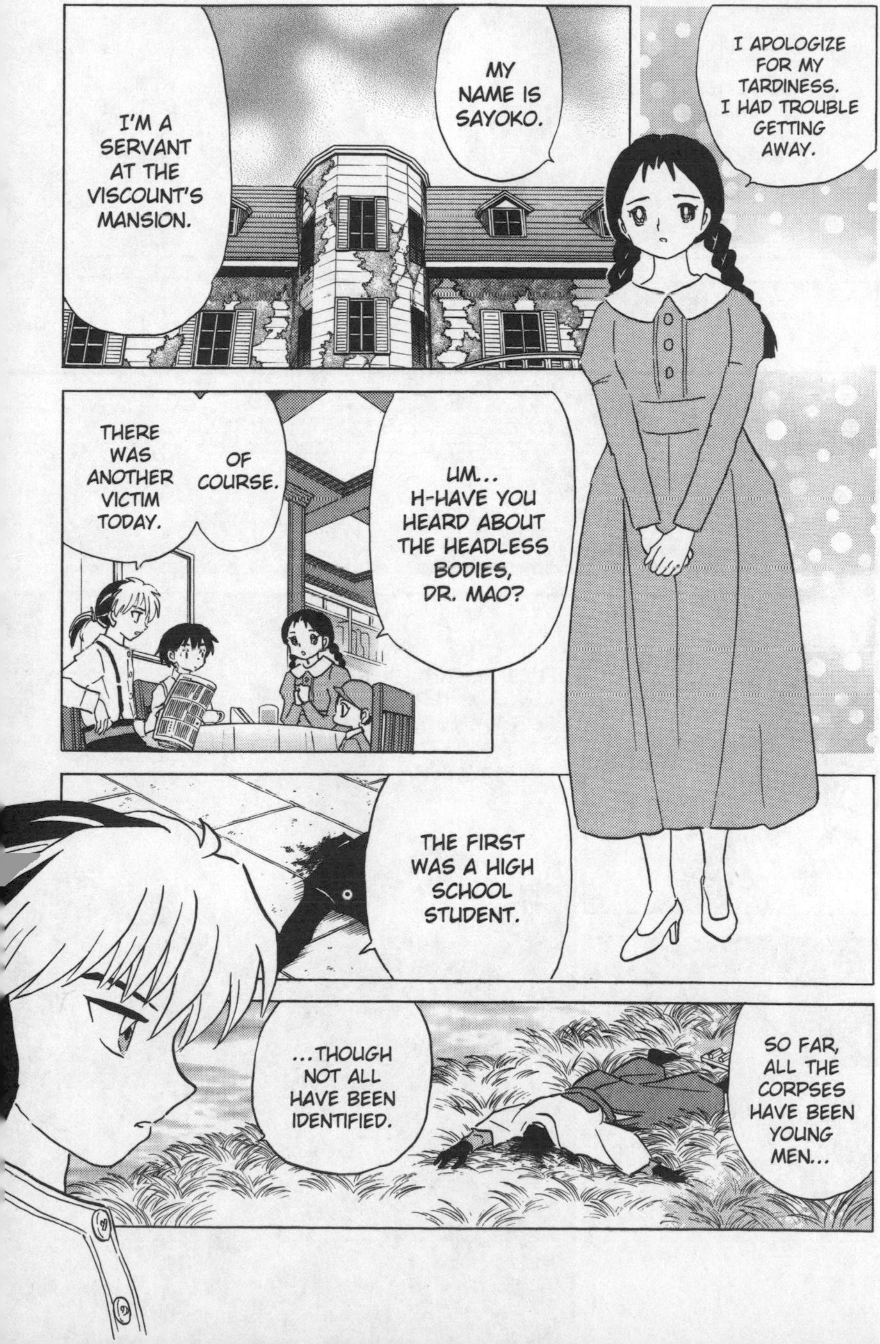
I APOLOGIZE FOR MY TARDINESS. I HAD TROUBLE GETTING AWAY.
MY NAME IS SAYOKO.
I'M A SERVANT AT THE VISCOUNT'S MANSION.
UM... H-HAVE YOU HEARD ABOUT THE HEADLESS BODIES, DR. MAO?
OF COURSE.
THERE WAS ANOTHER VICTIM TODAY.
THE FIRST WAS A HIGH SCHOOL STUDENT.
SO FAR, ALL THE CORPSES HAVE BEEN YOUNG MEN...
...THOUGH NOT ALL HAVE BEEN IDENTIFIED.

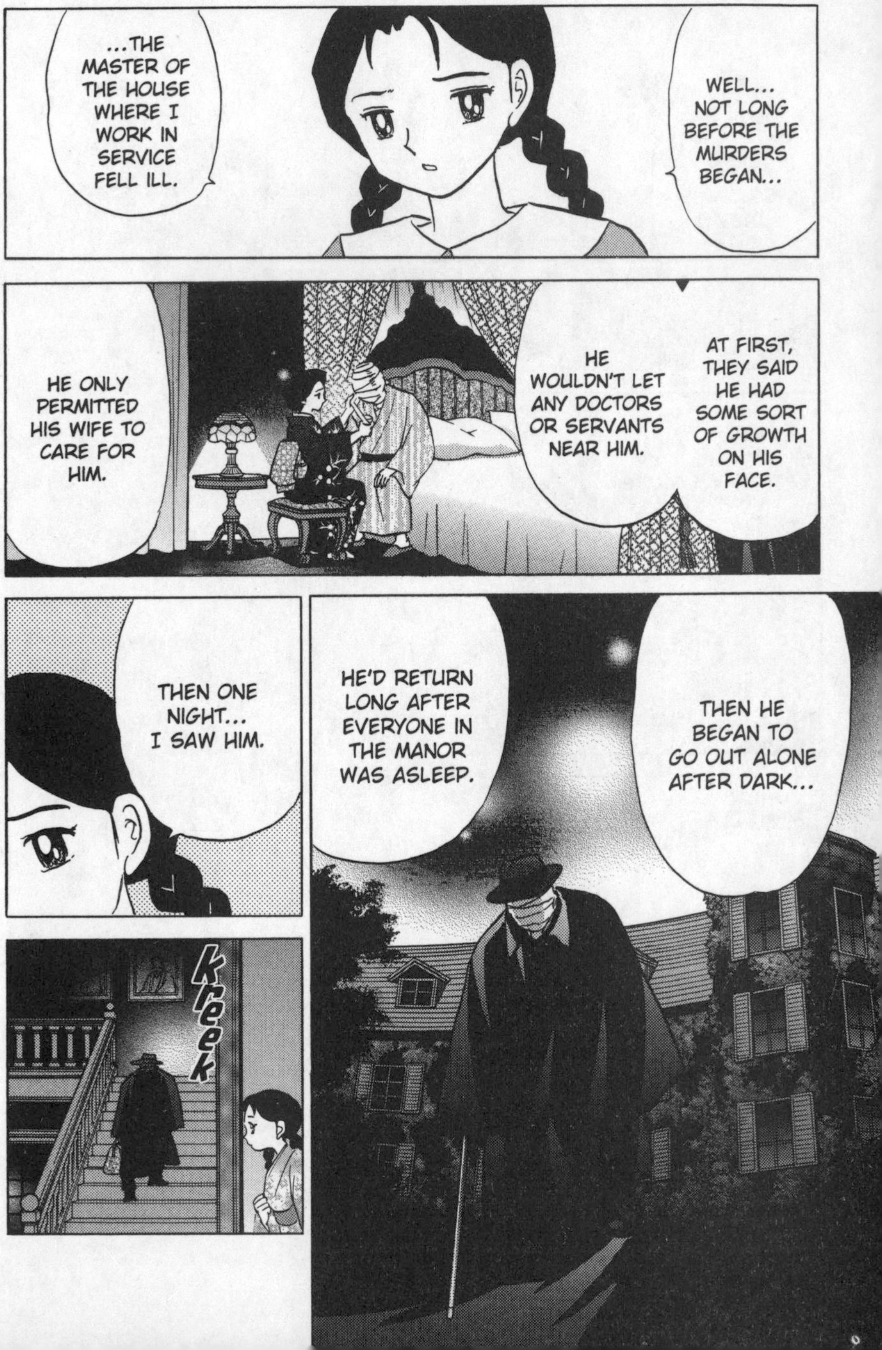
WELL... NOT LONG BEFORE THE MURDERS BEGAN...
...THE MASTER OF THE HOUSE WHERE I WORK IN SERVICE FELL ILL.
AT FIRST, THEY SAID HE HAD SOME SORT OF GROWTH ON HIS FACE.
HE WOULDN'T LET ANY DOCTORS OR SERVANTS NEAR HIM.
HE ONLY PERMITTED HIS WIFE TO CARE FOR HIM.
THEN HE BEGAN TO GO OUT ALONE AFTER DARK...
HE'D RETURN LONG AFTER EVERYONE IN THE MANOR WAS ASLEEP.
THEN ONE NIGHT... I SAW HIM.
kreek

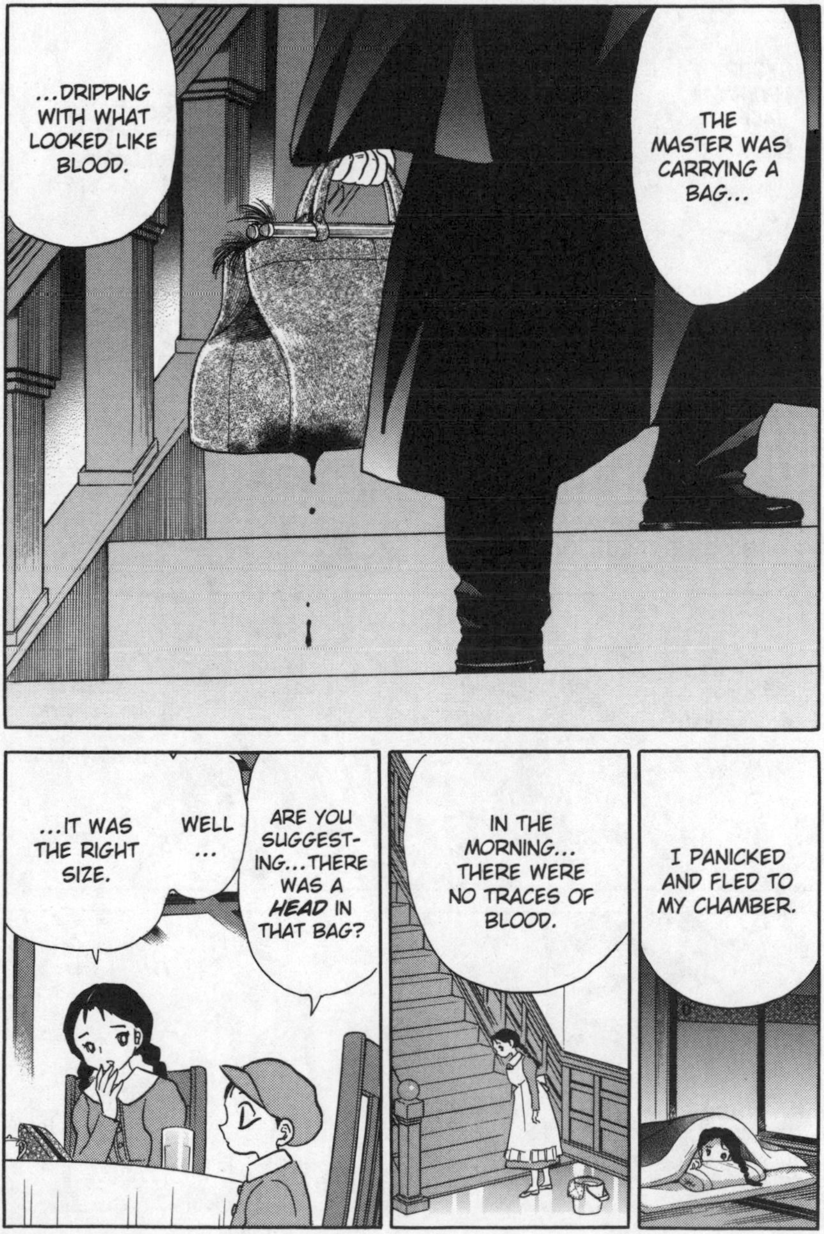
THE MASTER WAS CARRYING A BAG...
...DRIPPING WITH WHAT LOOKED LIKE BLOOD.
I PANICKED AND FLED TO MY CHAMBER.
IN THE MORNING... THERE WERE NO TRACES OF BLOOD.
ARE YOU SUGGEST-ING...THERE WAS A *HEAD* IN THAT BAG?
WELL...
...IT WAS THE RIGHT SIZE.

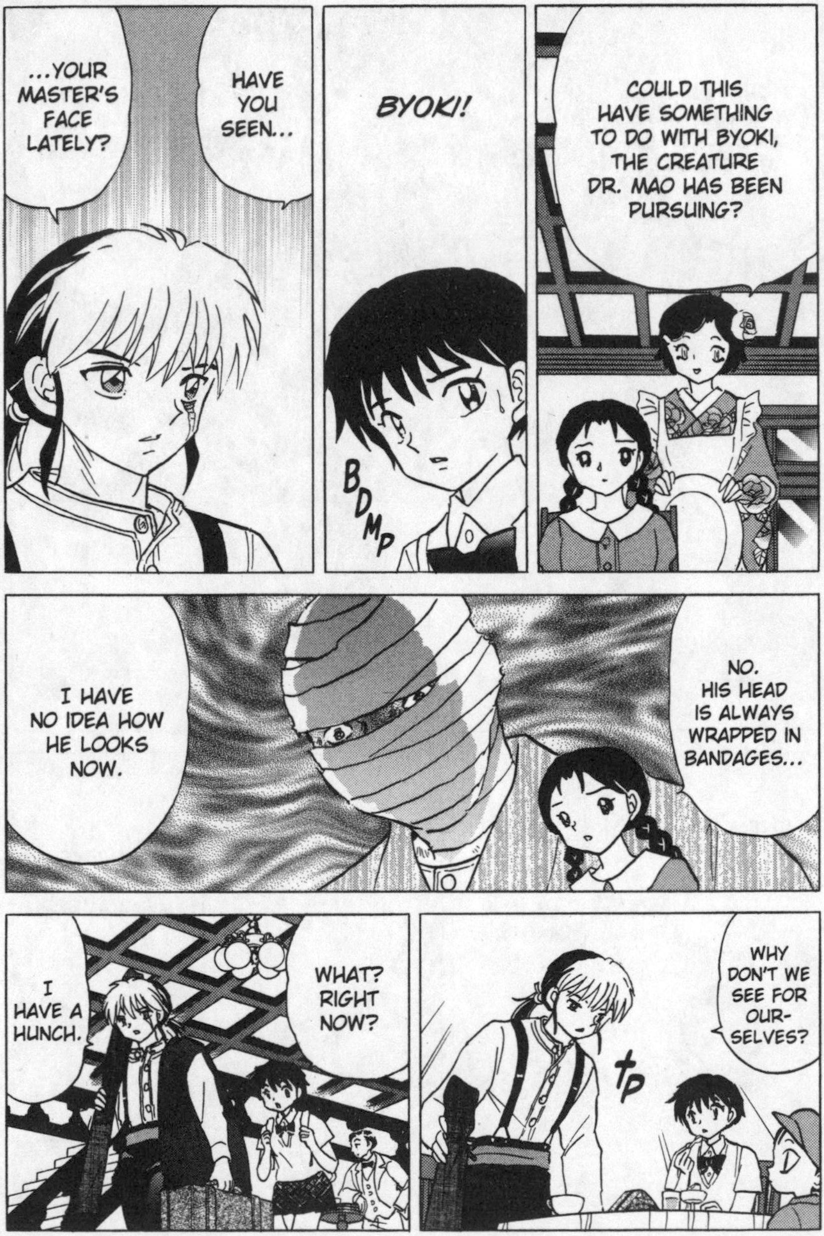

COULD THIS HAVE SOMETHING TO DO WITH BYOKI, THE CREATURE DR. MAO HAS BEEN PURSUING?
BYOKI!
BDMP
HAVE YOU SEEN...
...YOUR MASTER'S FACE LATELY?
NO. HIS HEAD IS ALWAYS WRAPPED IN BANDAGES...
I HAVE NO IDEA HOW HE LOOKS NOW.
WHY DON'T WE SEE FOR OUR-SELVES?
TP
WHAT? RIGHT NOW?
I HAVE A HUNCH.

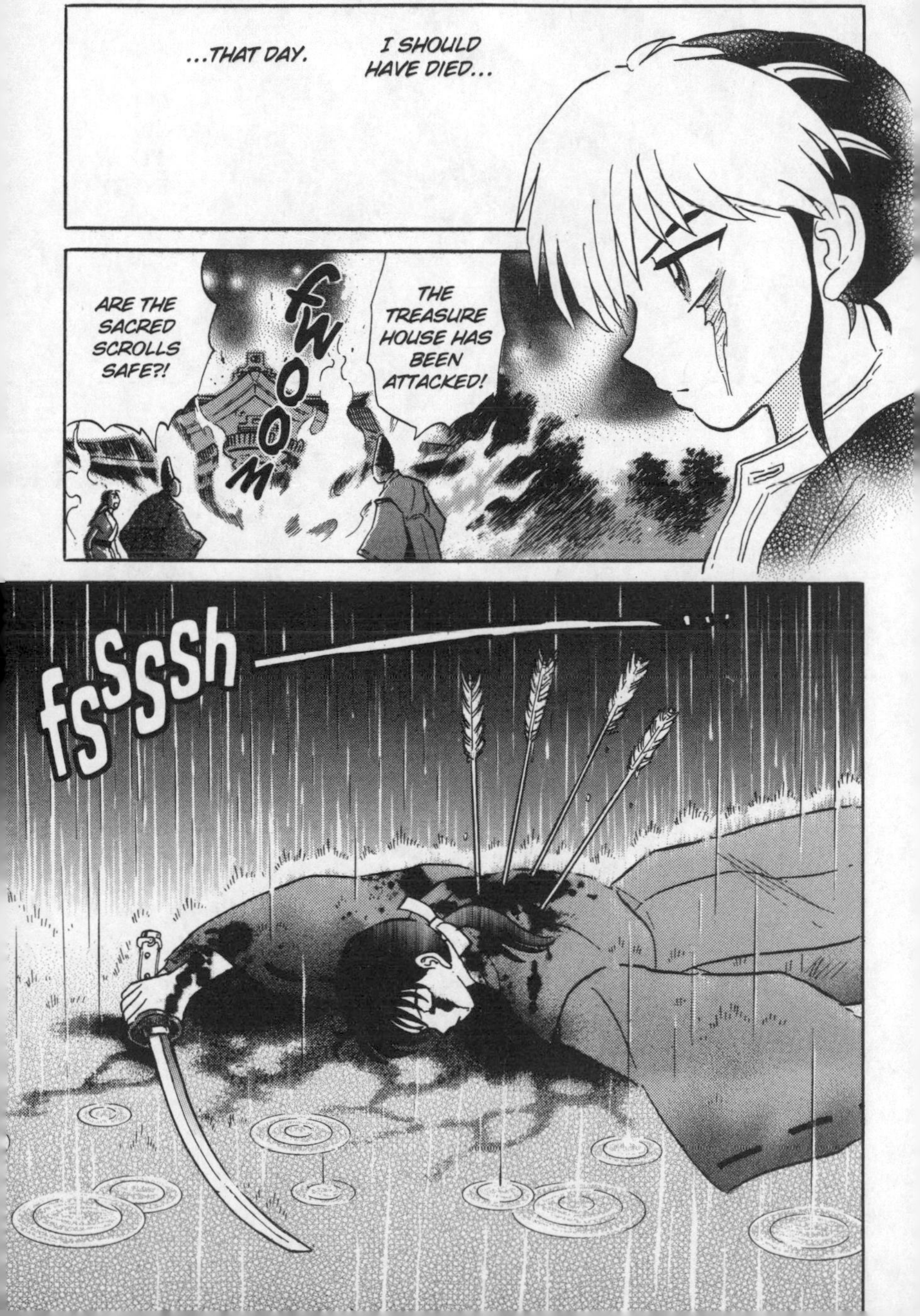
I SHOULD HAVE DIED...
...THAT DAY.
THE TREASURE HOUSE HAS BEEN ATTACKED!
fWOOM
ARE THE SACRED SCROLLS SAFE?!
fSSSSh
...

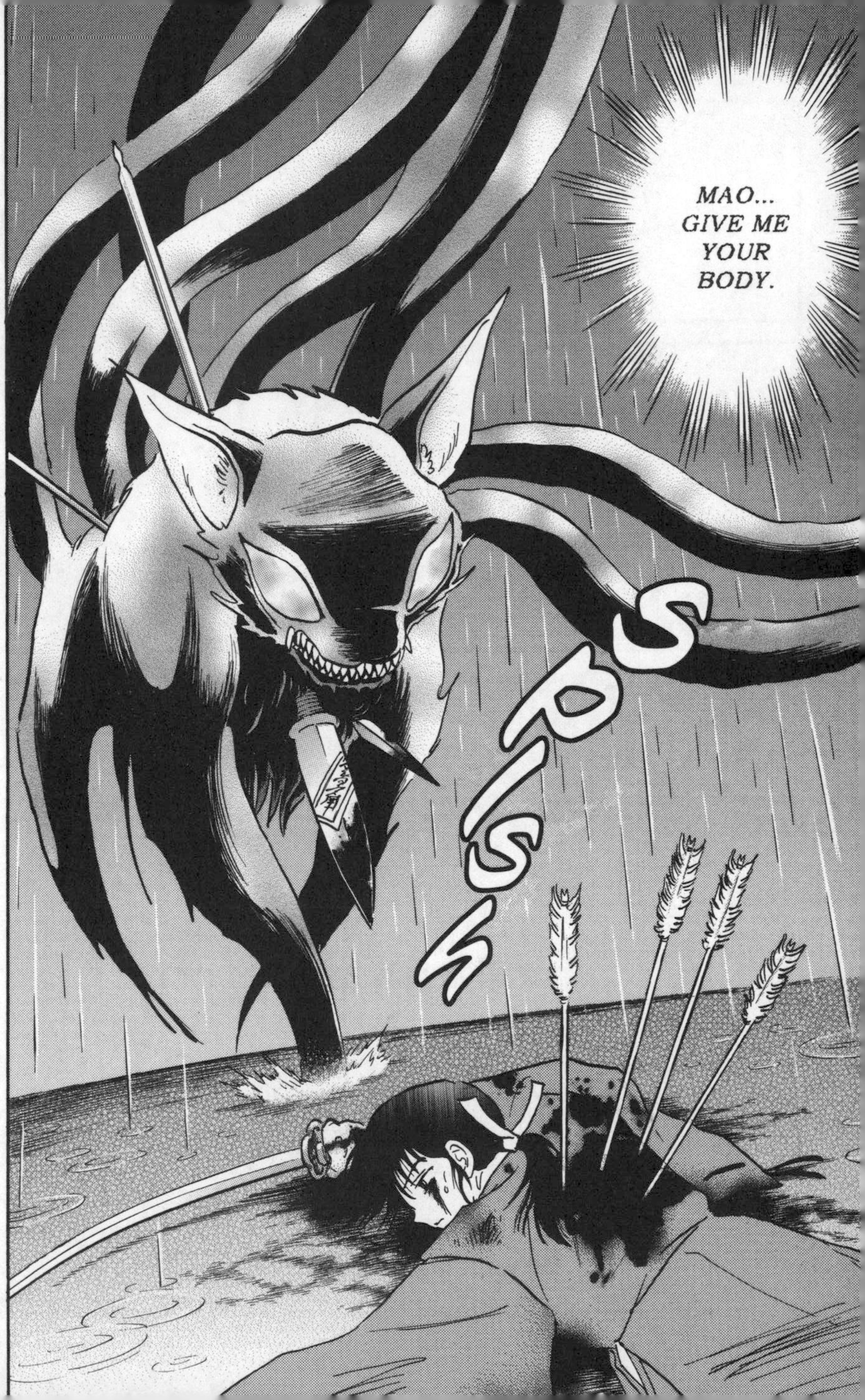
MAO... GIVE ME YOUR BODY.
SPRISH

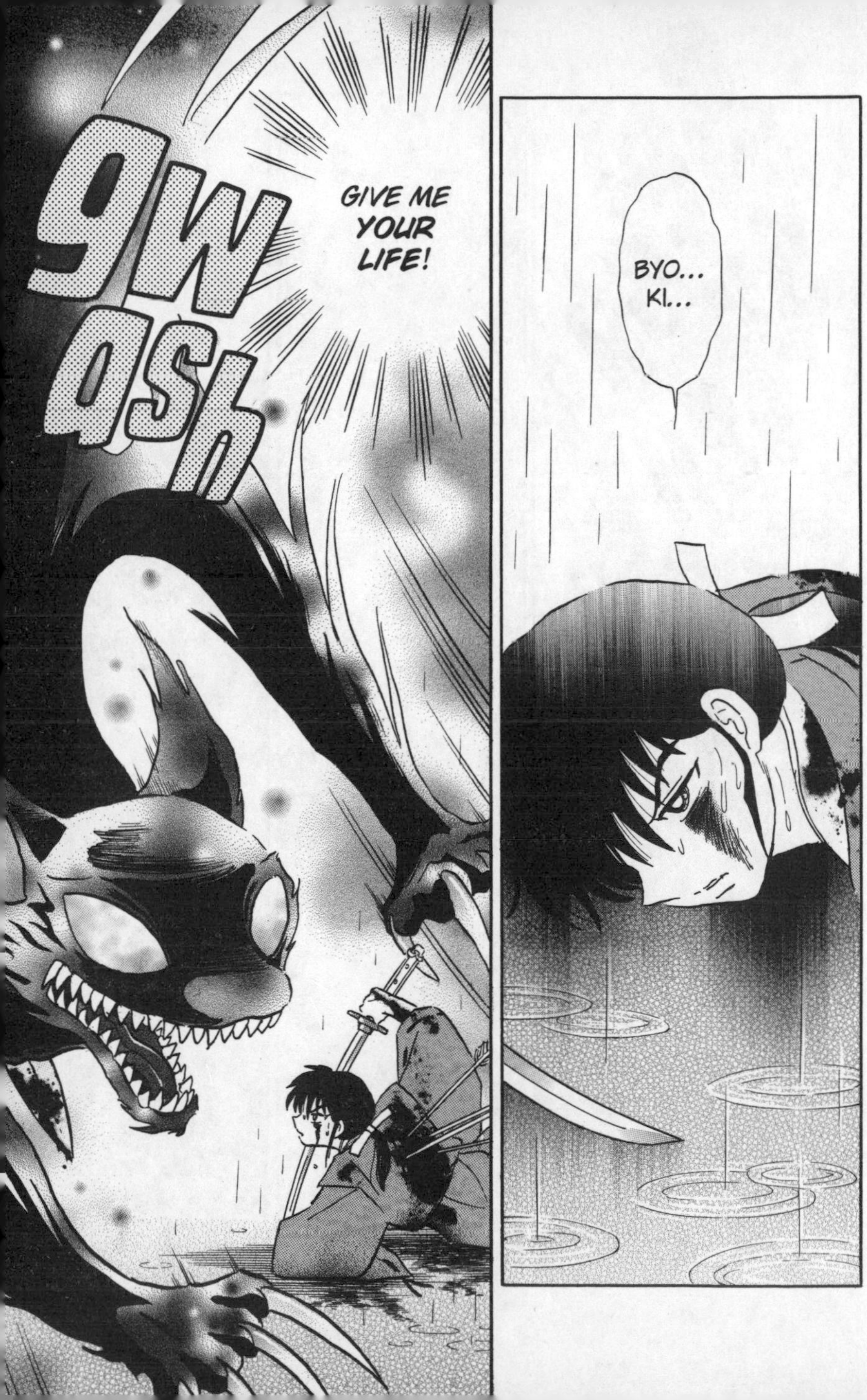
BYO... KI...
GWASH
GIVE ME YOUR LIFE!

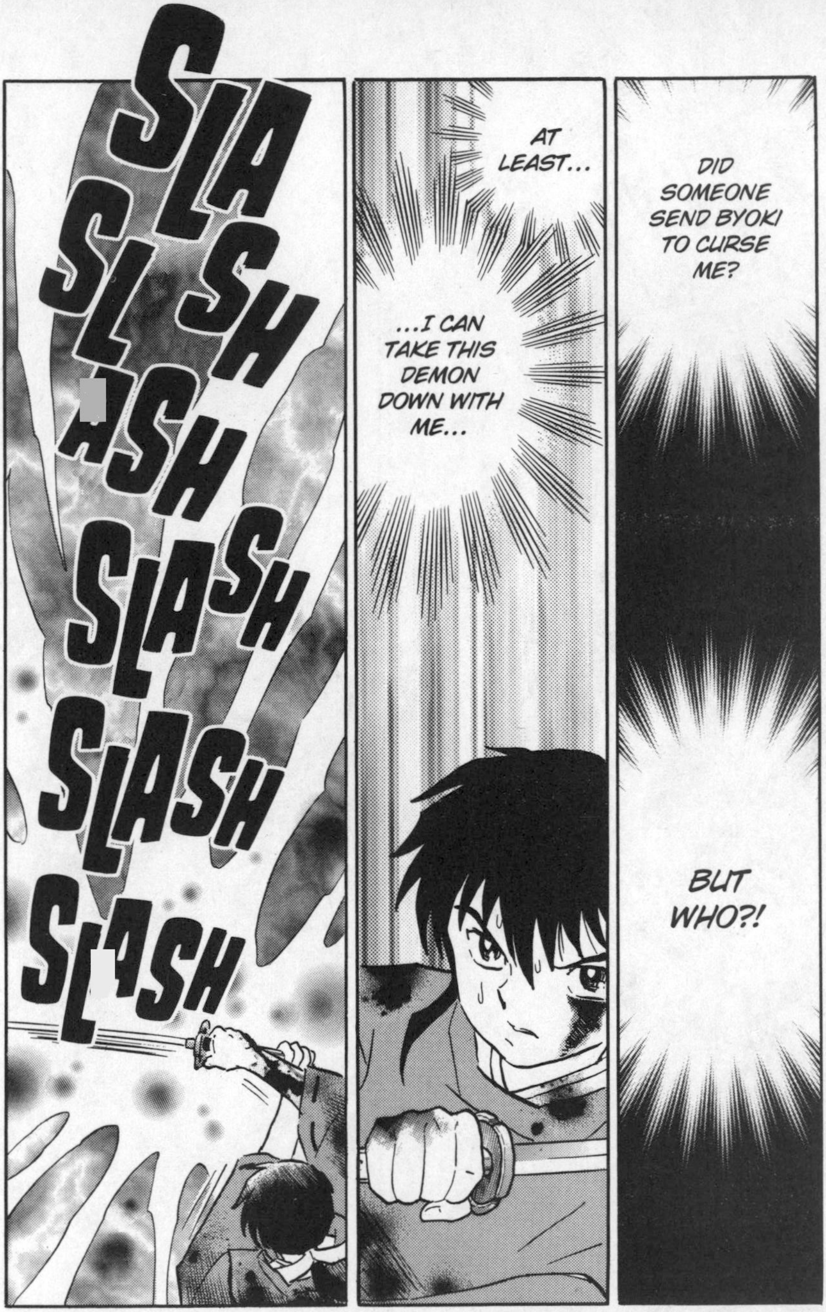
DID SOMEONE SEND BYOKI TO CURSE ME?
BUT WHO?!
AT LEAST...
...I CAN TAKE THIS DEMON DOWN WITH ME...
SLASH
SLASH
SLASH
SLASH
SLASH
SLASH

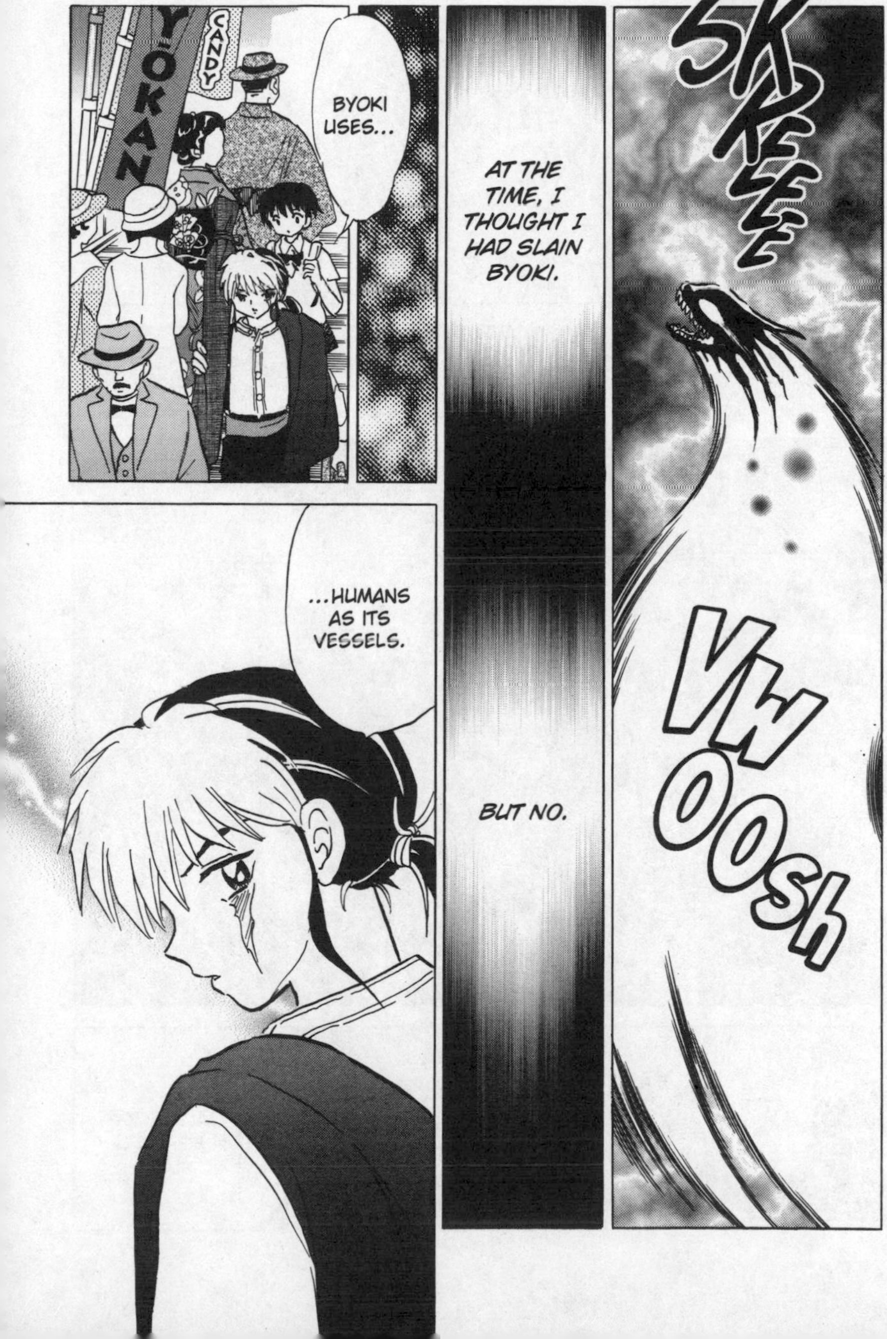
SKREEEE
VWOOOSh
AT THE TIME, I THOUGHT I HAD SLAIN BYOKI.
BUT NO.
YŌKAN
CANDY
BYOKI USES...
...HUMANS AS ITS VESSELS.

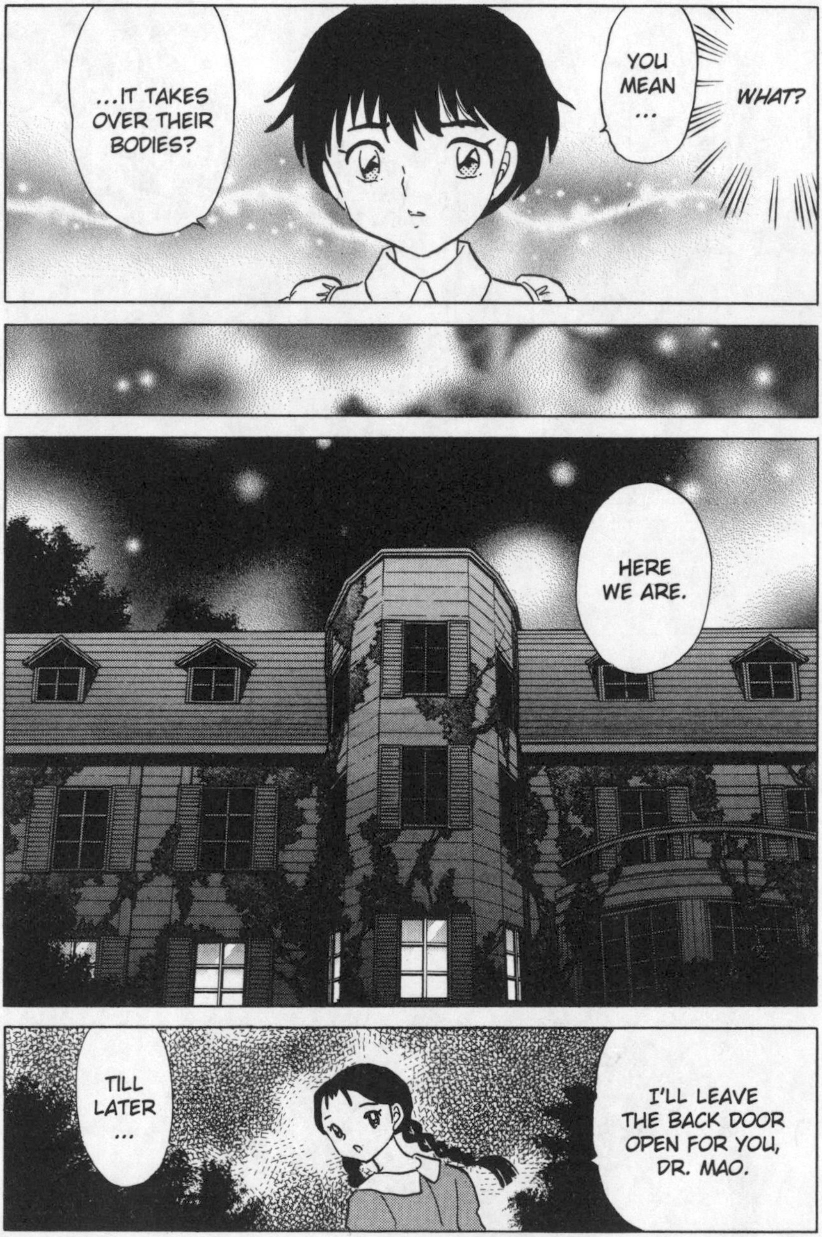
WHAT?
YOU MEAN ...
...IT TAKES OVER THEIR BODIES?
HERE WE ARE.
I'LL LEAVE THE BACK DOOR OPEN FOR YOU, DR. MAO.
TILL LATER ...

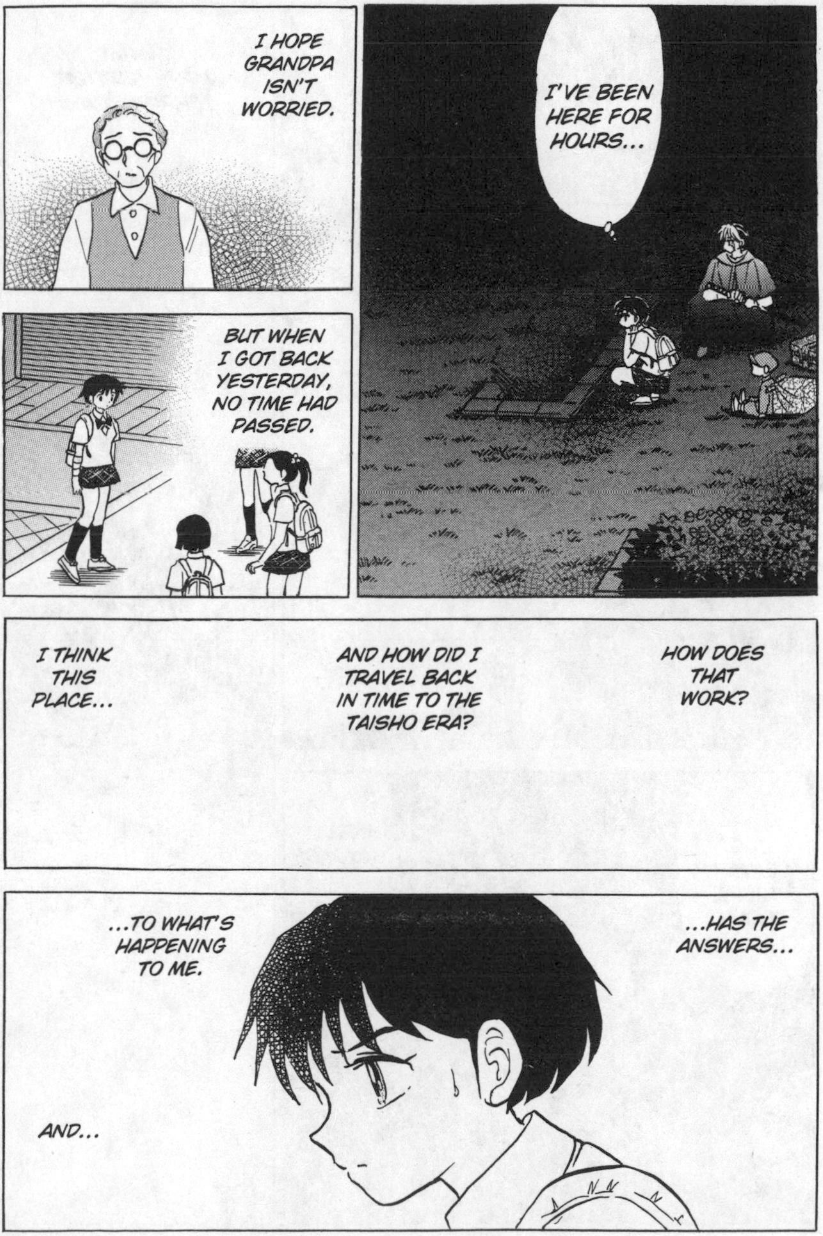
I'VE BEEN HERE FOR HOURS...
I HOPE GRANDPA ISN'T WORRIED.
BUT WHEN I GOT BACK YESTERDAY, NO TIME HAD PASSED.
HOW DOES THAT WORK?
AND HOW DID I TRAVEL BACK IN TIME TO THE TAISHO ERA?
I THINK THIS PLACE...
...HAS THE ANSWERS...
...TO WHAT'S HAPPENING TO ME.
AND...

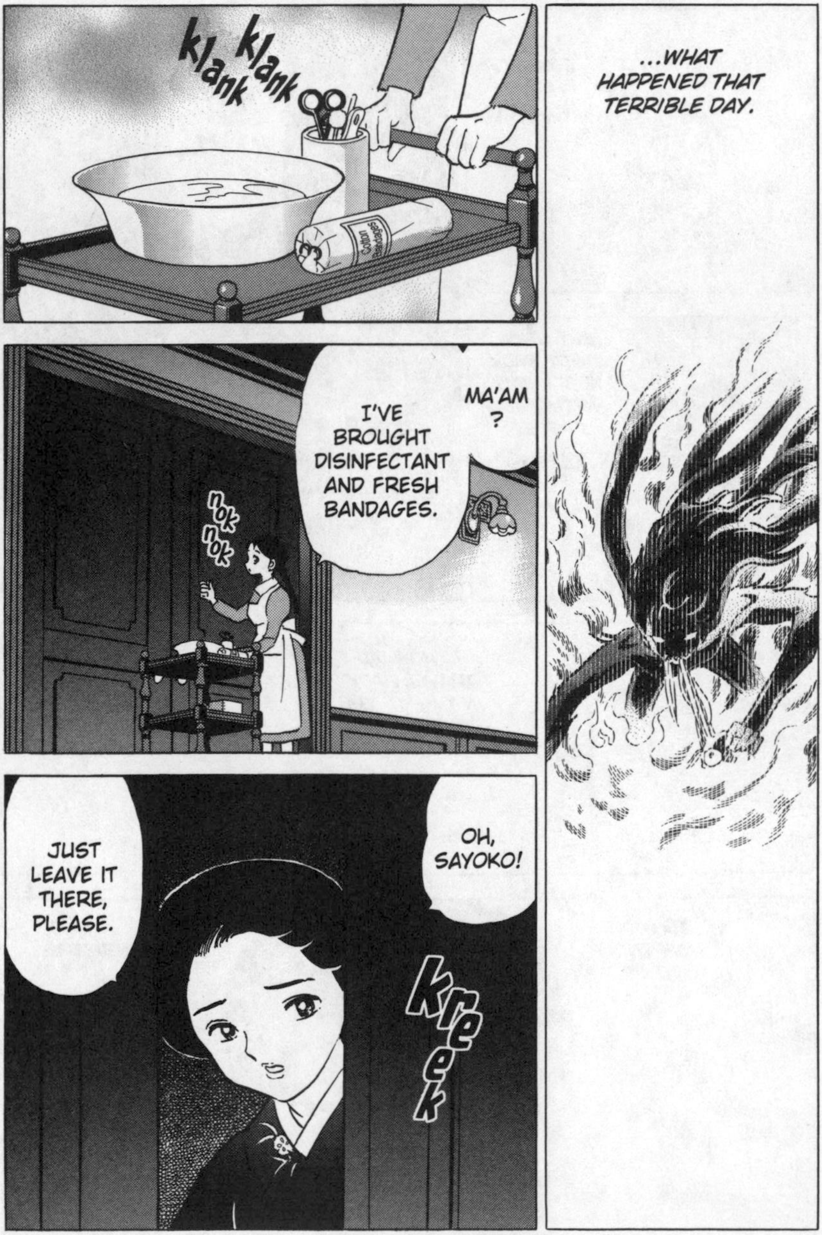
...WHAT HAPPENED THAT TERRIBLE DAY.
klank klank
Cotton Bandages
MA'AM ?
I'VE BROUGHT DISINFECTANT AND FRESH BANDAGES.
nok nok
OH, SAYOKO!
JUST LEAVE IT THERE, PLEASE.
kreek

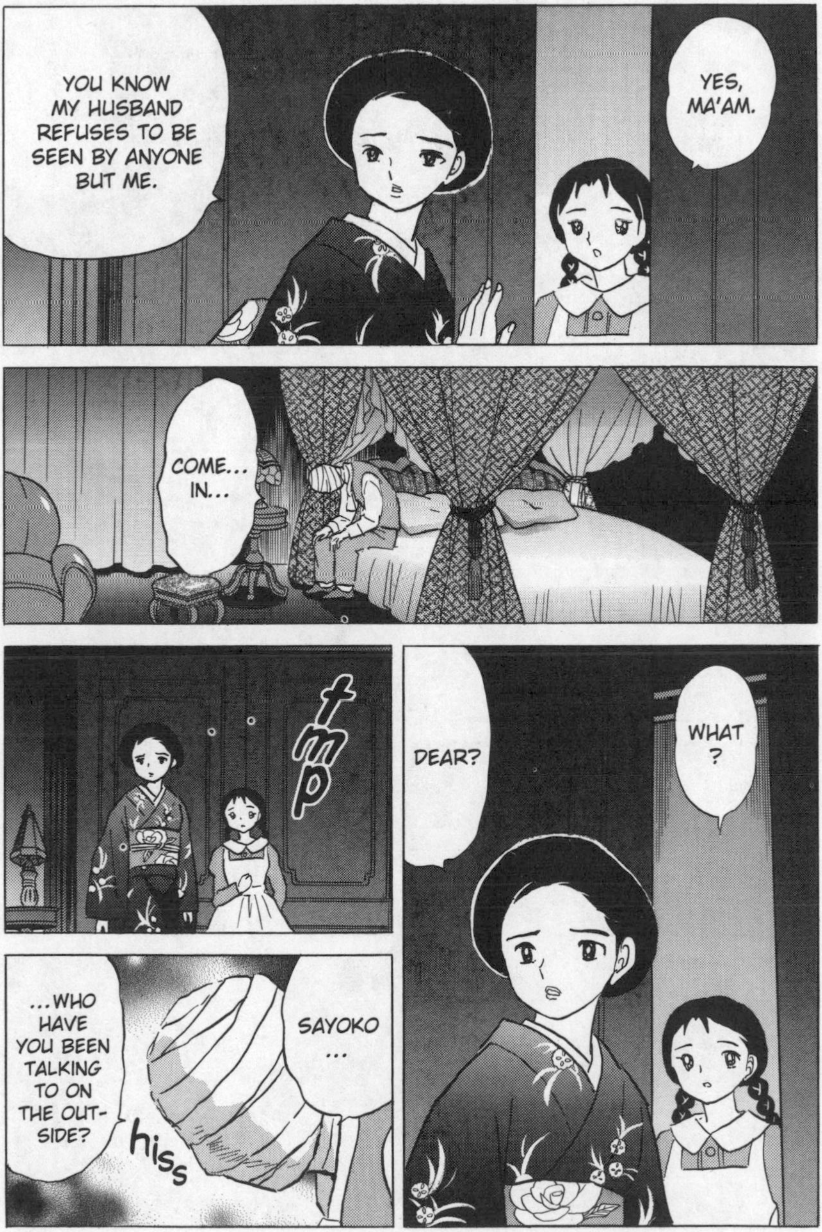
YES, MA'AM.
YOU KNOW MY HUSBAND REFUSES TO BE SEEN BY ANYONE BUT ME.
COME... IN...
WHAT ?
DEAR?
tmp
SAYOKO ...
...WHO HAVE YOU BEEN TALKING TO ON THE OUT-SIDE?
hiss

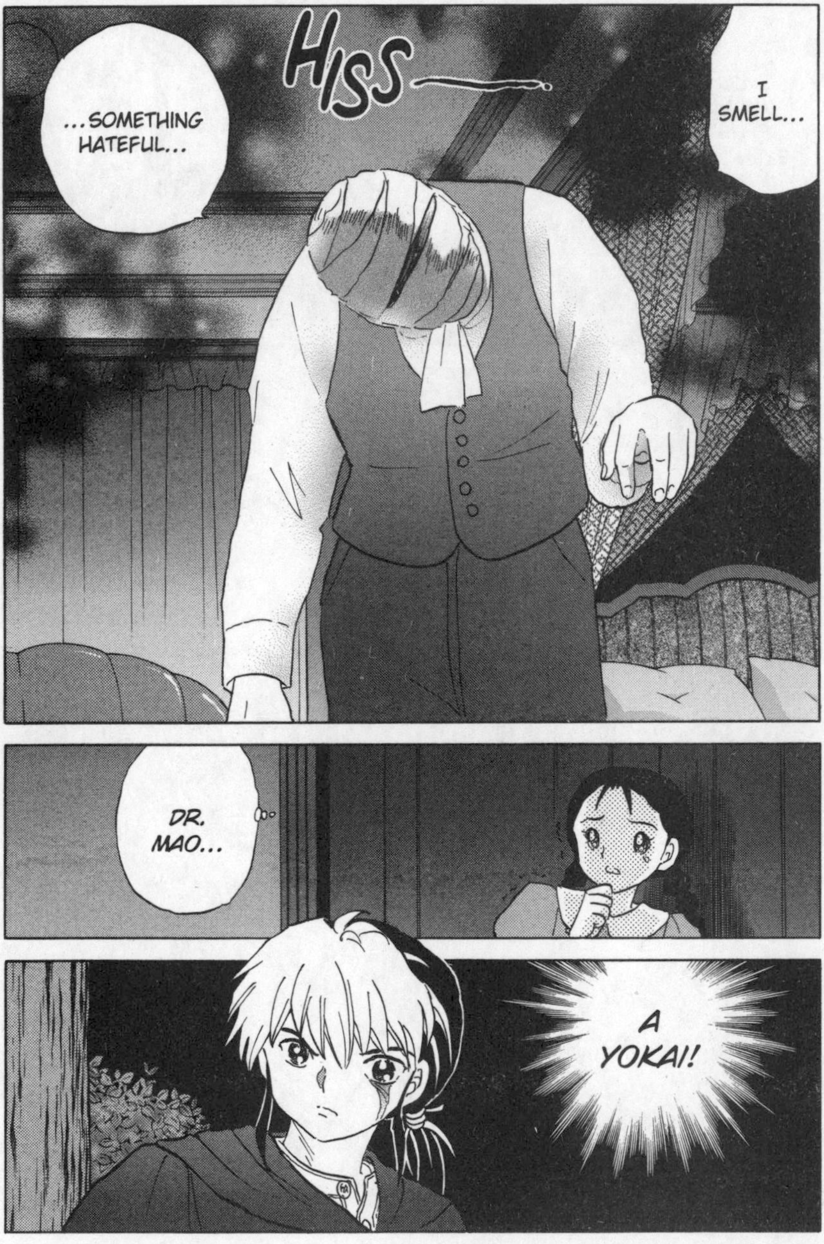

I SMELL...
HISS
...SOMETHING HATEFUL...
DR. MAO...
A YOKAI!

Chapter 4:
The Faceless Viscount

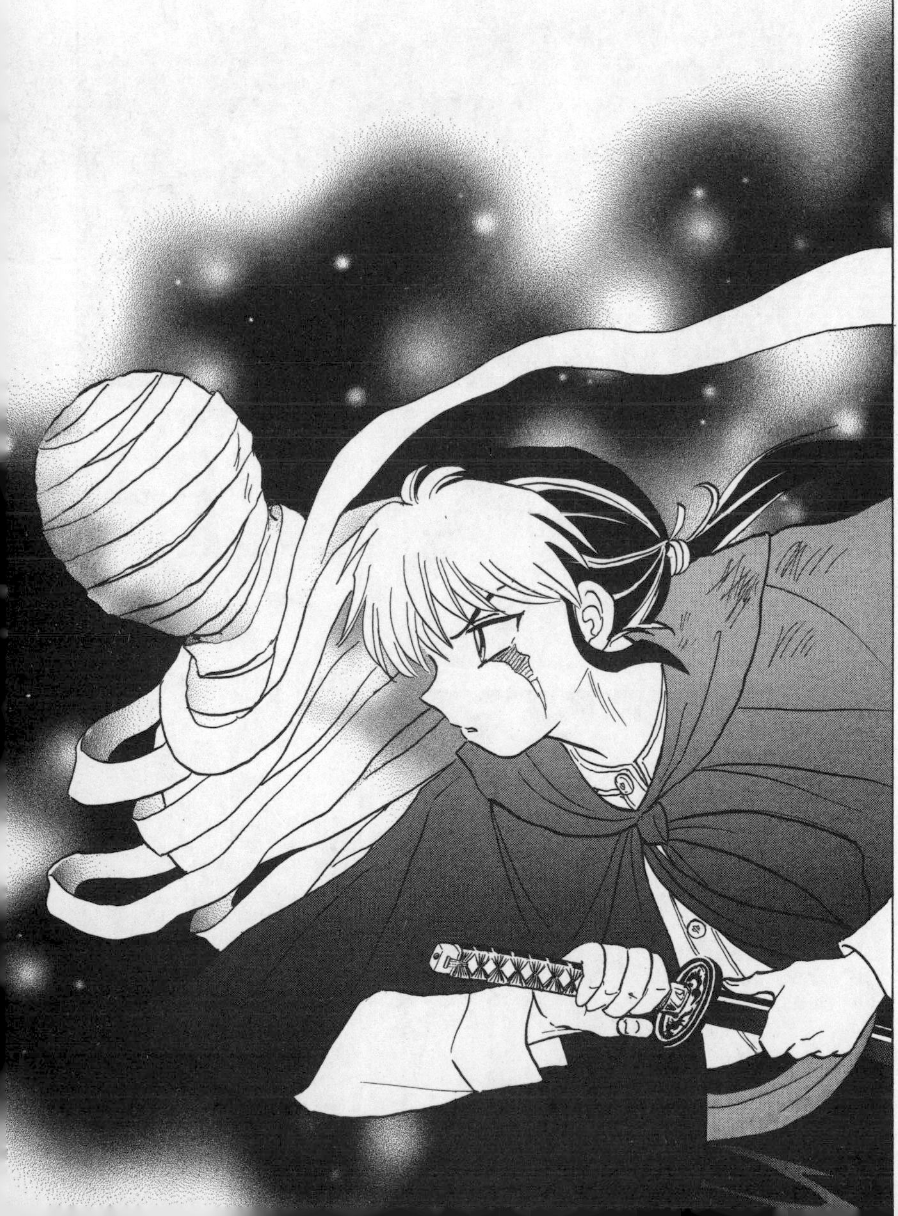

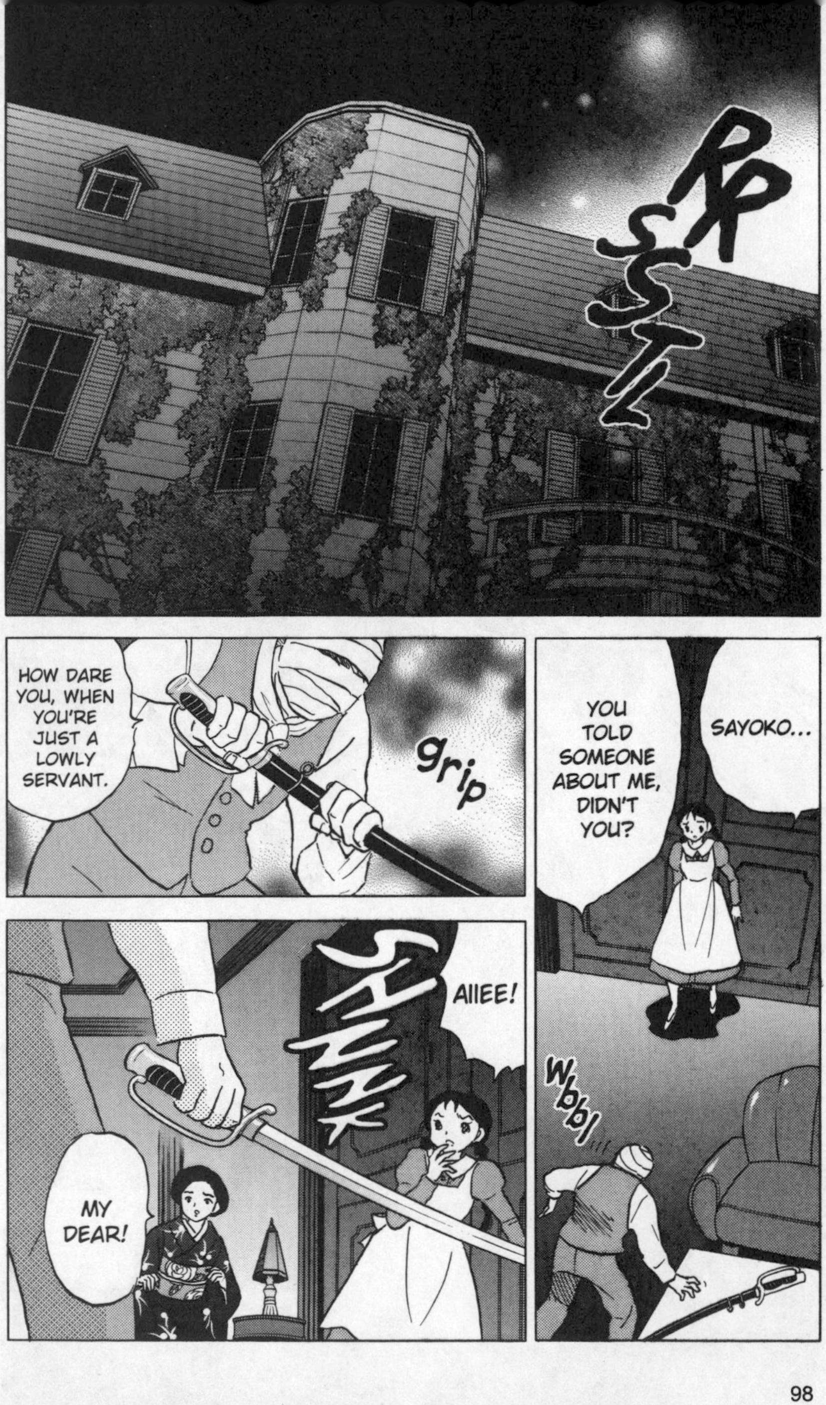
RRSSTL
SAYOKO...
YOU TOLD SOMEONE ABOUT ME, DIDN'T YOU?
HOW DARE YOU, WHEN YOU'RE JUST A LOWLY SERVANT.
grip
wbbl
SHNNK
AIIEE!
MY DEAR!

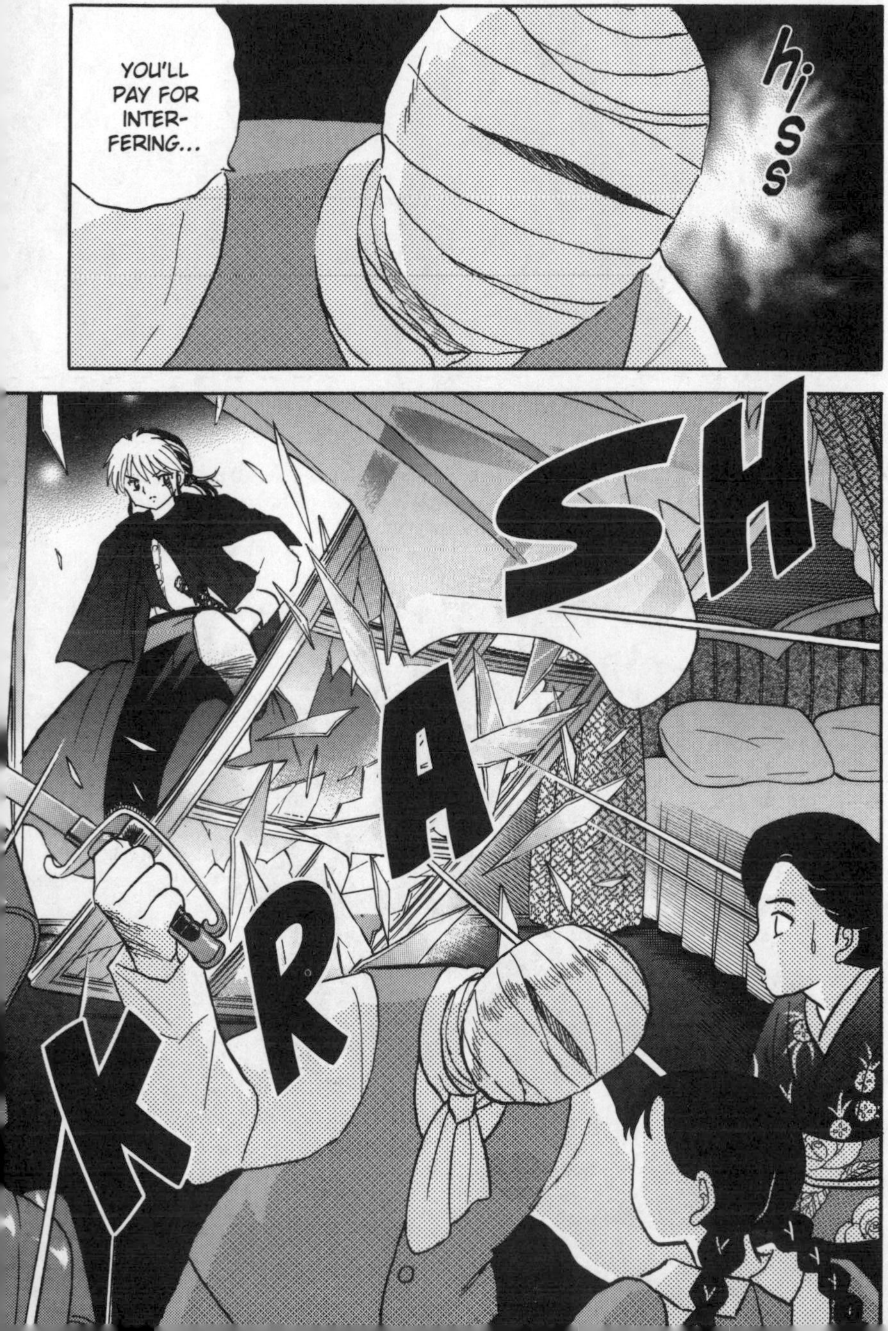
hiss
YOU'LL PAY FOR INTER-FERING...
KRASH

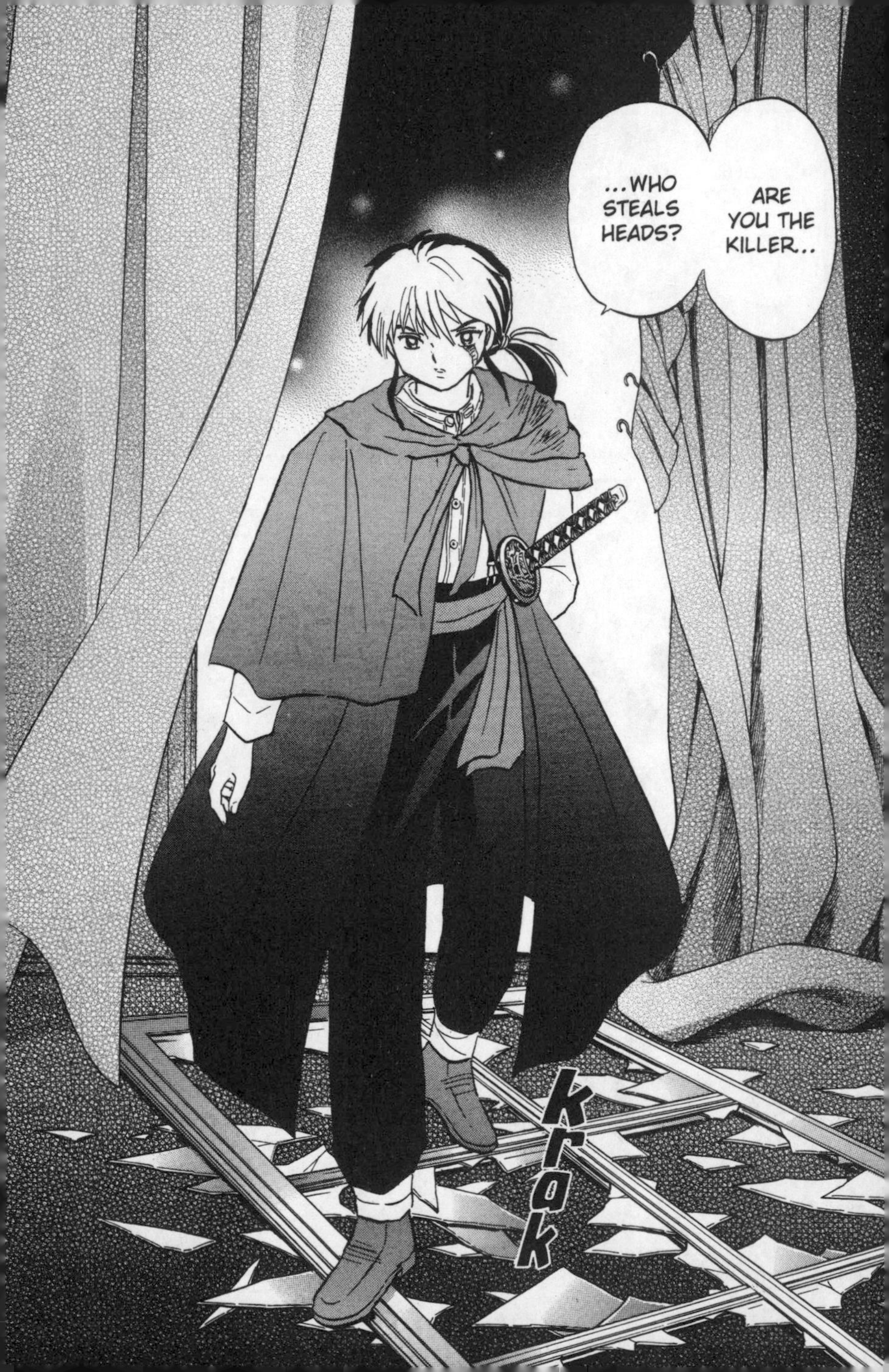
ARE YOU THE KILLER...
...WHO STEALS HEADS?
krak

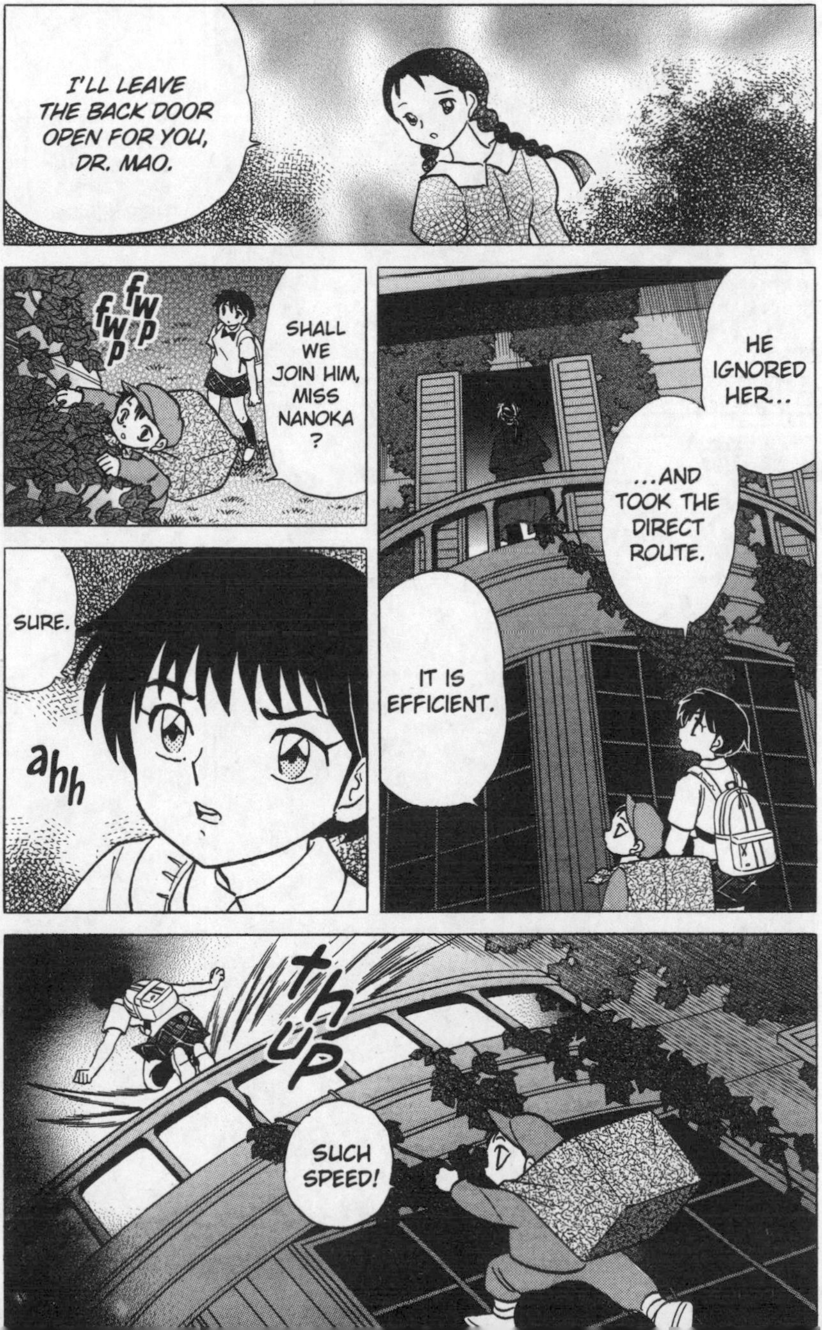
I'LL LEAVE THE BACK DOOR OPEN FOR YOU, DR. MAO.
HE IGNORED HER...
...AND TOOK THE DIRECT ROUTE.
IT IS EFFICIENT.
fwp fwp
SHALL WE JOIN HIM, MISS NANOKA?
SURE.
ahh
thup
SUCH SPEED!

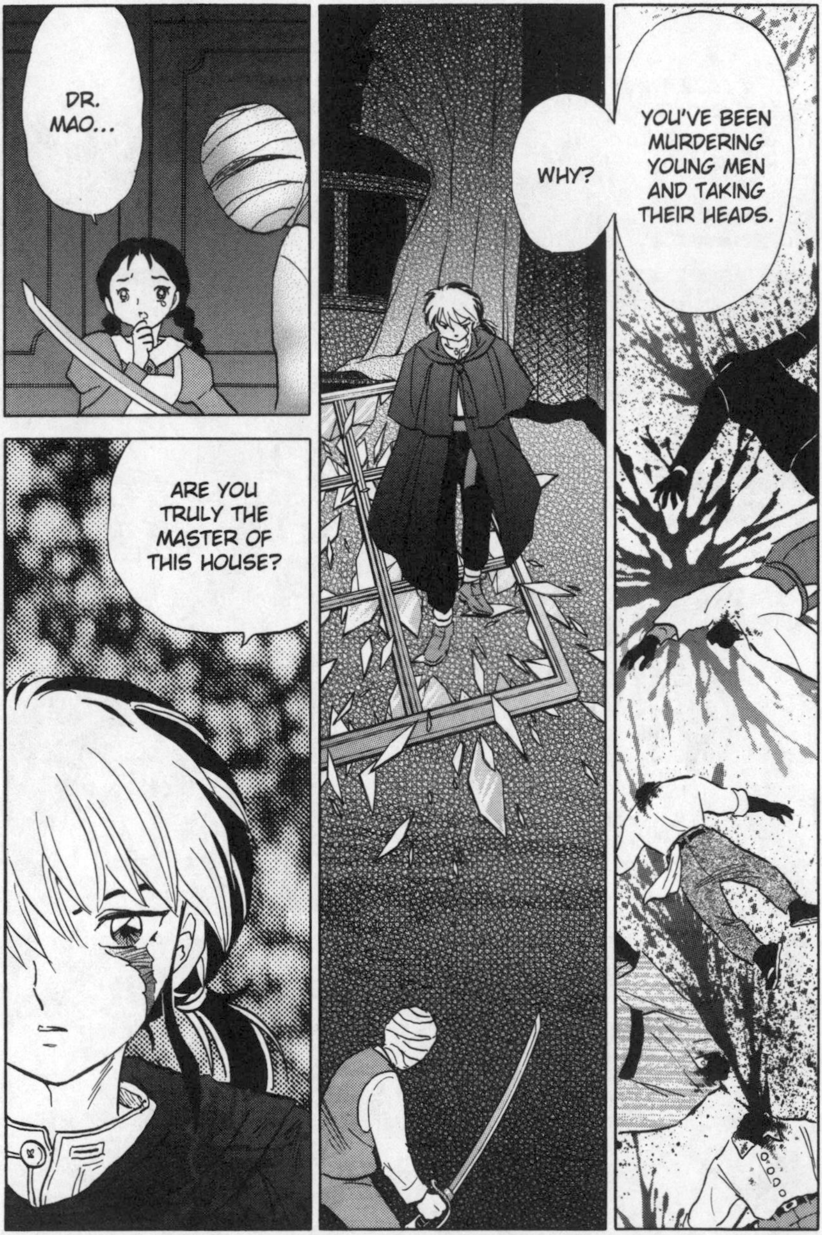
YOU'VE BEEN MURDERING YOUNG MEN AND TAKING THEIR HEADS.
WHY?
DR. MAO...
ARE YOU TRULY THE MASTER OF THIS HOUSE?

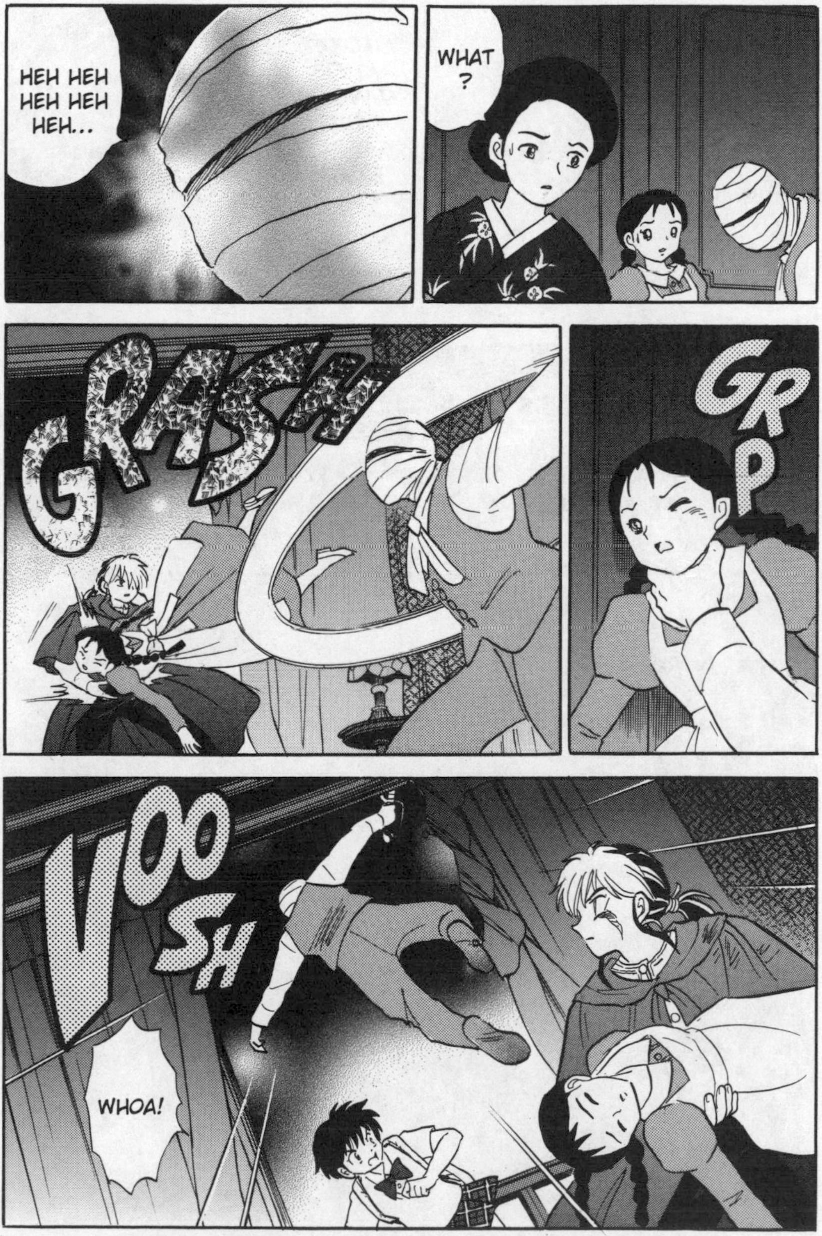
WHAT ?
HEH HEH HEH HEH HEH...
GRP
GRASH
VOOSH
WHOA!

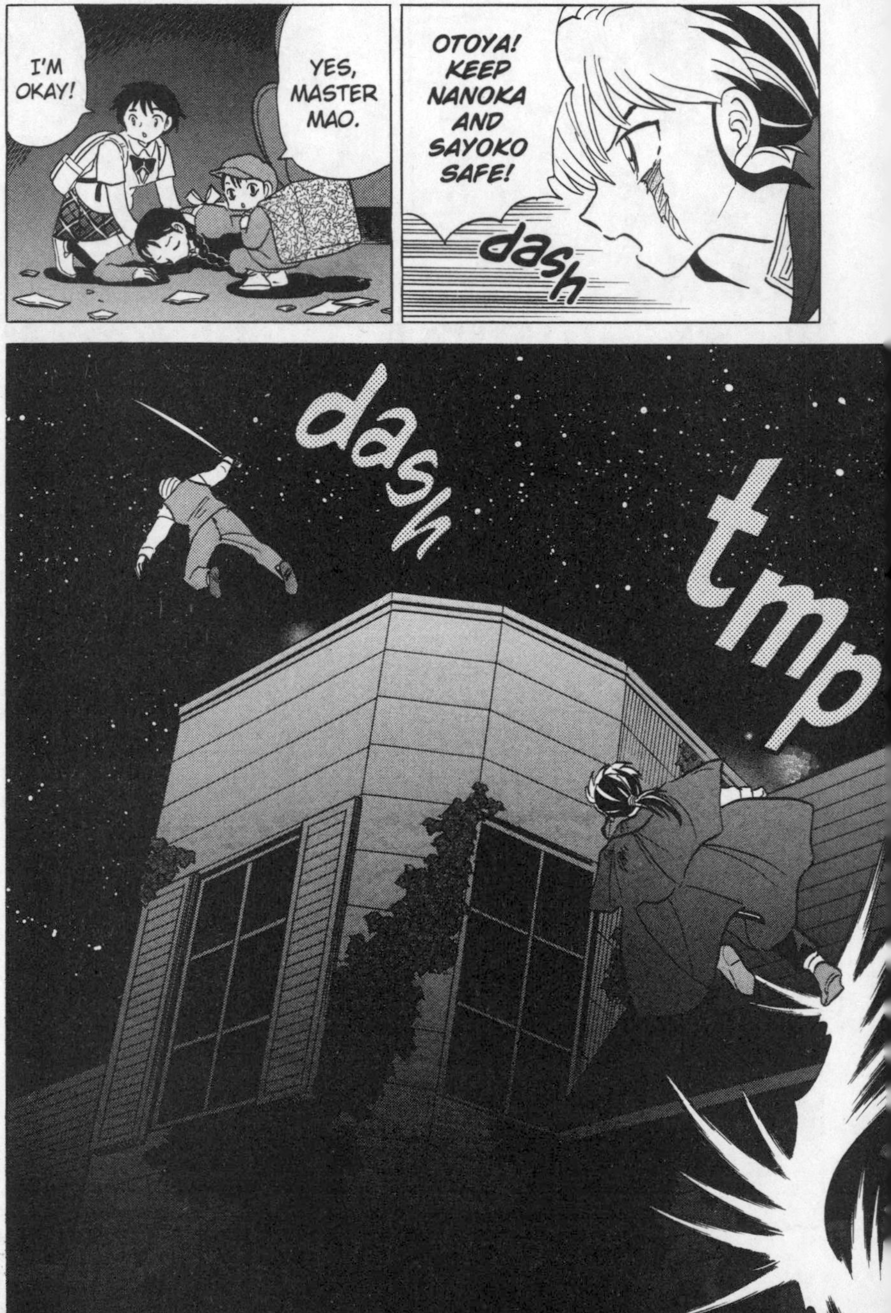
OTOYA! KEEP NANOKA AND SAYOKO SAFE!
dash
YES, MASTER MAO.
I'M OKAY!
dash
tmp

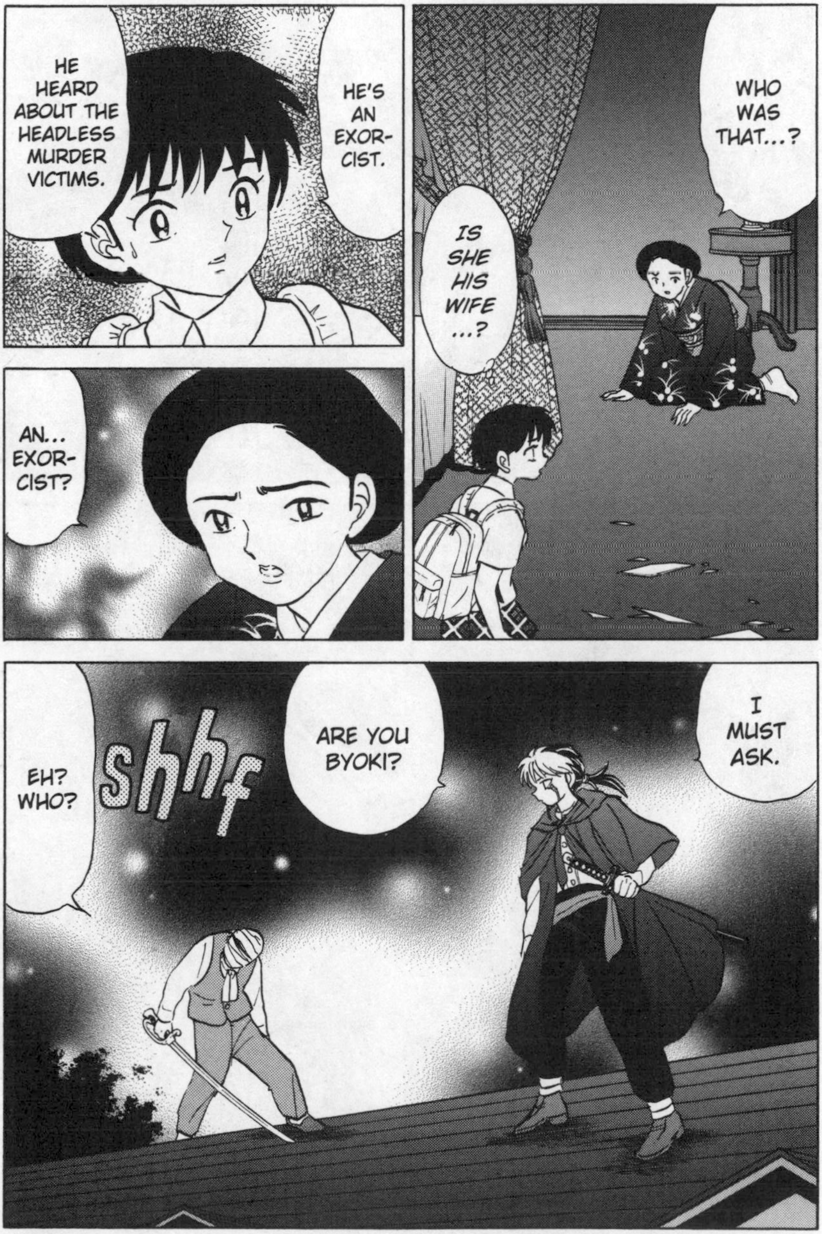
WHO WAS THAT...?
IS SHE HIS WIFE ...?
HE'S AN EXOR-CIST.
HE HEARD ABOUT THE HEADLESS MURDER VICTIMS.
AN... EXOR-CIST?
I MUST ASK.
ARE YOU BYOKI?
shhf
EH? WHO?

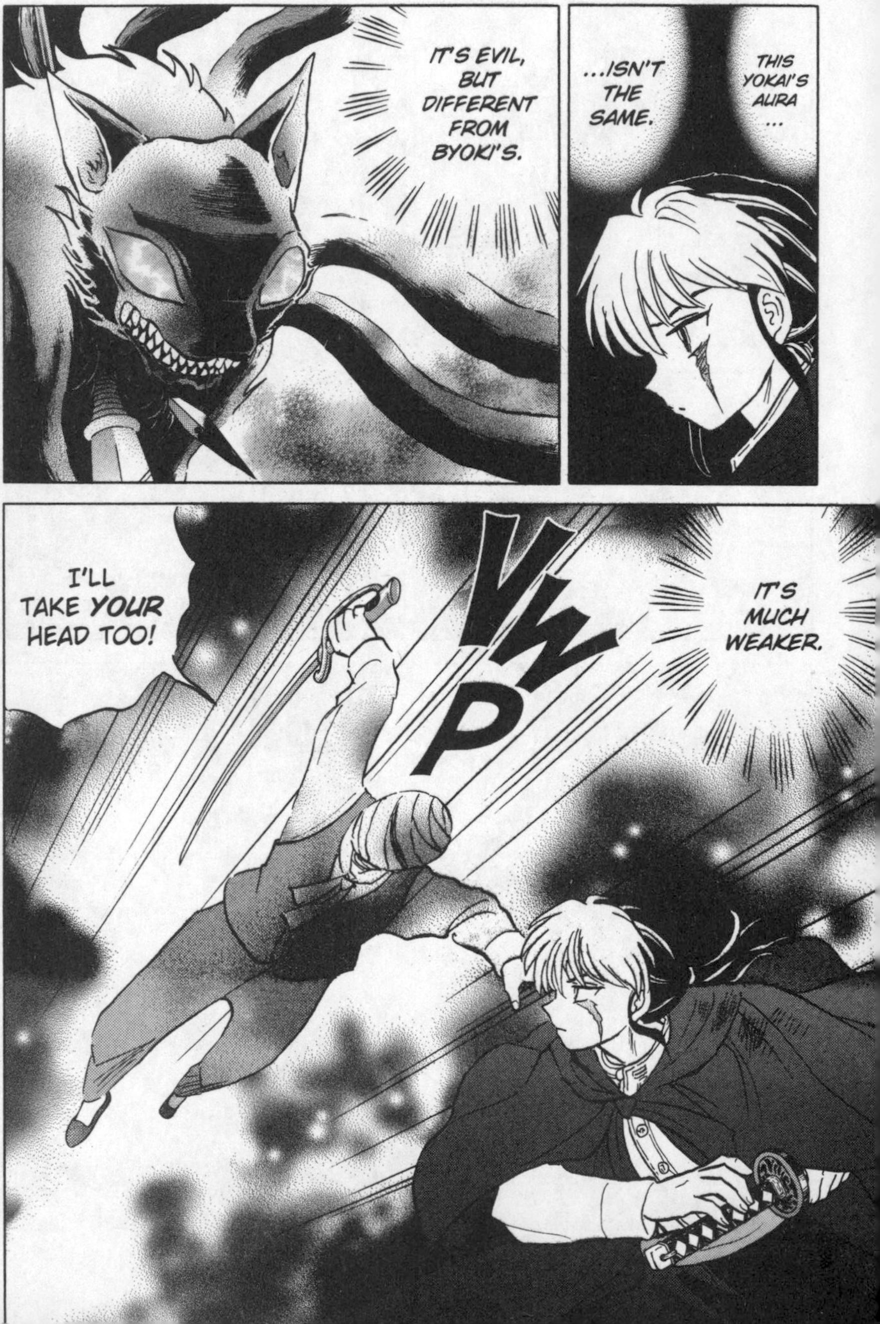
THIS YOKAI'S AURA ...
...ISN'T THE SAME.
IT'S EVIL, BUT DIFFERENT FROM BYOKI'S.
IT'S MUCH WEAKER.
VWP
I'LL TAKE *YOUR* HEAD TOO!

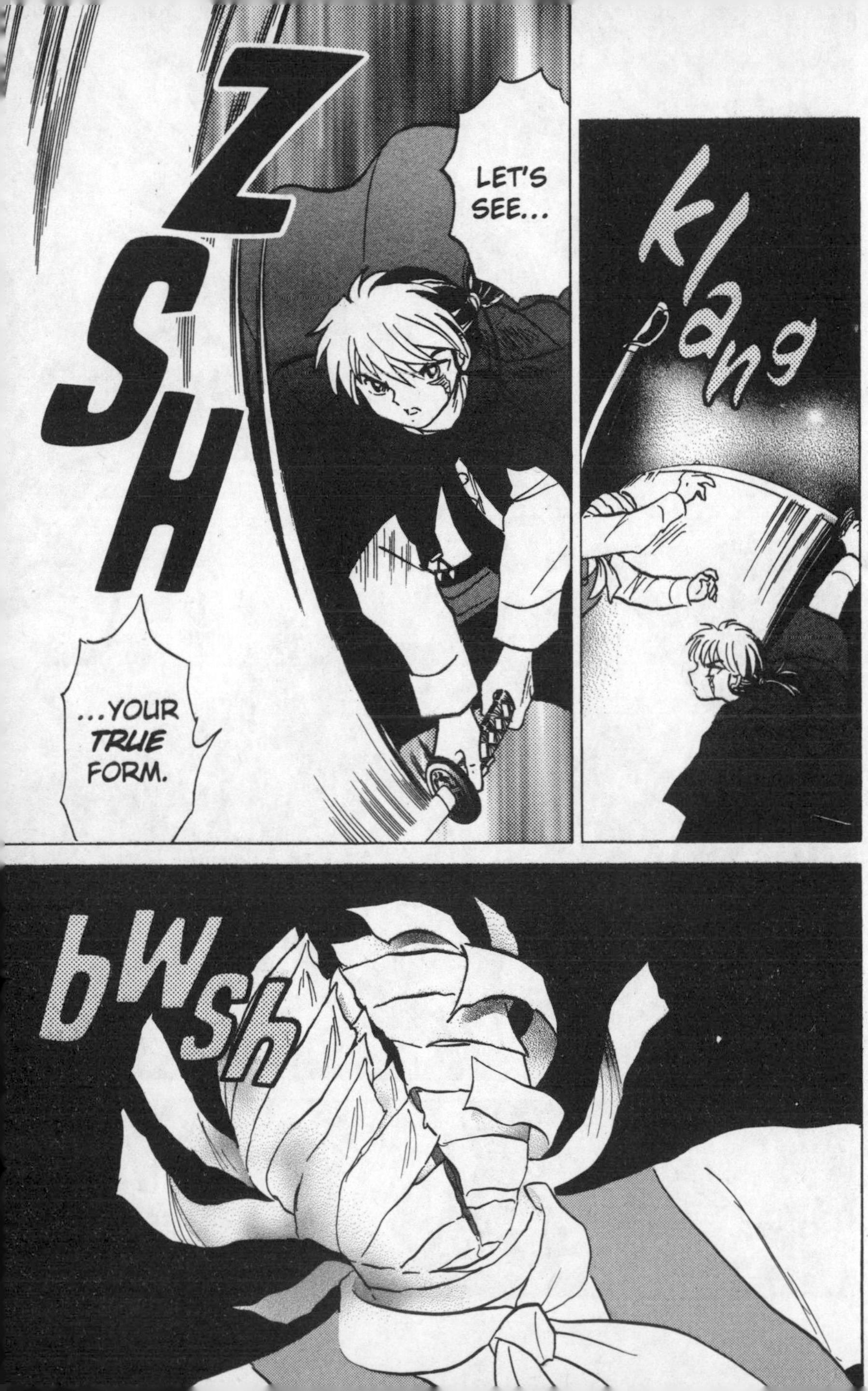
klang
ZSH
LET'S SEE...
...YOUR TRUE FORM.
bwsh

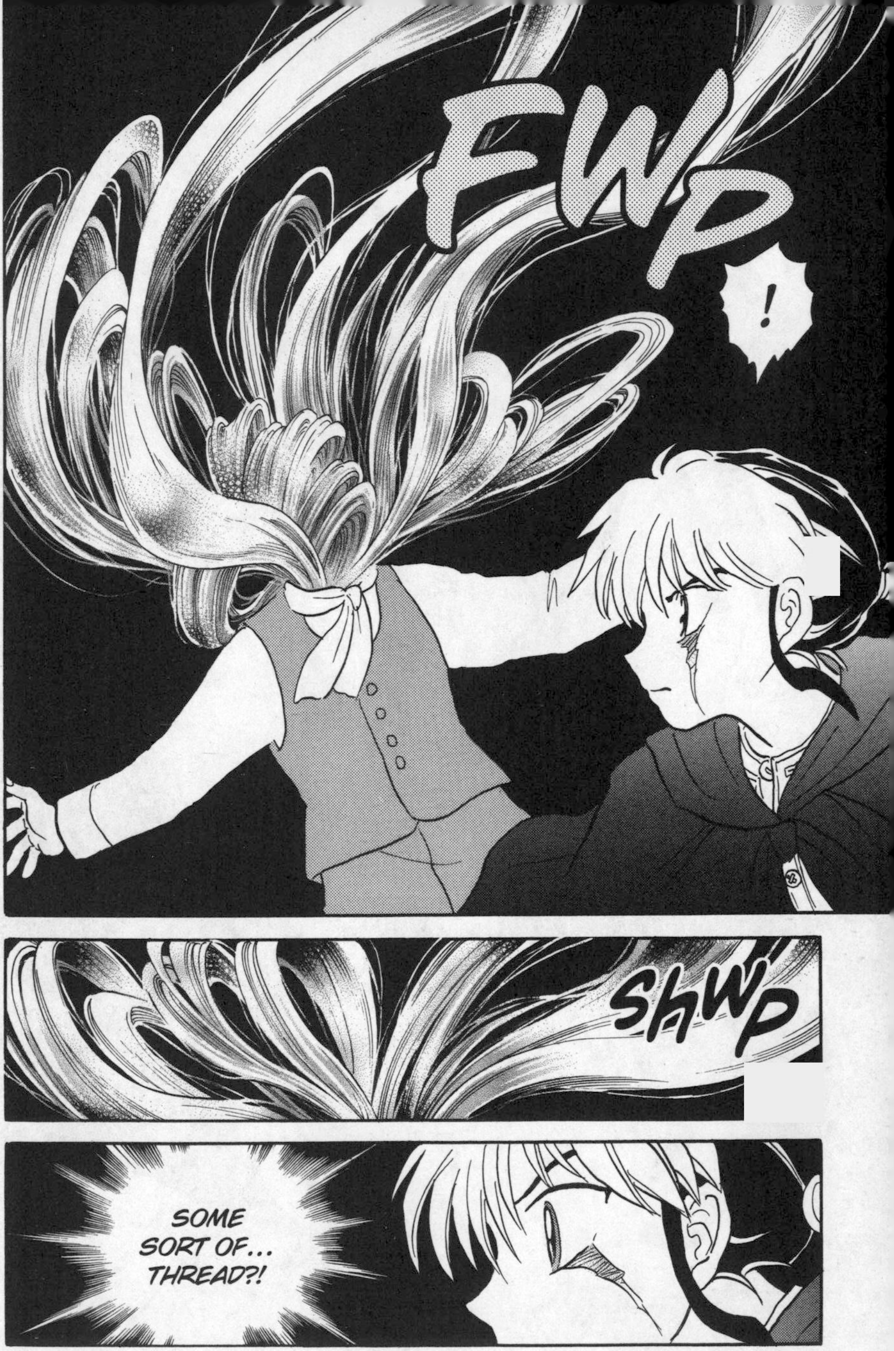
FWP
!
SHWP
SOME SORT OF... THREAD?!

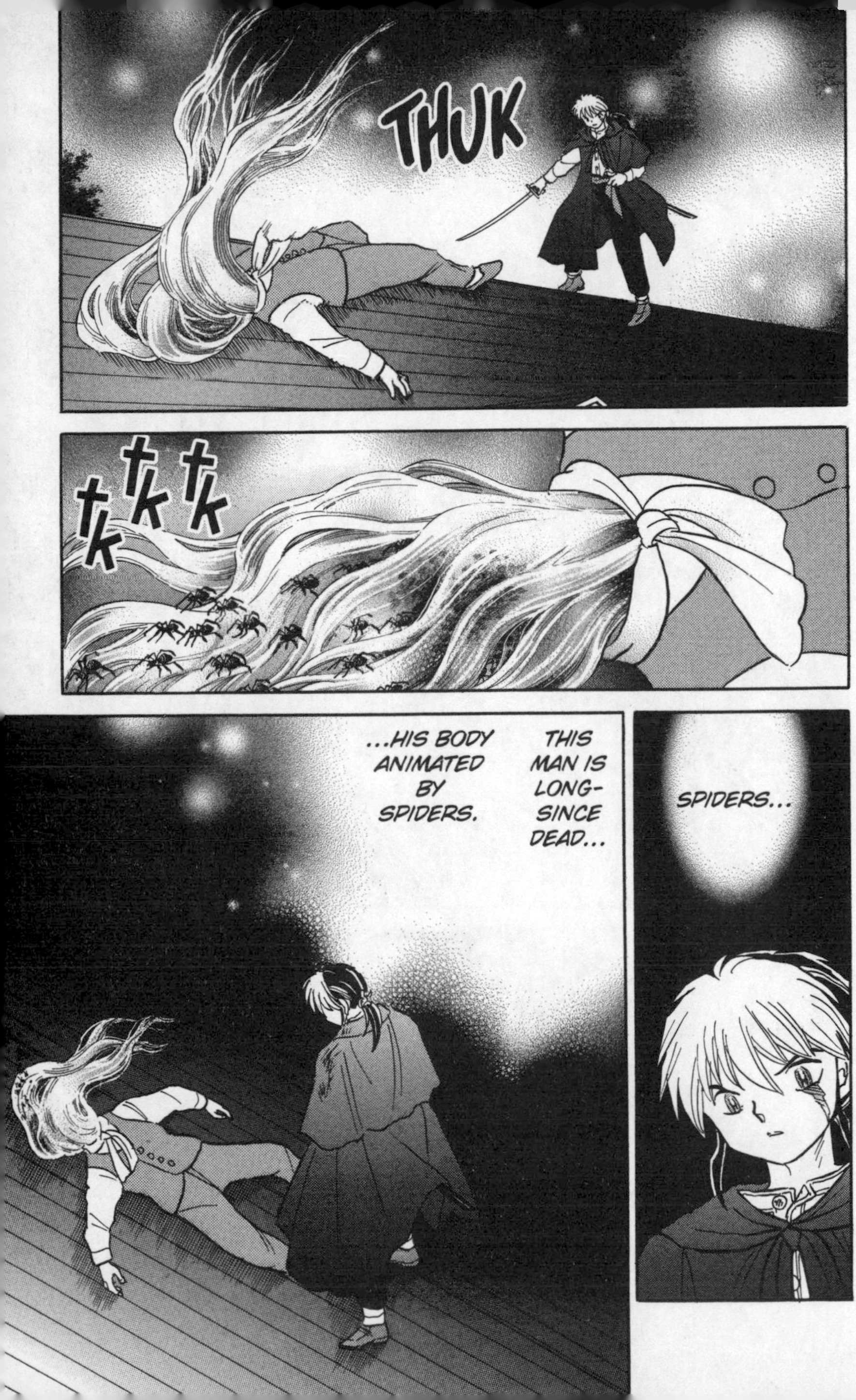
THUK
tk tk tk tk
SPIDERS...
THIS MAN IS LONG-SINCE DEAD...
...HIS BODY ANIMATED BY SPIDERS.

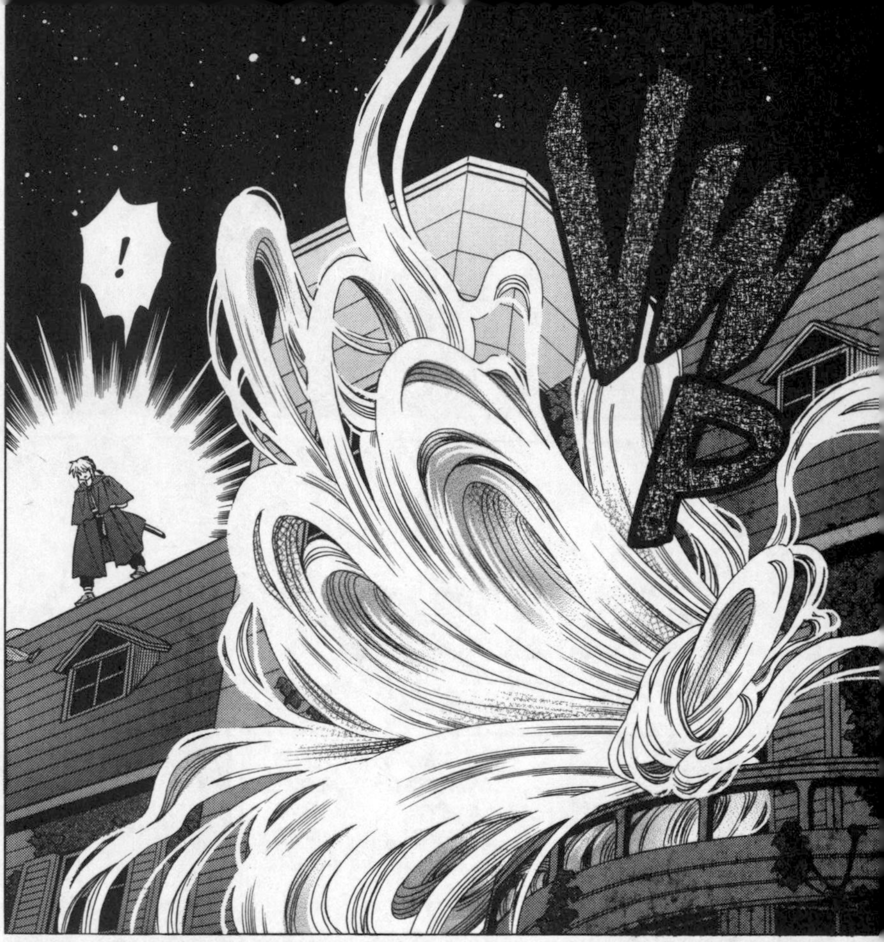
!
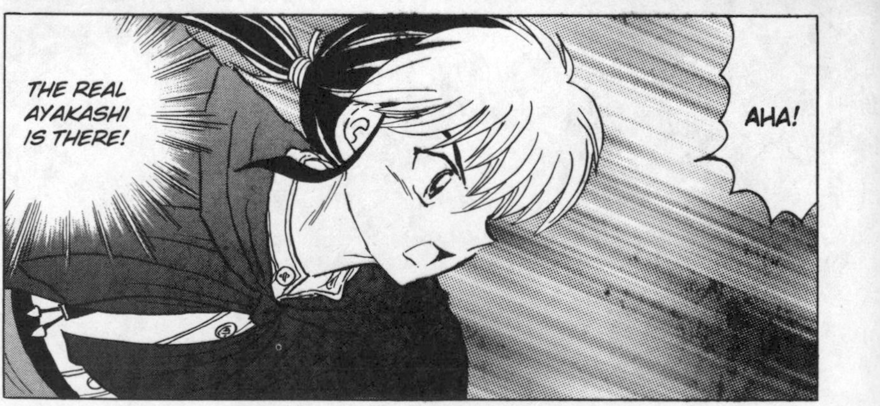
AHA!
THE REAL AYAKASHI IS THERE!

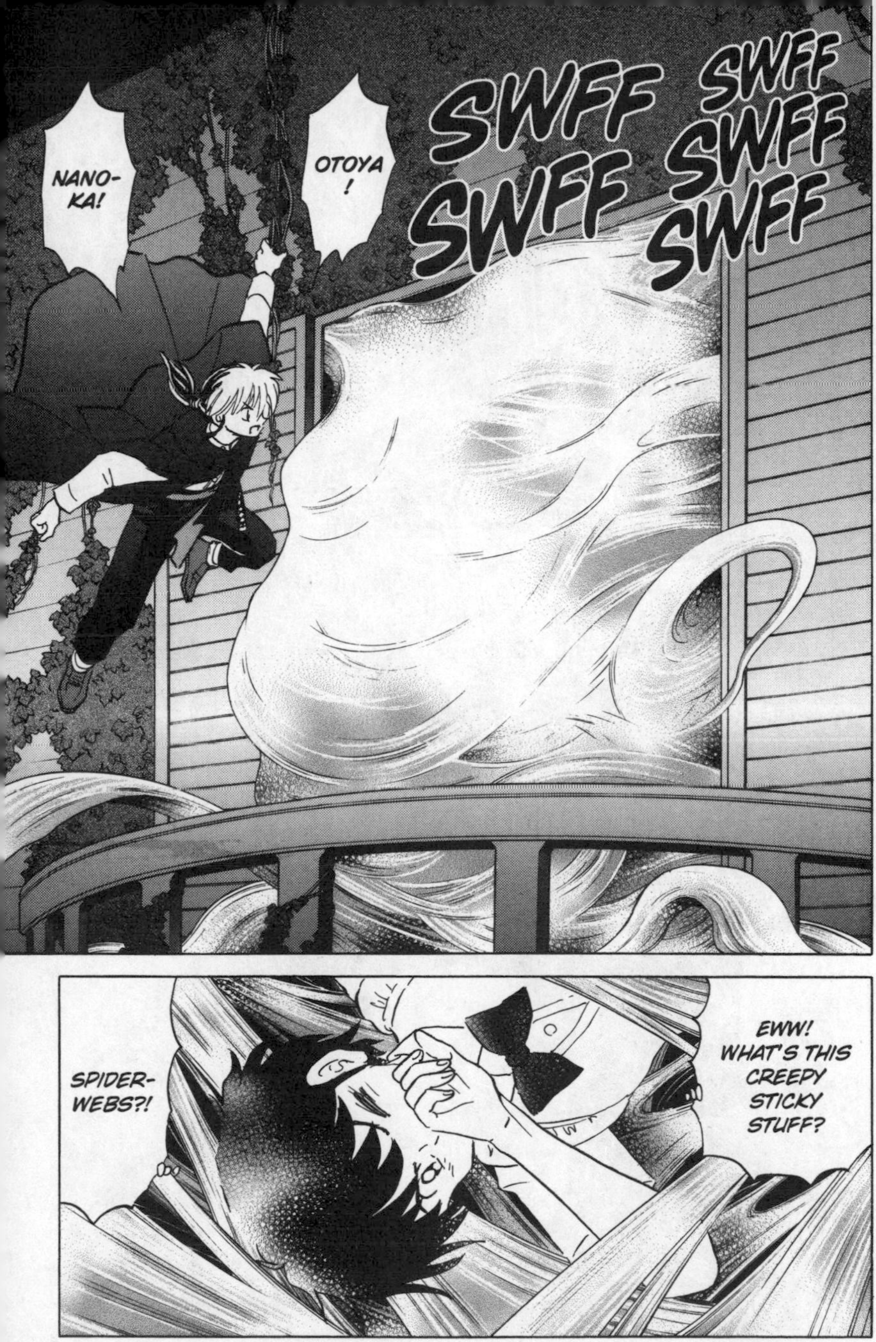
SWFF SWFF
SWFF SWFF
SWFF SWFF
OTOYA!
NANO-KA!
EWW! WHAT'S THIS CREEPY STICKY STUFF?
SPIDER-WEBS?!

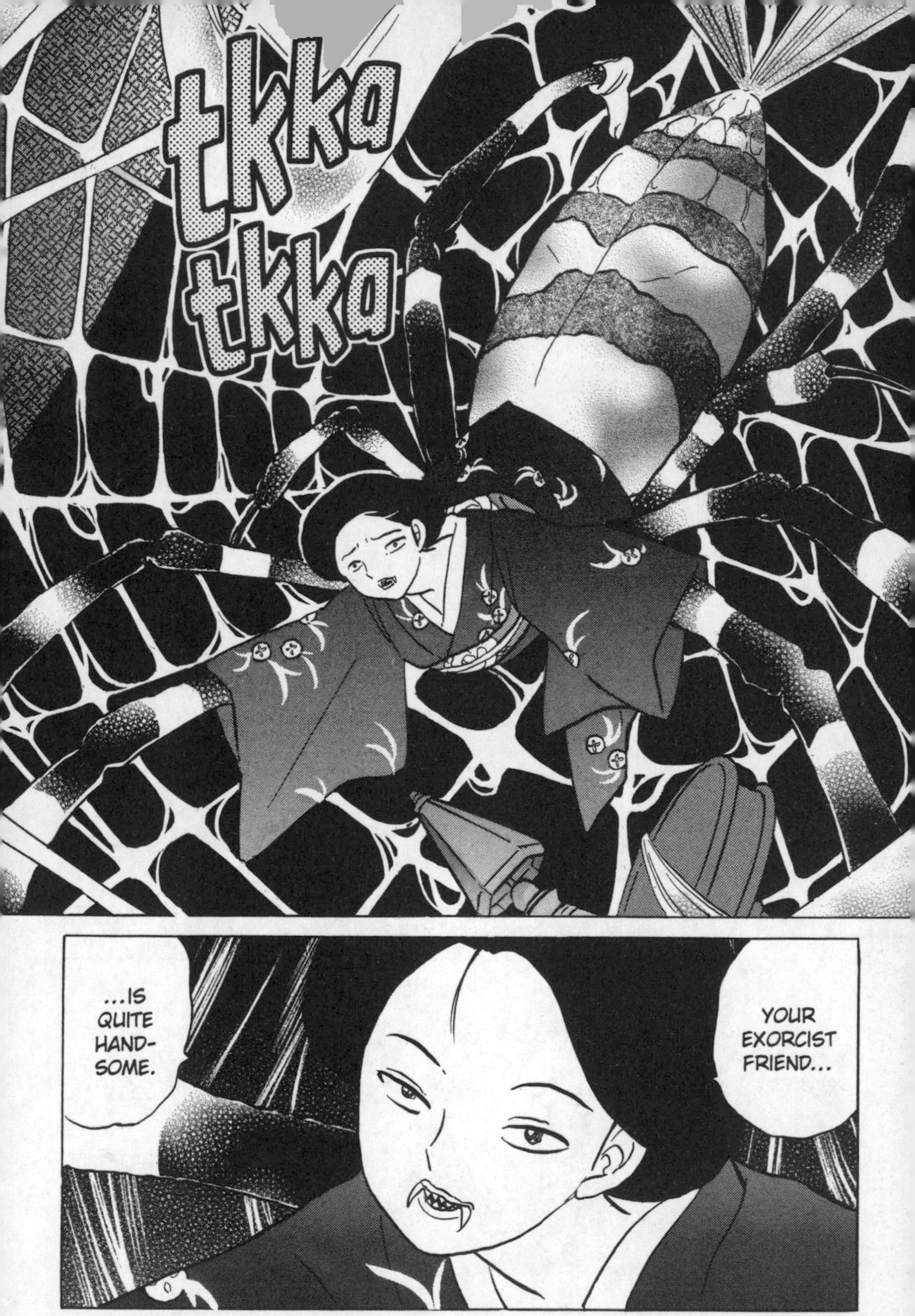
tkka
tkka
YOUR EXORCIST FRIEND...
...IS QUITE HAND-SOME.

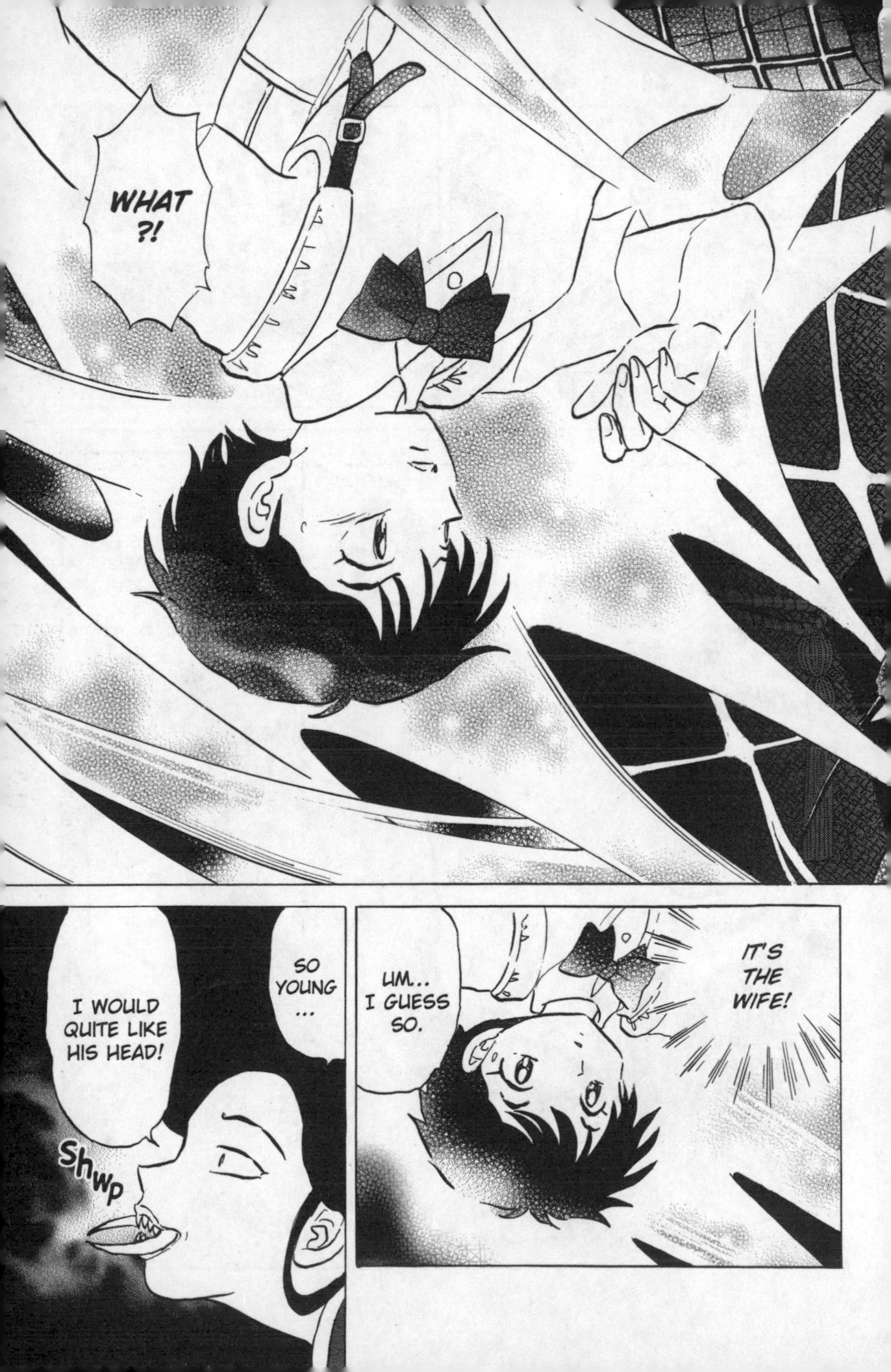
WHAT ?!
IT'S THE WIFE!
UM... I GUESS SO.
SO YOUNG ...
I WOULD QUITE LIKE HIS HEAD!
Shwp

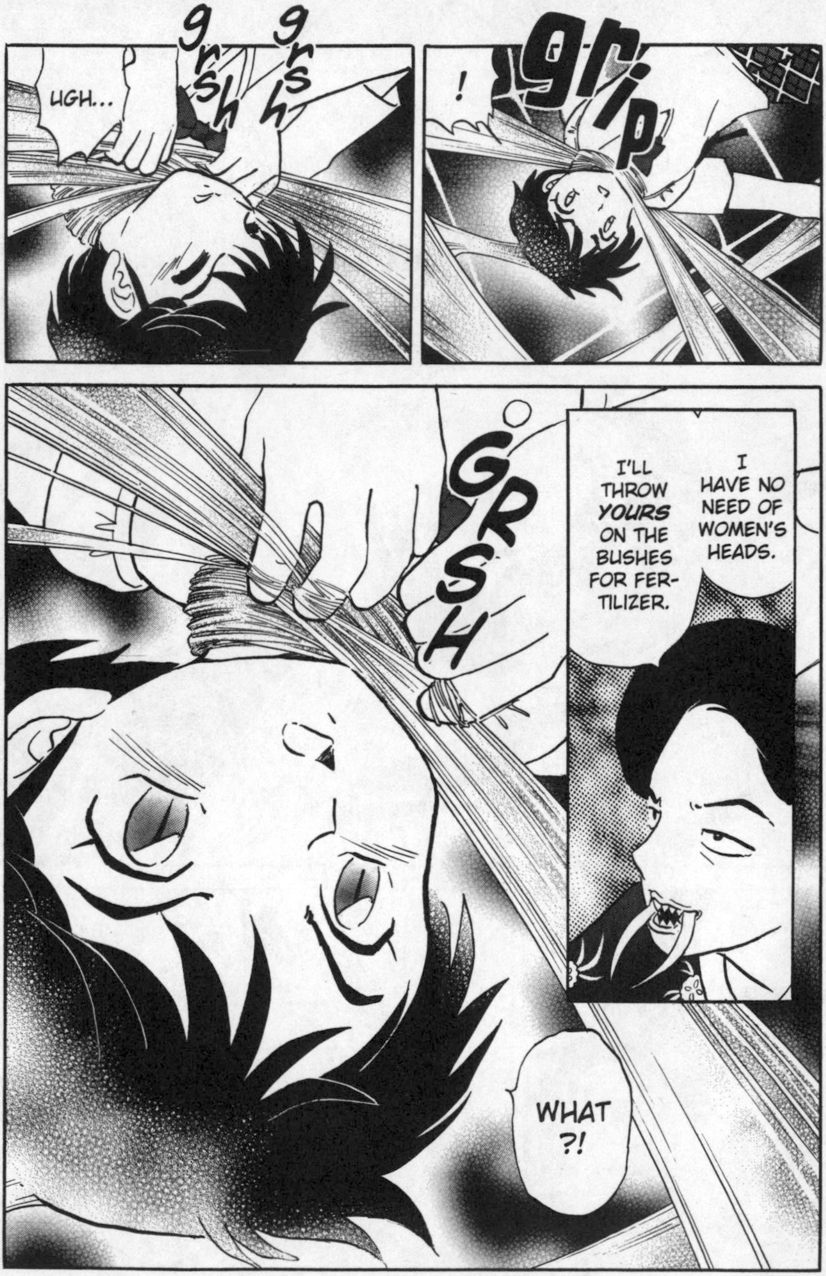
grip
!
grsh
grsh
UGH...
I HAVE NO NEED OF WOMEN'S HEADS.
I'LL THROW *YOURS* ON THE BUSHES FOR FER-TILIZER.
GRSH
WHAT?!

Chapter 5:
Spider Lady

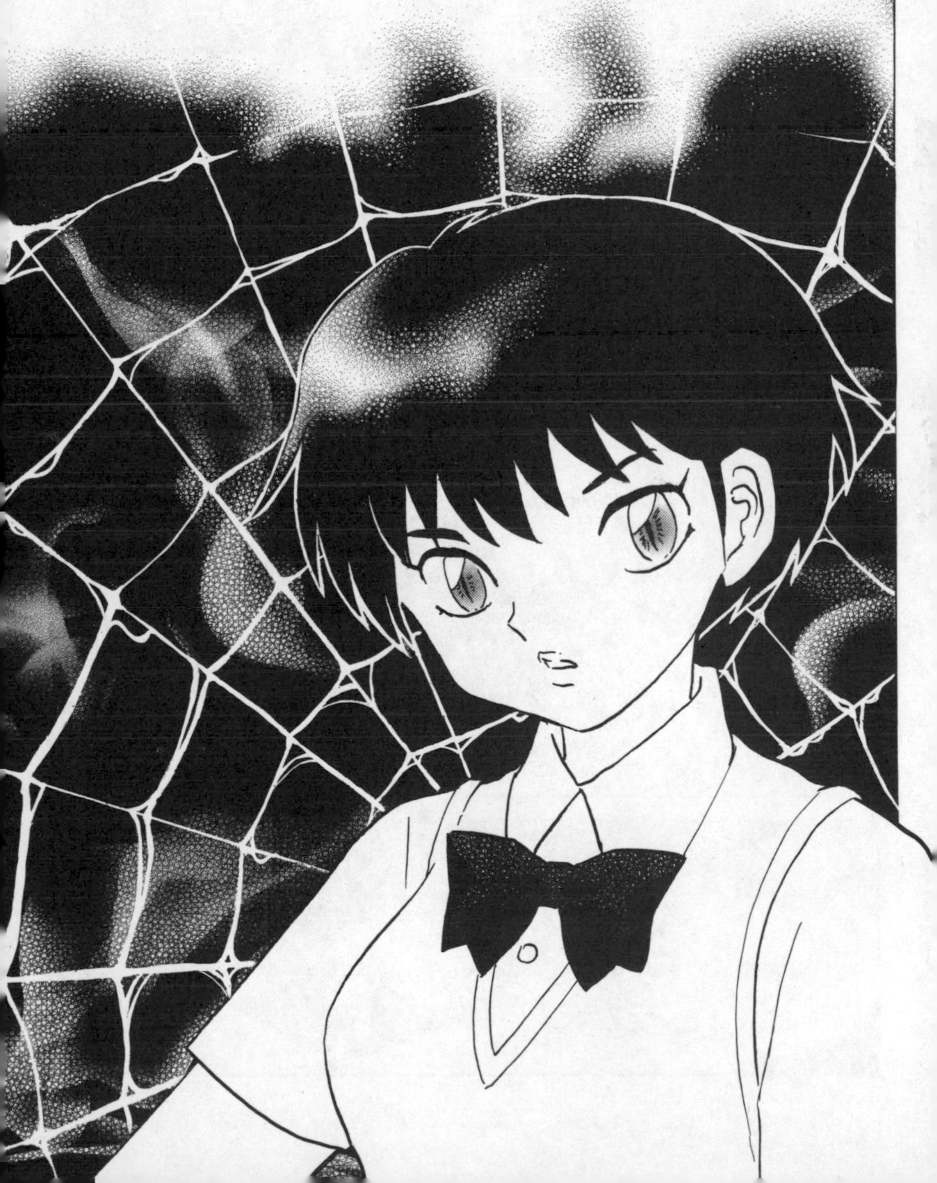

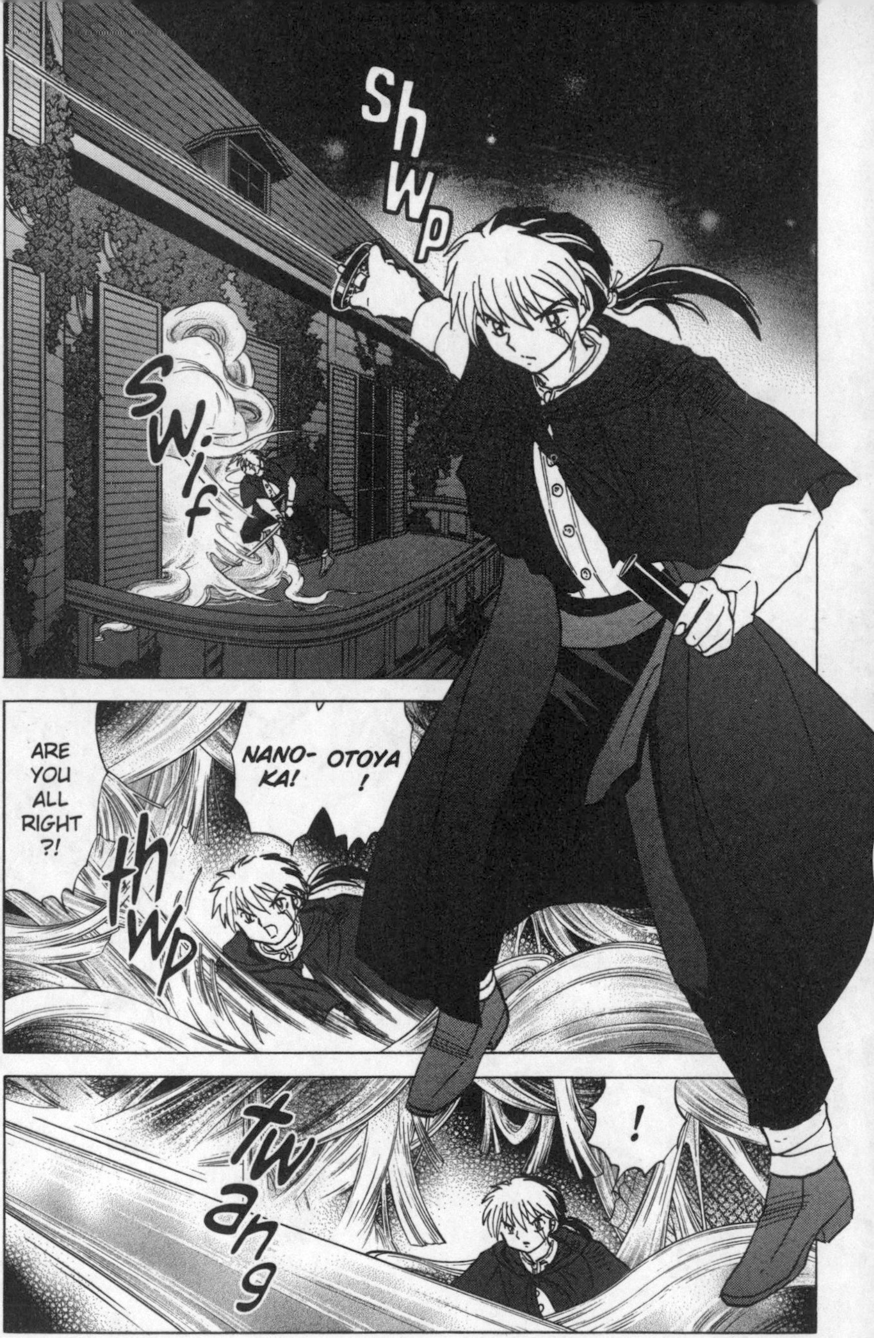
Shwp
Swif
OTOYA!
NANO-KA!
ARE YOU ALL RIGHT?!
thwp
!
twang

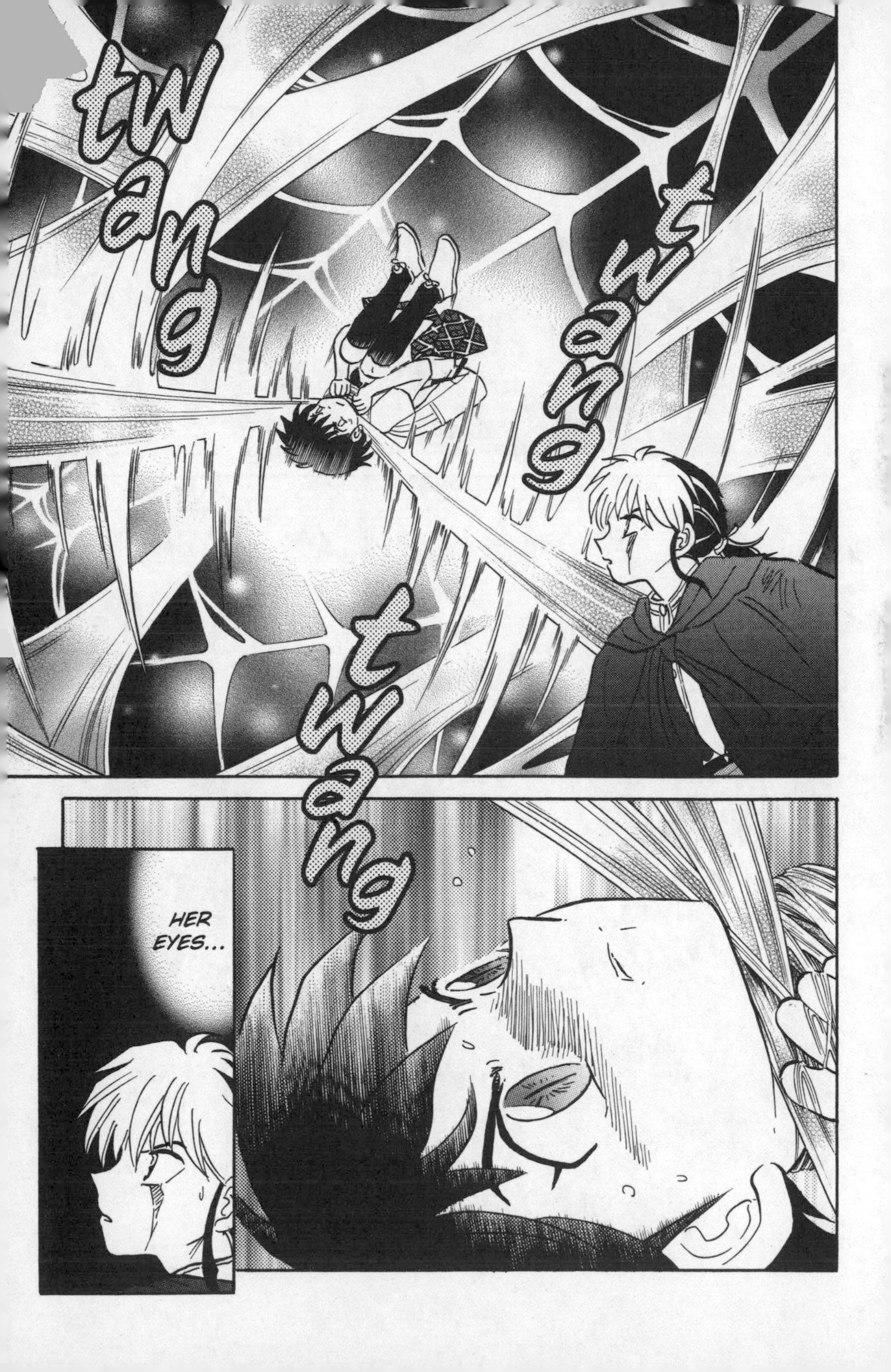
twang
twang
twang
HER EYES...

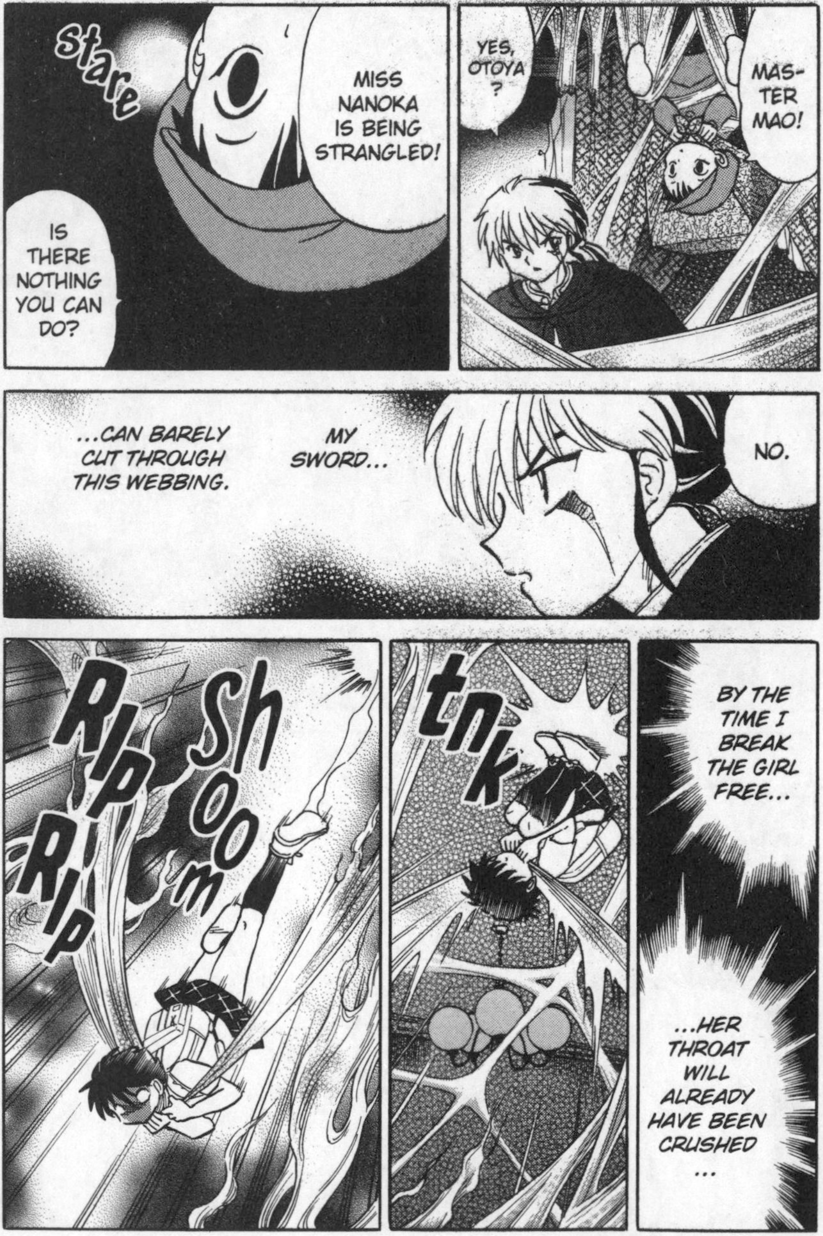
MASTER MAO!
YES, OTOYA?
MISS NANOKA IS BEING STRANGLED!
stare
IS THERE NOTHING YOU CAN DO?
NO.
MY SWORD...
...CAN BARELY CUT THROUGH THIS WEBBING.
BY THE TIME I BREAK THE GIRL FREE...
...HER THROAT WILL ALREADY HAVE BEEN CRUSHED...
tnk
Shoom
RIP RIP

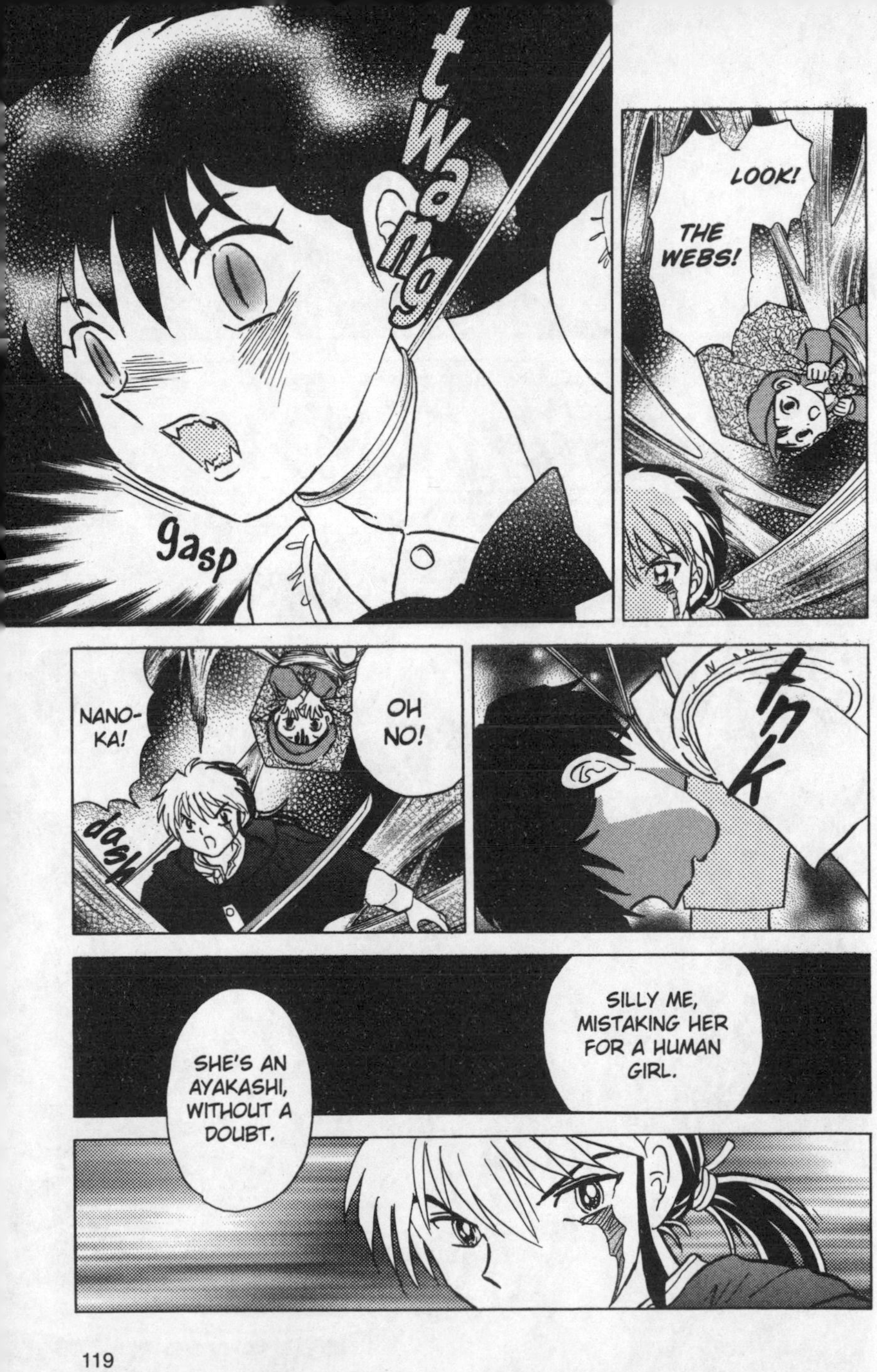
LOOK!
THE WEBS!
twang
gasp
trk
OH NO!
NANO-KA!
dash
SILLY ME, MISTAKING HER FOR A HUMAN GIRL.
SHE'S AN AYAKASHI, WITHOUT A DOUBT.

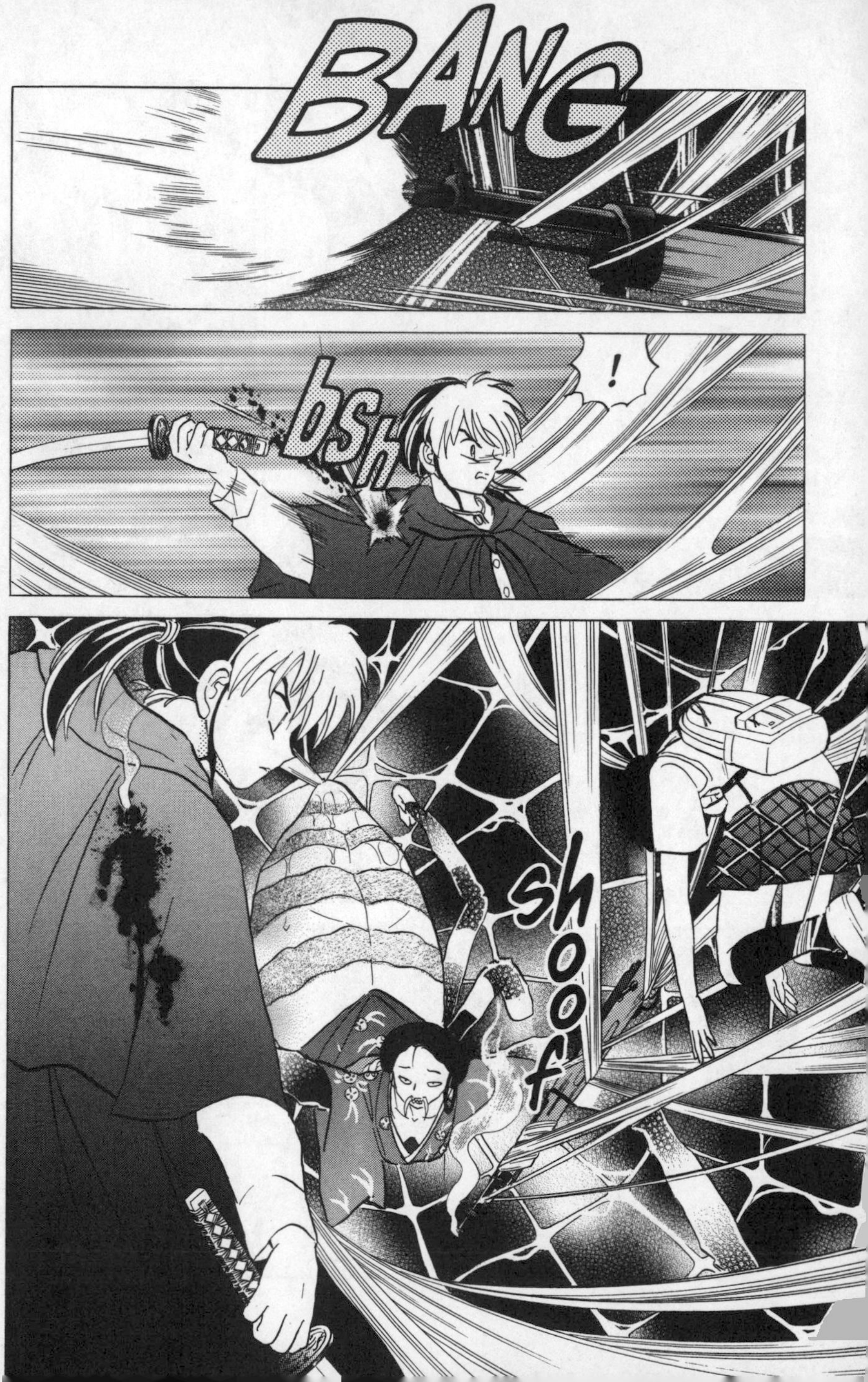
BANG
bsh
!
shoof

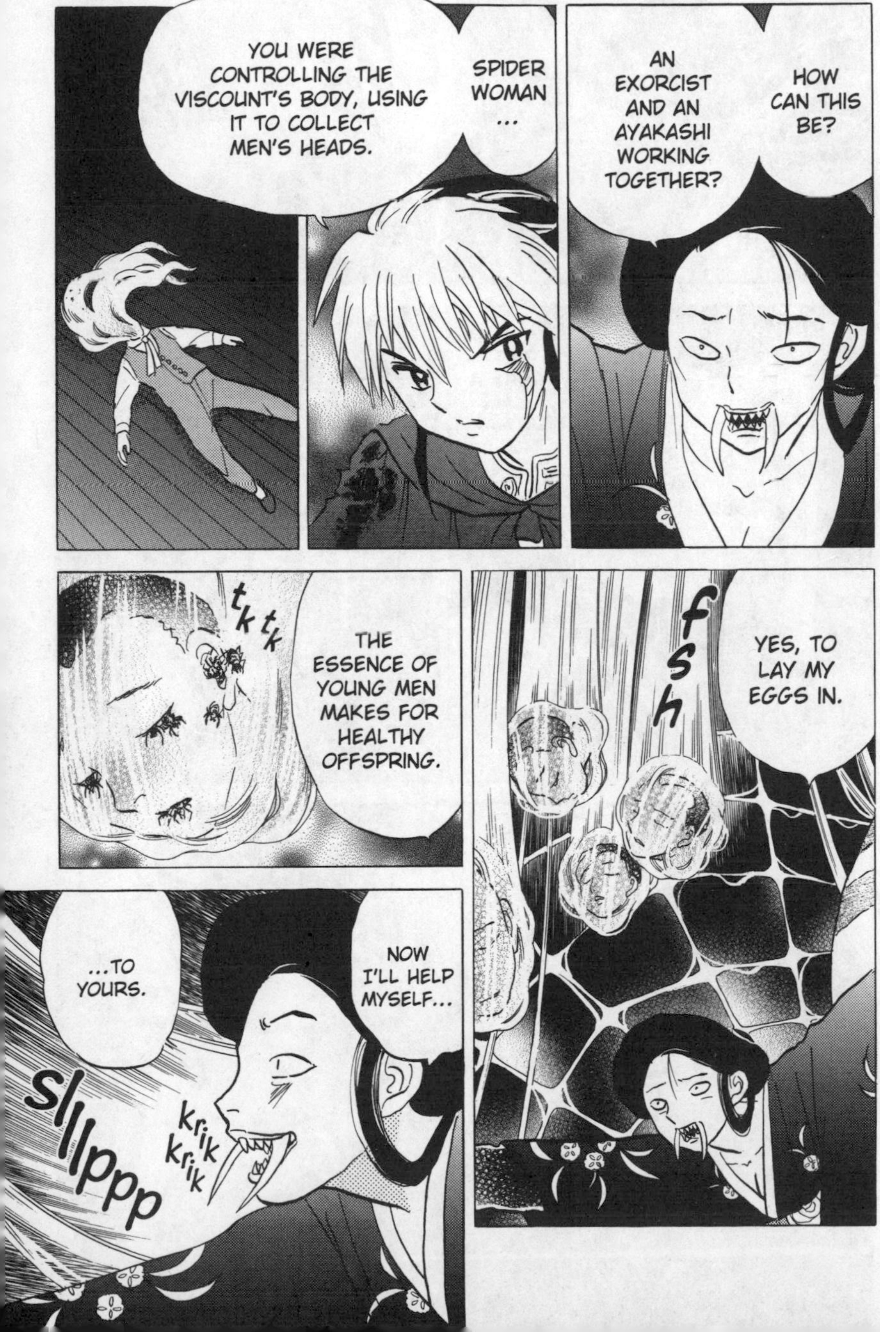
HOW CAN THIS BE?
AN EXORCIST AND AN AYAKASHI WORKING TOGETHER?
SPIDER WOMAN ...
YOU WERE CONTROLLING THE VISCOUNT'S BODY, USING IT TO COLLECT MEN'S HEADS.
fsh
YES, TO LAY MY EGGS IN.
tk tk
THE ESSENCE OF YOUNG MEN MAKES FOR HEALTHY OFFSPRING.
NOW I'LL HELP MYSELF...
...TO YOURS.
krik krik
sllppp

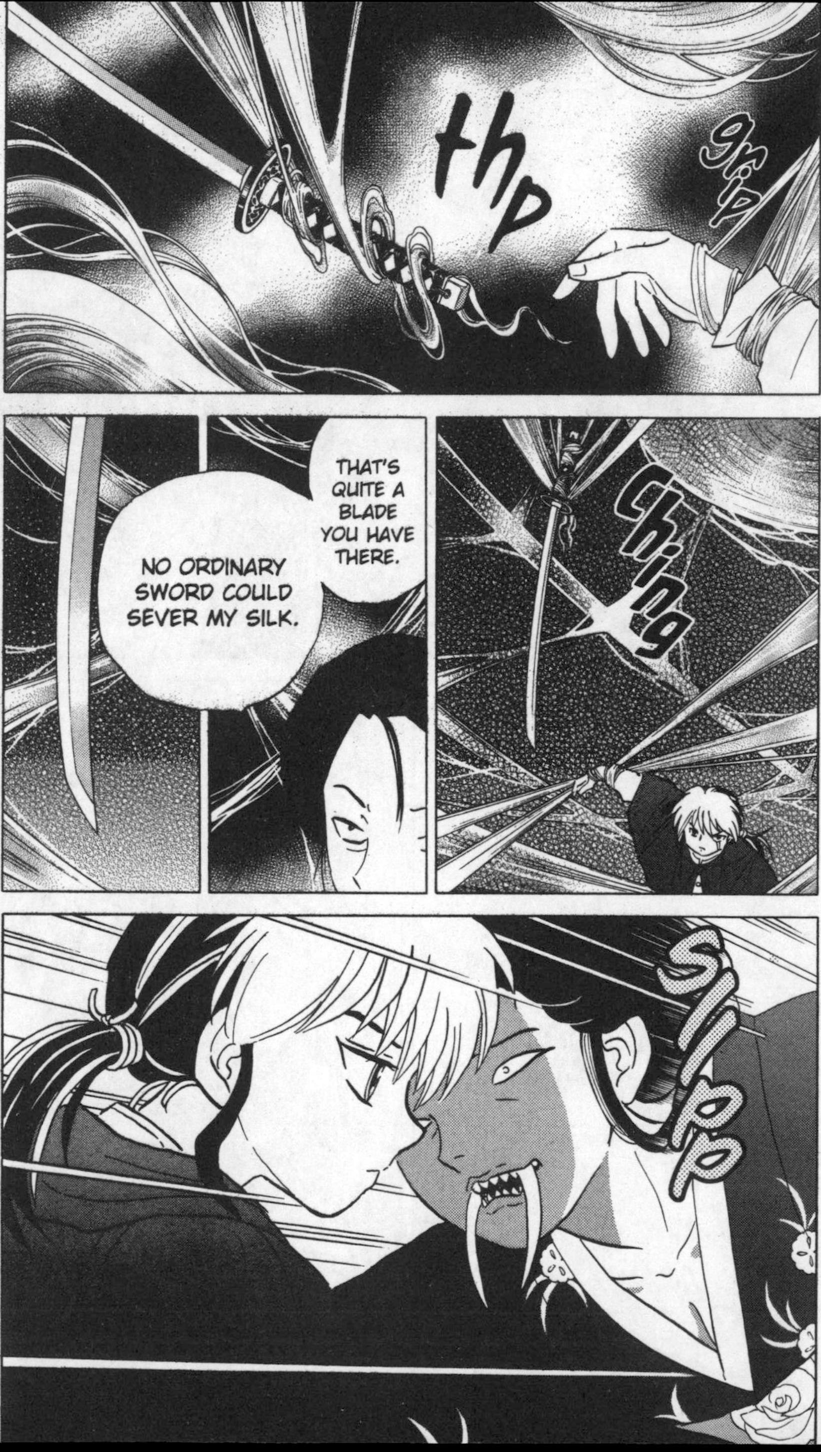
grip
thp
Ching
THAT'S QUITE A BLADE YOU HAVE THERE.
NO ORDINARY SWORD COULD SEVER MY SILK.
SLIPP

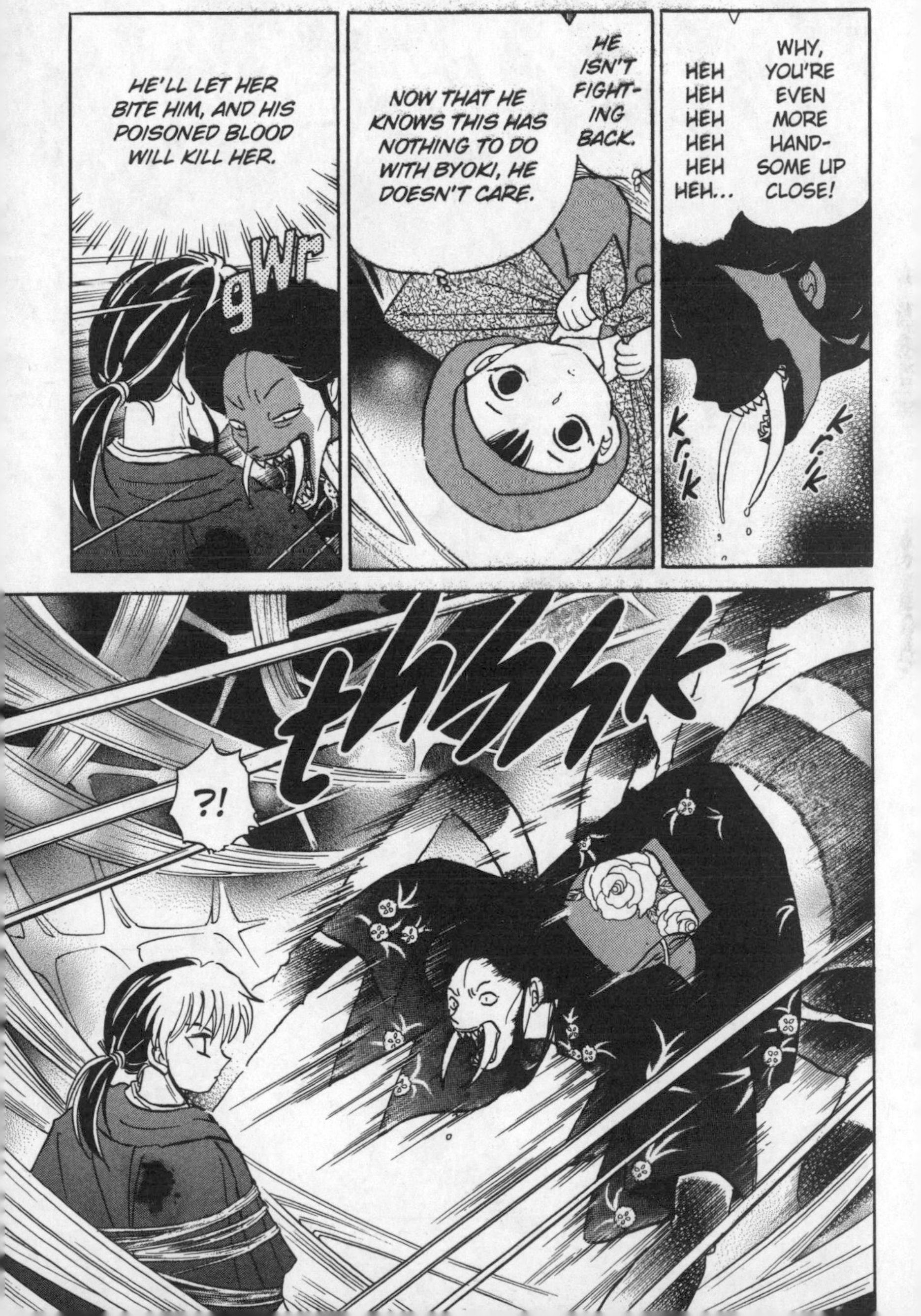
WHY, YOU'RE EVEN MORE HAND-SOME UP CLOSE!
HEH HEH HEH HEH HEH HEH...
krik
krik
HE ISN'T FIGHT-ING BACK.
NOW THAT HE KNOWS THIS HAS NOTHING TO DO WITH BYOKI, HE DOESN'T CARE.
HE'LL LET HER BITE HIM, AND HIS POISONED BLOOD WILL KILL HER.
gWr
thshk
?!

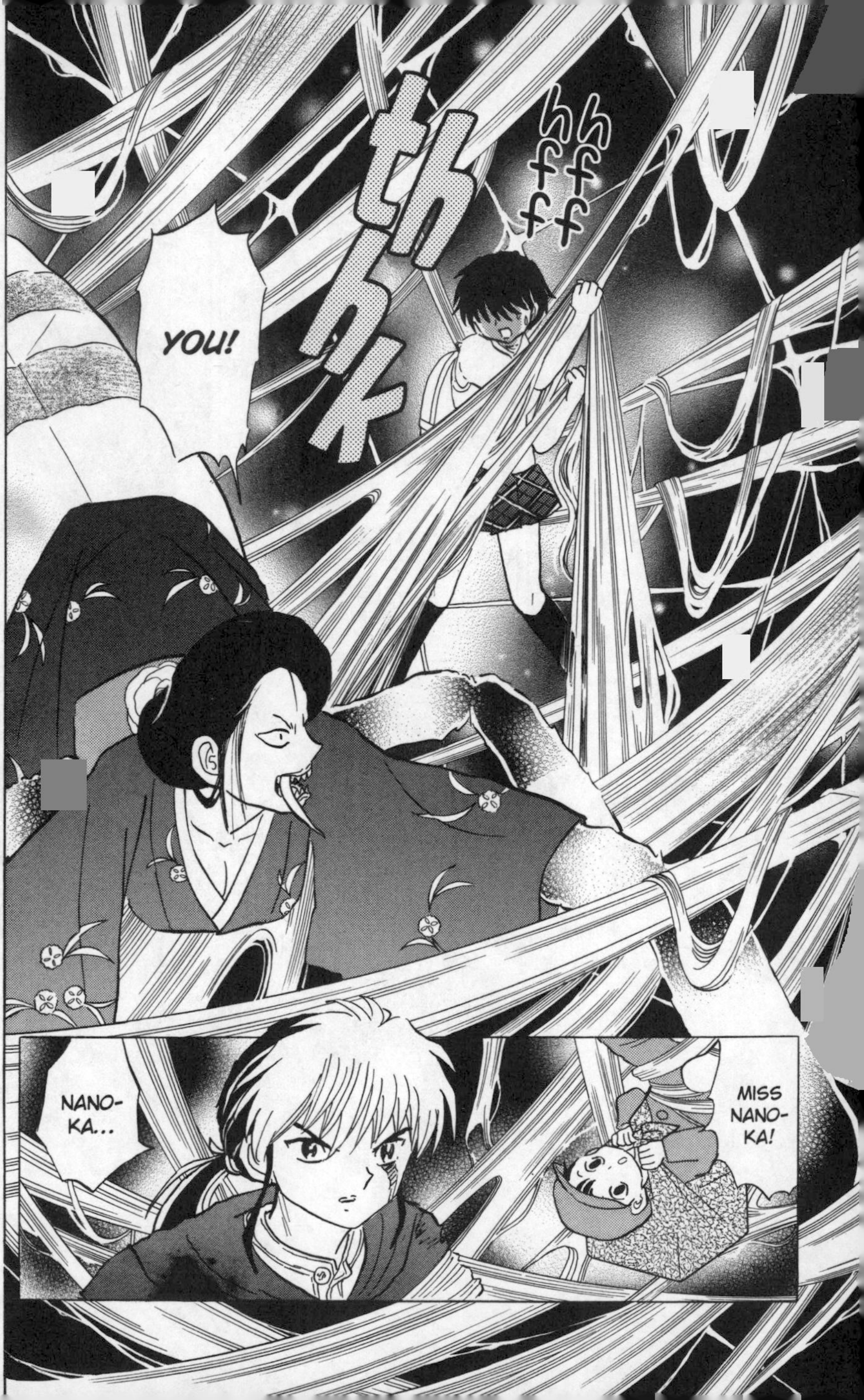
hff hff
YOU!
MISS NANO-KA!
NANO-KA...

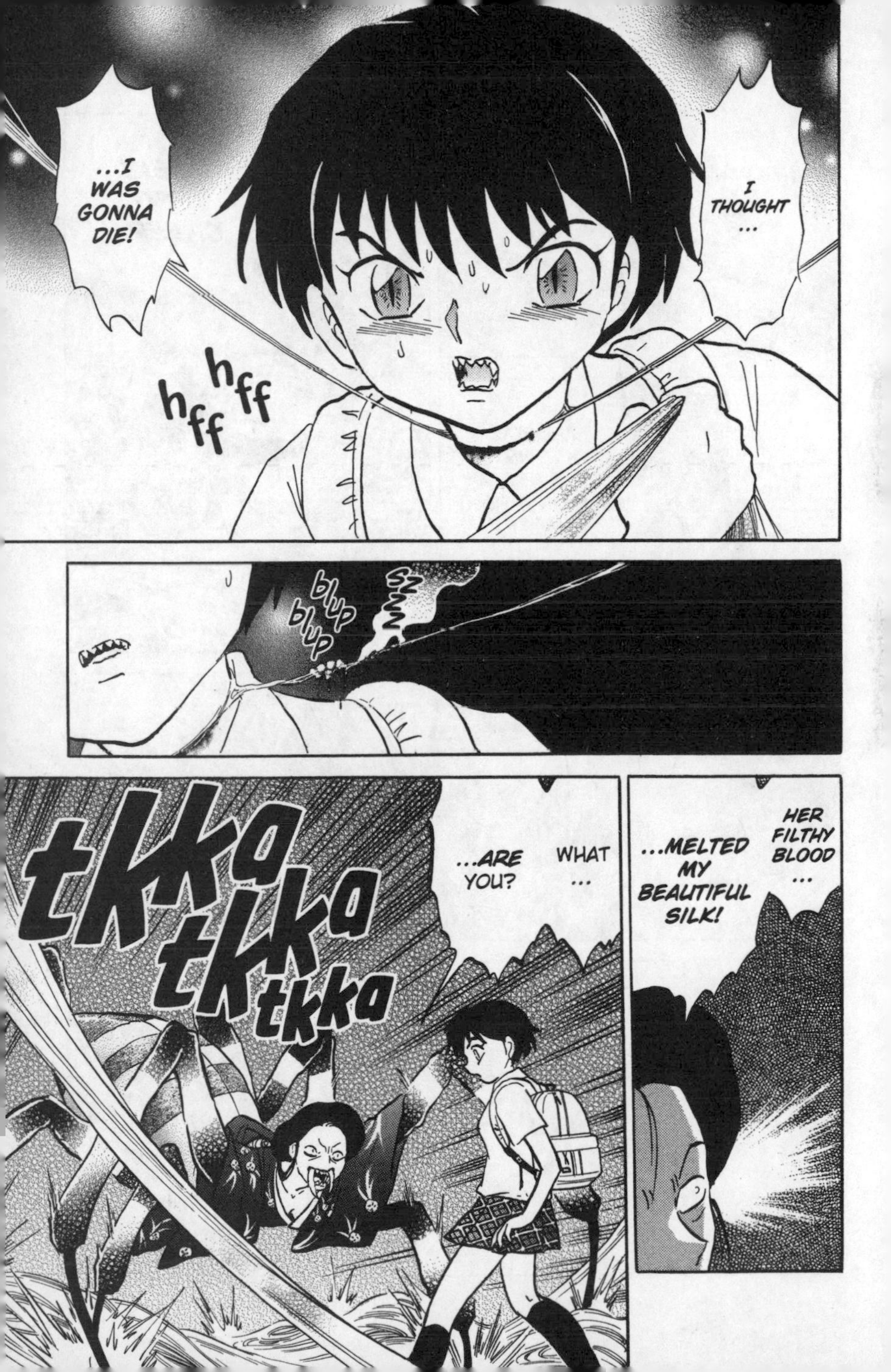
I THOUGHT ...
...I WAS GONNA DIE!
hff hff
SZZZ
blup blup
HER FILTHY BLOOD ...
...MELTED MY BEAUTIFUL SILK!
WHAT ...
...ARE YOU?
tkka tkka tkka tkka

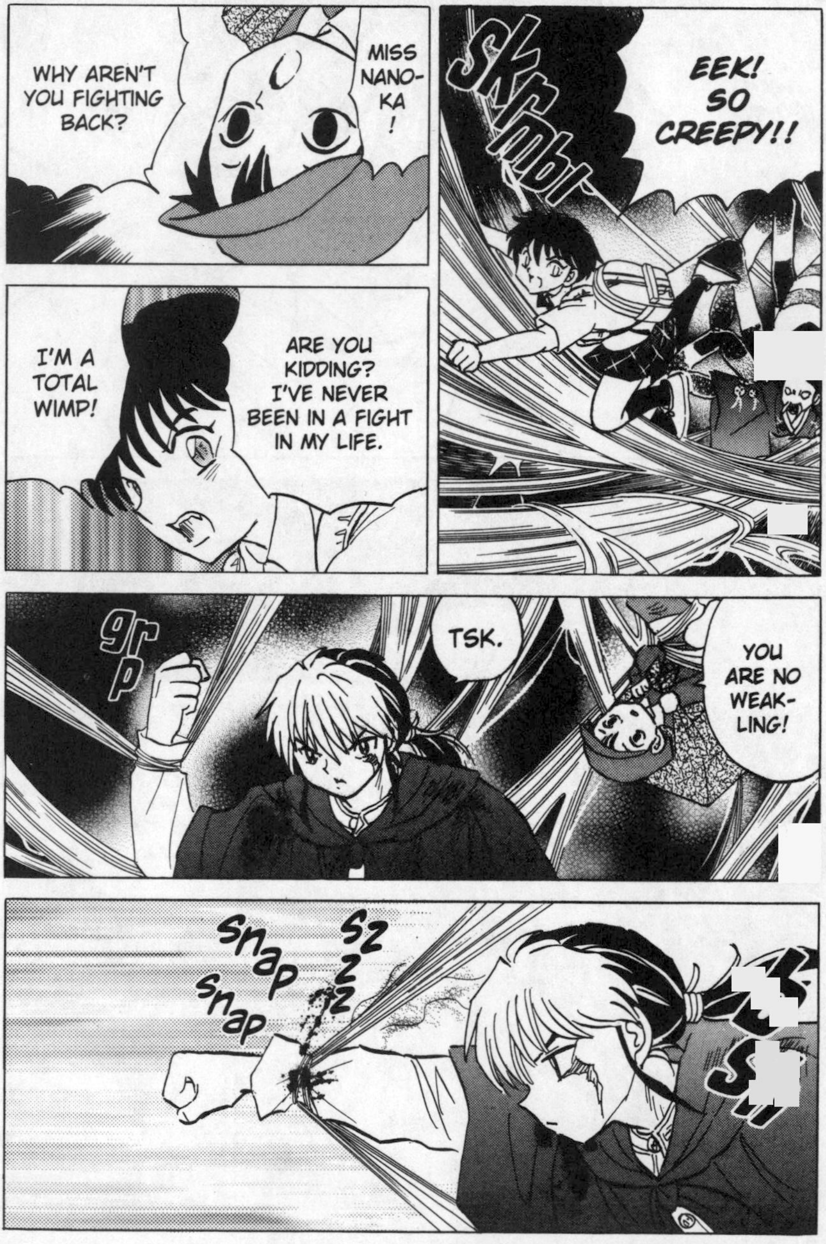
EEK! SO CREEPY!!
skrmbl
MISS NANO-KA!
WHY AREN'T YOU FIGHTING BACK?
ARE YOU KIDDING? I'VE NEVER BEEN IN A FIGHT IN MY LIFE.
I'M A TOTAL WIMP!
YOU ARE NO WEAK-LING!
TSK.
grp
szzz
snap
snap

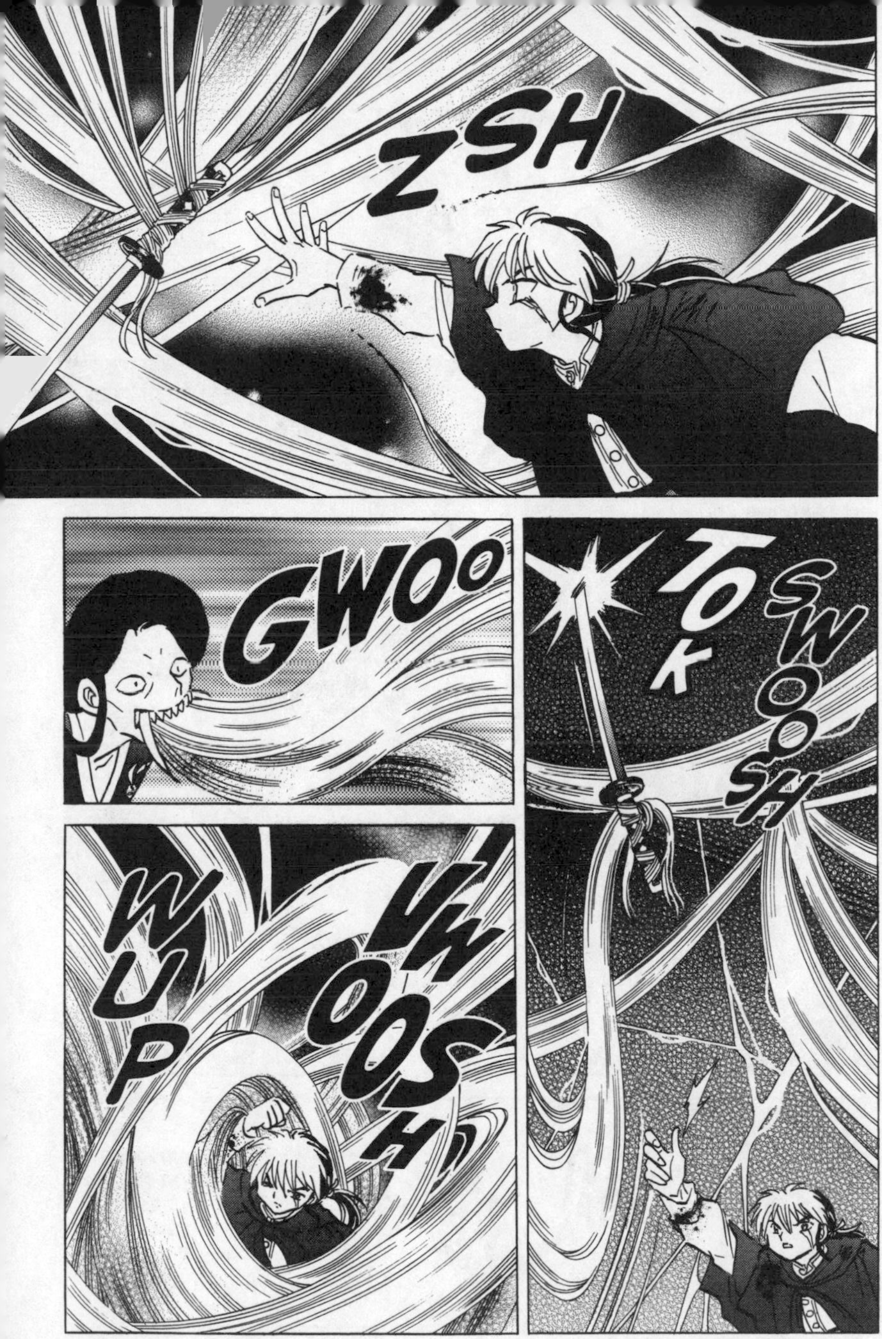
ZSH
TOK
SWOOSH
GWOO
WHOOSH
WUP

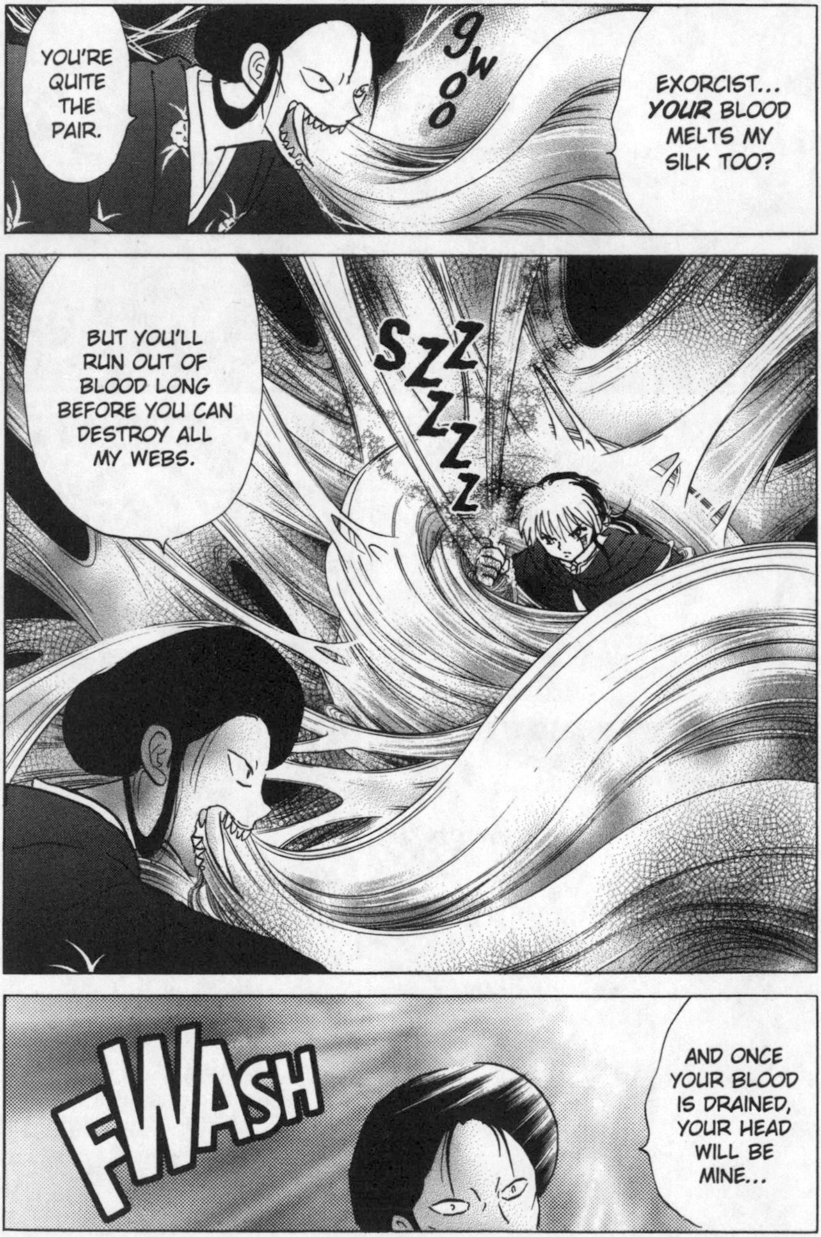
EXORCIST... YOUR BLOOD MELTS MY SILK TOO?
GWOOO
YOU'RE QUITE THE PAIR.
SZZZZZZ
BUT YOU'LL RUN OUT OF BLOOD LONG BEFORE YOU CAN DESTROY ALL MY WEBS.
AND ONCE YOUR BLOOD IS DRAINED, YOUR HEAD WILL BE MINE...
FWASH

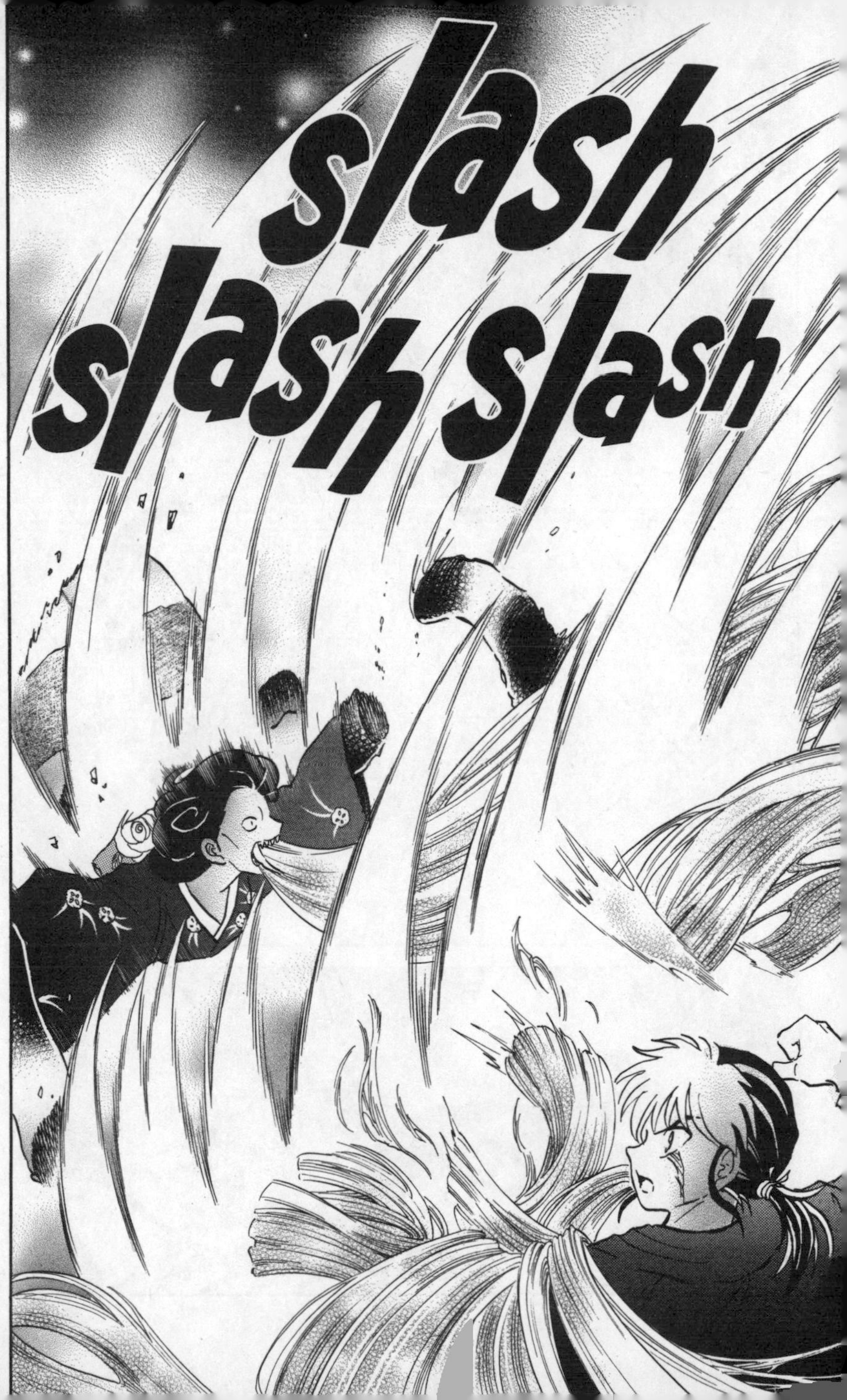
slash
slash slash slash

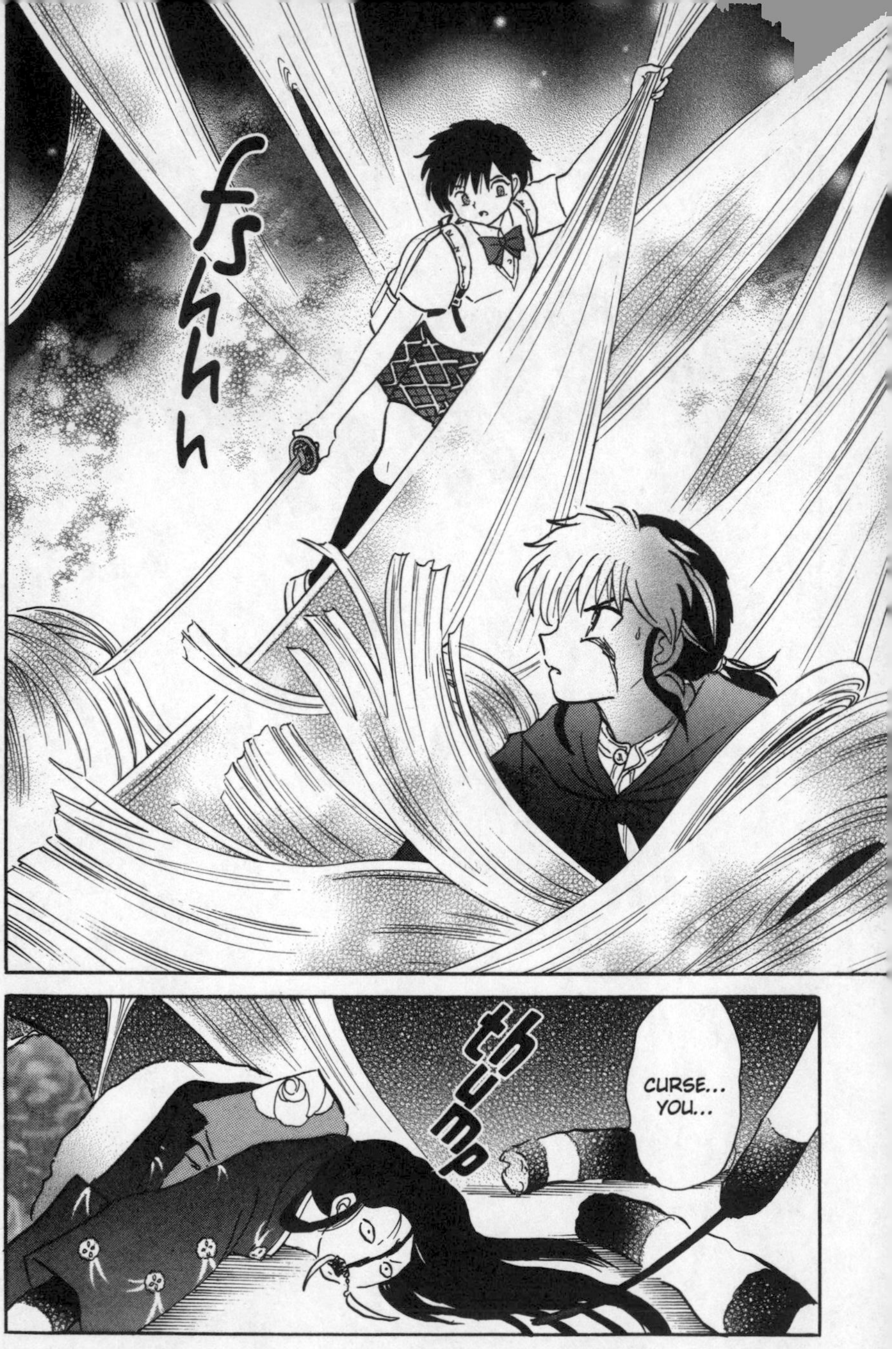
fshhhh
thump
CURSE... YOU...

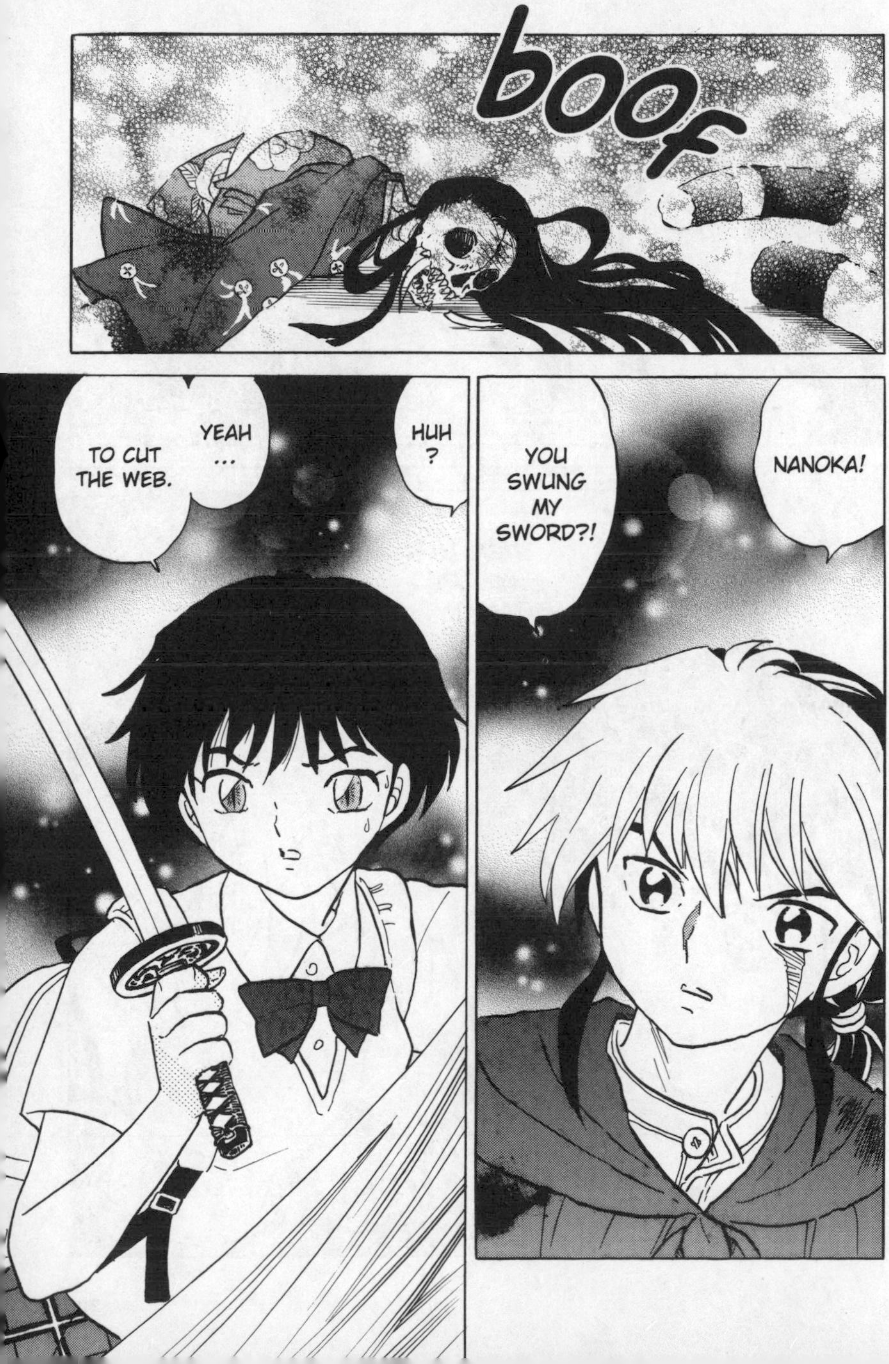
boof
NANOKA!
YOU SWUNG MY SWORD?!
HUH ?
YEAH ...
TO CUT THE WEB.

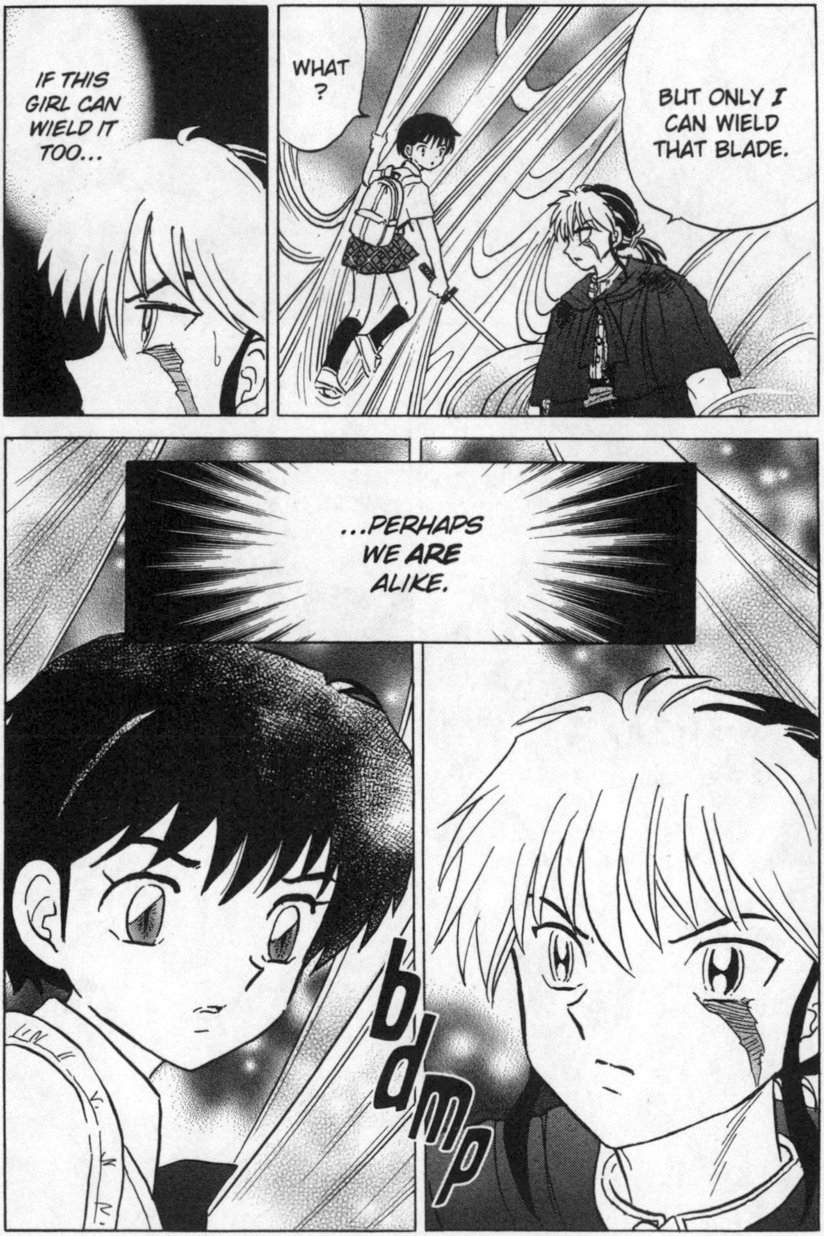
BUT ONLY *I* CAN WIELD THAT BLADE.
WHAT?
IF THIS GIRL CAN WIELD IT TOO...
...PERHAPS WE ARE ALIKE.
bdmp

Chapter 6: The Accursed

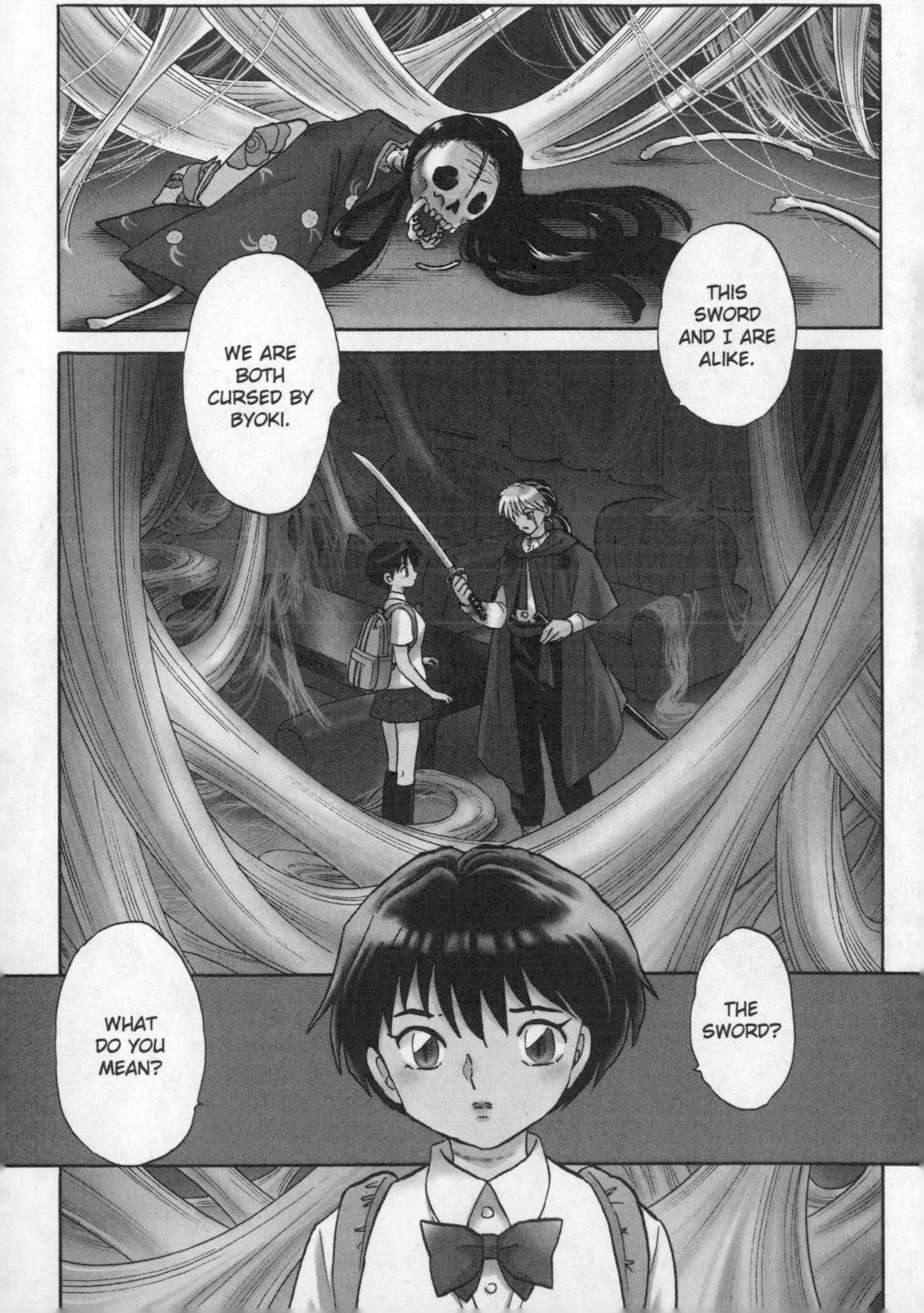
THIS SWORD AND I ARE ALIKE.
WE ARE BOTH CURSED BY BYOKI.
THE SWORD?
WHAT DO YOU MEAN?

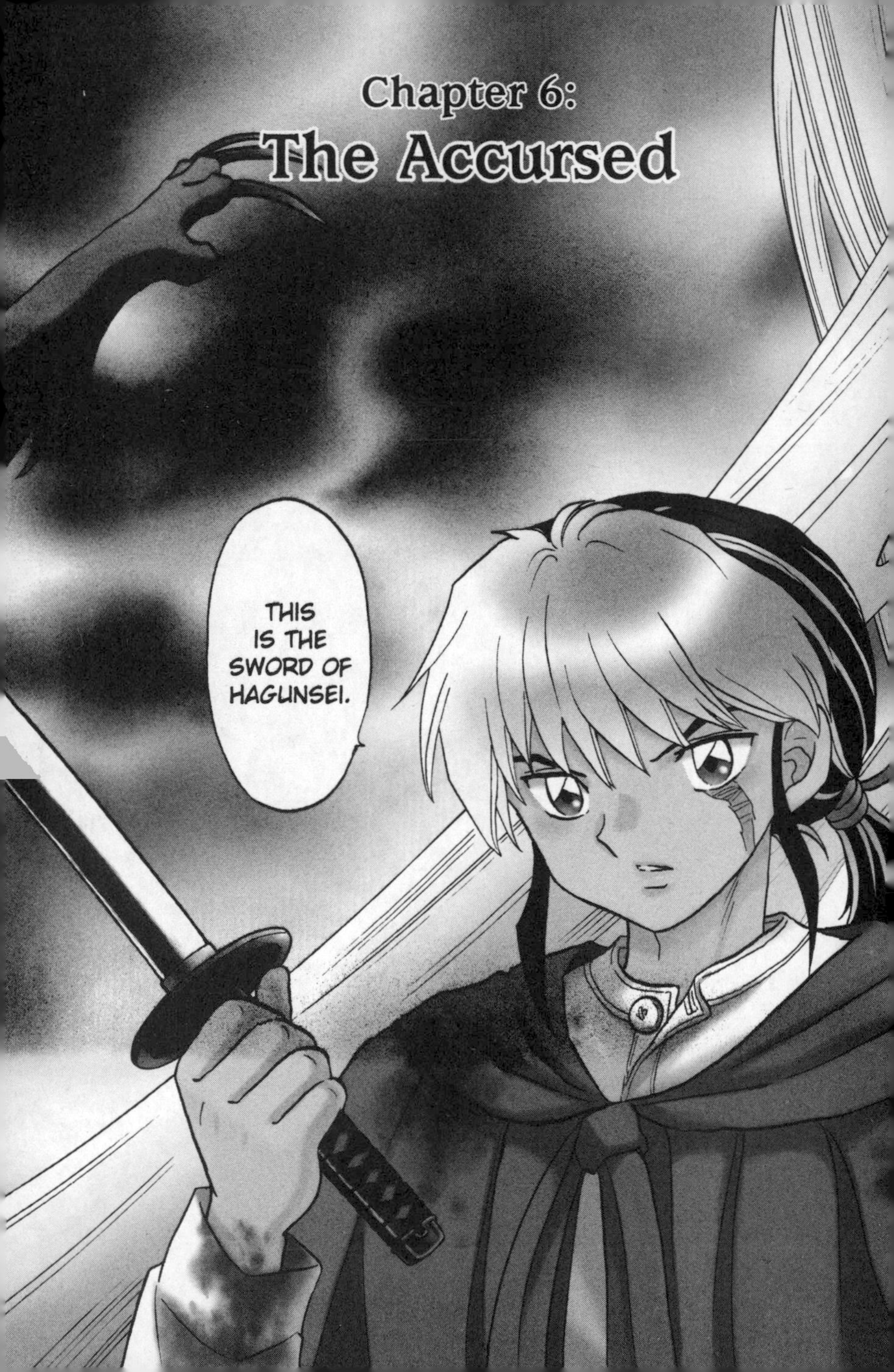
Chapter 6:
The Accursed
THIS IS THE SWORD OF HAGUNSEI.

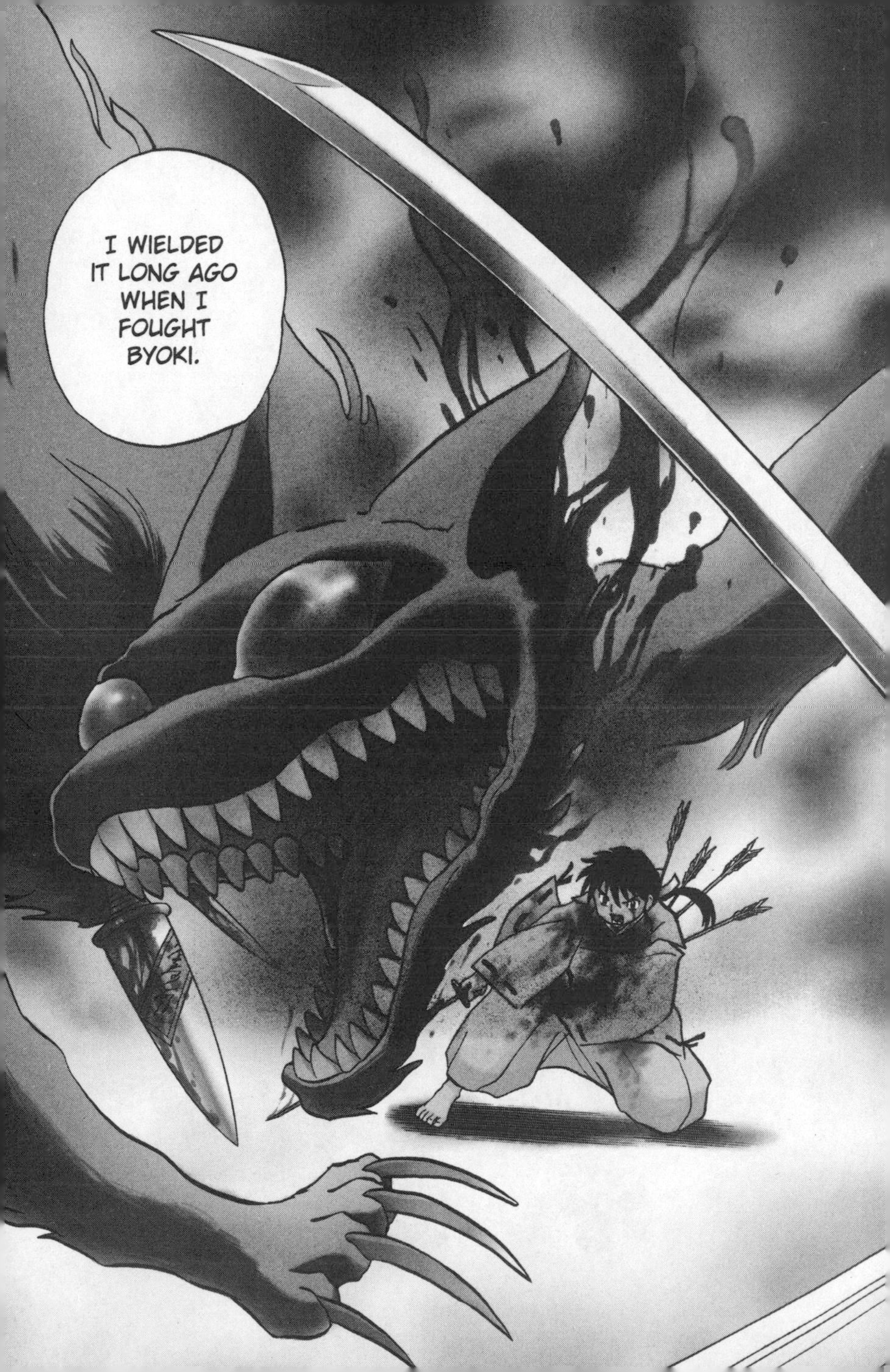
I WIELDED IT LONG AGO WHEN I FOUGHT BYOKI.

MAO

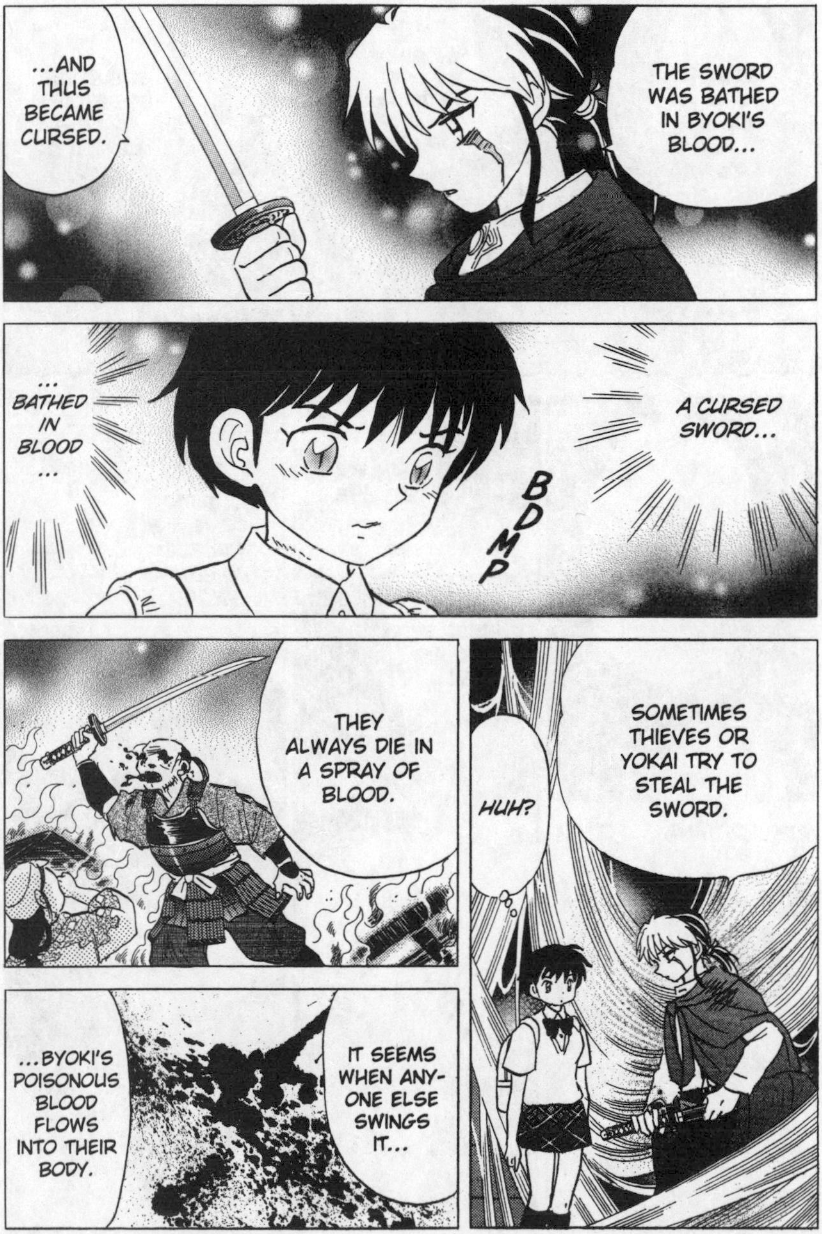
THE SWORD WAS BATHED IN BYOKI'S BLOOD...
...AND THUS BECAME CURSED.
A CURSED SWORD...
BDMP
...BATHED IN BLOOD...
SOMETIMES THIEVES OR YOKAI TRY TO STEAL THE SWORD.
HUH?
THEY ALWAYS DIE IN A SPRAY OF BLOOD.
IT SEEMS WHEN ANYONE ELSE SWINGS IT...
...BYOKI'S POISONOUS BLOOD FLOWS INTO THEIR BODY.

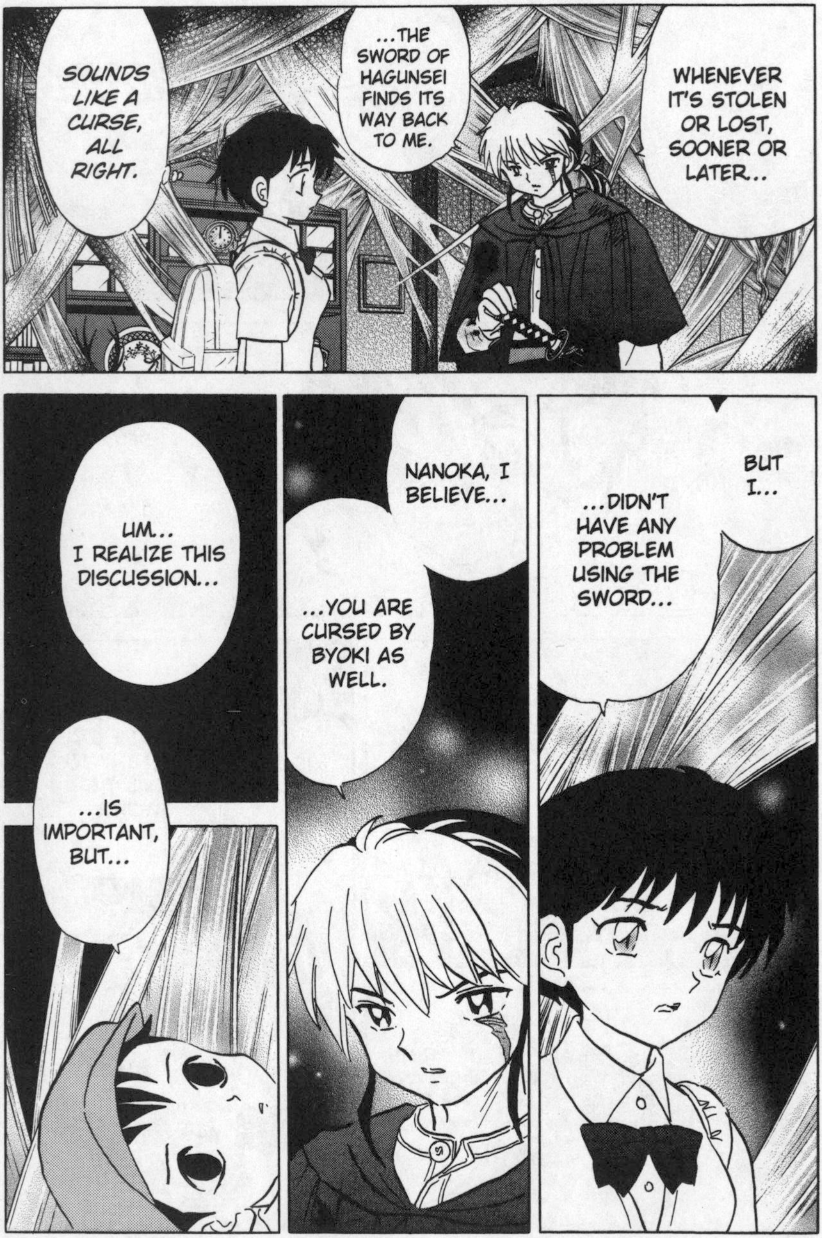
WHENEVER IT'S STOLEN OR LOST, SOONER OR LATER...
...THE SWORD OF HAGUNSEI FINDS ITS WAY BACK TO ME.
SOUNDS LIKE A CURSE, ALL RIGHT.
BUT I...
...DIDN'T HAVE ANY PROBLEM USING THE SWORD...
NANOKA, I BELIEVE...
...YOU ARE CURSED BY BYOKI AS WELL.
UM... I REALIZE THIS DISCUSSION...
...IS IMPORTANT, BUT...

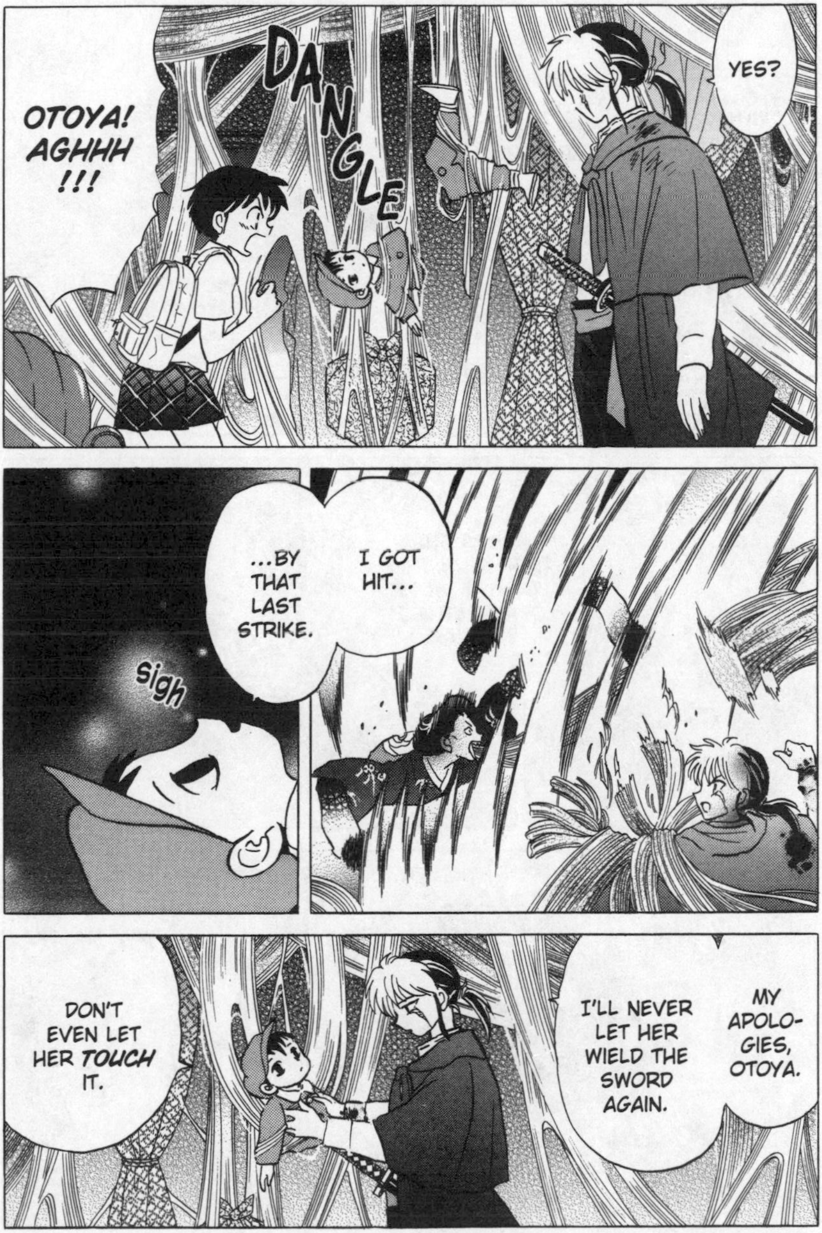
YES?
DANGLE
OTOYA! AGHHH !!!
I GOT HIT... ...BY THAT LAST STRIKE.
sigh
MY APOLOGIES, OTOYA.
I'LL NEVER LET HER WIELD THE SWORD AGAIN.
DON'T EVEN LET HER *TOUCH* IT.

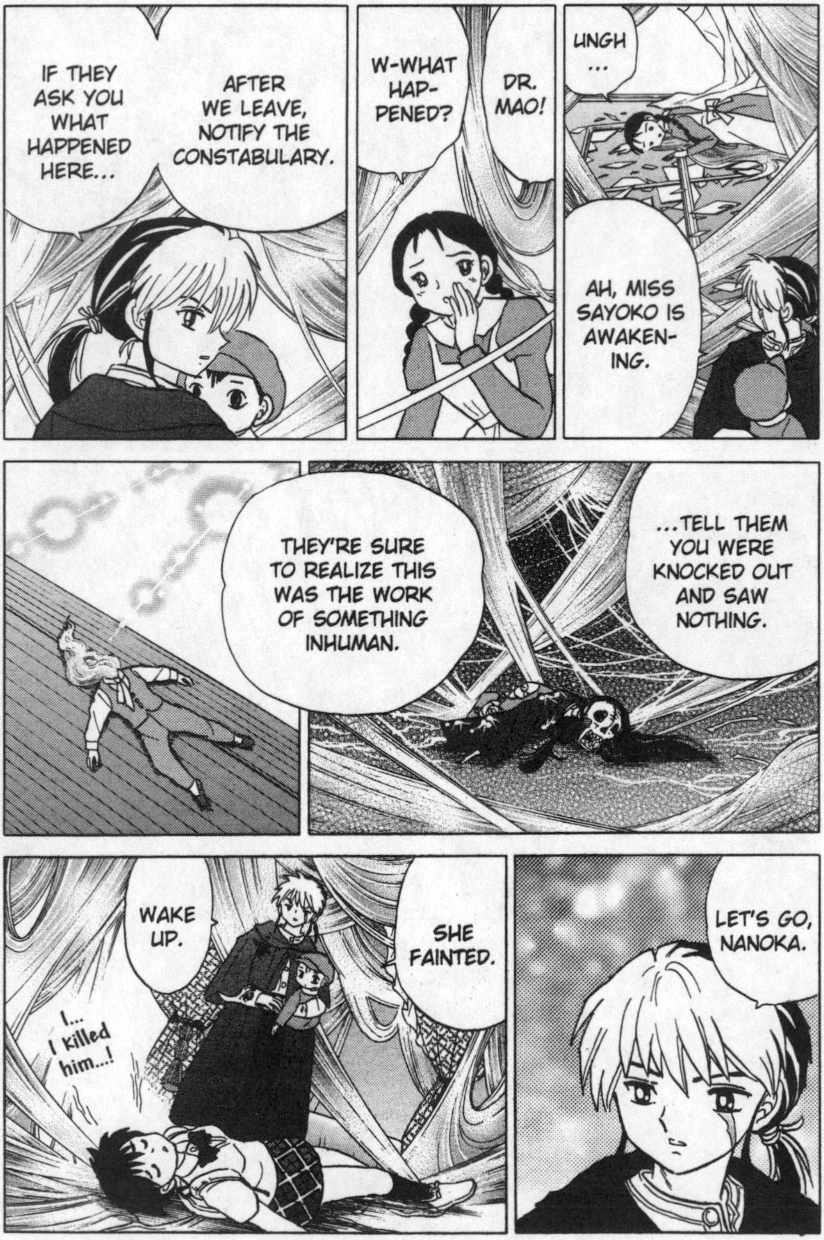
UNGH ...
AH, MISS SAYOKO IS AWAKEN-ING.
DR. MAO!
W-WHAT HAP-PENED?
AFTER WE LEAVE, NOTIFY THE CONSTABULARY.
IF THEY ASK YOU WHAT HAPPENED HERE...
...TELL THEM YOU WERE KNOCKED OUT AND SAW NOTHING.
THEY'RE SURE TO REALIZE THIS WAS THE WORK OF SOMETHING INHUMAN.
LET'S GO, NANOKA.
SHE FAINTED.
WAKE UP.
I... I killed him...!

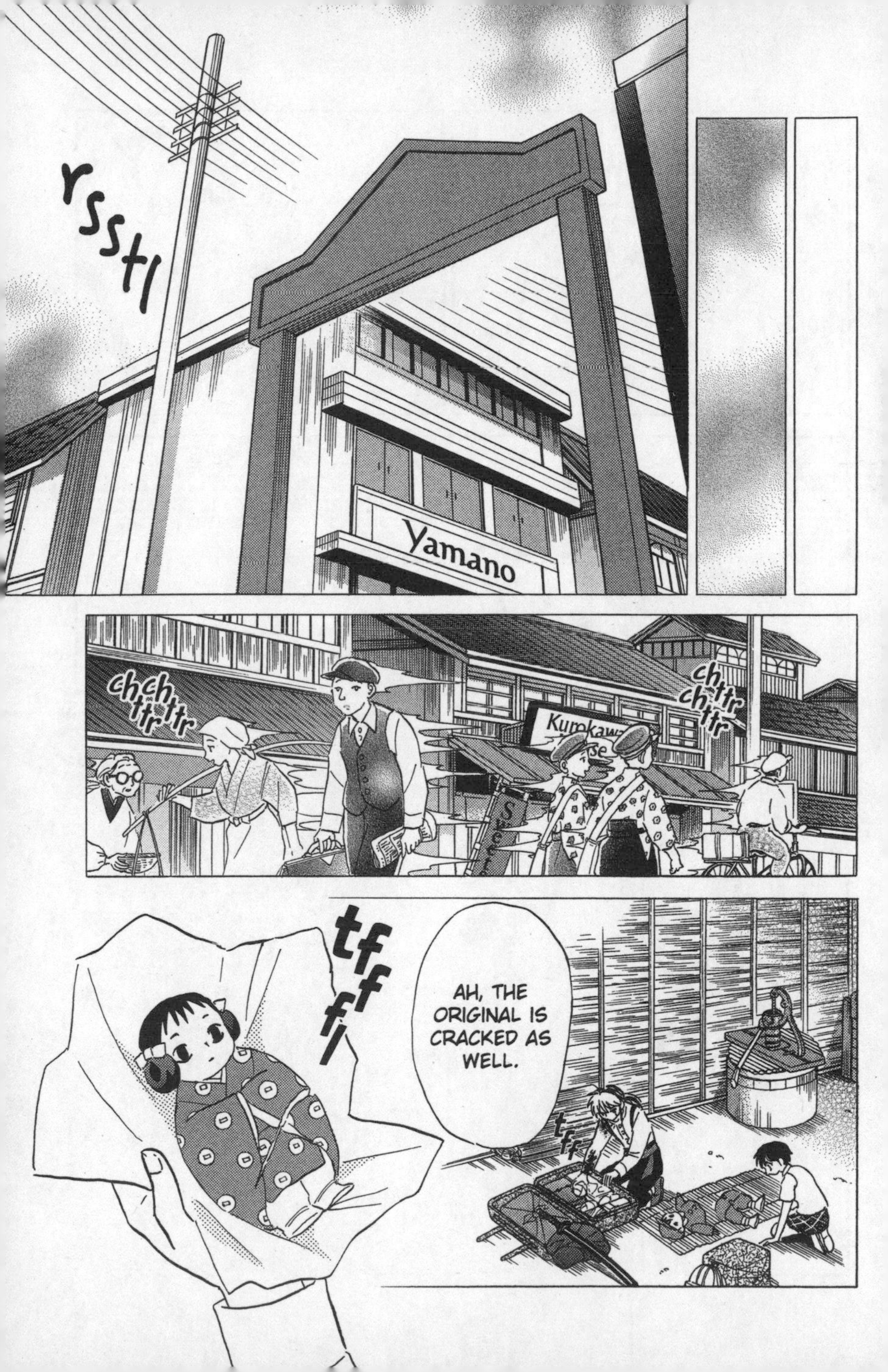
rsstl
Yamano
chttr chttr
chchttr ttr
tff
AH, THE ORIGINAL IS CRACKED AS WELL.
tfffi

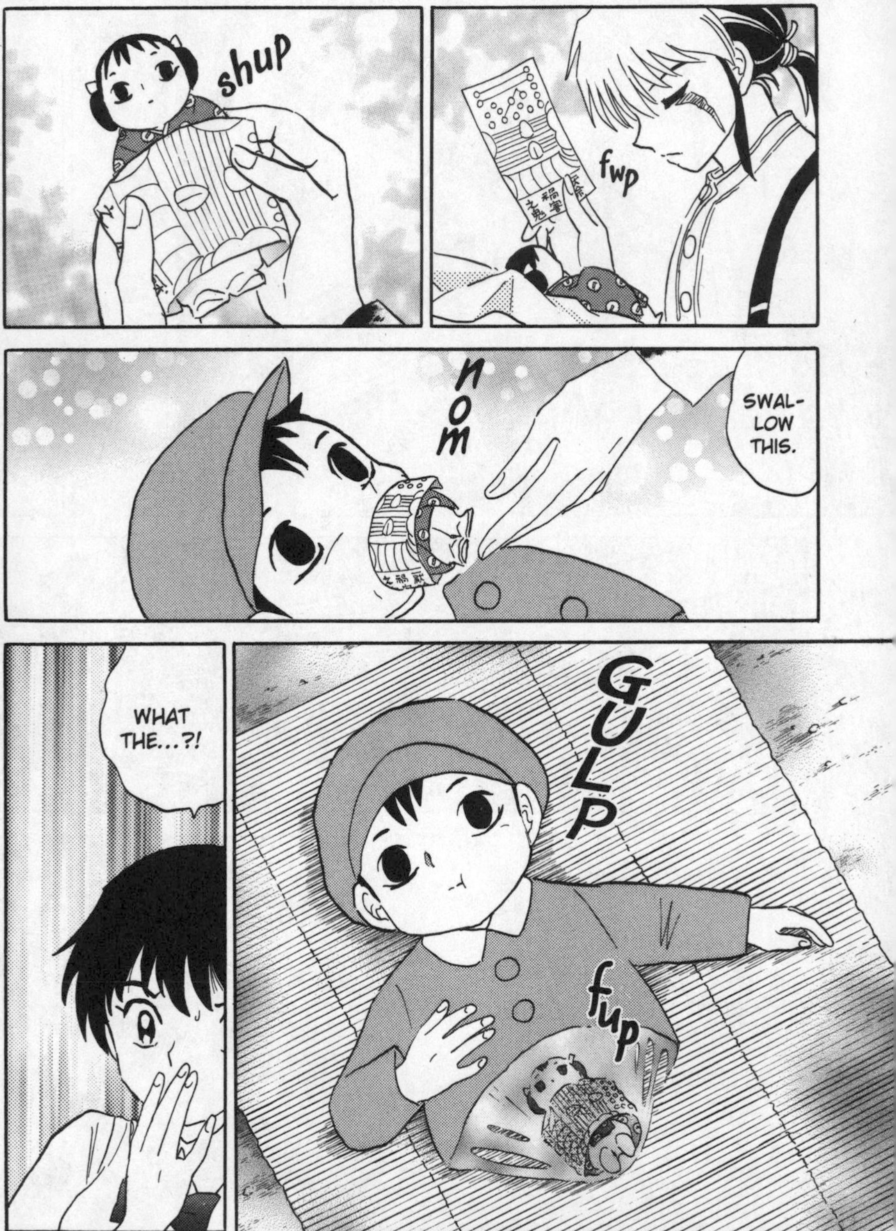
fwp
shup
SWAL-
LOW
THIS.
nom
GULP
fup
WHAT
THE...?!

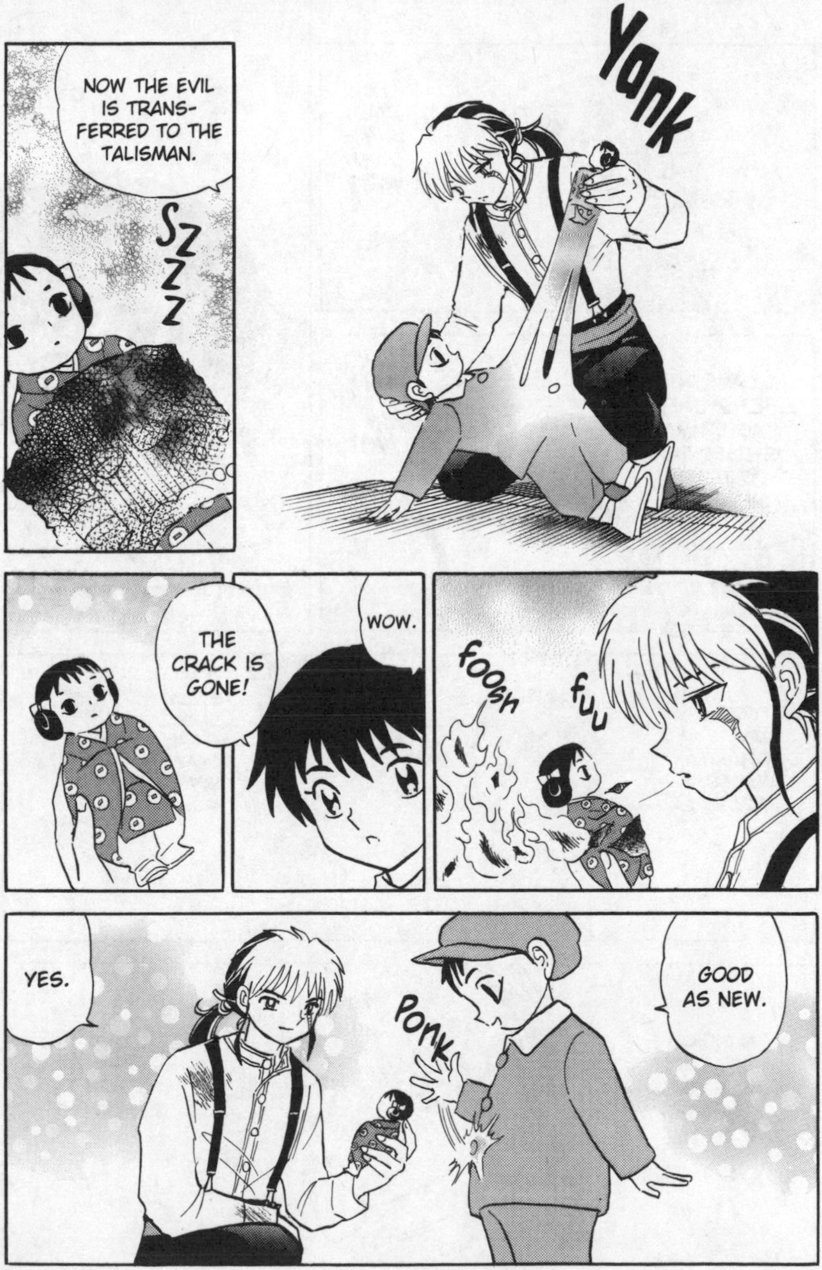
Yank
NOW THE EVIL IS TRANS-FERRED TO THE TALISMAN.
SZZZ
foosh
fuu
WOW.
THE CRACK IS GONE!
GOOD AS NEW.
Ponk
YES.

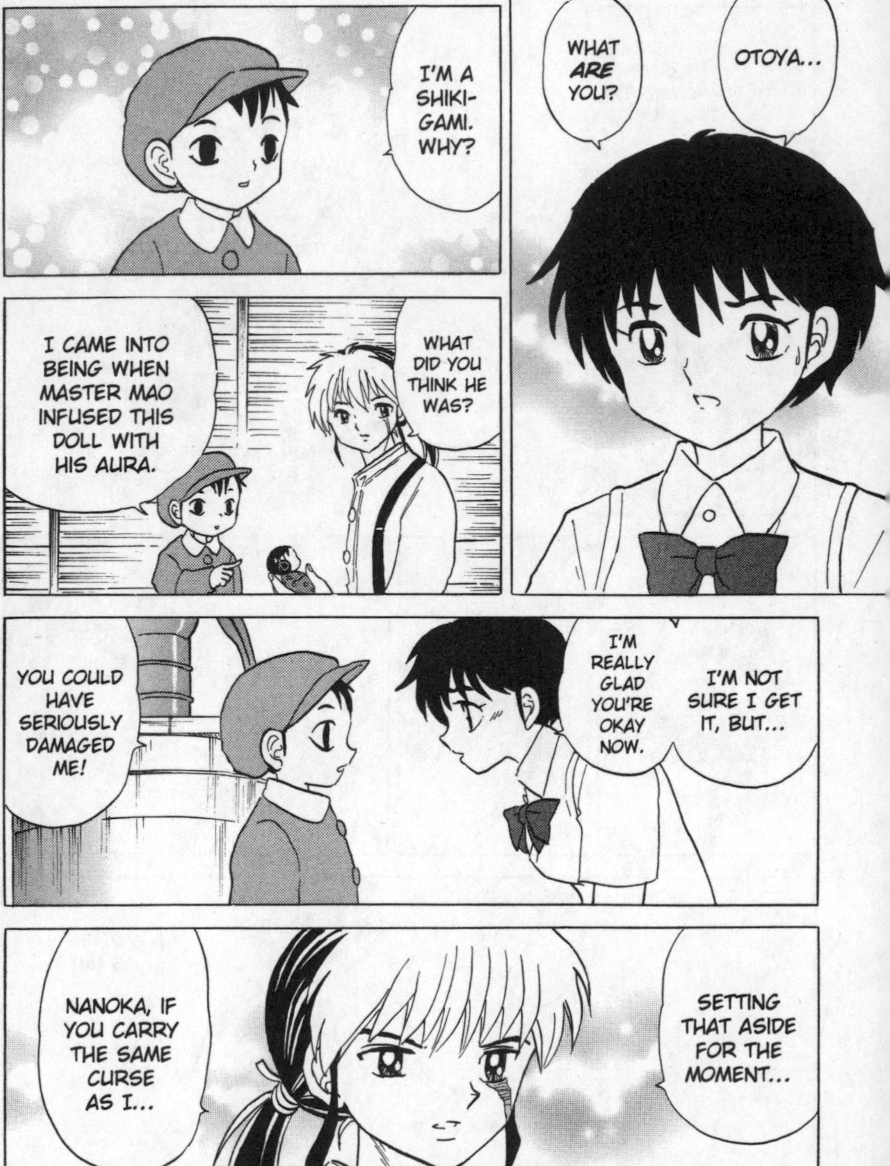
OTOYA...
WHAT *ARE* YOU?
I'M A SHIKI-GAMI. WHY?
WHAT DID YOU THINK HE WAS?
I CAME INTO BEING WHEN MASTER MAO INFUSED THIS DOLL WITH HIS AURA.
I'M NOT SURE I GET IT, BUT...
I'M REALLY GLAD YOU'RE OKAY NOW.
YOU COULD HAVE SERIOUSLY DAMAGED ME!
SETTING THAT ASIDE FOR THE MOMENT...
NANOKA, IF YOU CARRY THE SAME CURSE AS I...

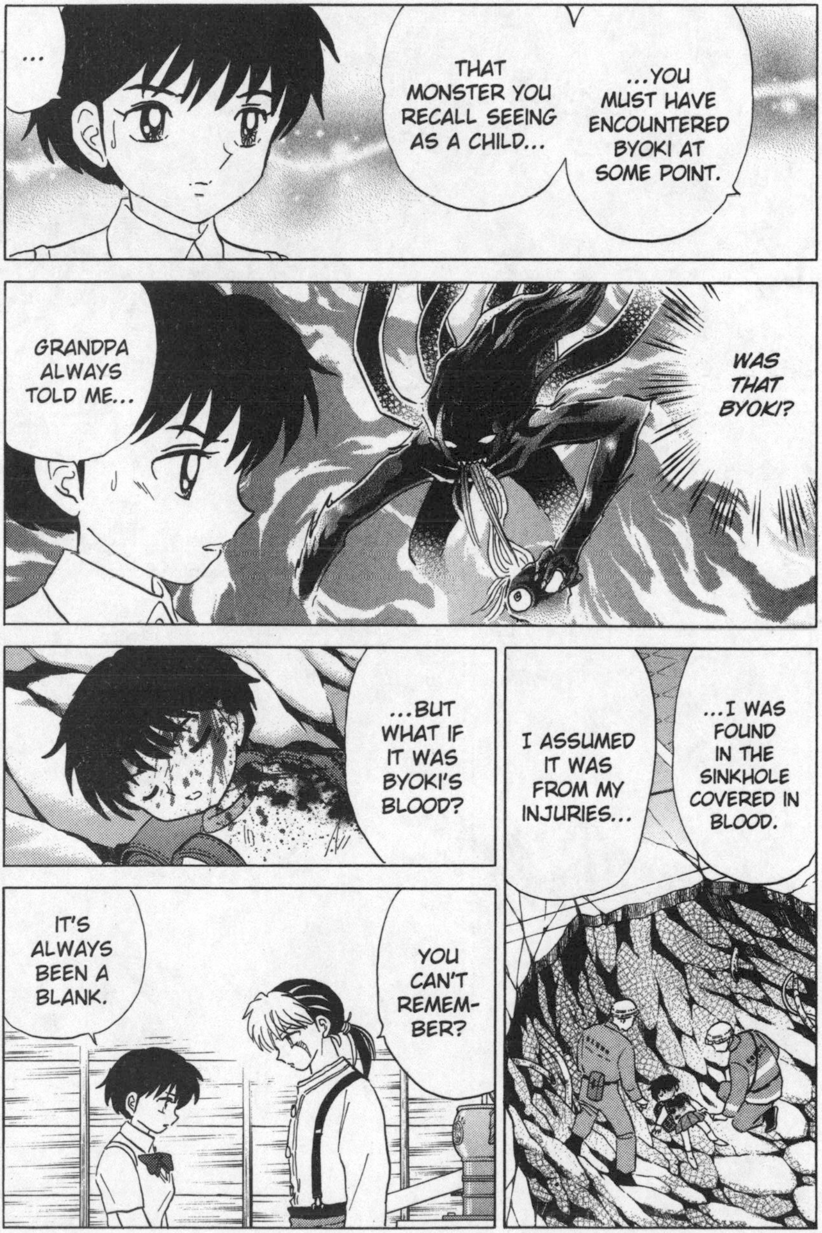

THAT MONSTER YOU RECALL SEEING AS A CHILD...
...YOU MUST HAVE ENCOUNTERED BYOKI AT SOME POINT.
...
WAS THAT BYOKI?
GRANDPA ALWAYS TOLD ME...
...I WAS FOUND IN THE SINKHOLE COVERED IN BLOOD.
I ASSUMED IT WAS FROM MY INJURIES...
...BUT WHAT IF IT WAS BYOKI'S BLOOD?
YOU CAN'T REMEM-BER?
IT'S ALWAYS BEEN A BLANK.

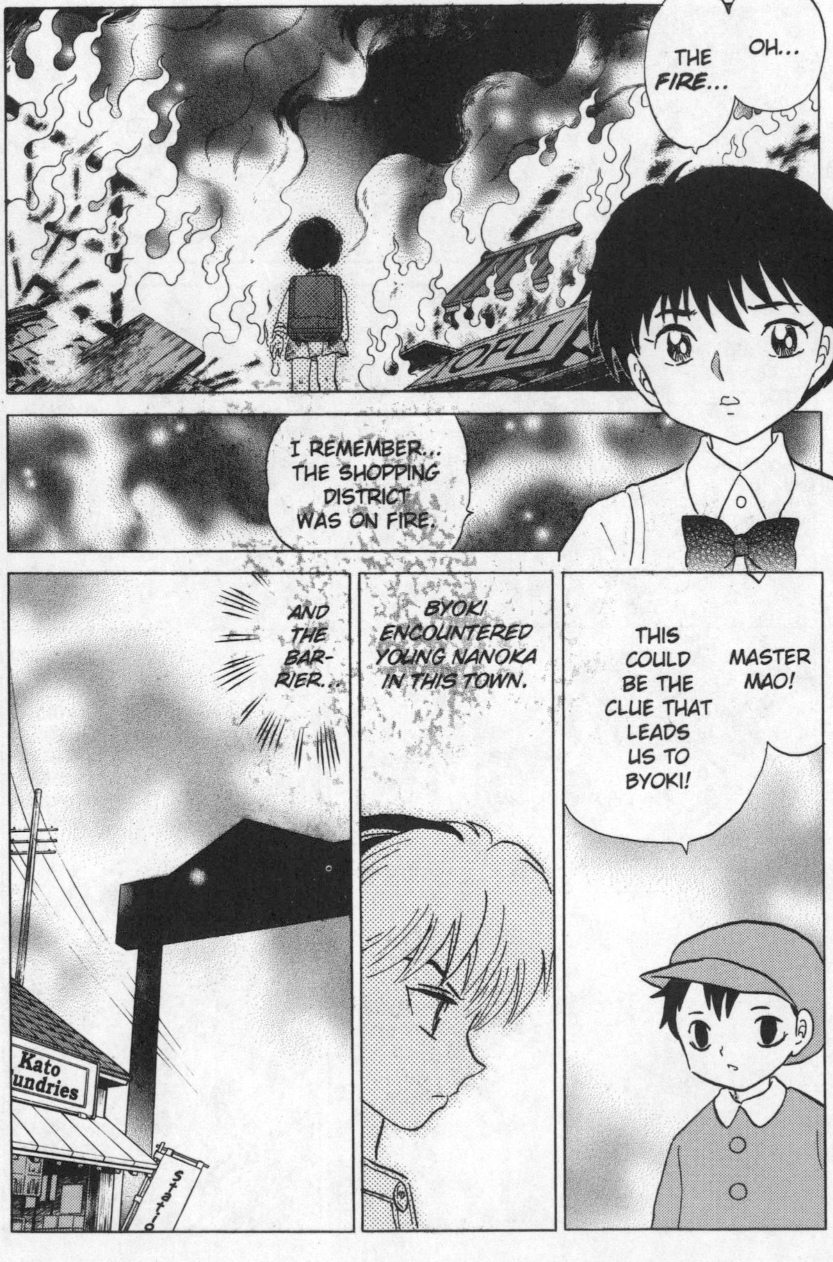
OH...
THE FIRE...
I REMEMBER... THE SHOPPING DISTRICT WAS ON FIRE.
MASTER MAO!
THIS COULD BE THE CLUE THAT LEADS US TO BYOKI!
BYOKI ENCOUNTERED YOUNG NANOKA IN THIS TOWN.
AND THE BAR-RIER...
Kato

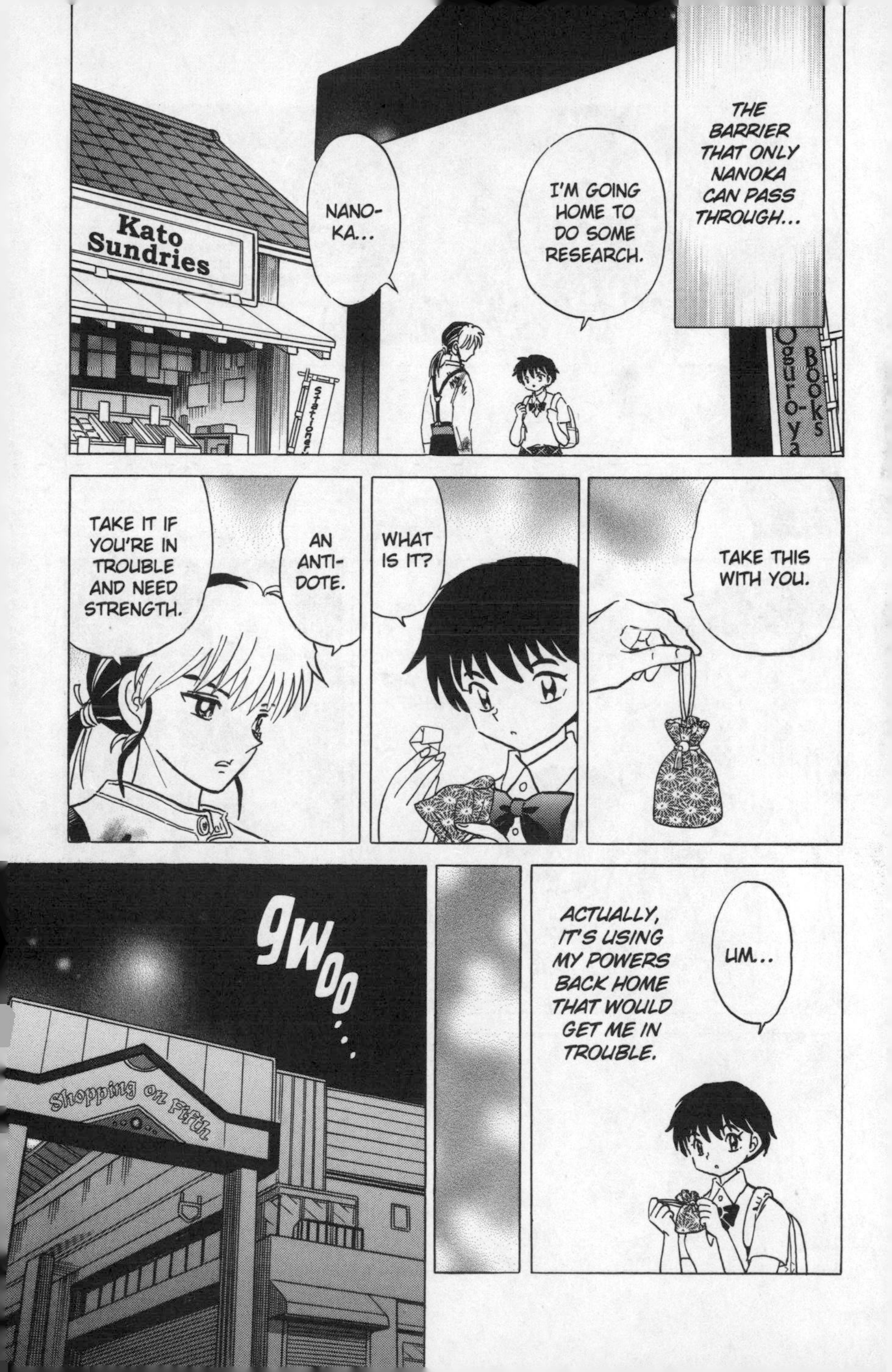
THE BARRIER THAT ONLY NANOKA CAN PASS THROUGH...
I'M GOING HOME TO DO SOME RESEARCH.
NANO-KA...
Kato Sundries
Oguro-ya Books
TAKE THIS WITH YOU.
WHAT IS IT?
AN ANTI-DOTE.
TAKE IT IF YOU'RE IN TROUBLE AND NEED STRENGTH.
UM...
ACTUALLY, IT'S USING MY POWERS BACK HOME THAT WOULD GET ME IN TROUBLE.
GWOO...
Shopping on Fifth

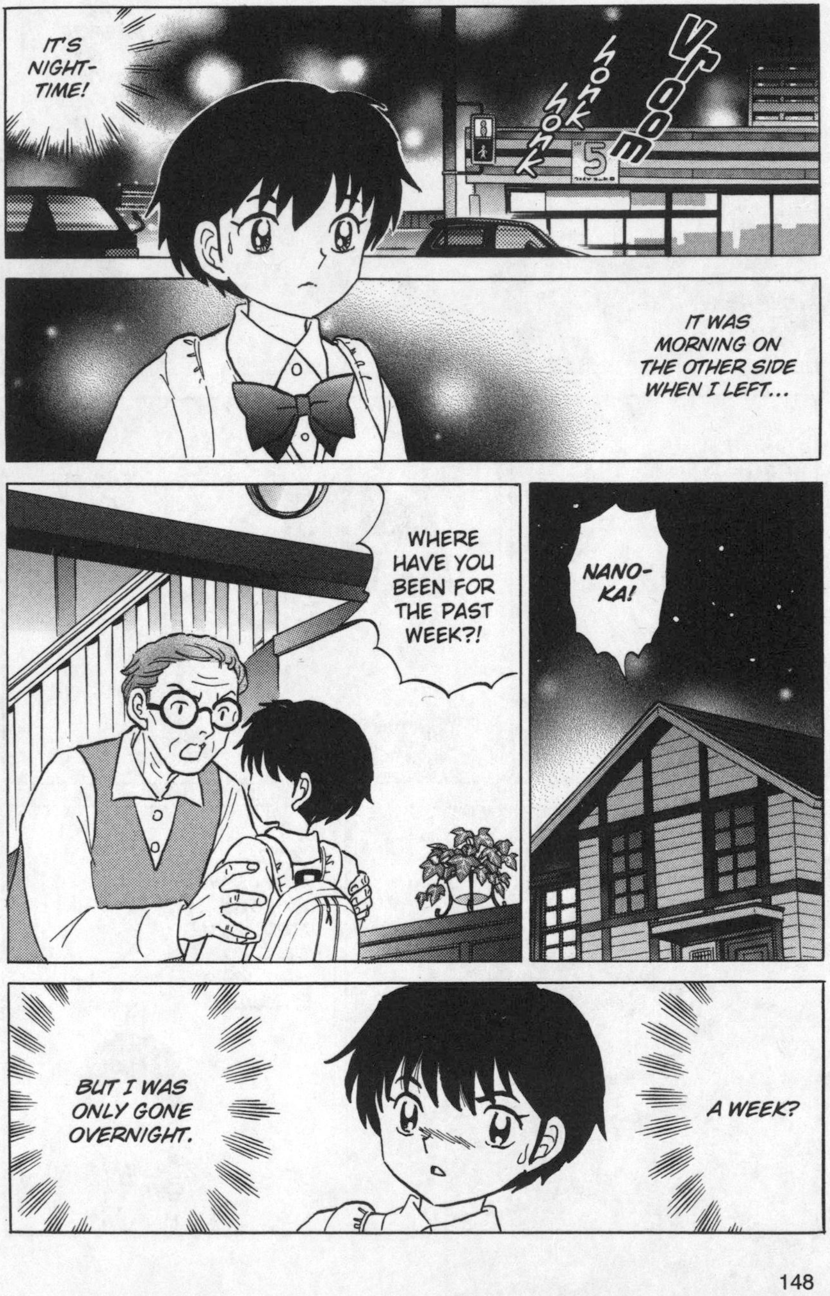
VROOM
honk honk
IT'S NIGHT-TIME!
IT WAS MORNING ON THE OTHER SIDE WHEN I LEFT...
NANO-KA!
WHERE HAVE YOU BEEN FOR THE PAST WEEK?!
A WEEK?
BUT I WAS ONLY GONE OVERNIGHT.

TIME MOVES UNPREDICTABLY BETWEEN THE TWO WORLDS...

WHAT?

UOZUMI HAS BEEN LOOKING ALL OVER FOR YOU!

YOUR GRANDFATHER COLLAPSED FROM WORRY! HE WAS AT DEATH'S DOOR!

LUCKY FOR ME, HE'S TOO RELIEVED TO BE REALLY MAD.

I'M SO SORRY, GRANDPA.

YOU'RE REALLY UNWELL, HUH?

NANOKA! YOU'RE BACK FROM THE HOSPITAL!

MORNING!

UM... YEAH.

OH...

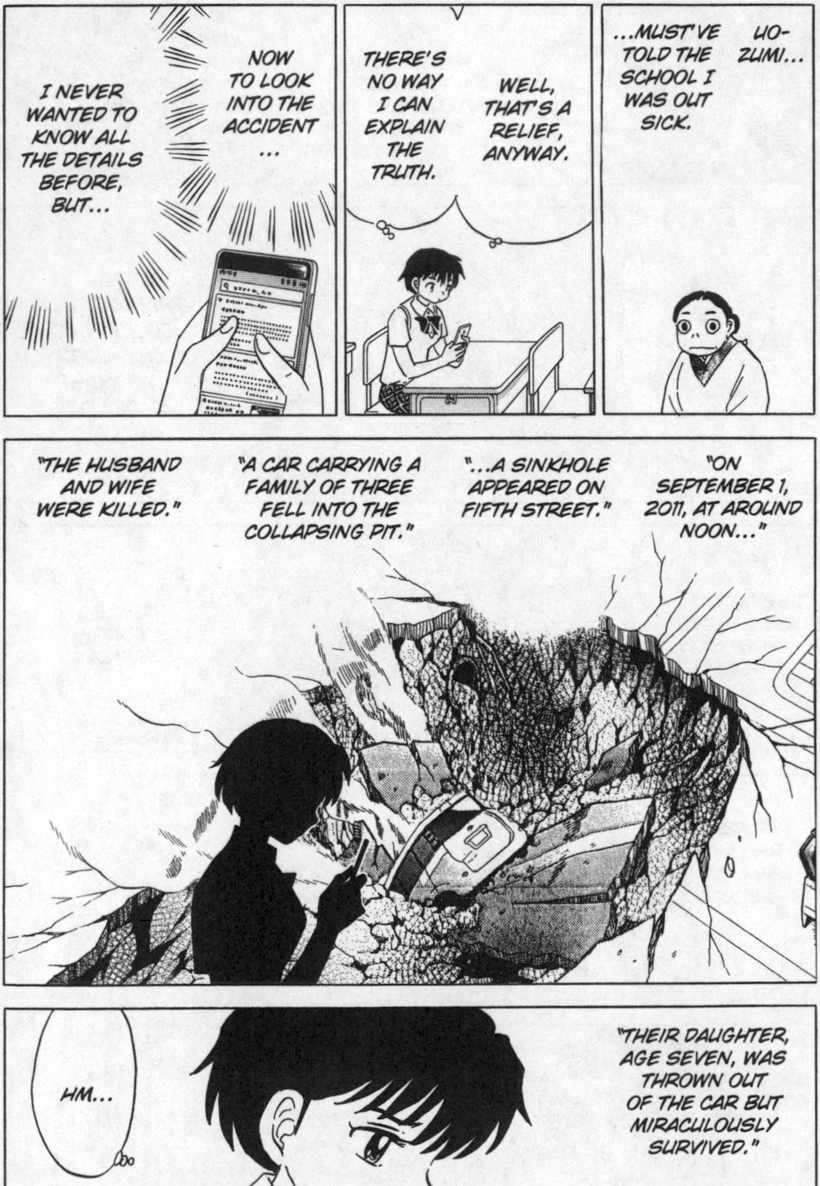
UO-ZUMI...
...MUST'VE TOLD THE SCHOOL I WAS OUT SICK.
WELL, THAT'S A RELIEF, ANYWAY.
THERE'S NO WAY I CAN EXPLAIN THE TRUTH.
NOW TO LOOK INTO THE ACCIDENT ...
I NEVER WANTED TO KNOW ALL THE DETAILS BEFORE, BUT...
"ON SEPTEMBER 1, 2011, AT AROUND NOON..."
"...A SINKHOLE APPEARED ON FIFTH STREET."
"A CAR CARRYING A FAMILY OF THREE FELL INTO THE COLLAPSING PIT."
"THE HUSBAND AND WIFE WERE KILLED."
"THEIR DAUGHTER, AGE SEVEN, WAS THROWN OUT OF THE CAR BUT MIRACULOUSLY SURVIVED."
HM...

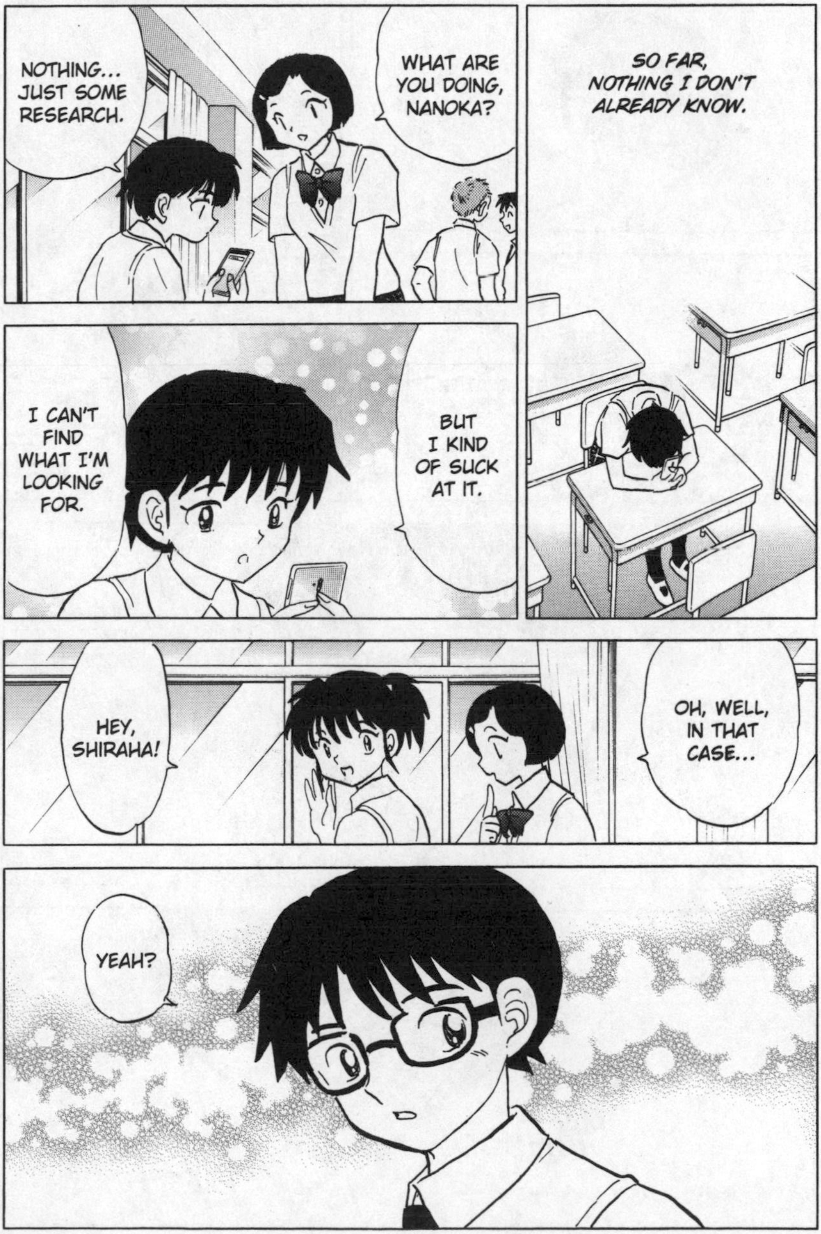
SO FAR, NOTHING I DON'T ALREADY KNOW.
WHAT ARE YOU DOING, NANOKA?
NOTHING... JUST SOME RESEARCH.
BUT I KIND OF SUCK AT IT.
I CAN'T FIND WHAT I'M LOOKING FOR.
OH, WELL, IN THAT CASE...
HEY, SHIRAHA!
YEAH?

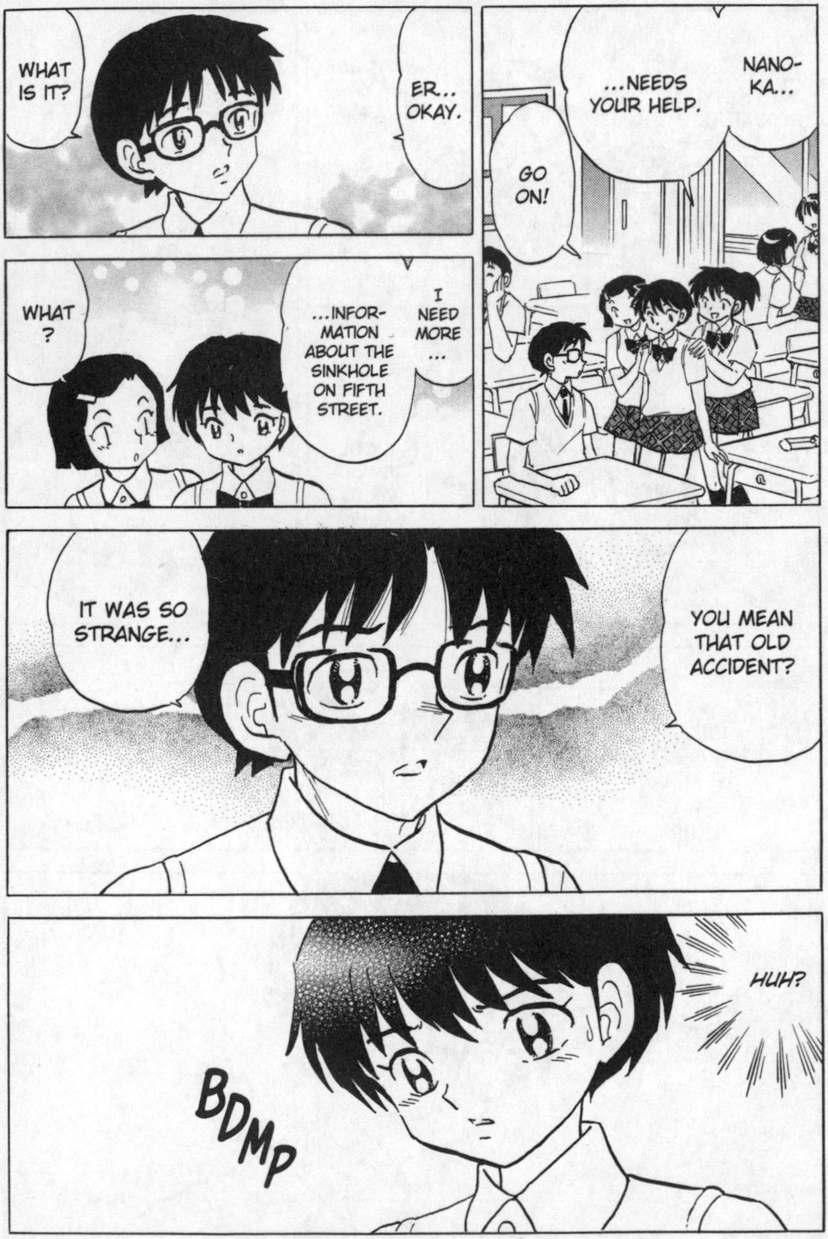
NANO-KA...
...NEEDS YOUR HELP.
GO ON!
ER... OKAY.
WHAT IS IT?
I NEED MORE ...
...INFOR-MATION ABOUT THE SINKHOLE ON FIFTH STREET.
WHAT ?
YOU MEAN THAT OLD ACCIDENT?
IT WAS SO STRANGE...
HUH?
BDMP

Chapter 7:
The Sinkhole

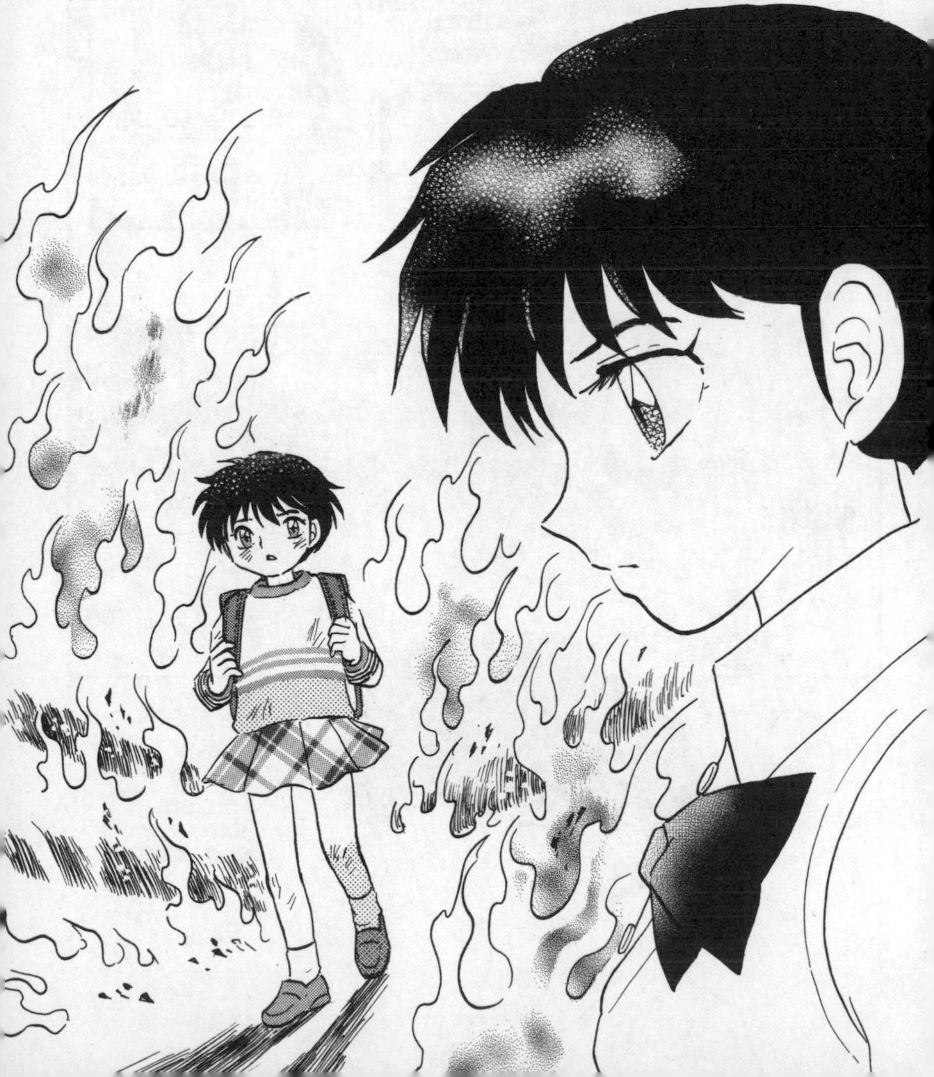

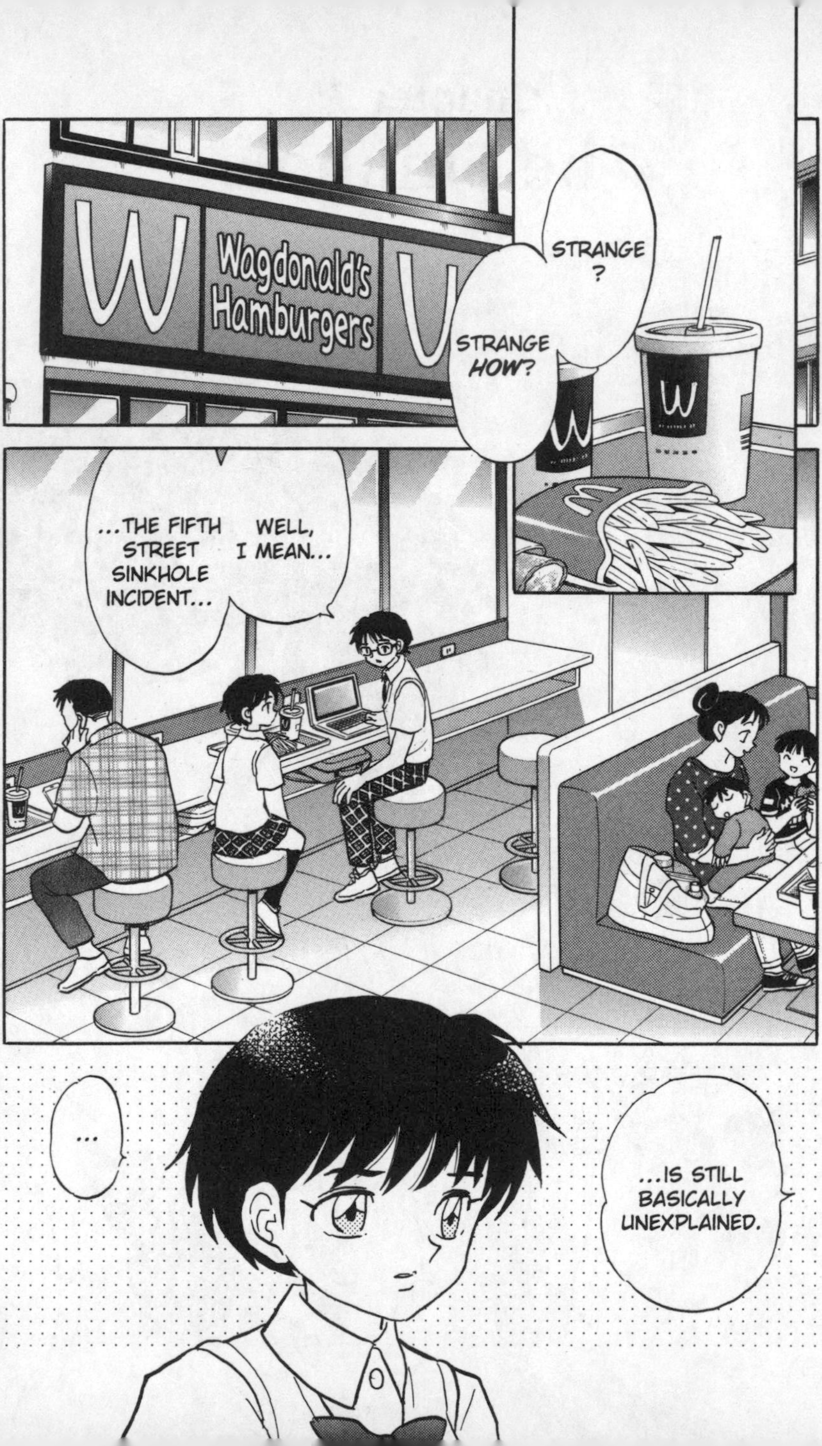
STRANGE ?
STRANGE HOW?
Wagdonald's Hamburgers
WELL, I MEAN...
...THE FIFTH STREET SINKHOLE INCIDENT...
...IS STILL BASICALLY UNEXPLAINED.
...

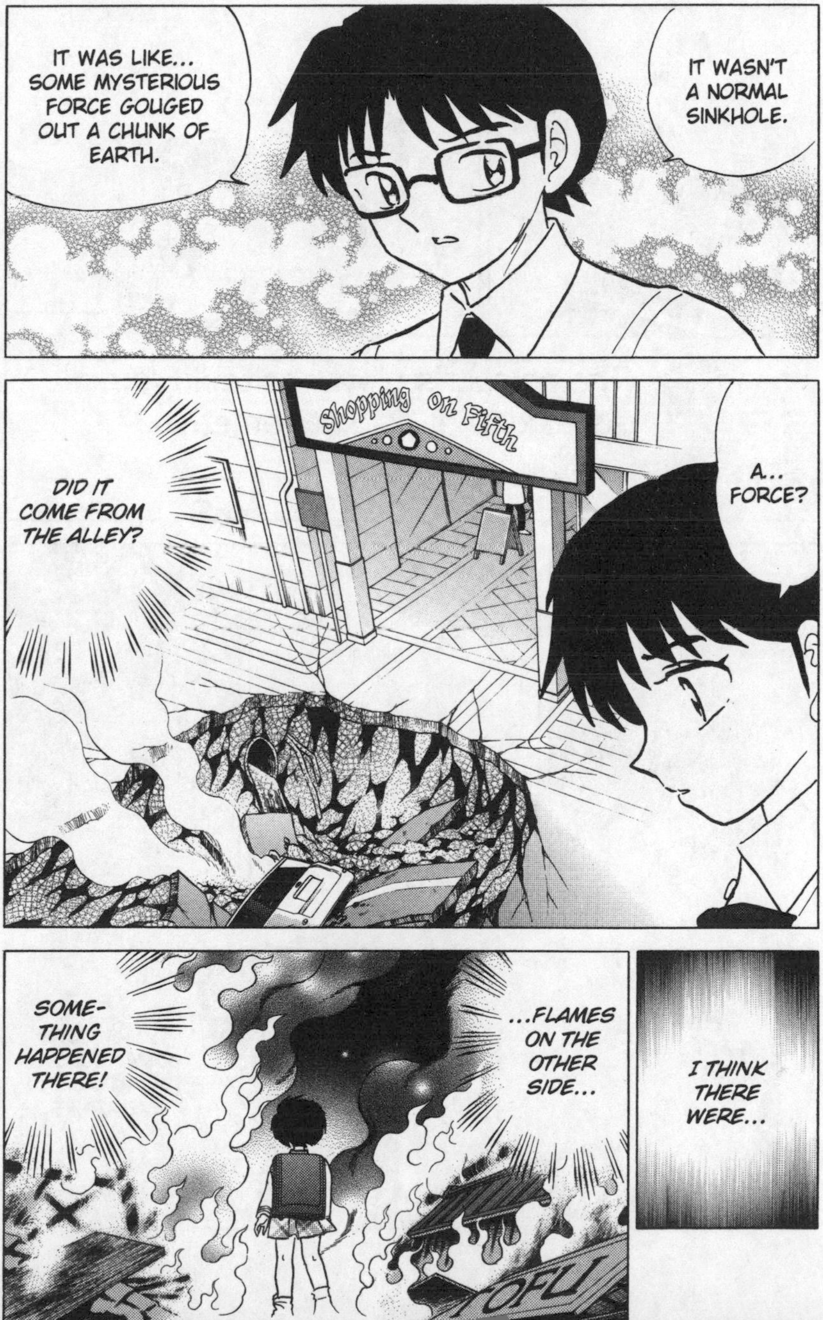
IT WASN'T A NORMAL SINKHOLE.
IT WAS LIKE... SOME MYSTERIOUS FORCE GOUGED OUT A CHUNK OF EARTH.
A... FORCE?
Shopping on Fifth
DID IT COME FROM THE ALLEY?
I THINK THERE WERE...
...FLAMES ON THE OTHER SIDE...
SOME-THING HAPPENED THERE!

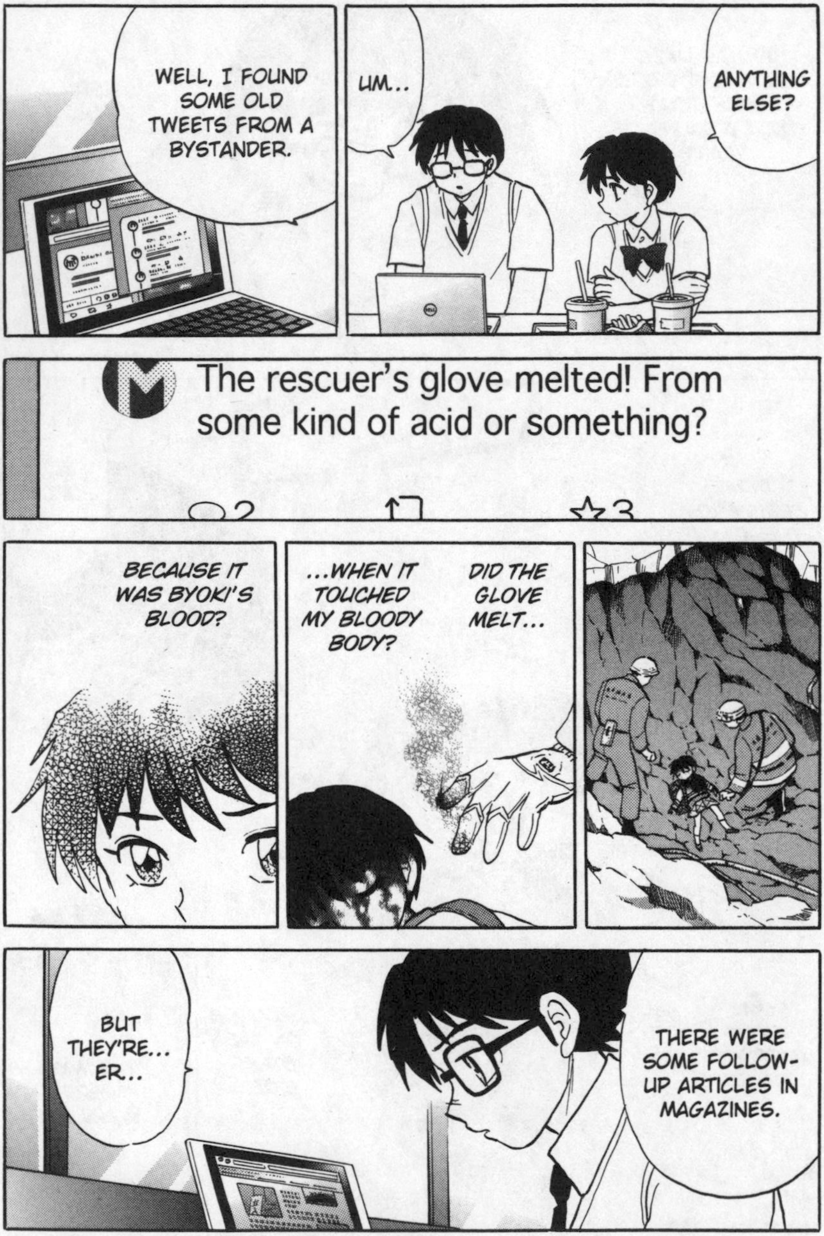
ANYTHING ELSE?
UM...
WELL, I FOUND SOME OLD TWEETS FROM A BYSTANDER.
The rescuer's glove melted! From some kind of acid or something?
2
3
DID THE GLOVE MELT...
...WHEN IT TOUCHED MY BLOODY BODY?
BECAUSE IT WAS BYOKI'S BLOOD?
THERE WERE SOME FOLLOW-UP ARTICLES IN MAGAZINES.
BUT THEY'RE... ER...

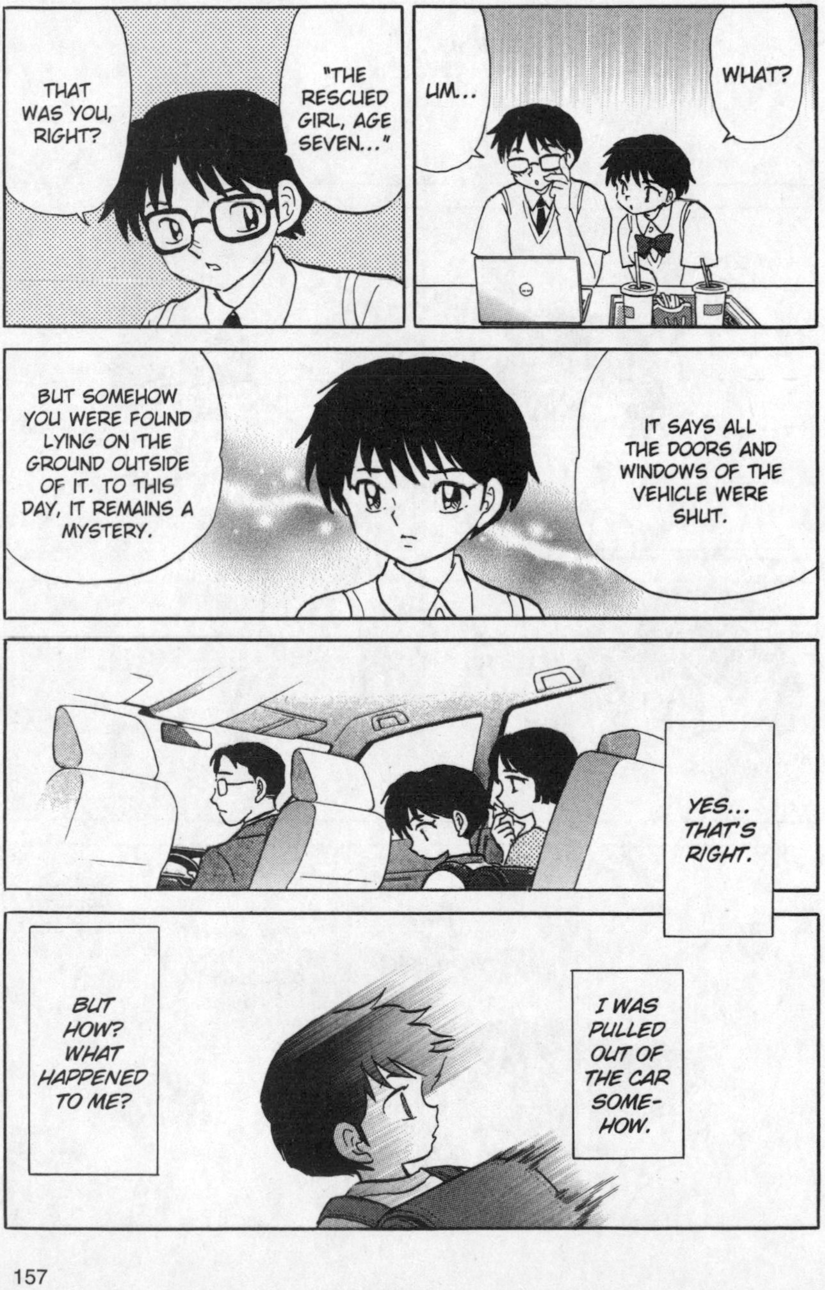
WHAT?
UM...
"THE RESCUED GIRL, AGE SEVEN..."
THAT WAS YOU, RIGHT?
IT SAYS ALL THE DOORS AND WINDOWS OF THE VEHICLE WERE SHUT.
BUT SOMEHOW YOU WERE FOUND LYING ON THE GROUND OUTSIDE OF IT. TO THIS DAY, IT REMAINS A MYSTERY.
YES... THAT'S RIGHT.
I WAS PULLED OUT OF THE CAR SOME-HOW.
BUT HOW? WHAT HAPPENED TO ME?

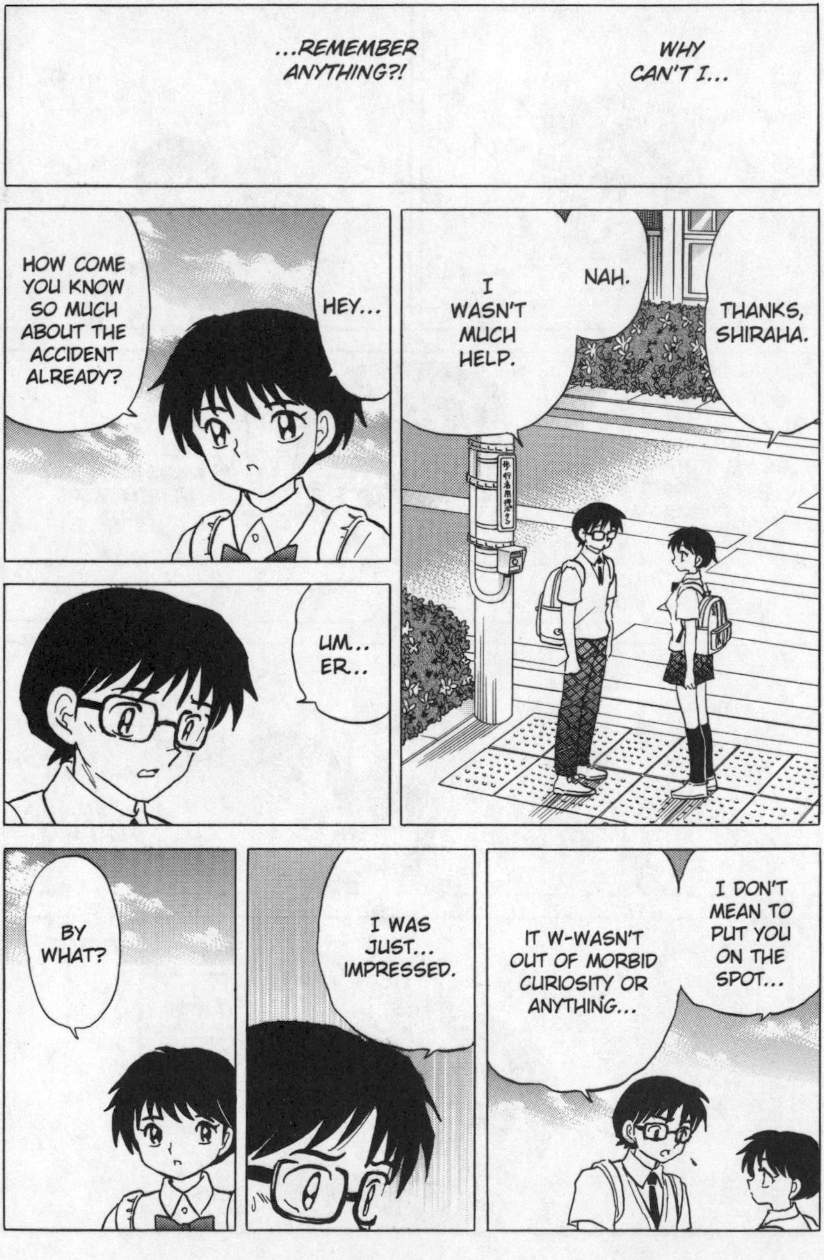
WHY CAN'T I...
...REMEMBER ANYTHING?!
THANKS, SHIRAHA.
NAH.
I WASN'T MUCH HELP.
HEY...
HOW COME YOU KNOW SO MUCH ABOUT THE ACCIDENT ALREADY?
UM... ER...
I DON'T MEAN TO PUT YOU ON THE SPOT...
IT W-WASN'T OUT OF MORBID CURIOSITY OR ANYTHING...
I WAS JUST... IMPRESSED.
BY WHAT?

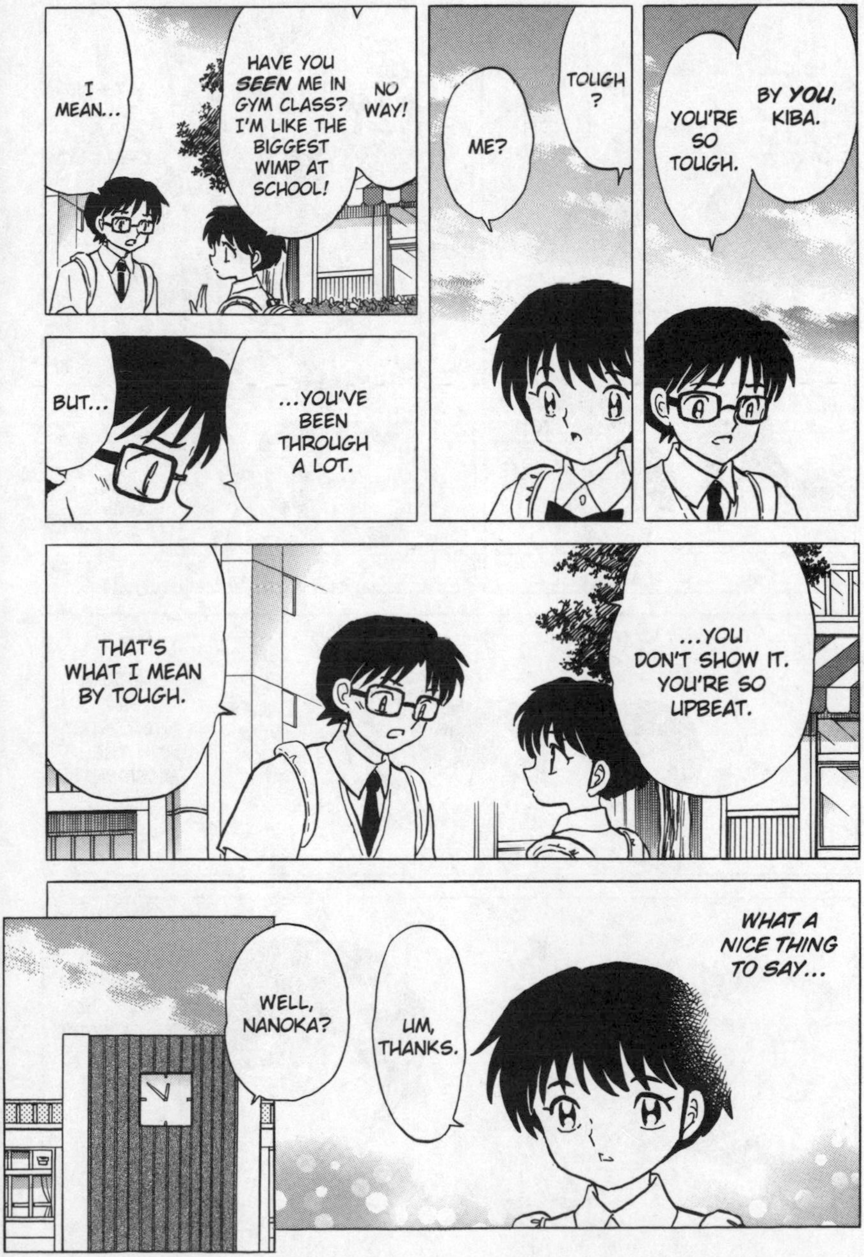
BY YOU, KIBA.
YOU'RE SO TOUGH.
TOUGH?
ME?
NO WAY!
HAVE YOU SEEN ME IN GYM CLASS? I'M LIKE THE BIGGEST WIMP AT SCHOOL!
I MEAN...
BUT...
...YOU'VE BEEN THROUGH A LOT.
...YOU DON'T SHOW IT. YOU'RE SO UPBEAT.
THAT'S WHAT I MEAN BY TOUGH.
WHAT A NICE THING TO SAY...
UM, THANKS.
WELL, NANOKA?

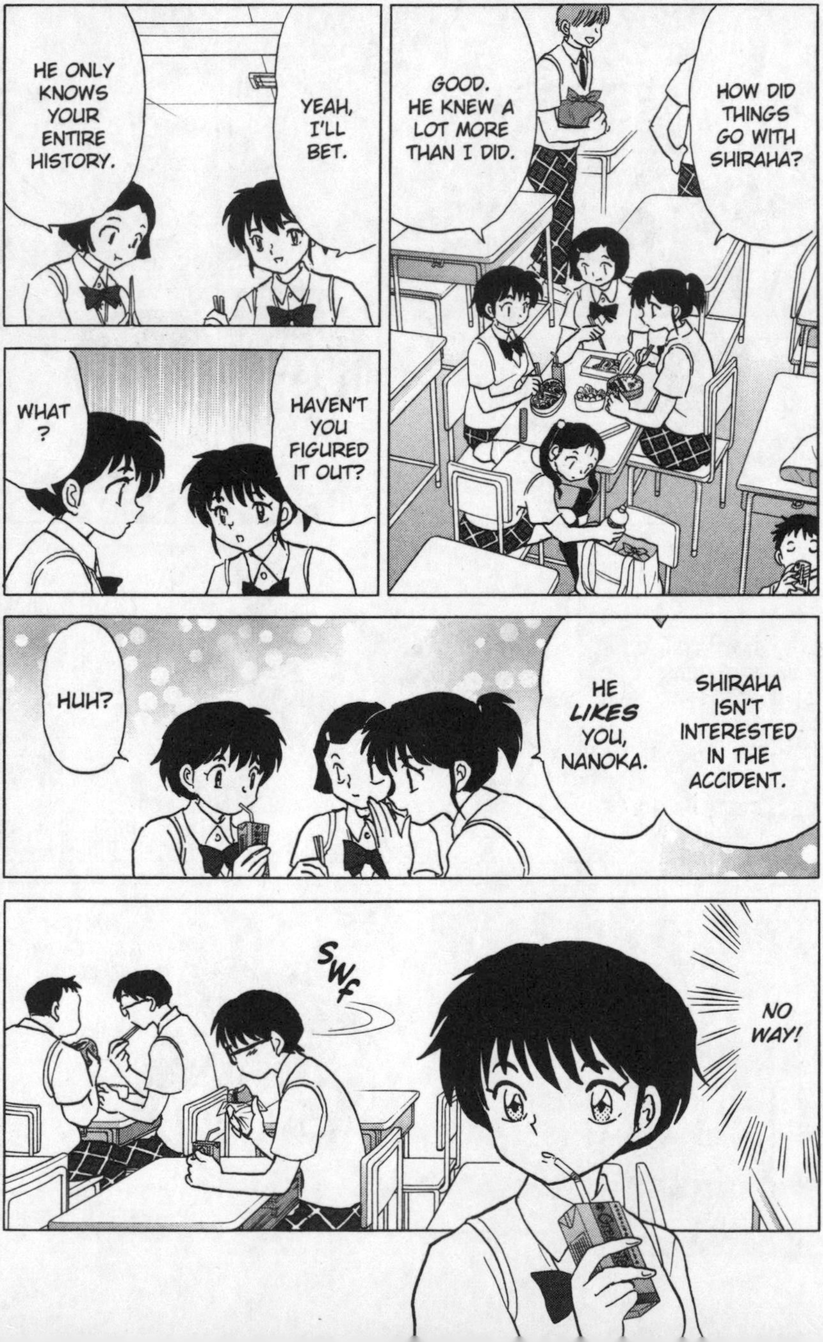
HOW DID THINGS GO WITH SHIRAHA?
GOOD. HE KNEW A LOT MORE THAN I DID.
YEAH, I'LL BET.
HE ONLY KNOWS YOUR ENTIRE HISTORY.
HAVEN'T YOU FIGURED IT OUT?
WHAT?
SHIRAHA ISN'T INTERESTED IN THE ACCIDENT.
HE *LIKES* YOU, NANOKA.
HUH?
NO WAY!
SWF

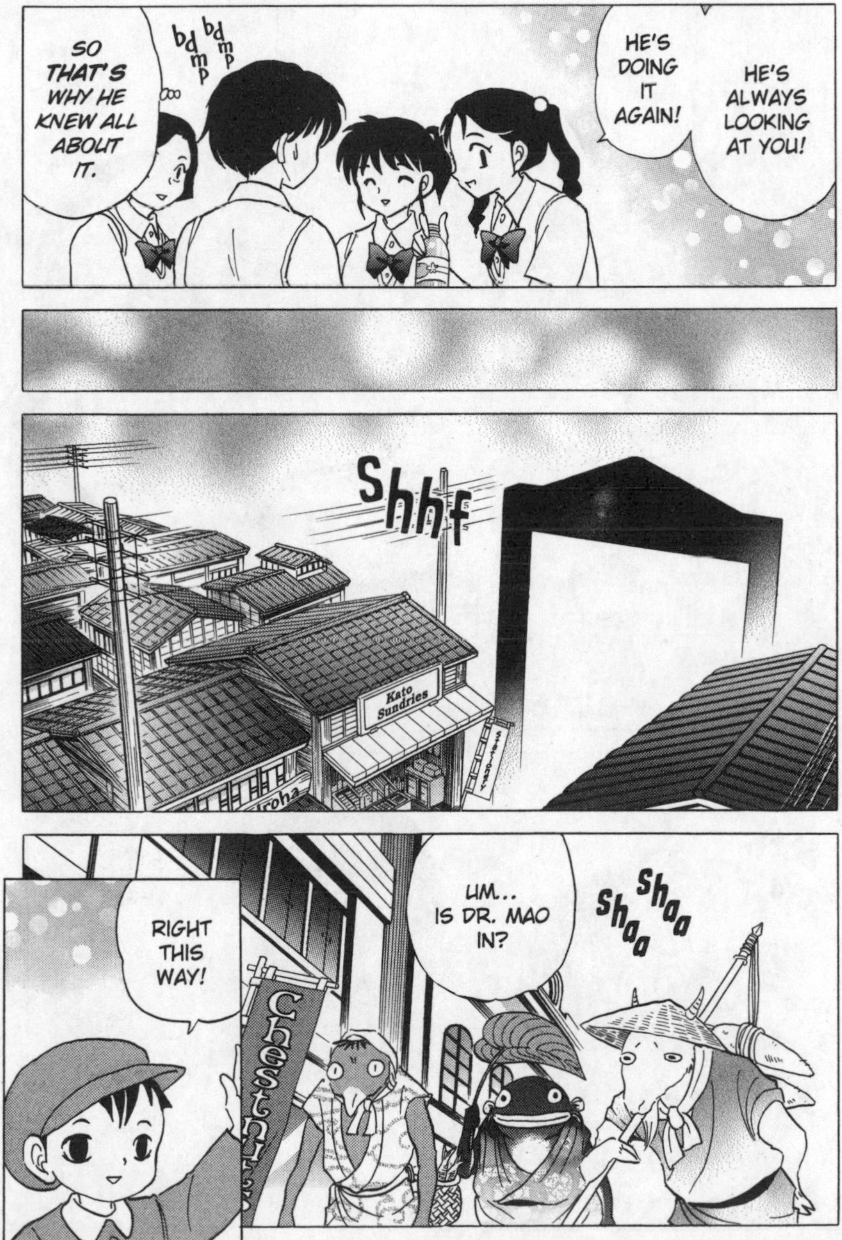
HE'S ALWAYS LOOKING AT YOU!
HE'S DOING IT AGAIN!
bdmp bdmp
SO THAT'S WHY HE KNEW ALL ABOUT IT.
Shhf
Kato Sundries
Stationery
Iroha
Shaa Shaa
UM... IS DR. MAO IN?
RIGHT THIS WAY!

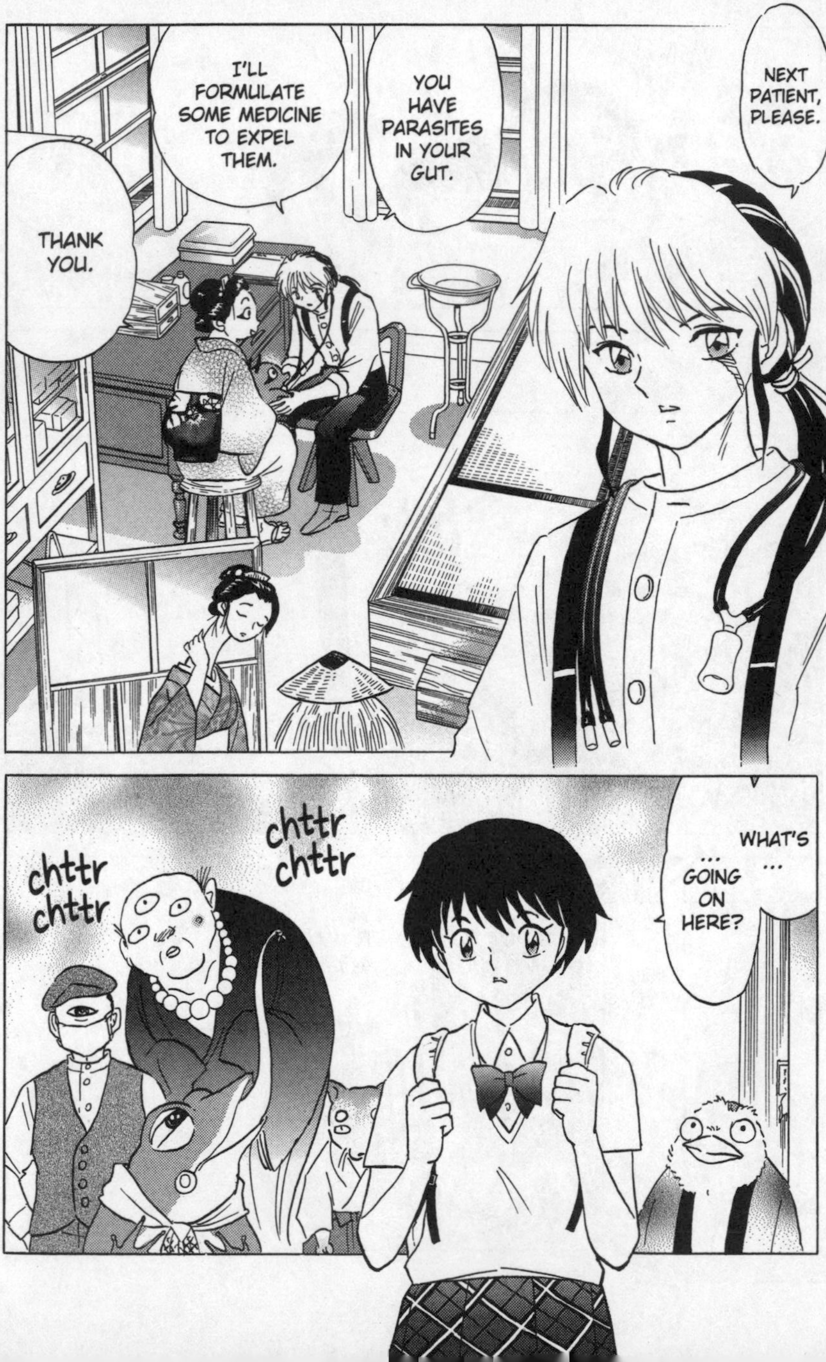
NEXT PATIENT, PLEASE.
YOU HAVE PARASITES IN YOUR GUT.
I'LL FORMULATE SOME MEDICINE TO EXPEL THEM.
THANK YOU.
WHAT'S ...
... GOING ON HERE?
chttr chttr
chttr chttr

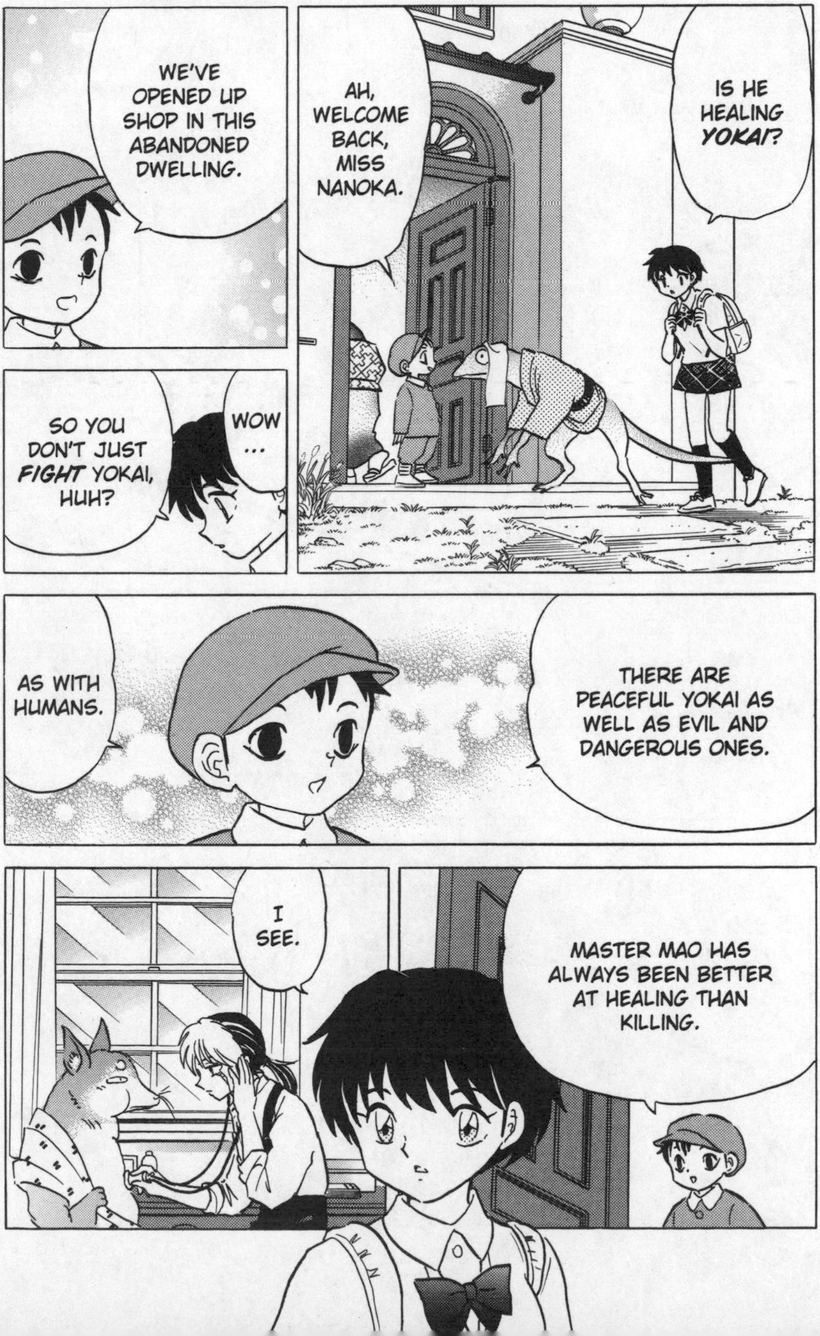
IS HE HEALING YOKAI?
AH, WELCOME BACK, MISS NANOKA.
WE'VE OPENED UP SHOP IN THIS ABANDONED DWELLING.
WOW ...
SO YOU DON'T JUST FIGHT YOKAI, HUH?
THERE ARE PEACEFUL YOKAI AS WELL AS EVIL AND DANGEROUS ONES.
AS WITH HUMANS.
MASTER MAO HAS ALWAYS BEEN BETTER AT HEALING THAN KILLING.
I SEE.

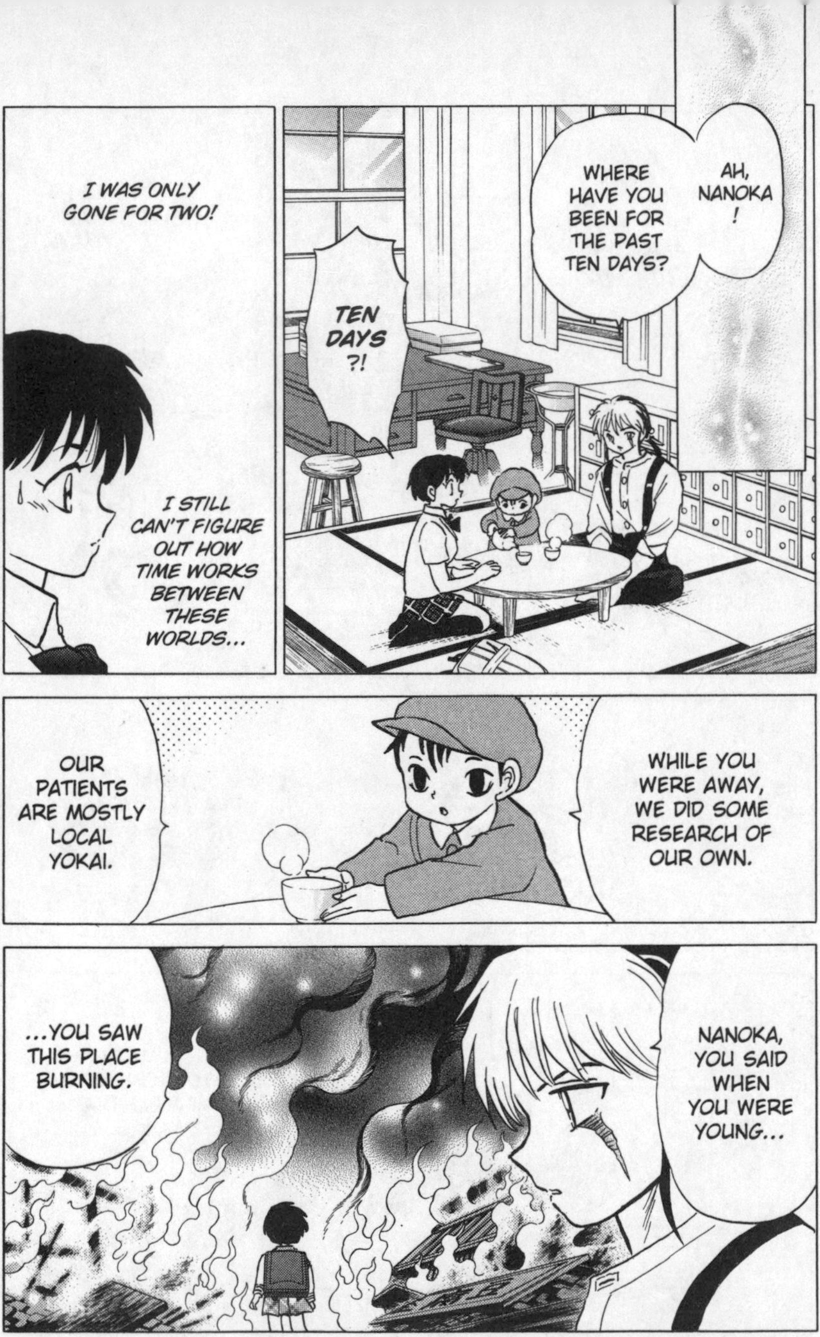
AH, NANOKA!
WHERE HAVE YOU BEEN FOR THE PAST TEN DAYS?
TEN DAYS ?!
I WAS ONLY GONE FOR TWO!
I STILL CAN'T FIGURE OUT HOW TIME WORKS BETWEEN THESE WORLDS...
WHILE YOU WERE AWAY, WE DID SOME RESEARCH OF OUR OWN.
OUR PATIENTS ARE MOSTLY LOCAL YOKAI.
NANOKA, YOU SAID WHEN YOU WERE YOUNG...
...YOU SAW THIS PLACE BURNING.

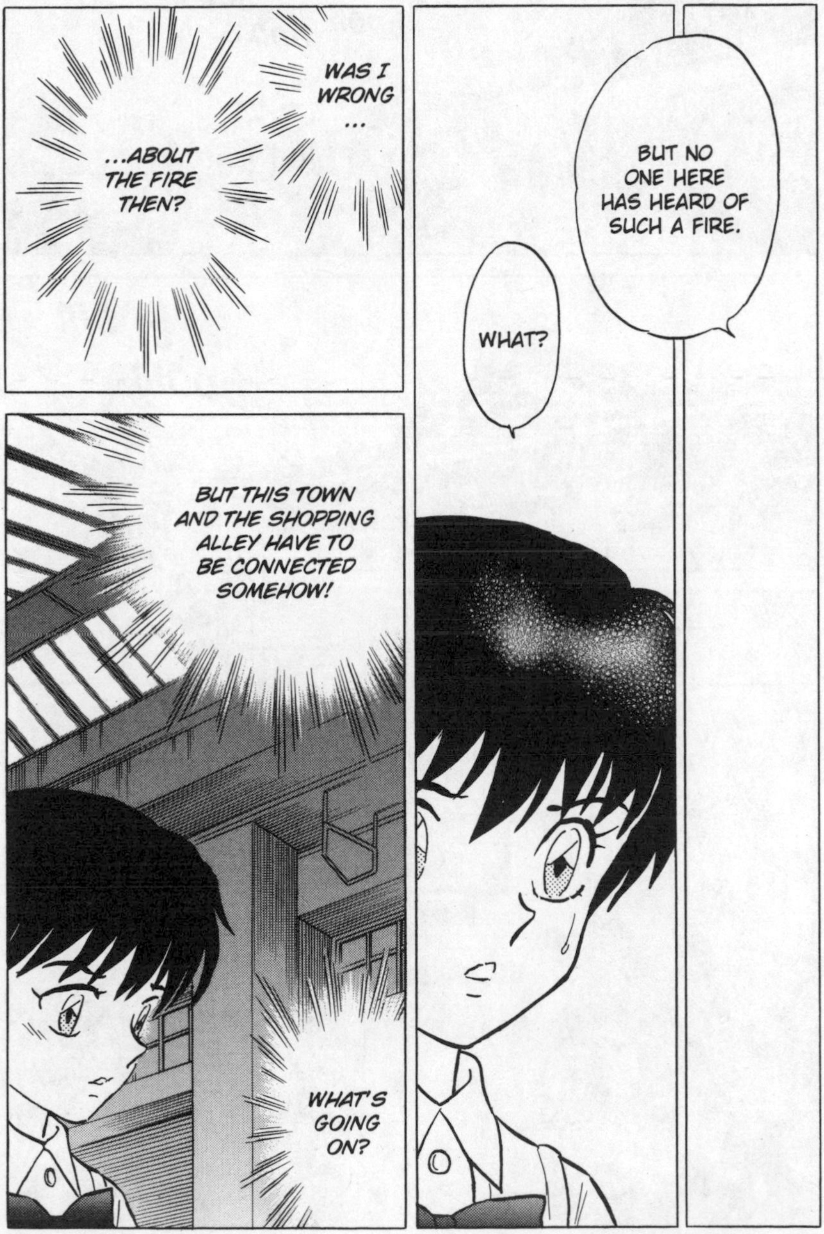
BUT NO ONE HERE HAS HEARD OF SUCH A FIRE.
WHAT?
WAS I WRONG ...
...ABOUT THE FIRE THEN?
BUT THIS TOWN AND THE SHOPPING ALLEY HAVE TO BE CONNECTED SOMEHOW!
WHAT'S GOING ON?

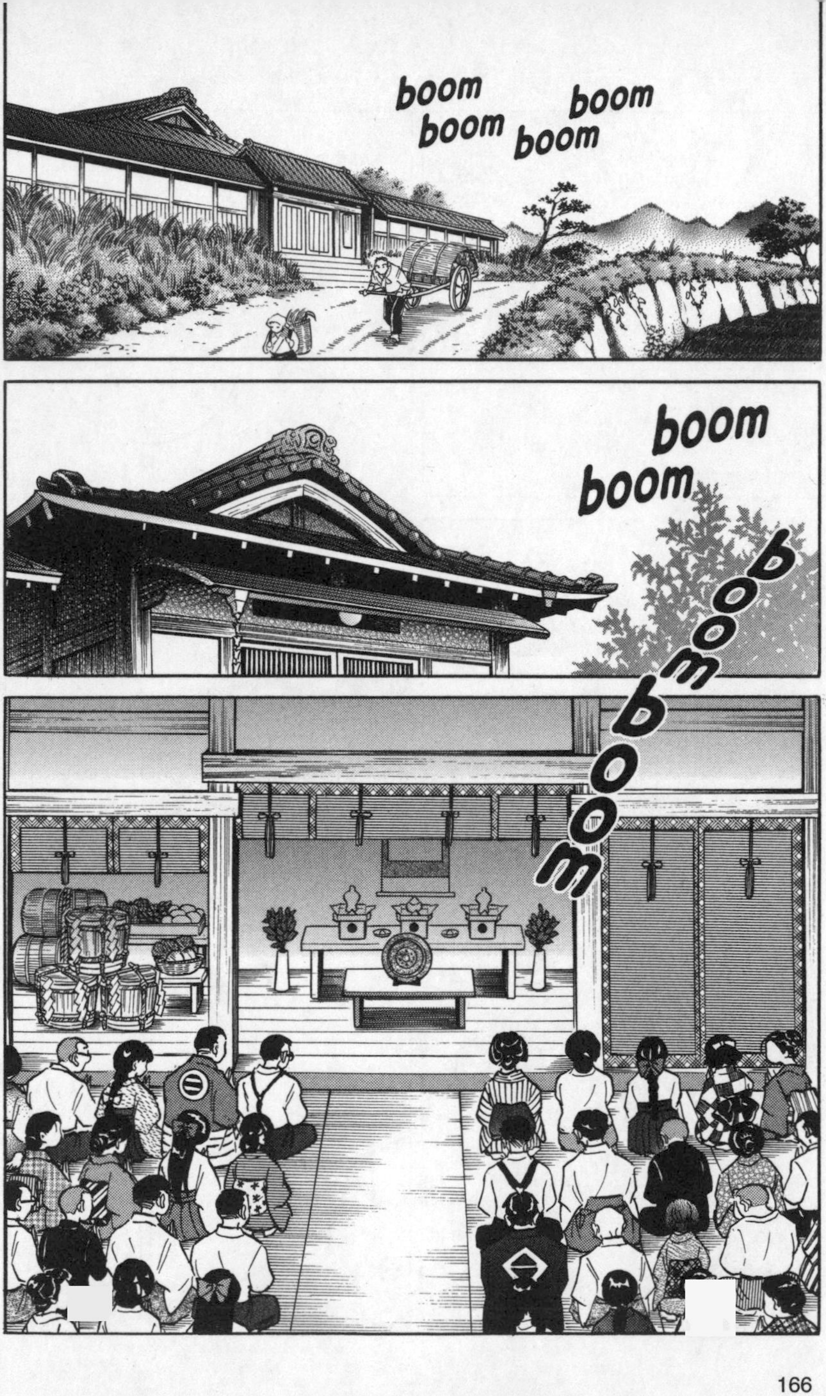
boom
boom
boom
boom
boom
boom
boom boom boom

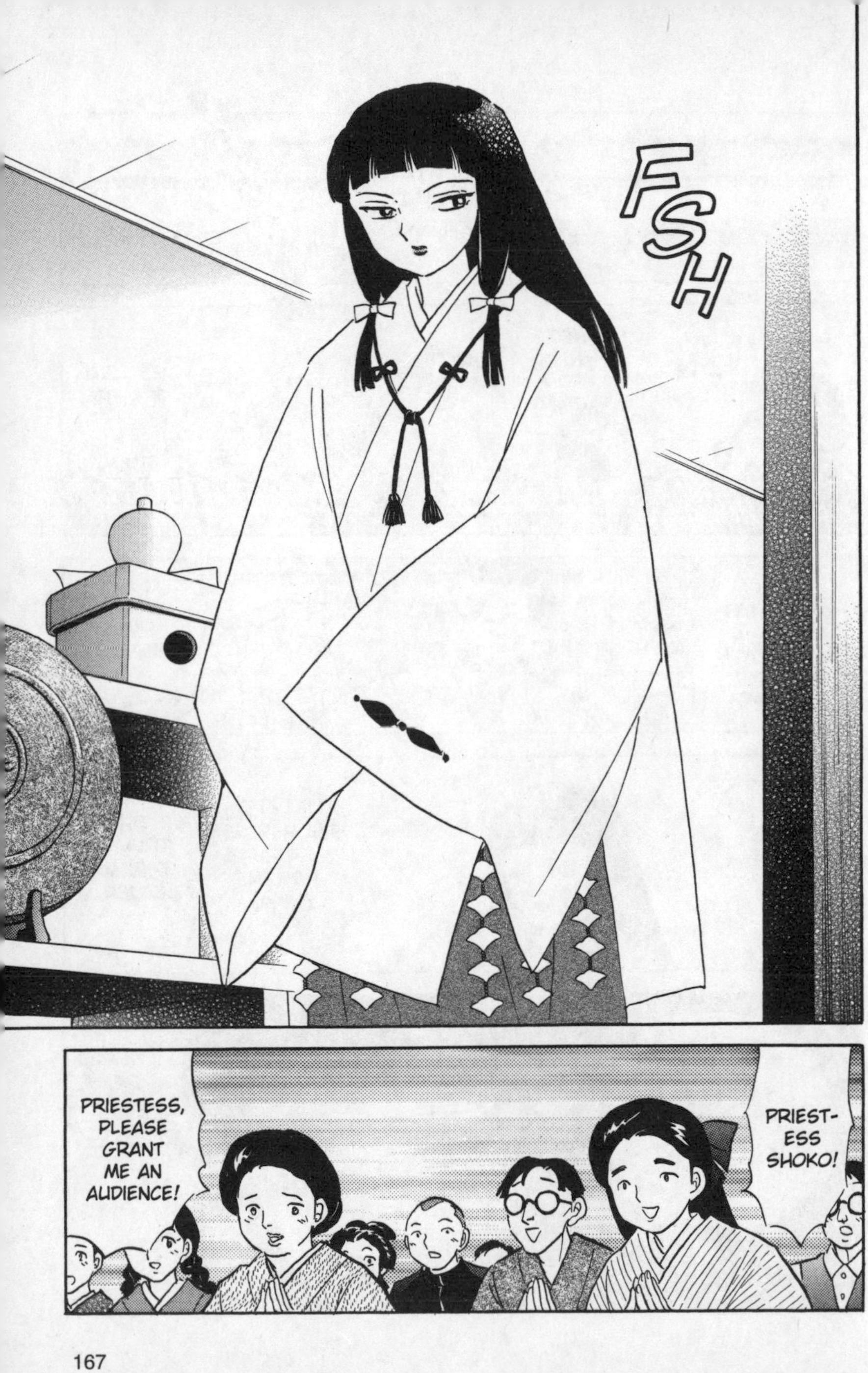
FSH
PRIEST-ESS SHOKO!
PRIESTESS, PLEASE GRANT ME AN AUDIENCE!

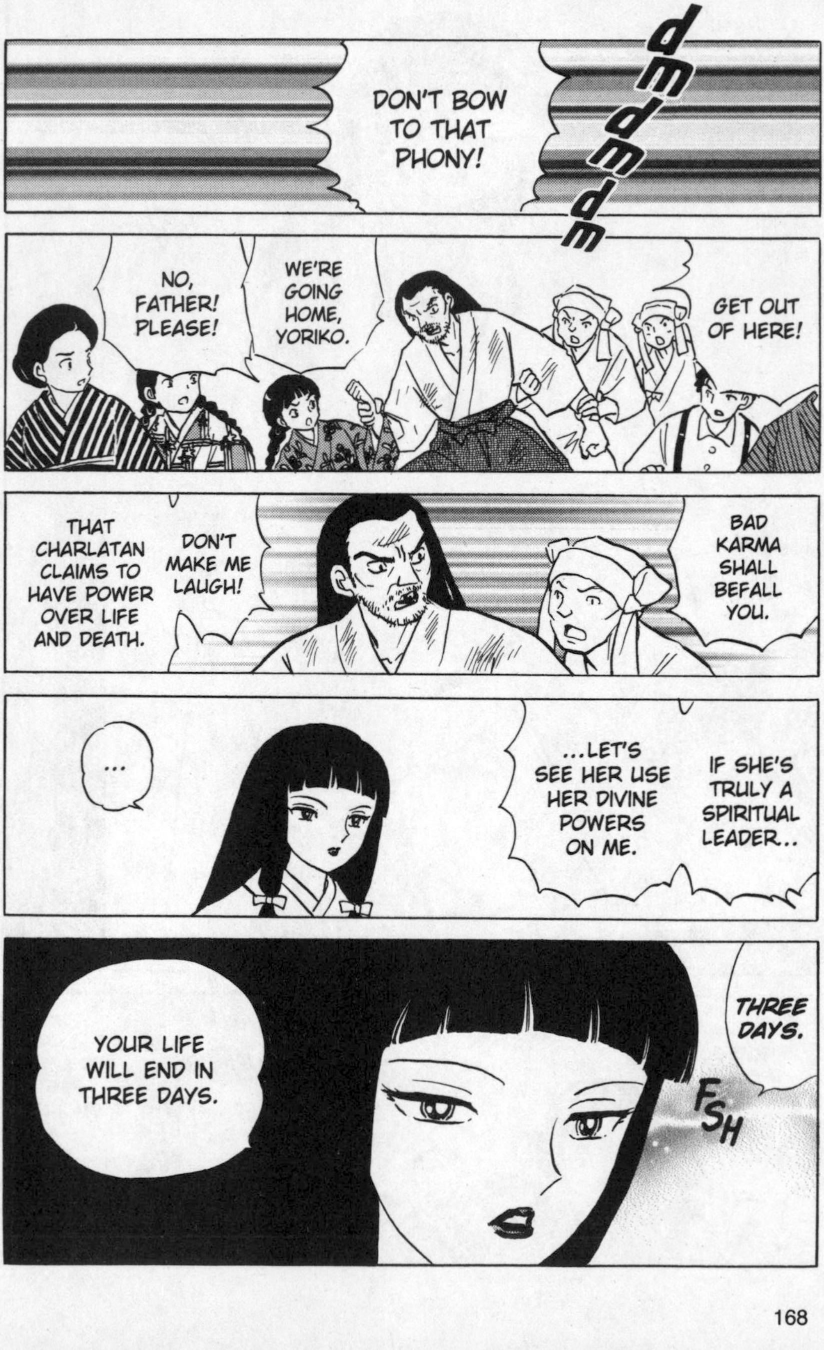
DON'T BOW TO THAT PHONY!
GET OUT OF HERE!
WE'RE GOING HOME, YORIKO.
NO, FATHER! PLEASE!
BAD KARMA SHALL BEFALL YOU.
DON'T MAKE ME LAUGH!
THAT CHARLATAN CLAIMS TO HAVE POWER OVER LIFE AND DEATH.
IF SHE'S TRULY A SPIRITUAL LEADER...
...LET'S SEE HER USE HER DIVINE POWERS ON ME.
...
THREE DAYS.
YOUR LIFE WILL END IN THREE DAYS.
FSH

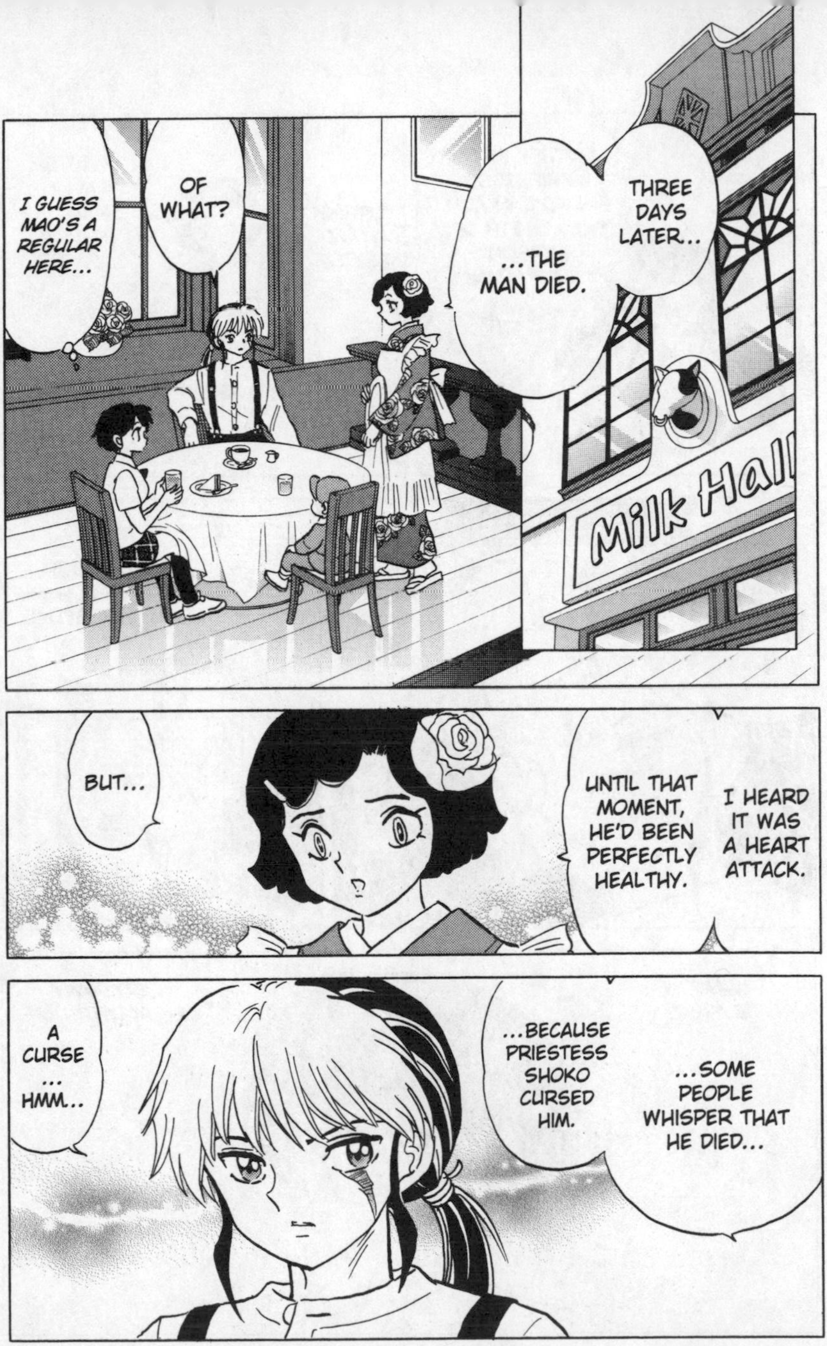
THREE DAYS LATER...
...THE MAN DIED.
OF WHAT?
I GUESS MAO'S A REGULAR HERE...
Milk Hall
I HEARD IT WAS A HEART ATTACK.
UNTIL THAT MOMENT, HE'D BEEN PERFECTLY HEALTHY.
BUT...
...SOME PEOPLE WHISPER THAT HE DIED...
...BECAUSE PRIESTESS SHOKO CURSED HIM.
A CURSE ... HMM...

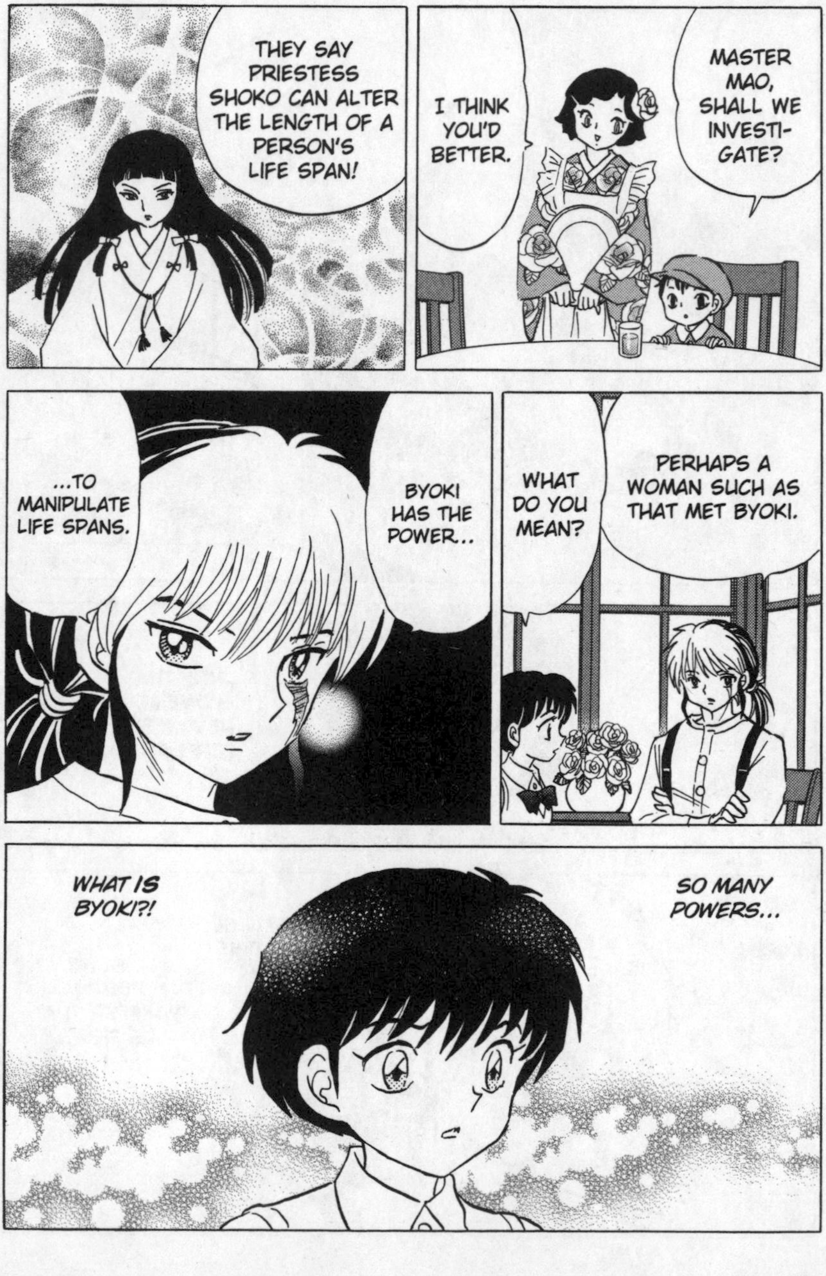
MASTER MAO, SHALL WE INVESTIGATE?
I THINK YOU'D BETTER.
THEY SAY PRIESTESS SHOKO CAN ALTER THE LENGTH OF A PERSON'S LIFE SPAN!
PERHAPS A WOMAN SUCH AS THAT MET BYOKI.
WHAT DO YOU MEAN?
BYOKI HAS THE POWER...
...TO MANIPULATE LIFE SPANS.
SO MANY POWERS...
WHAT IS BYOKI?!

Chapter 8:
Power over Life and Death

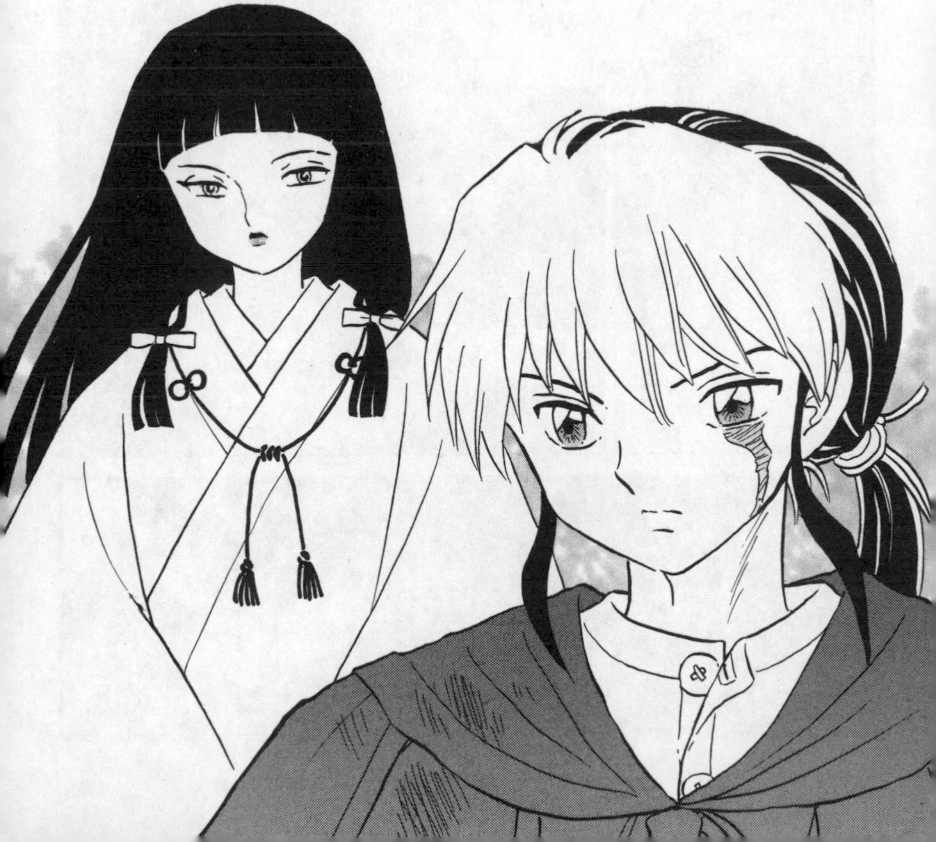

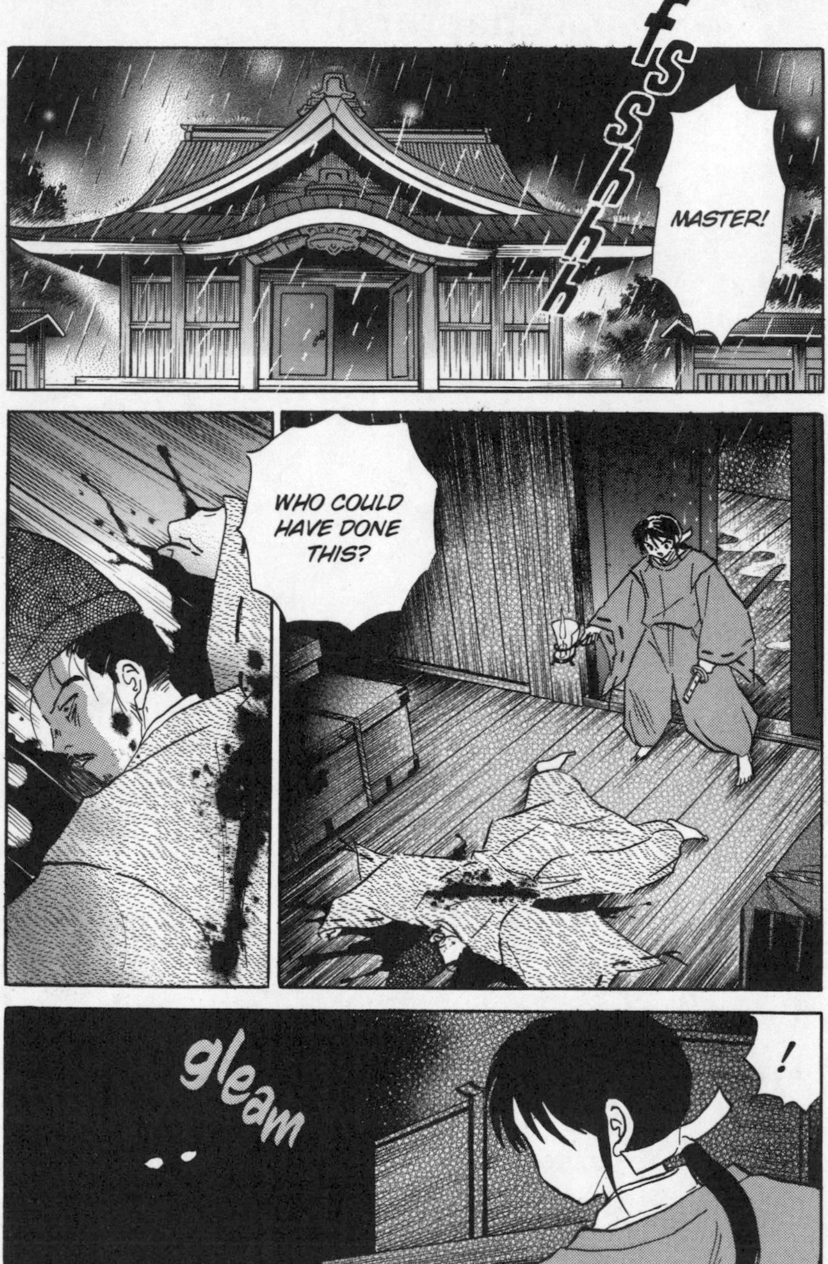
MASTER!
fsshhhh
WHO COULD HAVE DONE THIS?
!
gleam

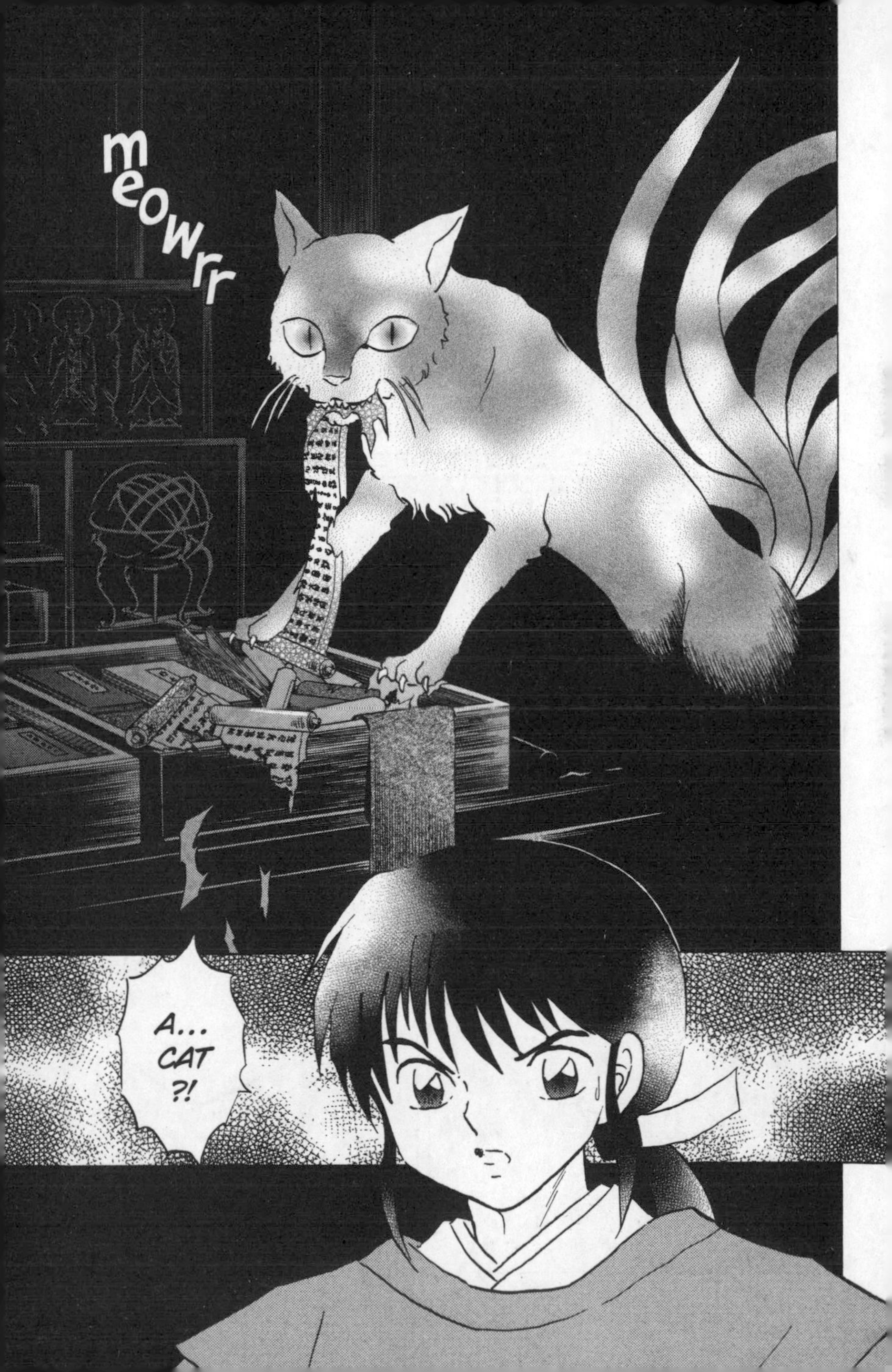
meowrr
A... CAT ?!

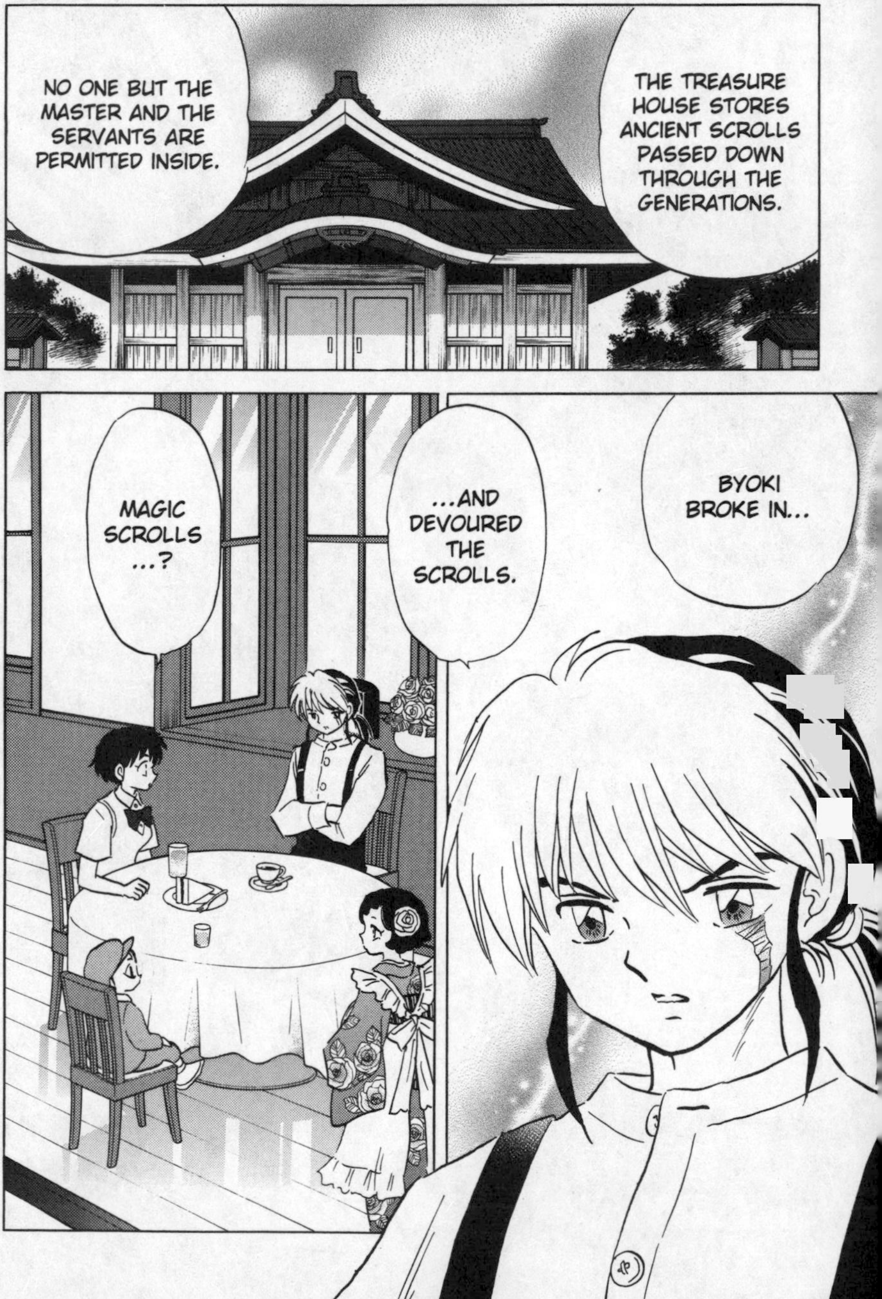
THE TREASURE HOUSE STORES ANCIENT SCROLLS PASSED DOWN THROUGH THE GENERATIONS.
NO ONE BUT THE MASTER AND THE SERVANTS ARE PERMITTED INSIDE.
BYOKI BROKE IN...
...AND DEVOURED THE SCROLLS.
MAGIC SCROLLS ...?

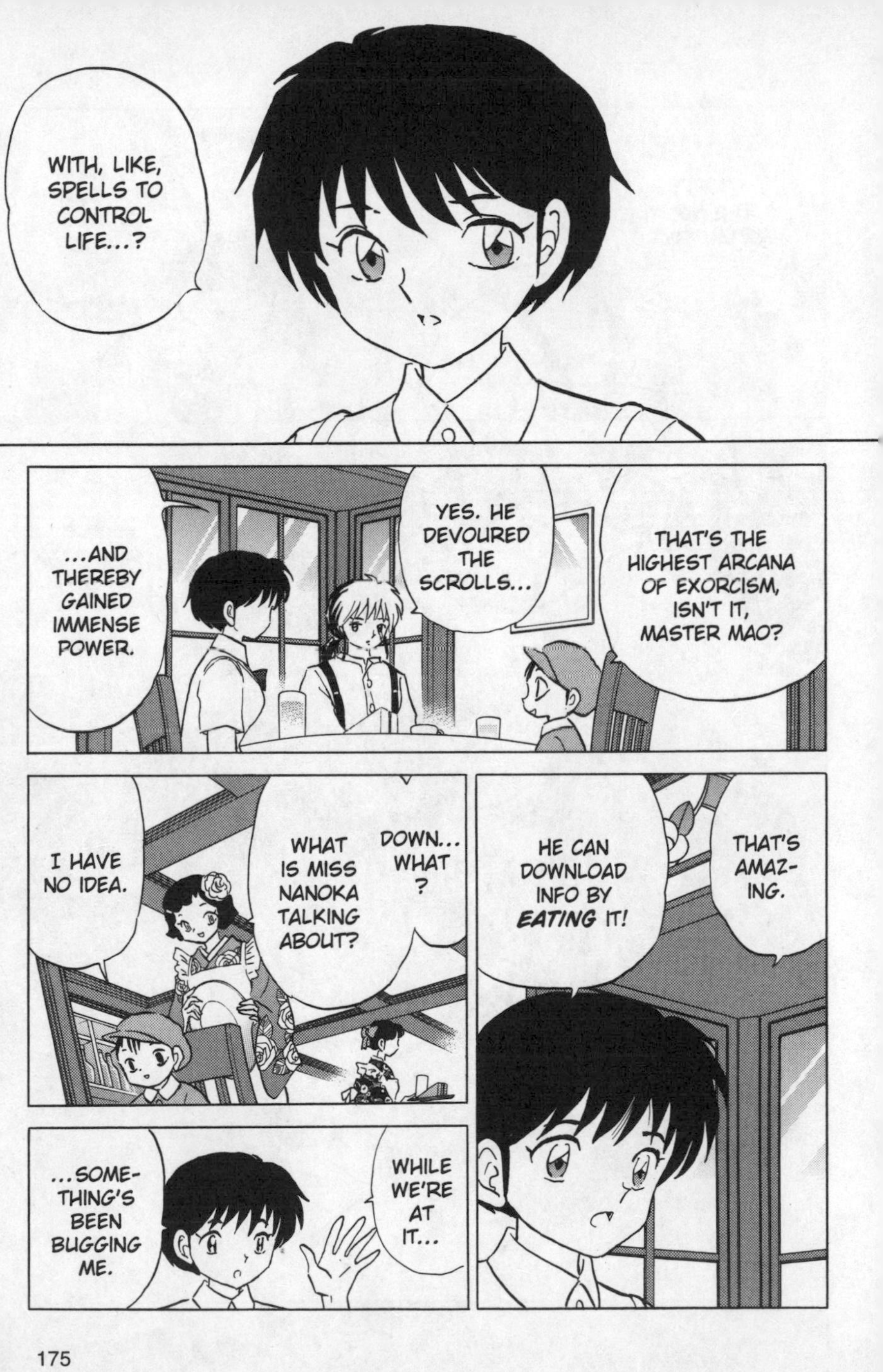
WITH, LIKE, SPELLS TO CONTROL LIFE...?
THAT'S THE HIGHEST ARCANA OF EXORCISM, ISN'T IT, MASTER MAO?
YES. HE DEVOURED THE SCROLLS...
...AND THEREBY GAINED IMMENSE POWER.
THAT'S AMAZ-ING.
HE CAN DOWNLOAD INFO BY *EATING* IT!
DOWN... WHAT?
WHAT IS MISS NANOKA TALKING ABOUT?
I HAVE NO IDEA.
WHILE WE'RE AT IT...
...SOME-THING'S BEEN BUGGING ME.

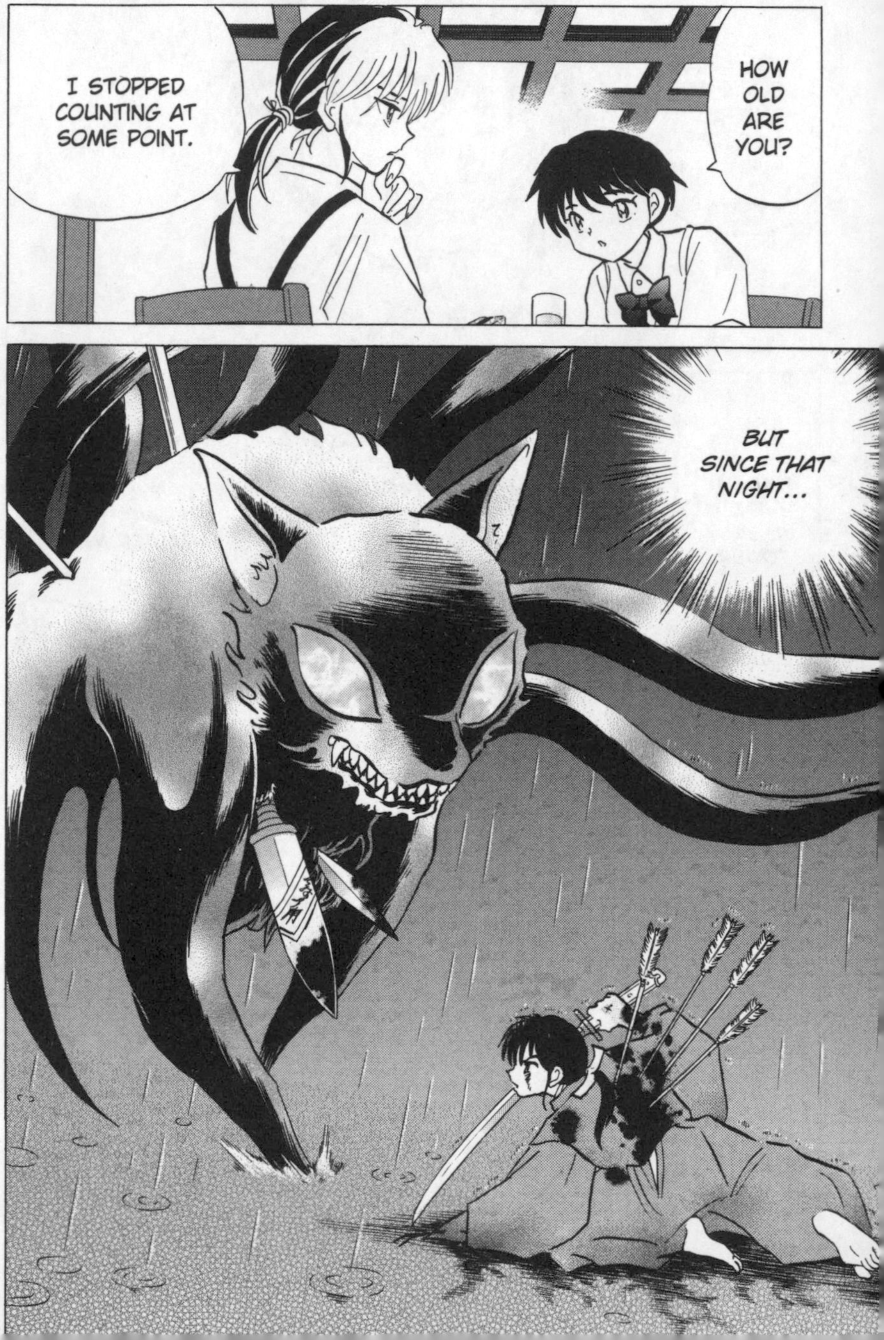
HOW OLD ARE YOU?
I STOPPED COUNTING AT SOME POINT.
BUT SINCE THAT NIGHT...

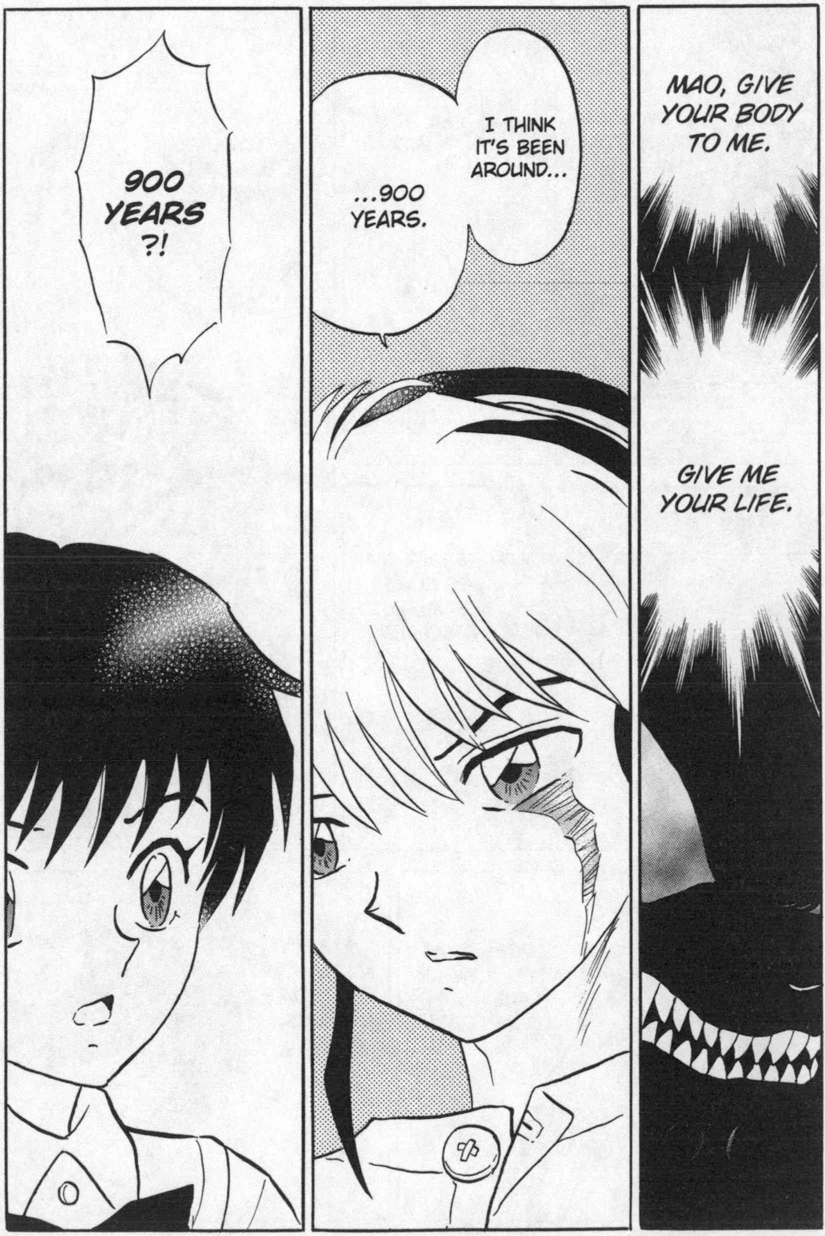
MAO, GIVE YOUR BODY TO ME.
GIVE ME YOUR LIFE.
I THINK IT'S BEEN AROUND...
...900 YEARS.
900 YEARS ?!

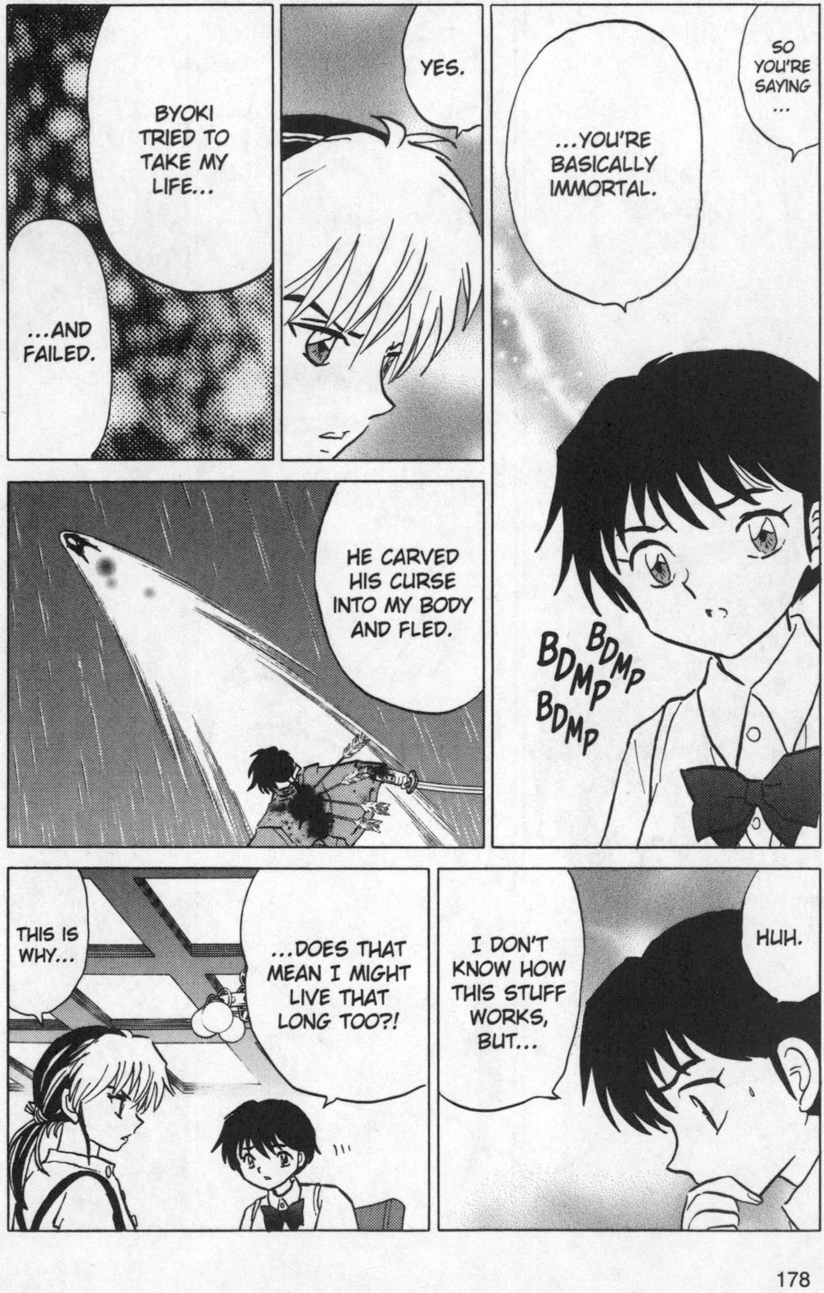
SO YOU'RE SAYING ...
...YOU'RE BASICALLY IMMORTAL.
BDMP BDMP BDMP
YES.
BYOKI TRIED TO TAKE MY LIFE...
...AND FAILED.
HE CARVED HIS CURSE INTO MY BODY AND FLED.
HUH.
I DON'T KNOW HOW THIS STUFF WORKS, BUT...
...DOES THAT MEAN I MIGHT LIVE THAT LONG TOO?!
THIS IS WHY...

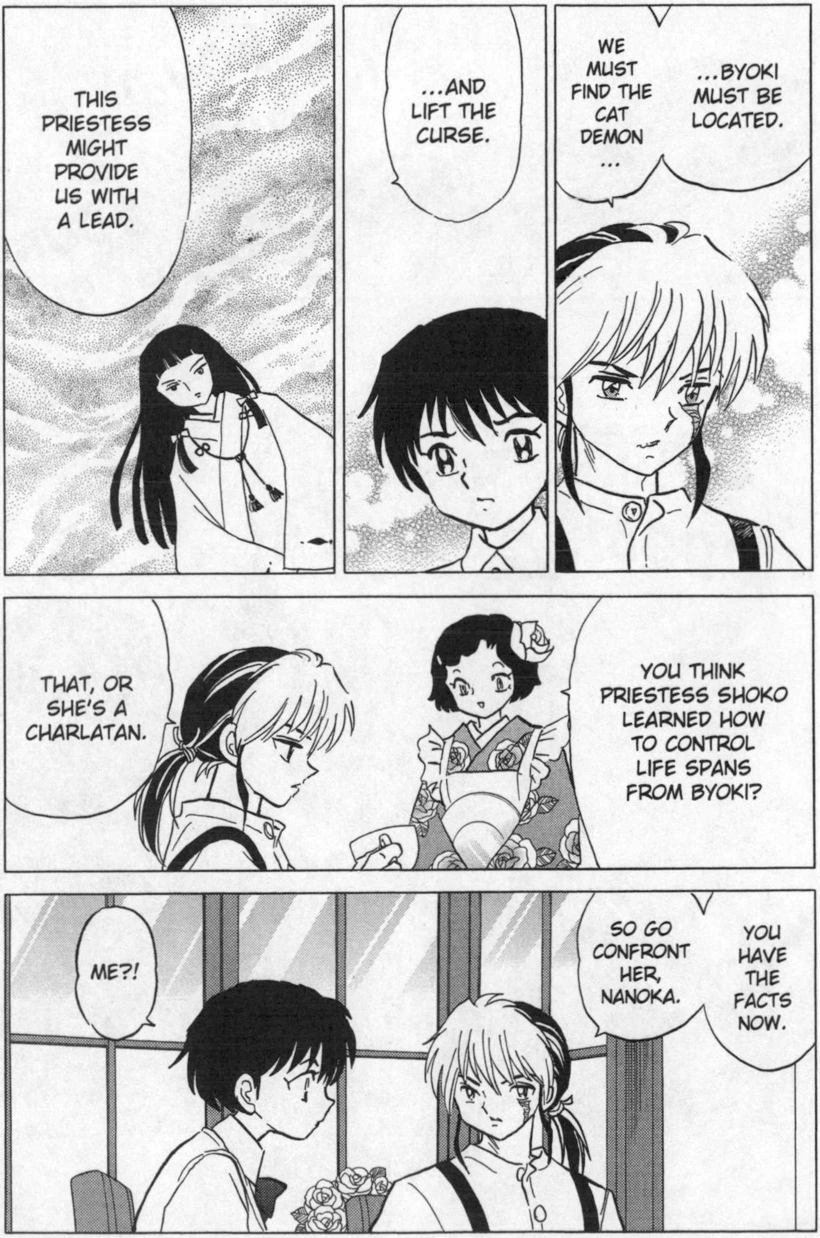
WE MUST FIND THE CAT DEMON ...
...BYOKI MUST BE LOCATED.
...AND LIFT THE CURSE.
THIS PRIESTESS MIGHT PROVIDE US WITH A LEAD.
YOU THINK PRIESTESS SHOKO LEARNED HOW TO CONTROL LIFE SPANS FROM BYOKI?
THAT, OR SHE'S A CHARLATAN.
YOU HAVE THE FACTS NOW.
SO GO CONFRONT HER, NANOKA.
ME?!

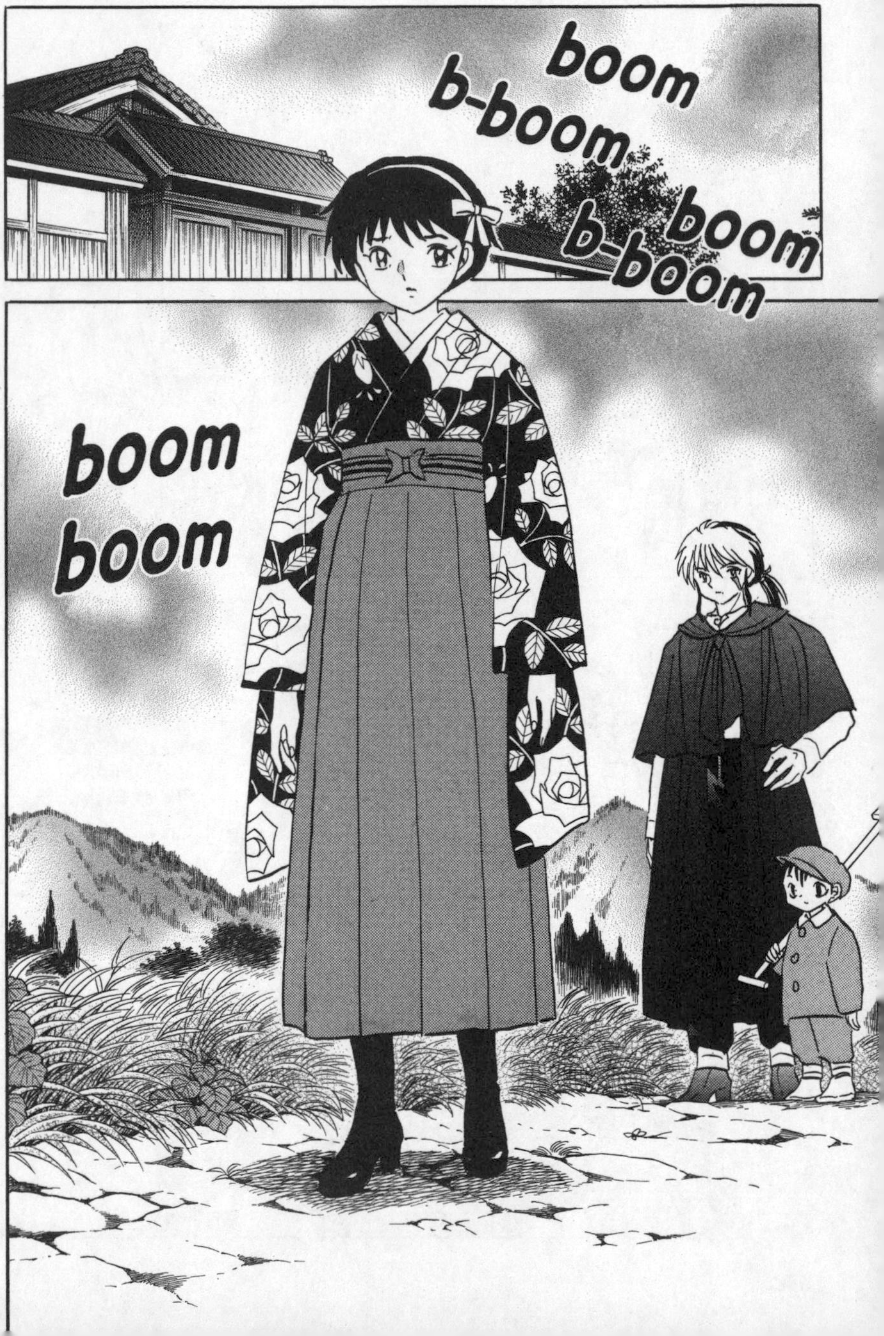
boom
b-boom
boom
b-boom
boom
boom

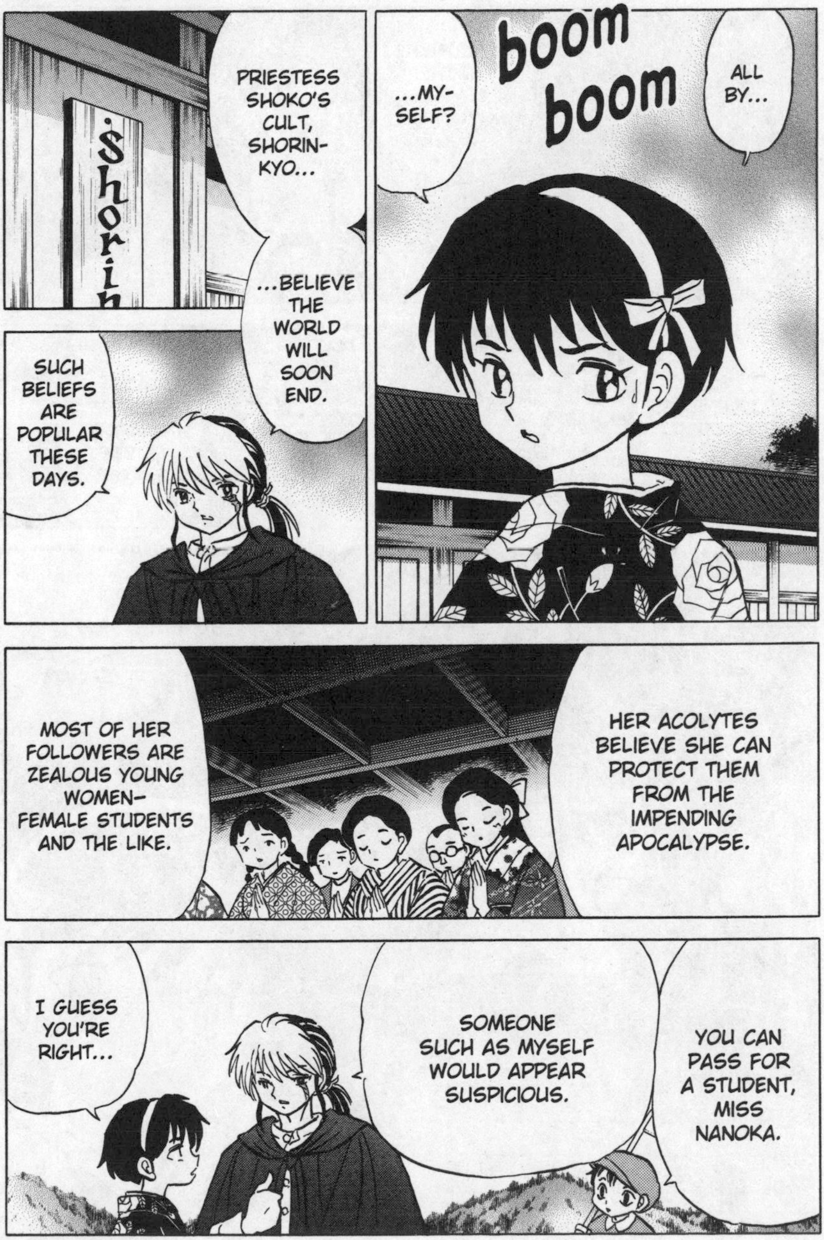
ALL BY...
boom boom
...MY-SELF?
PRIESTESS SHOKO'S CULT, SHORIN-KYO...
Shorin
...BELIEVE THE WORLD WILL SOON END.
SUCH BELIEFS ARE POPULAR THESE DAYS.
HER ACOLYTES BELIEVE SHE CAN PROTECT THEM FROM THE IMPENDING APOCALYPSE.
MOST OF HER FOLLOWERS ARE ZEALOUS YOUNG WOMEN—FEMALE STUDENTS AND THE LIKE.
YOU CAN PASS FOR A STUDENT, MISS NANOKA.
SOMEONE SUCH AS MYSELF WOULD APPEAR SUSPICIOUS.
I GUESS YOU'RE RIGHT...

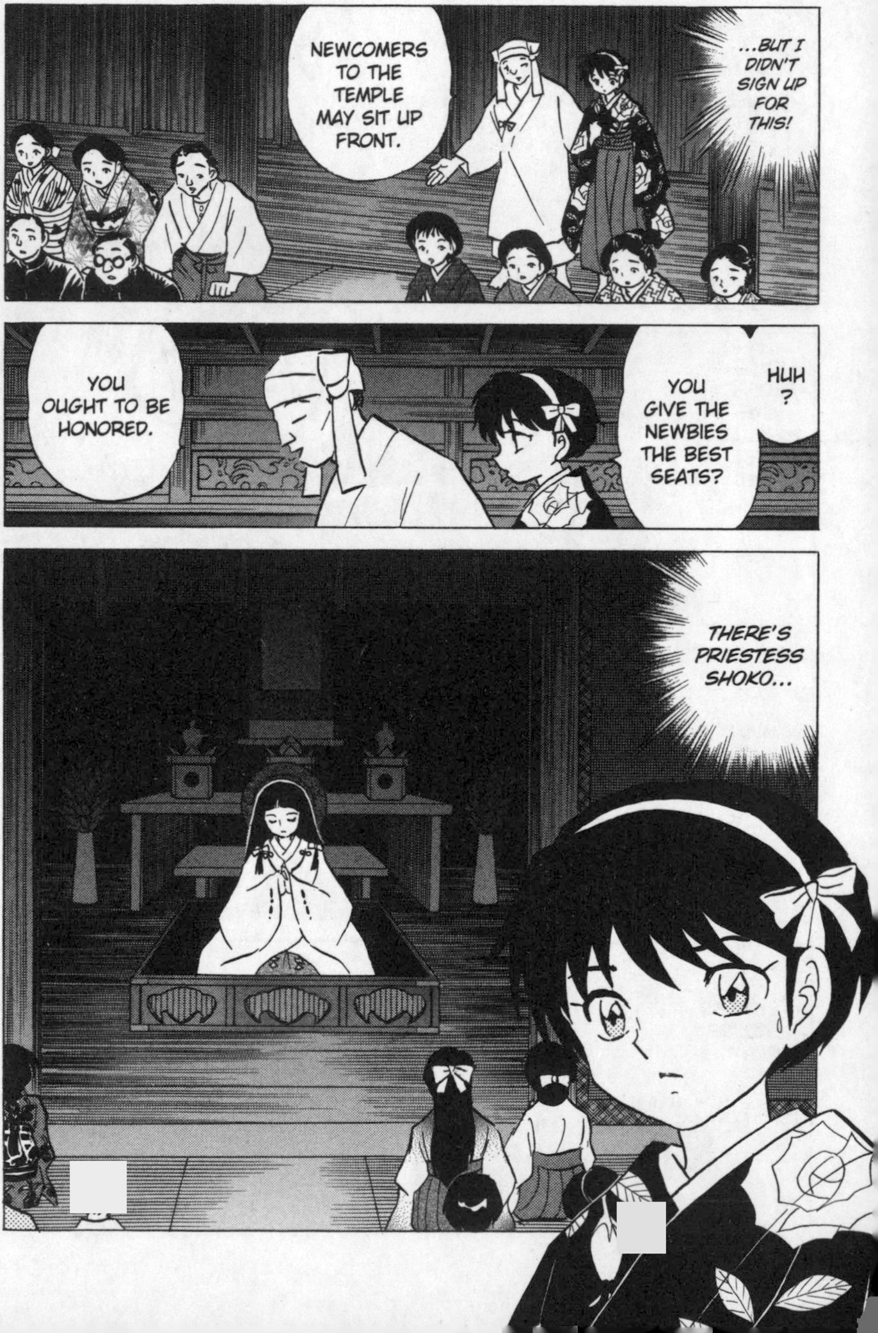
...BUT I DIDN'T SIGN UP FOR THIS!
NEWCOMERS TO THE TEMPLE MAY SIT UP FRONT.
HUH?
YOU GIVE THE NEWBIES THE BEST SEATS?
YOU OUGHT TO BE HONORED.
THERE'S PRIESTESS SHOKO...

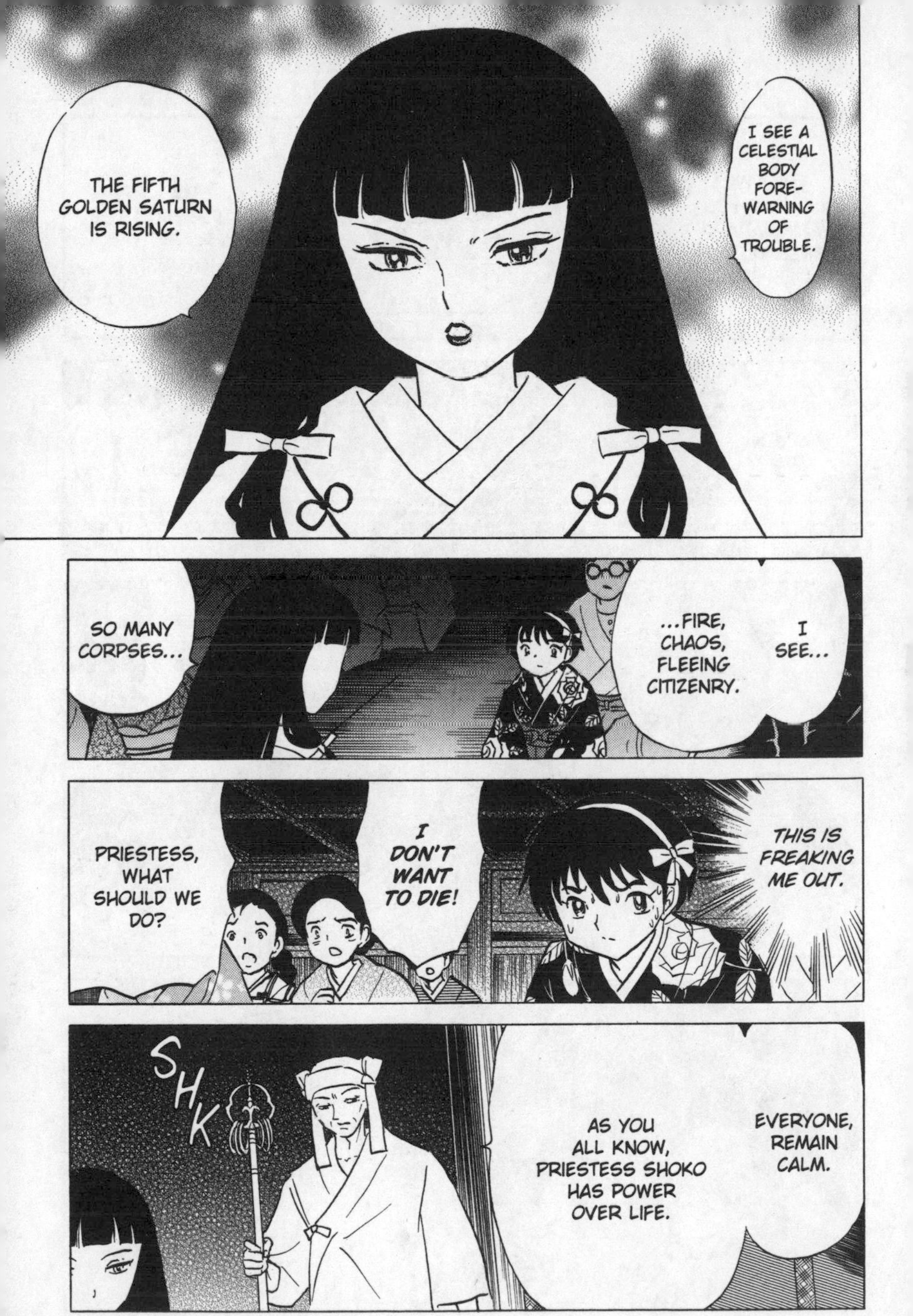
I SEE A CELESTIAL BODY FORE-WARNING OF TROUBLE.
THE FIFTH GOLDEN SATURN IS RISING.
I SEE...
...FIRE, CHAOS, FLEEING CITIZENRY.
SO MANY CORPSES...
THIS IS FREAKING ME OUT.
I DON'T WANT TO DIE!
PRIESTESS, WHAT SHOULD WE DO?
EVERYONE, REMAIN CALM.
AS YOU ALL KNOW, PRIESTESS SHOKO HAS POWER OVER LIFE.
SHK

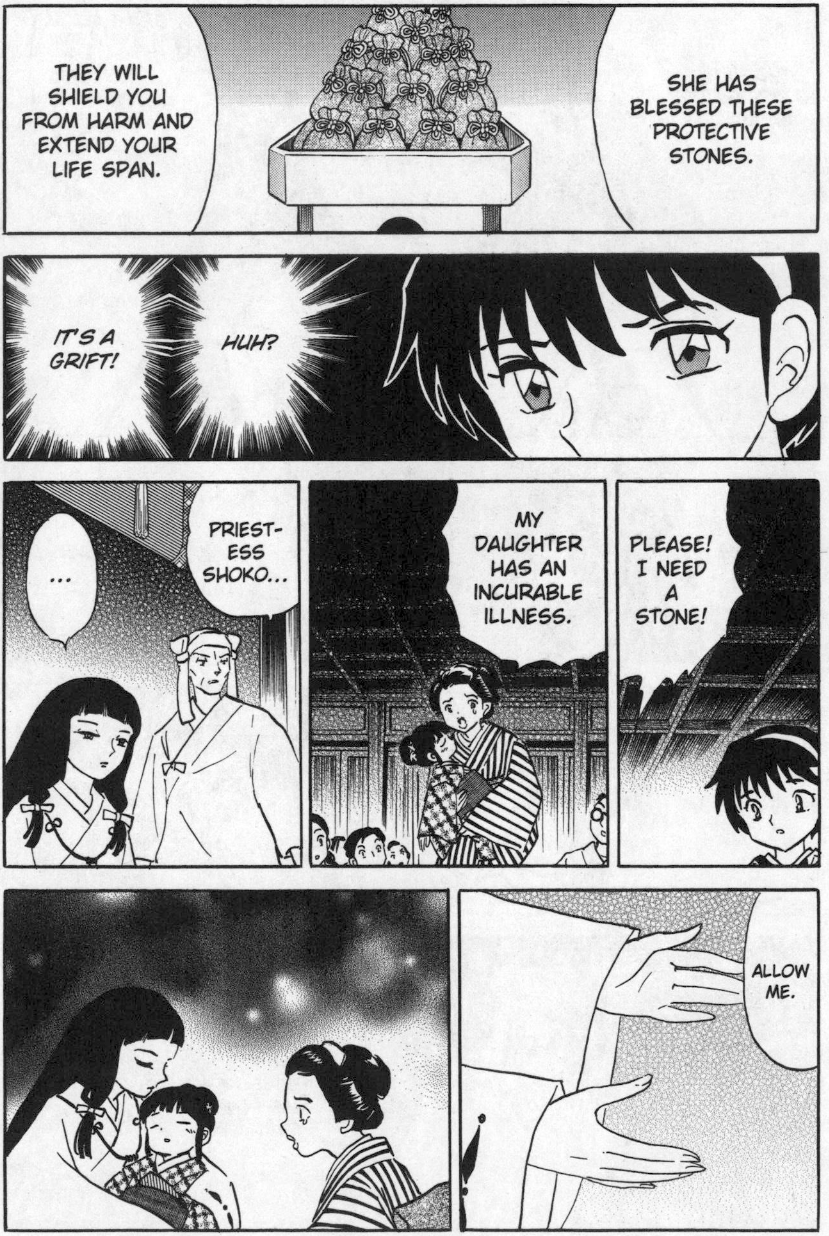
SHE HAS BLESSED THESE PROTECTIVE STONES.
THEY WILL SHIELD YOU FROM HARM AND EXTEND YOUR LIFE SPAN.
HUH?
IT'S A GRIFT!
PLEASE! I NEED A STONE!
MY DAUGHTER HAS AN INCURABLE ILLNESS.
PRIEST-ESS SHOKO...
...
ALLOW ME.

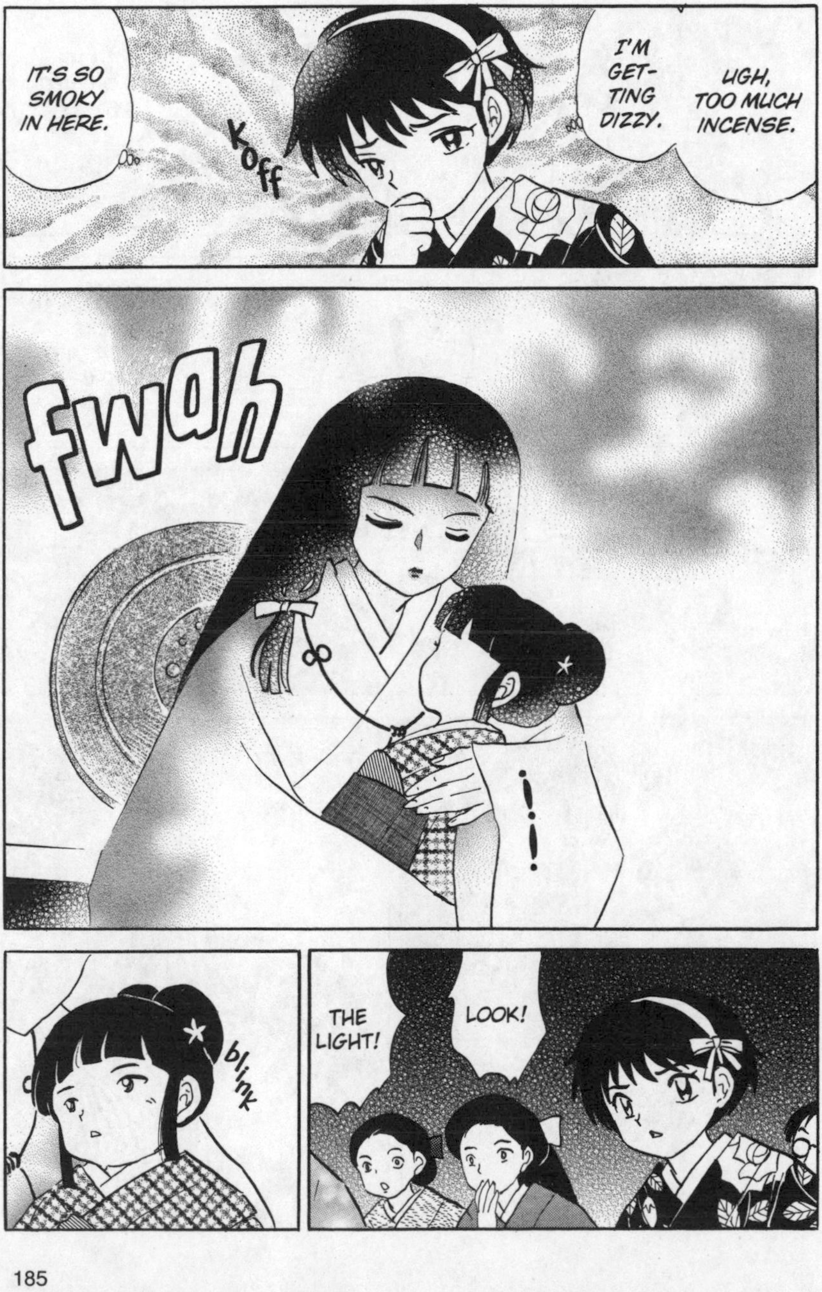
UGH, TOO MUCH INCENSE.
I'M GET-TING DIZZY.
koff
IT'S SO SMOKY IN HERE.
fwah
!!
LOOK!
THE LIGHT!
blink

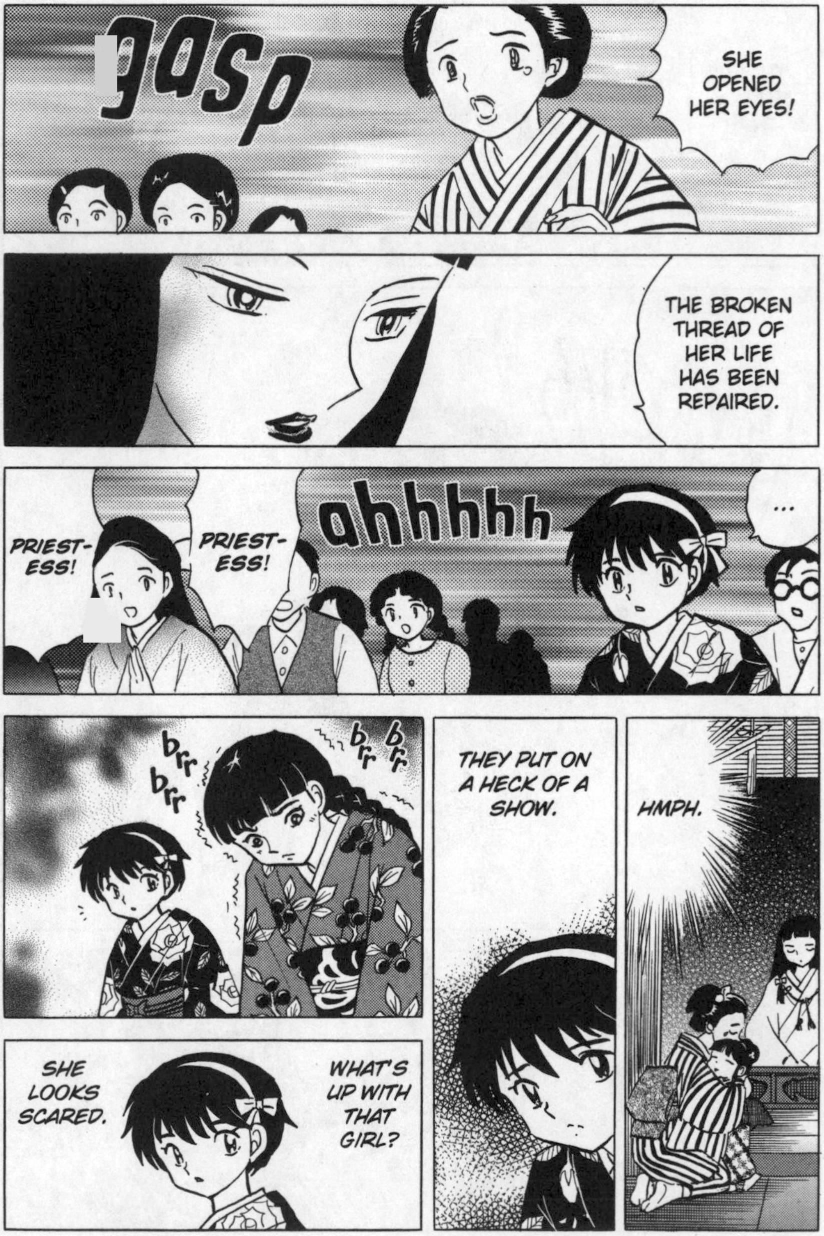
SHE OPENED HER EYES!
gasp
THE BROKEN THREAD OF HER LIFE HAS BEEN REPAIRED.
...
ahhhhh
PRIEST-ESS!
PRIEST-ESS!
HMPH.
THEY PUT ON A HECK OF A SHOW.
brr
brr
brr
brr
WHAT'S UP WITH THAT GIRL?
SHE LOOKS SCARED.

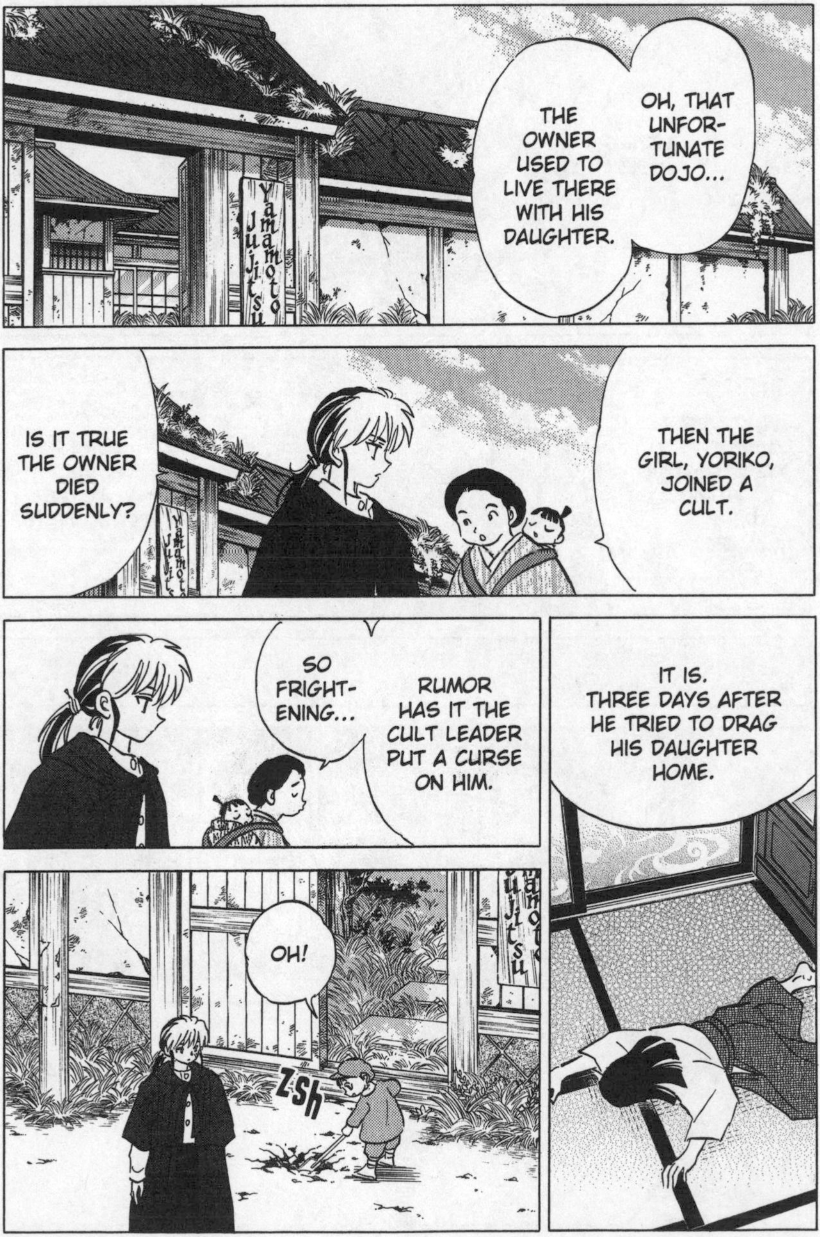
OH, THAT UNFOR-TUNATE DOJO...
THE OWNER USED TO LIVE THERE WITH HIS DAUGHTER.
Yamamoto Jujitsu
THEN THE GIRL, YORIKO, JOINED A CULT.
IS IT TRUE THE OWNER DIED SUDDENLY?
IT IS. THREE DAYS AFTER HE TRIED TO DRAG HIS DAUGHTER HOME.
RUMOR HAS IT THE CULT LEADER PUT A CURSE ON HIM.
SO FRIGHT-ENING...
Jujitsu Yamamoto
OH!
Z-Sh

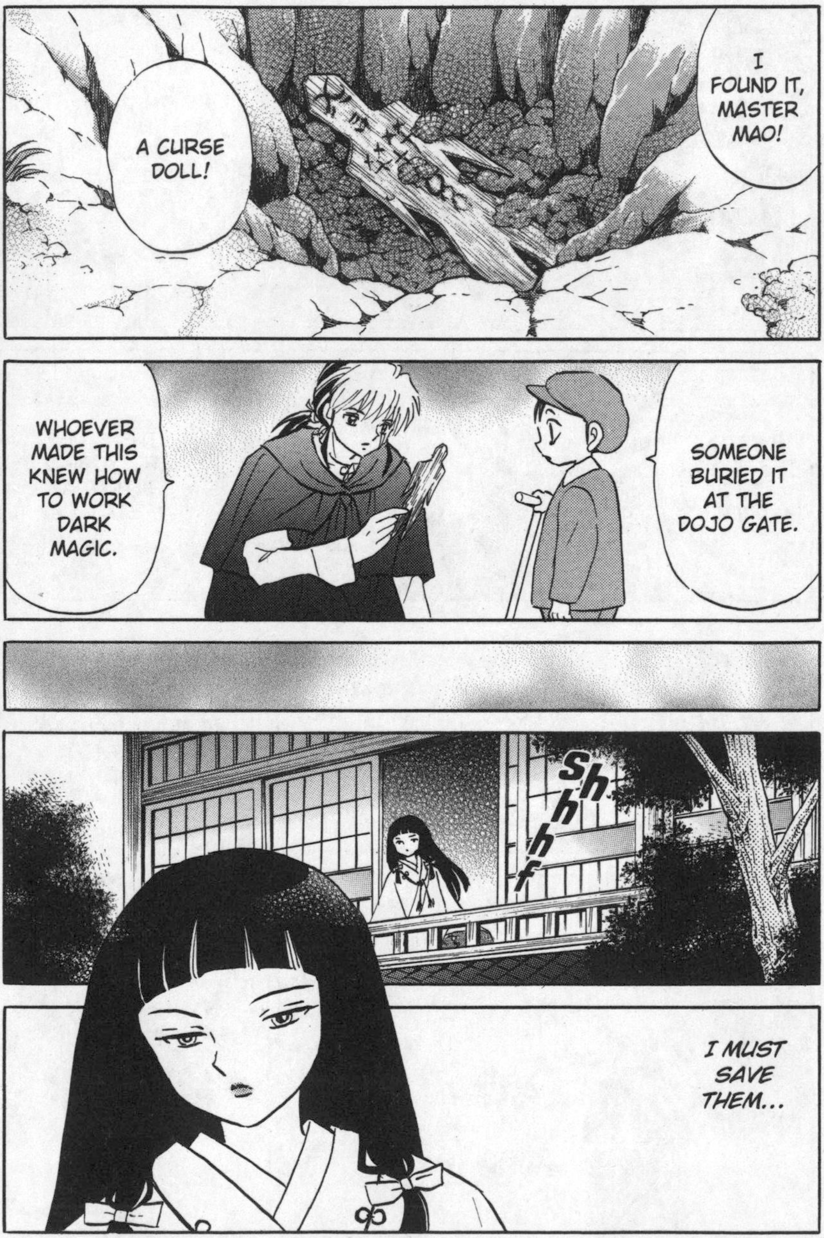
I FOUND IT, MASTER MAO!
A CURSE DOLL!
SOMEONE BURIED IT AT THE DOJO GATE.
WHOEVER MADE THIS KNEW HOW TO WORK DARK MAGIC.
Shhhf
I MUST SAVE THEM...

TO BE CONTINUED...

Rumiko Takahashi

The spotlight on Rumiko Takahashi's career began in 1978 when she won an honorable mention in Shogakukan's prestigious New Comic Artist Contest for *Those Selfish Aliens*. Later that same year, her boy-meets-alien comedy series, *Urusei Yatsura*, was serialized in *Weekly Shonen Sunday*. This phenomenally successful manga series was adapted into anime format and spawned a TV series and half a dozen theatrical-release movies, all incredibly popular in their own right. Takahashi followed up the success of her debut series with one blockbuster hit after another—*Maison Ikkoku* ran from 1980 to 1987, *Ranma ½* from 1987 to 1996, and *Inuyasha* from 1996 to 2008. Other notable works include *Mermaid Saga*, *Rumic Theater*, and *One-Pound Gospel*.

Takahashi was inducted into the Will Eisner Comic Awards Hall of Fame in 2018. She won the prestigious Shogakukan Manga Award twice in her career, once for *Urusei Yatsura* in 1981 and the second time for *Inuyasha* in 2002. A majority of the Takahashi canon has been adapted into other media such as anime, live-action TV series, and film. Takahashi's manga, as well as the other formats her work has been adapted into, have continued to delight generations of fans around the world. Distinguished by her wonderfully endearing characters, Takahashi's work adeptly incorporates a wide variety of elements such as comedy, romance, fantasy, and martial arts. While her series are difficult to pin down into one simple genre, the signature style she has created has come to be known as the "Rumic World." Rumiko Takahashi is an artist who truly represents the very best from the world of manga.

MAO

VOLUME 1
Shonen Sunday Edition

STORY AND ART BY
RUMIKO TAKAHASHI

MAO Vol. 1
by Rumiko TAKAHASHI
© 2019 Rumiko TAKAHASHI
All rights reserved.
Original Japanese edition published by SHOGAKUKAN.
English translation rights in the United States of America,
Canada, the United Kingdom, Ireland, Australia and New
Zealand arranged with SHOGAKUKAN.

Original Cover Design: Chie SATO + Bay Bridge Studio

Translation/Junko Goda
English Adaptation/Shaenon Garrity
Touch-up Art & Lettering/Susan Daigle-Leach
Cover & Interior Design/Yukiko Whitley
Editor/Annette Roman

Printed in the U.S.A.

Published by VIZ Media, LLC
P.O. Box 77010
San Francisco, CA 94107

10 9 8 7 6 5 4 3 2
First printing, September 2021
Second printing, November 2021

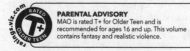

VIZ MEDIA
viz.com

SHONEN SUNDAY
shonensunday.com

Coming in Volume 2...

Nanoka, Mao and his helper Otoya investigate the strange cult of Priestess Shoko in hopes of bringing her to justice, but cursed dolls and scrolls of eternal life may be more than they bargained for. Will the priestess's doomsday prophecy come true? Back in the present, Nanoka and friend-zoned Shiraha do some historical research that uncovers a cataclysmic event yet to occur in Mao's timeline. Then Mao's curiosity gets him on the wrong side of a group of blood suckers and in need of a rescue by Nanoka—again!

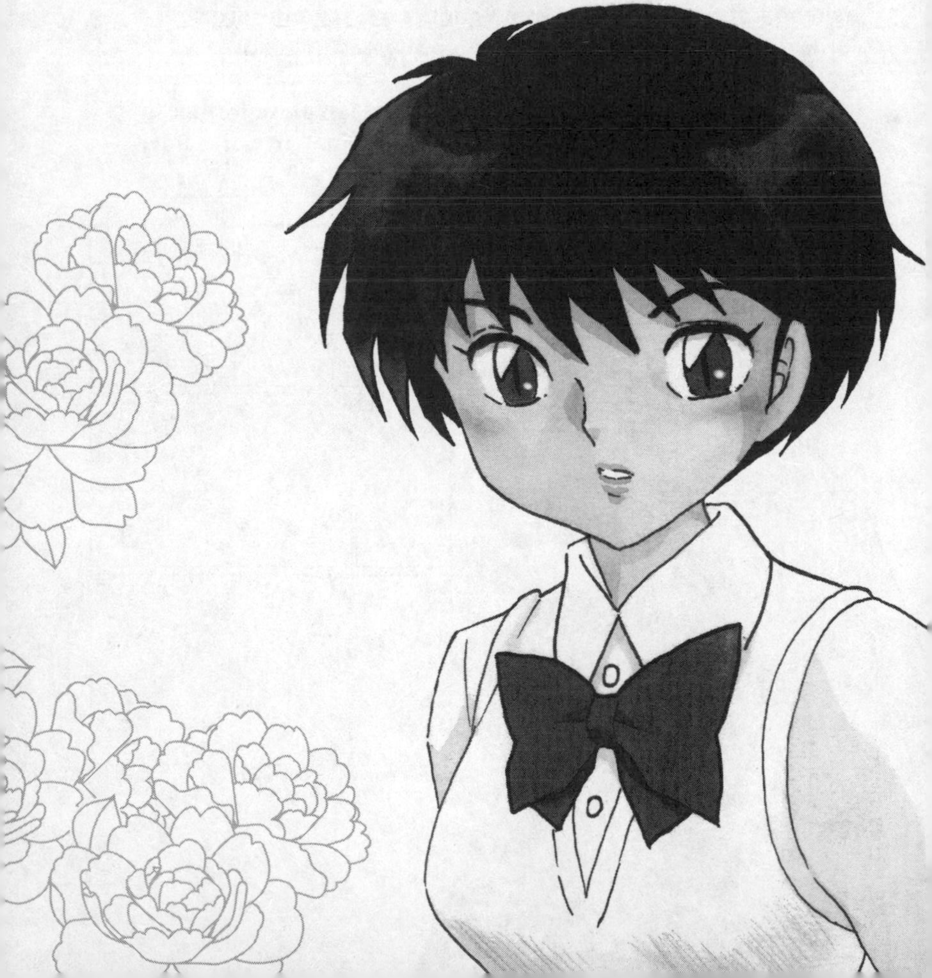

Hey! You're Reading in the Wrong Direction!

This is the end of this graphic novel!

To properly enjoy this VIZ graphic novel, please turn it around and begin reading from right to left. Unlike English, Japanese is read right to left, so Japanese comics are read in reverse order from the way English comics are typically read.

This book has been printed in the original Japanese format in order to preserve the orientation of the original artwork. Have fun with it!

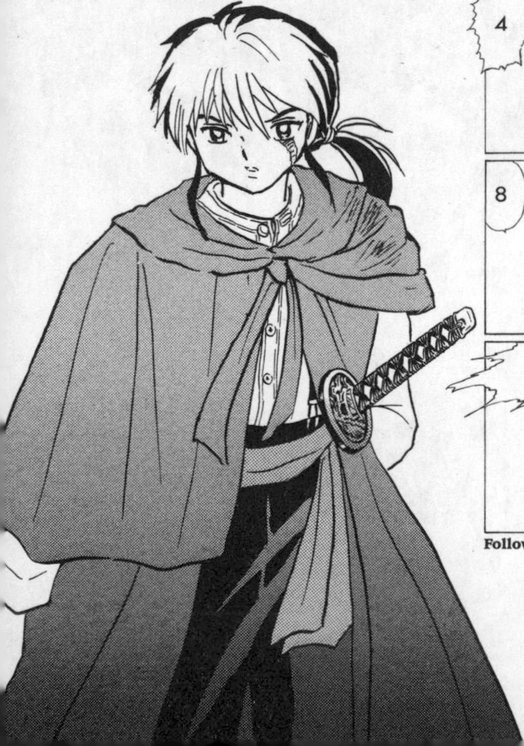

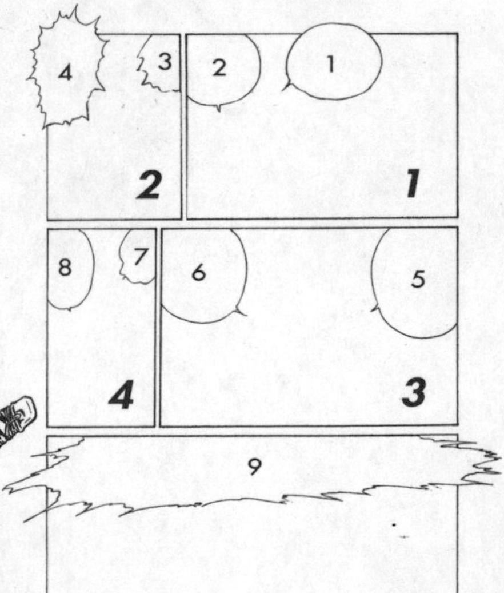
1
1
2
2
3
4
3
5
6
4
7
8
5
9

Follow the action this way